Chess Highlights of the 20th Century

Graham Burgess

First published in the UK by Gambit Publications Ltd 1999

A copy of the British Library Cataloguing in Publication data is available from the British Library

ISBN 1 901983 21 8

DISTRIBUTION:

Worldwide (except USA): Biblios Distribution Services, Star Rd, Partridge Green, West Sussex, RH13 8LD, England.
USA: BHB International, Inc., 41 Monroe Turnpike, Trumbull, CT 06611, USA.

For all other enquiries (including a full list of all Gambit Chess titles) please contact the publishers, Gambit Publications Ltd, 69 Masbro Rd, Kensington, London W14 0LS.
Fax +44 (0)20 7371 1477. E-mail 100617.2702@compuserve.com.
Or visit the Gambit Publications web site at http://www.gambitchess.co.uk

Edited by Graham Burgess
Typeset by John Nunn
Printed in Great Britain by Redwood Books, Trowbridge, Wilts.

10 9 8 7 6 5 4 3 2 1

Cover photographs
Front, top: Garry Kasparov playing Deep Blue in 1997
Front, bottom left: Joseph Blackburne (leading British player at the start of the 20th Century)
Front, bottom centre: Michael Adams (leading British player at the end of the 20th Century)
Front, bottom right: Judit Polgar, the strongest woman player in history
Back, top left: José Raúl Capablanca, World Champion 1921-7
Back, top centre: The 1957 Botvinnik vs Smyslov World Championship match
Back, top right: Alexander Alekhine, World Champion 1927-35, 37-46
Back, bottom left: Mikhail Tal, World Champion 1960-1
Back, bottom centre: Bobby Fischer, World Champion 1972-5
Back, bottom right: Anatoly Karpov, World Champion 1975-85

Gambit Publications Ltd
Managing Director: GM Murray Chandler
Chess Director: GM John Nunn
Editorial Director: FM Graham Burgess
Assistant Editor: GM John Emms
German Editor: WFM Petra Nunn

Contents 1900-1919

Symbols and Bibliography   8
Introduction   9

1900   10
Tournament victories for Pillsbury,
Schlechter and Lasker

1901   12
Sensational results by Capablanca

1902   14
Good results for Schlechter and
Janowski

1903   16
Victories for Tarrasch and Chigorin

1904   18
Marshall triumphs at Cambridge
Springs

1905   20
Great results for Tarrasch and Maroczy

1906   22
Pillsbury dies, leaving Marshall as the
leading American player

1907   24
Lasker outclasses Marshall

1908   26
Lasker fends off Tarrasch's challenge

1909   28
Capablanca achieves an astonishing
match victory over Marshall

1910   30
Lasker retains his world title through
two (?) challenges

1911   32
Another sensational result for
Capablanca

1912   34
A good year for Rubinstein

1913   36
A mixed year for Capablanca

1914   38
Lasker edges out Capablanca in the
St Petersburg tournament

1915   40
No major tournaments due to the war

1916   41
The war rages on

1917   42
No major events

1918   43
International chess slowly resumes
as the war ends

1919   44
Good results for Spielmann,
Bogoljubow and Capablanca

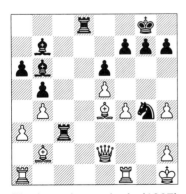

Black to play and win (1907)

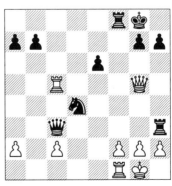

Black to play and win (1912)

Contents 1920-1939

1920	45
The hypermoderns make their mark	
1921	46
Capablanca becomes World Champion	
1922	48
Another good year for Alekhine	
1923	50
Successes for Alekhine and Nimzowitsch	
1924	52
Lasker triumphs at New York	
1925	54
Efim Bogoljubow wins at Moscow	
1926	56
A sensational result for Nimzowitsch	
1927	58
Capablanca loses the World Championship to Alekhine	
1928	60
An excellent year for Capablanca	
1929	62
Alekhine retains the World Title	

1930	64
Alekhine dominant at San Remo	
1931	66
A great result for Alekhine	
1932	68
A year of few major tournaments	
1933	70
Botvinnik shows his class	
1934	72
Alekhine remains Champion	
1935	74
Alekhine loses the world title to Euwe	
1936	76
Vintage performances by Capablanca	
1937	78
Alekhine regains the world title	
1938	80
The AVRO tournament – a triumph for Keres and Fine	
1939	82
World War II throws international chess into chaos	

White to play and win (1925)

White to play and win (1938)

Contents 1940-1959

1940   84
Chess continues in the USSR
and Germany

1941   86
Botvinnik proves his 'Absolute'
superiority

1942   88
Alekhine and Keres fight it out in
Nazi tournaments

1943   90
Sverdlovsk becomes the centre
of chess activity in the USSR

1944   92
Less chess as the war escalates

1945   94
The USSR dominates the first
post-war chess matches

1946   96
Alekhine dies

1947   98
FIDE organizes new World
Championship

1948   100
Botvinnik wins the World
Championship

1949   102
David Bronstein emerges as a
new star

1950   104
Chess and Politics mix

1951   106
A rusty Botvinnik survives
Bronstein's challenge

1952   108
Excellent performances by
Botvinnik, Keres and Kotov

1953   110
Smyslov triumphs at Zurich

1954   112
Botvinnik hangs on in another
drawn World Championship match

1955   114
Bronstein's brilliant result

1956   116
Smyslov is the Challenger again

1957   118
Smyslov is the new World
Champion

1958   120
Botvinnik regains the world title

1959   122
Tal is to challenge Botvinnik

Black to play and win (1948)

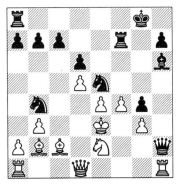

Black to play and win (1958)

Contents 1960-1979

1960   124
Tal becomes World Champion • Fischer has a mixed year

1961   126
Tal becomes the youngest Ex-World Champion

1962   128
Both glory and agony for Fischer

1963   130
Petrosian defeats Botvinnik • Fischer's 'exhibition'

1964   132
Spassky becomes a Candidate

1965   134
Spassky dominates the Candidates matches

1966   136
Petrosian shows his class by retaining his title

1967   138
Fischer quits the Interzonal while leading

1968   140
Spassky is to challenge again • Dismay at another Fischer withdrawal

1969   142
Spassky is World Champion • Karpov – a new Soviet star

1970   144
Fischer is back on track • USSR narrowly beats the Rest of the World

1971   146
Fischer ruthless: 6-0 twice!

1972   148
Fischer is World Champion • Chess is headline news around the world

1973   150
Karpov and Mecking become Candidates

1974   152
Karpov is Fischer's challenger

1975   154
Karpov becomes World Champion by default to the dismay of Fischer's fans

1976   156
Karpov proves he is a worthy Champion • Korchnoi defects

1977   158
Korchnoi wins through a tempestuous Candidates cycle

1978   160
Karpov remains Champion after a thrilling match

1979   162
Garry Kasparov achieves sensational results • Tal has a great year

White to play and win (1963)

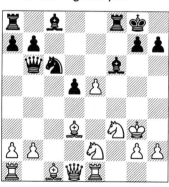

Black to play and win (1976)

Contents 1980-1999

1980   164
A mixed year for Karpov • England emerges as a chess power

1981   166
Karpov comfortably defends his title

1982   168
Kasparov gathers momentum, but political storms are brewing

1983   170
Candidates cycle in crisis • Kasparov faces a stern challenge from Korchnoi

1984   172
Kasparov fights desperately for survival in a marathon match

1985   174
Outrage as match is cancelled • Kasparov is the new Champion

1986   176
Kasparov defends his title • Startling successes by Andrei Sokolov

1987   178
Kasparov survives a scare in Seville

1988   180
The GMA makes chess more democratic and organizes the World Cup

1989   182
Kasparov wins the World Cup

1990   184
Kasparov wins an exciting match

1991   186
Anand enters the world elite • The World Cup collapses

1992   188
Fischer is back • Short beats Karpov

1993   190
Kasparov and Short split from FIDE

1994   192
The PCA organizes a series of high-profile events

1995   194
Kasparov retains the PCA title

1996   196
Kasparov beats Deep Blue, after losing the first game

1997   198
Kasparov loses a bizarre rematch against Deep Blue

1998   200
Anand dominates tournament chess

1999   202
Kasparov reconfirms his dominance

Conclusion   204
Index of Games   205

White to play and win (1984)

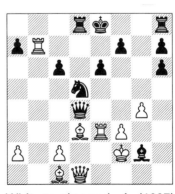

White to play and win (1997)

Symbols

+	check
++	double check
x	capture
#	checkmate
!!	brilliant move
!	good move
!?	interesting move
?!	dubious move
?	bad move
??	blunder
0-0	castles kingside
0-0-0	castles queenside
1-0	the game ends in a win for White
½-½	the game ends in a draw
0-1	the game ends in a win for Black
Ch	Championship

W or *B* by a diagram indicates White or Black to play.

Bibliography

Non-Chess

Chronicle of the World, Dorling Kindersley, 1996

The Times *Concise Atlas of World History*, Times Books, 1994

Chronicle of the 20th Century (CD-ROM), DK Multimedia, 1996

The Guinness Book of the 20th Century, Guinness Publishing, 1997

Pears Cyclopaedia 1999-2000, Penguin Books, 1999

Chess

B. Cafferty and M. Taimanov, *The Soviet Championships*, Cadogan, 1998

I. Belov, A. Shakarov, V. Tsaturian and L. Vilensky, *Antology* (sic) *of Chess Beauty*, 1996

K. Whyld, *Guinness Chess the Records*, Guinness Books, 1986

J. Gaige, *Chess Personalia*, McFarland, 1987

Dr. P. Feenstra Kuiper, *Hundert Jahre Schach-Turniere 1851-1950*, W. Ten Have, 1964

Dr. P. Feenstra Kuiper, *Hundert Jahre Schach-Zweikämpfe 1851-1950*, W. Ten Have, 1967

D. Hooper and K. Whyld, *The Oxford Companion to Chess*, Oxford University Press, 1992

S. Gligorić and R. Wade, *The World Chess Championship*, Batsford, 1973

B. Kazić, *International Championship Chess*, Batsford, 1974

R. Eales, *Chess: The History of a Game*, Batsford, 1985

G. Burgess, J. Nunn and J. Emms, *The Mammoth Book of the World's Greatest Chess Games*, Robinson, 1998

Mega Database '99 (CD-ROM), ChessBase GmbH 1998

In addition, many biographies and games collections were consulted.

Photographs

All photographs were supplied from the library of the *British Chess Magazine*. Photographer credits: Michael Adams (photograph no. 33); Lesley Collett (24, 29); Calle Erlandsson (Tal picture on the back cover); Catherine Jaeg (28); Dagobert Kohlmeyer (31, 32, 39); Helen Milligan (37); Rosa de las Nieves (Kasparov vs Deep Blue and J.Polgar pictures on the front cover, Karpov picture on the back cover, 34, 35); Petra Nunn (Michael Adams picture on front cover); Cathy Rogers (36)

Acknowledgements

I would like to thank John Nunn for suggesting that I write this book in the first place, and for his helpful comments throughout. My mother, Aileen Burgess, deserves thanks for reading through the non-chess content. Finally, I should thank Ken Whyld for his assistance in checking historical facts.

Introduction

The aim of this book is to present a selection of the best and most entertaining chess games from the 20th Century, together with year-by-year accounts of the main chess news stories. It is intended as a book to dip into both for entertainment and instruction.

Chess does not exist in a vacuum, but rather reflects and is affected by events outside our 64 squares. With this in mind, the book also contains brief accounts of the events and achievements that made world news in each year.

In selecting the chess games to include, I have sought to strike a balance between presenting the best and most important chess games, and choosing less familiar material. All the games have been carefully analysed using both carbon-based and silicon-based brains, and in many cases the new notes differ substantially in their conclusions from the 'traditional' accounts of these games. I have for the most part avoided a discussion of the opening play, and join the games in the early middlegame. This, I feel, makes for the fairest comparison between different eras. How opening play has developed during the 20th Century is certainly an interesting topic, but to do it justice would require a whole book.

The chess news from each year falls into a number of broad categories. First comes the World Championship, and qualifying events for it, such as Interzonals and Candidates events. Next is news of the most important tournaments of the year, followed by team chess. In general, I have only mentioned national championships when there is something exceptional to report, such as a player becoming Champion at an unusually early age. I have made an exception for the USSR Championships, as these were such strong events as always to merit attention.

Then I discuss notable achievements in junior, women's and correspondence chess, before listing notable chess-player births and deaths. Please note that I use square brackets when referring to future events, to distinguish them from the discussion of events of the year in question, for which the present tense is used.

In the non-chess world news I have focused on the stories that made the greatest impact on the world. Thus you will find most space devoted to scientific discoveries, inventions, conflicts, wars, disasters, social upheavals and technological breakthroughs. Naturally, I have devoted particular attention to events that had particular influence on the chess world, such as the rise and fall of the Soviet Union. I have aimed to provide enough concise information about each key issue to assist the reader to delve deeper into a particular subject.

I hope this book helps you become a better chess-player and proves to be a useful source of chess information. Perhaps setting chess history in its wider context will even spark an interest in other areas.

Graham Burgess
October 1999

1900

Tournament victories for Pillsbury, Schlechter and Lasker • Steinitz dies

At the start of 1900, the World Champion is Emanuel Lasker (born 1868); he has been Champion since 1894. His last title defence was in 1897, when he comfortably defeated Wilhelm Steinitz (World Champion 1886-94) in a return match. Lasker is clearly the best player in the world, but he is by no means dominant. The pursuing group includes Siegbert Tarrasch and Dawid Janowski, who are both around the peak of their careers, while the world elite has recently been joined by Geza Maroczy and the talented young American, Harry Nelson Pillsbury. Carl Schlechter and Frank Marshall are two other players who are making rapid progress. The top British player is Joseph Blackburne, while the leading Russian is Mikhail Chigorin; both players are towards the end of their careers.

Emanuel Lasker wins the Paris tournament with 14½/16, ahead of Pillsbury (12½), Marshall and Maroczy (both 12). A game from the event:

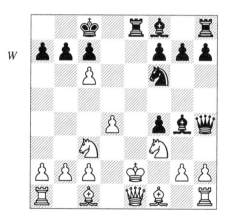

M. Chigorin – J. Mortimer
Paris 1900

A wild Steinitz Gambit – a typically bold opening by Chigorin – has led to a bizarre position, where it seems that the white king and queen are in terrible danger. However, it turns out that the black king is threatened too, while the black queen is also attacked. The key for White in the subsequent play is to find the best squares for his king.

10 ♔d2! ♕h5 11 ♕f2 ♗b4

Black threatens 12...♘e4+.

12 ♗d3 ♖e3

12...♘d5 13 cxb7+ ♔b8 14 a3 doesn't look sufficient for Black either.

With the text-move Black appears to have seized the initiative. White's solution is simple: attack!

13 cxb7+ ♔b8 14 ♘e5! ♖e2+

14...♗xc3+ 15 bxc3 ♖e2+ 16 ♗xe2 ♘e4+ 17 ♔e1 ♘xf2 18 ♖b1 and the threat of mate on c6 is decisive.

15 ♕xe2 ♗xe2 16 ♗xe2 ♘e4+

16...♗xc3+ 17 ♔d1! (this gains a tempo on the queen; 17 bxc3? ♘e4+ lets Black escape) 17...♕h4 18 bxc3 ♘e4 19 ♗f3 and again the black king's predicament proves fatal.

17 ♔d3! ♘f2+ 18 ♔c4!

The king is safe enough here, as the black pieces are in no position to attack it.

18...♕h6 19 ♗f3 c5

There is nothing better; Black is lost.

20 ♘d7+ ♔c7 21 ♗xf4+ ♕xf4 22 ♘d5+ ♔xd7 23 ♘xf4 ♖xh1 24 dxc5 ♗a5 25 b4 ♗c7 26 ♖d1+ ♔e8 27 ♗c6+ 1-0

Harry Nelson Pillsbury and Carl Schlechter jointly win the German Open Championship, one of the strongest tournaments of the year, scoring 12/15. Here is an eventful game involving one of the winners:

A. Halprin – H. Pillsbury
German Open Ch, Munich 1900

1 e4 e5 2 ♘f3 ♘c6 3 ♗b5 ♘f6 4 0-0 ♘xe4 5 d4 ♘d6 6 dxe5 ♘xb5 7 a4 d6

This game was played in the last round. Halprin, one of the backmarkers in this tournament, had been specially prepared in this sharp opening line.

8 e6! fxe6 9 axb5 ♘e7 10 ♘c3 ♘g6 11 ♘g5

11 ♕d4 is possibly more testing; it was played by Murray Chandler 89 years later.

11...♗e7 12 ♕h5 ♗xg5 13 ♗xg5 ♕d7

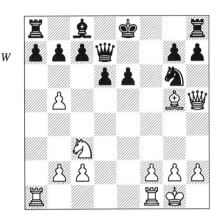

14 b6!

Pillsbury had faced 14 ♖a3 two rounds earlier, and won without undue difficulty. White's actual move is more critical, as it damages Black's structure and weakens his control of d6 and b6...

14...cxb6 15 ♘d5!?

...which White immediately exploits. The threat of ♘xb6 forces Black's reply.

15...exd5 16 ♖fe1+ ♔f8

For a piece and two pawns, White has managed to catch the black king in the centre. All his pieces are ready to attack, while Black's are mostly undeveloped.

17 ♖a3 ♘e5

Black must defend against ♖f3+.

18 ♖xe5

Sacrificing further material to keep the initiative.

18...dxe5 19 ♖f3+ ♔g8 20 ♗h6

White has many threats, including 21 ♗xg7.

20...♕e7

Not 20...gxh6? losing to 21 ♖g3+ ♔f8 22 ♕xe5.

21 ♗xg7

White must act quickly. 21 ♖g3 ♗e6 is safe enough for Black.

21...♔xg7

Now the game ends in perpetual check. Neither side can avoid it.

22 ♖g3+ ♔f8 23 ♖f3+ ♔g7 24 ♖g3+ ♔f8
½-½

Chess News in Brief

Henry Atkins wins the British Championship – one of 12 victories, spanning 1895-1925.

Richard Teichmann wins the London tournament.

Lipschütz wins the New York tournament.

Emanuel Lasker tours Great Britain and Germany, giving simultaneous displays.

Wilhelm Steinitz (born 1836; World Champion 1886-94) dies, in poverty, in New York.

World News in Brief

As the new century begins, the United Kingdom remains a major world power, with an empire that includes Canada, India, Australia, New Zealand, large parts of Africa, and many other territories dotted around the globe. However, economically, Britain is being overtaken by the United States and Germany, while the difficulties the British are experiencing in the ongoing Boer War have suggested that maintaining a large empire may no longer be tenable for a small country.

Russia and China disagree on the route of the new railroad; Russia invades Manchuria.

Count Ferdinand Zeppelin's airship *LZ1* makes its maiden flight over Lake Constance.

The Paris Metro underground railway is opened.

Sigmund Freud publishes *Die Traumdeutung*, an attempt to interpret dreams.

The German physicist Max Planck puts forward the quantum theory, under which energy is not transmitted as a wave, but rather as discrete packets, or *quanta*. This is entirely at odds with the Classical theory, but manages to explain several hitherto bewildering phenomena. It sparks heated debate amongst physicists and mathematicians.

1901

Sensational results by the Cuban prodigy Capablanca • Janowski wins the Monte Carlo tournament

The young Cuban, José Raúl Capablanca (born 1888) achieves sensational results, culminating in a match victory over Corzo, the Cuban Champion, by a score of 4 wins, 6 draws and 3 losses (having lost the first two games). As the two following games show, his play is extremely mature.

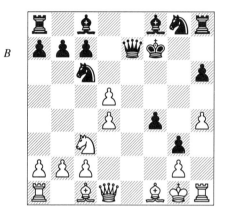

J. Corzo – J. Capablanca
Match (game 8), Havana 1901

This wild position has arisen from the Hamppe-Allgaier Gambit. Capablanca 'accidentally' improved over the theory of the day (which he didn't know), and now exploits the vulnerable white king.

11...②xd4! 12 ♕xd4

12 ♗xf4? gives Black a choice of strong moves, including 12...♕f6.

12...♕c5

White's king is in real danger of being mated.

13 ②e2 ♕b6!

Threatening 14...♗c5.

14 ♕xb6

14 ♗e3 fxe3 15 ♕xh8 ♗g7 16 ♕h7 ♕f6 17 ②xg3 ♕f2+ 18 ♔h2 ②f6 wins for Black. 14 b4!? looks best, but 14...♗xb4 15 ♗e3 ♗c5 16 ♕xc5 (or 16 ♕xf4+ ②f6) 16...fxe3 is pleasant for Black.

14...axb6

Thus Black has managed to activate his queen's rook.

15 ②d4 ♗c5 16 c3 ♖a4

Threatening 17...♖xd4.

17 ♗e2 ♗xd4+ 18 cxd4 ♖xd4 19 b3

It looks as if Black's rooks are in trouble.

19...②f6 20 ♗b2 ♖d2 21 ♗h5+ ②xh5!

Capablanca simply sacrifices the exchange, seeing that his attack will be swift and deadly.

22 ♗xh8 f3 23 gxf3 ②f4 24 ♗e5 ♖g2+ 25 ♔f1 ♖f2+ 26 ♔e1 ②d3+ 0-1

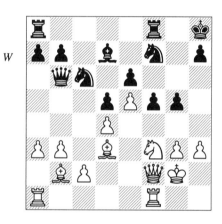

J. Capablanca – J. Corzo
Match (game 11), Havana 1901

Black has just advanced his g-pawn toward the white king, but immediately finds himself undermined on this flank.

20 g4! ②e7 21 ♕e3 ♖g8 22 ♖ae1

White calmly consolidates, as Black has no good way to resolve the tension.

22...②g6 23 gxf5 ②f4+ 24 ♔h2 ②xd3

24...exf5 loses to 25 ②xg5.

25 ♕xd3 exf5 26 c4!

Now Capablanca undermines the remnant of Black's central pawn-chain.

26...♕e6 27 cxd5 ♕xd5 28 e6!

This magnificent combination is based on the black king's vulnerability on the long diagonal.

28...♗b5 29 ♕xb5

Not the only good move, but strong and very attractive.

29...♕xb5 30 d5+ ♖g7 31 exf7 h6

31...♖f8 32 ♘xg5 wins without undue difficulty.

32 ♘d4 ♕xf1

32...♕d7 loses to 33 ♘xf5.

33 ♖xf1 ♖xf7 34 ♖xf5 ♖xf5 35 ♘xf5+ ♔h7 36 ♘e7

There remains only a straightforward technical task for White, which the 12-year-old negotiates with impressive maturity.

36...♖f8 37 ♔g2 h5 38 d6 g4 39 hxg4 hxg4 40 ♗e5 ♔h6 41 d7 ♖d8 42 ♘g8+ ♖xg8 43 ♗f6 ♔g6 44 d8♕ ♖xd8 45 ♗xd8 b5 46 ♔f2 ♔f5 47 ♔e3 ♔e5 48 ♔d3 ♔d5 49 ♔c3 g3 50 ♗h4 g2 51 ♗f2 a5 52 b4 ♔e4 53 ♗b6 ♔d5 54 ♔d3 ♔c6 55 ♗g1 ♔d5 56 ♗h2 ♔c6 57 ♔d4 a4 58 ♔e5 ♔b6 59 ♔d5 ♔a6 60 ♔c5!

Not 60 ♔c6?? g1♕ 61 ♗xg1 stalemate.

1-0

Dawid Janowski wins the Monte Carlo tournament, ahead of Schlechter, von Scheve and Chigorin. A game from the event:

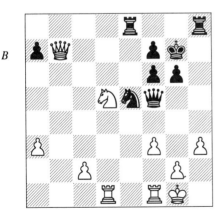

G. Marco – J. Mieses
Monte Carlo 1901

White has been pursuing his own plans without giving sufficient thought to the safety of his king.

26...♖xh3! 27 gxh3?

27 ♘e3 ♕g5 28 f4 ♕g3 29 fxe5 ♕h2+ 30 ♔f2 gives Black excellent winning chances,

e.g. 30...♕g3+ 31 ♔g1 ♕xe3+ 32 ♖f2 ♖xe5 33 gxh3 ♖g5+ 34 ♕g2 ♕xh3 or 30...♖xe3 31 ♔xe3 ♕xe5+ 32 ♔d3 ♕e3+ 33 ♔c4 ♖e4+.

Or 27 ♘c7, and then:

a) 27...♖e7 28 gxh3 ♕g5+ 29 ♔h1 ♕g3 30 ♖d2 ♖xc7 31 ♕xc7 ♕xh3+ 32 ♔g1 ♕g3+ is a draw.

b) 27...♘xf3+ 28 ♕xf3 ♖xf3 29 ♘xe8+ ♔f8 30 ♖xf3 ♕c5+ is unclear.

c) 27...♖eh8 28 gxh3 ♖xh3 29 ♔g2 ♘g4 is probably a draw; for example, 30 ♕e4 ♖h2+ 31 ♔g3 ♖h3+ 32 ♔g2 ♖h2+ 33 ♔g1 ♖h1+, etc.

27...♕g5+?

27...♘xf3+! 28 ♖xf3 (other moves are mated by force) 28...♕xf3 and there is no good answer to the threats of ...♖xe2 and ...♕xd1+.

28 ♔f2?

After 28 ♔h1 ♖h8 29 ♔h2 ♕h4 30 ♘f4 ♕xf4+ 31 ♔g2 ♕g5+ 32 ♔f2 ♕h4+ Black's attack should be enough to win: 33 ♔e3 ♖e8 34 ♔d2 ♕f4+ 35 ♔c3 ♕e3+ or 33 ♔e2 ♕c4+ 34 ♔d2 ♖xh3.

28...♘d3+! 29 ♖xd3 ♕h4+ 30 ♔g1 ♕g3+ 31 ♔h1 ♕xh3+ 32 ♔g1 ♕g3+ 33 ♔h1 ♖h8#
(0-1)

Chess News in Brief

Harry Nelson Pillsbury dominates the Buffalo tournament, scoring 9/10.

World Champion Emanuel Lasker tours the United States.

Max Euwe [World Champion 1935-7; FIDE President 1970-8] is born.

World News in Brief

President McKinley of the United States is assassinated.

The six states of Australia unite to form a federal commonwealth.

Queen Victoria of Great Britain dies at the age of 81. She has reigned for 63 years.

Guglielmo Marconi succeeds in transmitting the first wireless message across the Atlantic.

The Swede, Alfred Nobel, who has made a fortune following his invention of dynamite, establishes the Nobel Prizes, to be awarded each year for outstanding achievements in sciences, the arts and for those who further the cause of peace in the world.

1902

Good results for Schlechter and Janowski in a quiet year for chess

Dawid Janowski wins the German Open Championship with 13½/17, ahead of Pillsbury (12) and Atkins (11½). A critical game:

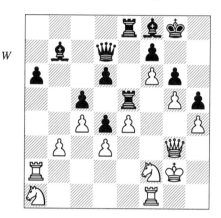

H. Pillsbury – D. Janowski
German Open Ch, Hannover 1902

White has been under pressure for some time, and now relaxes his guard, allowing a decisive combination.

37 ♘h3? ♖xe4! 38 dxe4 ♖xe4

White is unable to save both his king and queen.

39 ♔h2 ♖e3 40 ♕xe3 dxe3 41 ♘c2 d5 42 ♘xe3 d4 43 ♘g2 ♗xg2 44 ♖xg2 ♗d6+ 45 ♘f4 ♕f5 46 ♖gf2

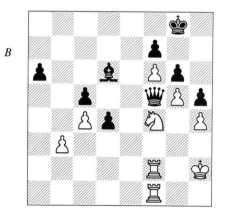

With White tied down, the black queen now picks off several pawns.

46...♕g4 47 ♔h1 ♕xh4+ 48 ♔g1 ♕g3+ 49 ♔h1 ♕xb3 50 ♔g2 ♕xc4 51 ♖e1 d3 52 ♖e8+ ♔h7 53 ♘xd3 ♕xd3 54 ♖fe2 ♕g3+ 55 ♔h1 ♕h3+ 56 ♔g1 c4 57 ♖f2 ♕g4+ 58 ♔f1 ♗c5 59 ♖d2 ♕xg5 0-1

Another game from the tournament sees a brave sacrifice by the English-born American player William Napier.

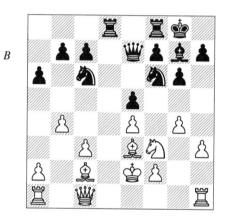

C. von Bardeleben – W. Napier
German Open Ch, Hannover 1902

White has disregarded king safety and made some seemingly random pawn thrusts. As a result, Black now executes a very logical sacrifice, but it is surprising how resilient White's position turns out to be.

17...♘d4+!? 18 cxd4 exd4 19 ♗xd4

19 ♗g5? d3+ 20 ♗xd3 ♖xd3 21 e5 ♖xf3 22 ♔xf3 ♕xe5 is very good for Black.

19...♘xe4 20 ♕e3 ♗xd4 21 ♘xd4 ♕xb4

21...♖fe8 is met by 22 ♔f1.

22 ♗xe4 ♖xd4 23 ♗d3?

23 ♖hb1! makes a real fight of it: 23...♕c4+ (23...♕a4 24 f3) 24 ♗d3 ♕d5 (24...♖xd3 25 ♕xd3 ♖e8+ 26 ♔d2 ♕f4+ 27 ♔c3) 25 ♖b3 ♖d8 is still not clear.

23...♕a4

Black wins after 23...♖fd8!, e.g. 24 ♖ad1 ♕a4.

24 ♔f1 ♖e8 25 ♕f3

25 ♕g3? loses to 25...♕c6 and ...♕c3.

25...♖f4

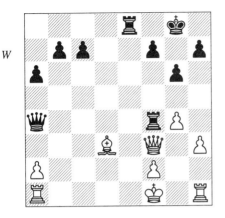

W

26 ♕d1

26 ♕d5! is a better try: 26...♖e3 (threatening 27...♖xf2+; 26...♖d4 27 ♗c2!) 27 ♖h2 ♖d4 28 ♗c2 ♕b4 29 ♕g5.

26...♕d4 27 ♖h2 ♕d6! 28 ♖g2 ♖d4 29 ♖g3 ♖d8 30 ♔e2 c5

Black will regain the piece with a decisive advantage.

31 ♕b3 ♖xd3 32 ♖xd3 ♕e5+ 33 ♖e3 ♕xa1 34 ♖e7 c4 35 ♕xc4 ♕d1+ 36 ♔e3 ♕e1+ 37 ♕e2 ♕c3+ 38 ♔f4 ♖d4+ 39 ♖e4 ♕c7+ 40 ♔g5 f6+ 41 ♔xf6 ♖d6+ 0-1

Carl Schlechter scores an impressive 7½-2½ match victory over Dawid Janowski at Karlsbad. After Janowski lost the first four games, the match result was never in doubt.

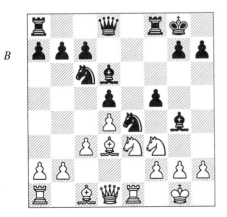

B

D. Janowski – C. Schlechter
Match (game 1), Karlsbad 1902

White has just played 12 ♘f1-e3?. It is surprising how severely this careless move is punished.

12...♗xh2+! 13 ♔xh2 ♘xf2 14 ♗xf5?!

14 ♕c2 ♘xd3 15 ♕xd3 ♗xf3 is hopeless for White, since 16 gxf3 ♕h4+ picks up the e1-rook.

14...♘xd1 15 ♗xg4 ♖xf3! 16 ♖xd1 ♕h4+ 17 ♗h3 ♖af8 18 gxf3 ♖xf3 19 ♖f1 ♖xh3+ 20 ♔g1 ♖h1+ 21 ♔g2 ♕h3+ 22 ♔f2 ♖h2+ 23 ♔e1 ♕h4+ 0-1

Chess News in Brief

The first radio match is played, between *SS Campania* and *SS Philadelphia* in the Atlantic Ocean.

The Monte Carlo tournament is won by Maroczy with 14¾/20, ahead of Pillsbury (14½) and Janowski (14). A draw is scored as a quarter of a point each, with a second game being played to decide the destination of the remaining half-point.

Pillsbury tours Germany.

Mario Monticelli [Italian grandmaster] is born.

World News in Brief

Germany, Austria and Italy renew their alliance for 12 more years.

Riots in Russia force concessions from Tsar Nicholas II.

Protests in Ireland result in the declaration of a state of emergency.

In South Africa, the Boer War ends, with British sovereignty recognized.

In Martinique, Mount Pelée erupts, wiping out the town of St Pierre.

The Aswan Dam on the River Nile in Egypt is completed.

The Lumière brothers experiment with 'moving photographs' in which a series of photographs are projected in quick succession to give the illusion of movement.

Henry Ford starts to pursue his dream of making automobiles that are affordable to ordinary members of the public.

Thomas Edison invents the electrical storage battery.

1903

Good results for Tarrasch and Chigorin

Siegbert Tarrasch wins the Monte Carlo tournament (now using a normal scoring system) with 20/26, ahead of Maroczy (19), Pillsbury (18½) and Schlechter (17). A game from the event:

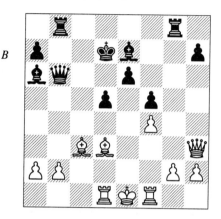

A. Reggio – J. Mieses
Monte Carlo 1903

White has just overlooked a cunning idea.
22...♖g3!
22...♖xg2 23 ♕xg2 ♕e3+ 24 ♕e2 ♗h4+ 25 ♖f2 ♗xf2+ 26 ♔f1 gives White more chances of surviving.
23 ♕xg3
23 hxg3 ♕e3+ 24 ♗e2 ♕xe2#.
23...♗h4! 24 ♗xa6 ♗xg3+ 25 hxg3 ♕xa6
It is difficult for White to coordinate his pieces, and his king is still exposed to attack. Black has excellent winning chances.
26 ♖h1 ♖g8 27 ♖xh7+ ♔c6 28 ♖h6 ♔b5 29 ♖xd5+?! exd5 30 ♖xa6 ♔xa6 31 ♔f2 ♔b5 32 b3 ♔c5 33 ♔f3 d4 34 ♗d2 ♔d5 35 ♗e1 ♖c8 36 g4 fxg4+ 37 ♔xg4 ♖c2 38 g3 d3 39 ♔g5 d2 0-1

Mikhail Chigorin wins the Gambit tournament in Vienna with 13/18, ahead of Marshall (11½), Marco (11) and Pillsbury (10). Evidently his aggressive style of play is well-suited to a tournament in which the King's Gambit is the mandatory opening. However, the following game went against him:

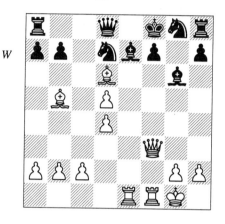

G. Maroczy – M. Chigorin
Gambit tournament, Vienna 1903

15 ♖xe7! ♘xe7 16 ♖e1 ♔g7
16...♔g8 17 ♖xe7 ♘b6 (or 17...♕b6 18 ♖xd7 ♕xb5 19 ♕f6) 18 ♖e8+ ♕xe8 19 ♗xe8 ♖xe8 20 ♗e5 is very good for White.
17 ♗xe7 ♕a5 18 ♕e2 ♘f8?

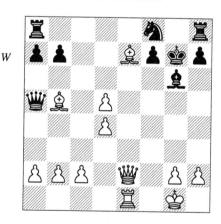

19 ♗f6+! ♔g8 20 ♕e5 h6
20...♕xb5 21 ♗xh8 f6 22 ♕xf6 ♕d7 23 ♖e7 and White wins.
21 ♗xh8 f6 22 ♕e7
22 ♕xf6! ♕xe1+ 23 ♗f1 is another way to finish off.
22...♔xh8
22...♗f7 allows a choice of wins, e.g. 23 ♖e3 or 23 c3.
23 ♕xf6+ 1-0

Chigorin wins the Russian Championship with 15/18, ahead of O.Bernstein (14), Yurevich (13½), Salwe (13) and Rubinstein (11½). This is the third 'All-Russian' Championship, and also Chigorin's third victory. The following game is noteworthy as it witnesses a modern attacking scheme typical of the King's Indian.

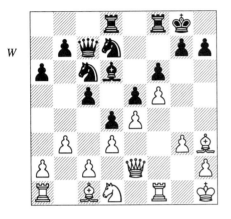

M. Chigorin – A. Rubinstein
Russian Ch, Kiev 1903

19 ♗g4! b5 20 ♗h5 ♖b8 21 g4 ♗e7 22 h4 ♖fc8 23 g5 ♘d8 24 c4

24...dxc3 25 ♘xc3 would allow the knight to d5, so White manages to block the queenside.
24...♘f8 25 ♖g1 ♘b7 26 ♘f2 ♘d6 27 ♘g4 ♔h8? 28 gxf6 gxf6 29 ♘h6 ♘g6 30 fxg6 ♗f8 31 ♘f7+ ♘xf7 32 gxf7 ♕e7 33 ♖g8# (1-0)

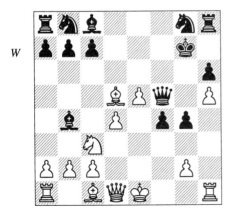

R. Spielmann – M. Eljaschoff
Munich 1903

Here we have the aftermath of an Allgaier Gambit that has not gone well for Black.
13 0-0 f3 14 ♘e4! ♕xh5
14...♘e7 15 ♘g3 ♕d7 does little for Black's queenside development; White can choose between 16 ♗xf3 and 16 ♗e4.
15 ♘g3 ♕h4 16 ♖xf3!! gxf3 17 ♕xf3 ♘f6
The only move to keep the game going.
18 exf6+
18 ♘h5+ allows 18...♔f8!.
18...♔f8 19 ♗f4 ♘a6
19...♗d6 20 ♗xd6+ cxd6 21 ♕e3! ♖h7 22 ♖e1 ♗d7 23 ♗xb7 is a win for White, while after 19...c6 20 ♕e4 ♕xf6 21 ♗b3 Black cannot avoid a serious loss of material.
20 ♕e4! ♕g4 21 ♗xb7!
Diverting the piece that defends the black queen.
21...♗xb7 22 ♗xh6+ ♖xh6 23 ♕xg4
Black has more than enough material for the queen, but his king is too vulnerable.
23...♖h7 24 ♕g6 ♖f7 25 c3 ♗d6 26 ♘f5 ♗e4 27 ♕h6+ ♔g8 28 ♕g5+ ♔f8 29 ♘h6 1-0

Chess News in Brief
Lasker completes a tour of the USA.

World News in Brief
Colombia and the USA sign a treaty to allow the Panama Canal to proceed. Later in the year, after Colombia makes additional demands, US-backed rebels take over the Panama isthmus and declare it a republic.

Turks massacre 50,000 Bulgarian civilians, notably at the village of Monastir.

The royal family of Serbia are assassinated.

The Russian socialists split into two groups, with Vladimir Lenin heading the *Bolsheviks*.

Marie Curie wins a Nobel Prize for discovering radiation. She rightly hopes it will play a part in treating diseases, but fails to anticipate its harmful effects.

Near Kitty Hawk, North Carolina, Orville and Wilbur Wright achieve the first powered flight in their biplane, *Flyer I*. The flight lasts for 12 seconds and covers about 37 metres.

The first coast-to-coast car journey across the USA is completed.

1904

Triumph for Marshall at Cambridge Springs

Frank Marshall wins the Cambridge Springs tournament with a sensational 13/15 ahead of a world-class field including Lasker, Janowski, Schlechter and Pillsbury. World Champion Lasker, in his first tournament since 1900, suffers two bad losses, but produces some exciting chess.

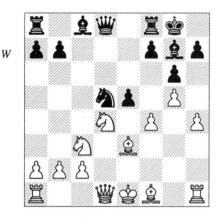

Em. Lasker – W. Napier
Cambridge Springs 1904

Lasker has responded to his opponent's Dragon Sicilian in rather crude fashion, and faces a crisis in the centre. He has no choice but to go forward.

15 ♘f5!

15 ♘xd5 exd4 is good for Black.

15...♘xc3 16 ♕xd8 ♖xd8 17 ♘e7+ ♔h8

Best. 17...♔f8 is met by 18 ♗c5 ♘e4 19 ♗a3.

18 h5!

Lasker perceives that, despite the exchange of queens, his best course is to continue the attack against the black king. Although there is an obvious risk, it is the only way to make sense of his earlier kingside advances and exploit the restricted black king.

18...♖e8!

Napier finds the best reply, which is based on counterplay against the white king.

19 ♗c5 gxh5

Probably best, but 19...exf4 is playable. Then 20 ♗c4 (20 hxg6 fxg6 21 ♗c4 can be met by

21...b6, transposing, or 21...♗f5!?) 20...b6! 21 hxg6 fxg6 22 ♔f1 ♗f5 is unclear.

20 ♗c4?

A brave but mistaken choice. White should play 20 bxc3 ♗f8 21 ♗b5 ♖xe7! 22 ♗xe7 ♗xe7 23 ♖xh5 ♗g4 24 ♖h4 ♗f5, with a likely draw.

20...exf4?!

Best is 20...♘e4! 21 ♗xf7 ♗g4! 22 ♗xe8 ♖xe8 23 ♗a3 ♘g3 24 ♖h2 exf4, with overwhelming compensation for the exchange.

21 ♗xf7 ♘e4?!

Black can still probably hold the balance by 21...♖f8 22 ♗xh5 ♘e4 23 ♘g6+ ♔g8.

22 ♗xe8 ♗xb2 23 ♖b1 ♗c3+ 24 ♔f1 ♗g4

This looks very awkward for White, but Lasker has a fantastic defensive resource.

25 ♗xh5! ♗xh5 26 ♖xh5 ♘g3+

26...♘d2+ loses to 27 ♔f2 ♘xb1 28 g6 ♔g7 29 ♖h7+ ♔f6 30 g7.

27 ♔g2 ♘xh5 28 ♖xb7 a5

The prolonged exchange of tactical blows has led to a seemingly quiet position, but one that very much favours White.

29 ♖b3! ♗g7 30 ♖h3 ♘g3 31 ♔f3 ♖a6?!

Even the better 31...♖e8 32 ♗d6 ♘f1 33 ♔xf4 should be a win for White.

32 ♔xf4 ♘e2+ 33 ♔f5 ♘c3 34 a3 ♘a4 35 ♗e3 1-0

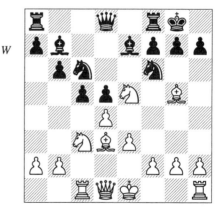

C. Schlechter – Em. Lasker
Cambridge Springs 1904

Schlechter decides that he has no objection to an exchange on e5.

11 0-0 ♘xe5 12 dxe5 ♘e8 13 ♗f4 f5?! 14 ♕c2! g5

Lasker allows himself to be provoked into a rash pawn advance.

15 ♗g3 f4? 16 ♗xh7+ ♔h8 17 ♕g6

With threats of 18 ♗g8 and 18 ♕h6. Black has no adequate defence.

17...♘f6 18 exf6 ♖xf6 19 ♕h5 ♔g7 20 ♕xg5+ ♔xh7 21 ♗xf4

The overall result is that White has won two pawns. He need only be a little accurate to make sure Black doesn't get counterplay on the g-file.

21...♖g6 22 ♕h5+ ♔g7 23 ♖fd1 d4 24 ♗g3 ♖g5 25 ♗e5+ ♔g8

25...♗f6? 26 ♕xg5+.

26 ♕h8+ ♔f7 27 ♕h7+ ♔e6 28 ♗g3 dxc3 29 ♖xd8 cxb2 30 ♖dd1 bxc1♕ 31 ♖xc1 ♖d8 32 f4 ♖gd5 33 e4 ♖d1+ 34 ♖xd1 ♖xd1+ 35 ♔f2 ♖d4 36 f5+ ♔d7 37 e5 1-0

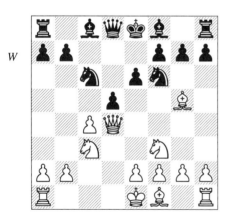

H. Pillsbury – Em. Lasker
Cambridge Springs 1904

This position had arisen in an earlier game Pillsbury-Lasker, St Petersburg 1895/6, which ended in a famous victory for Black. This time Pillsbury is ready.

7 ♗xf6! gxf6

7...♘xd4 8 ♗xd8 ♘c2+ 9 ♔d2 ♘xa1 is insufficient for Black.

8 ♕h4 dxc4

8...d4 is boldly met by 9 0-0-0.

9 ♖d1 ♗d7 10 e3 ♘e5

A risky move, inviting White to attack, and typical of Lasker's style. However, in this game his defensive skills are not up to their usual standard.

11 ♘xe5 fxe5 12 ♕xc4 ♕b6 13 ♗e2 ♕xb2

13...♗c6 is more solid.

14 0-0 ♖c8 15 ♕d3 ♖c7 16 ♘e4 ♗e7 17 ♘d6+ ♔f8

17...♗xd6 18 ♕xd6 is awkward for Black, as 18...♕c3? loses to 19 ♗b5.

18 ♘c4 ♕b4 19 f4?!

Pillsbury attacks relentlessly, but it is unconvincing. 19 ♘xe5 is better.

19...exf4?

19...♗b5 looks good. Then 20 ♕e4? (20 ♖c1 ♖xc4 21 ♖xc4 ♕xc4 22 ♕xc4 ♗xc4 23 ♗xc4 leaves White playing for a draw) 20...♗xc4 21 ♕xe5 f6 22 ♕xc7 ♗xe2 23 ♖b1 ♕c5 is no good for White.

20 ♕d4 f6 21 ♕xf4 ♕c5 22 ♘e5 ♗e8 23 ♘g4 f5 24 ♕h6+ ♔f7 25 ♗c4!

The bishop is tactically defended, and generates all manner of threats.

25...♖c6 26 ♖xf5+! ♕xf5 27 ♖f1 ♕xf1+ 28 ♔xf1 ♗d7 29 ♕h5+! ♔g8 30 ♘e5 1-0

Chess News in Brief

Geza Maroczy wins the Monte Carlo tournament, ahead of Schlechter and Marshall.

William Napier wins the British Championship.

World News in Brief

War breaks out between Russia and Japan over control of Manchuria. The Russian fleet suffers a catastrophic defeat at the hands of the Japanese navy.

The American occupation of Cuba is ended.

The Trans-Siberian Railway opens. It is an extraordinary engineering feat, linking European Russian with Vladivostok and China across some of the world's most inhospitable terrain.

The New York underground railway opens.

1905

Excellent results for Tarrasch and Maroczy •
Mixed performances by Marshall and Janowski

Geza Maroczy wins the Ostend tournament, ahead of Janowski and Tarrasch. The most exciting games involve these three players.

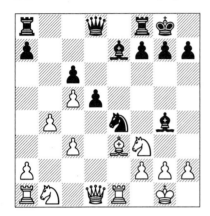

G. Maroczy – S. Tarrasch
Ostend 1905

Black has emerged from a dubious opening with good compensation for a pawn that White unwisely grabbed.

12...♗f6 13 ♗d4 ♖e8 14 a4

Planning to activate the rook via a2. Instead, 14 ♗xf6? ♕xf6 15 ♕d4 ♗xf3 16 ♕xf6 ♘xf6 17 ♖xe8+ ♖xe8 18 gxf3 ♖e1+ leaves White hopelessly tied up.

14...♗xd4 15 cxd4

15 ♕xd4 loses material to 15...♗xf3 16 gxf3 ♕g5+ 17 ♔f1 ♘g3+ followed by 18...♖e1+, 19...♕c1+ and 20...♕b2+.

15...♗xf3 16 gxf3?!

16 ♕xf3 ♘xc5! regains the pawn with some advantage, but White can fight for survival.

16...♕g5+ 17 ♔f1 ♘f6

The knight is heading for f4.

18 ♖e3

18 ♖a3 ♖xe1+ 19 ♕xe1 ♕h4 is good for Black.

18...♖xe3!

18...♘h5 is also good.

19 fxe3 ♕xe3 20 ♖a3 ♕f4 21 ♕d2 ♕f5 22 ♖b3 ♖e8 23 ♔g2 ♖e6!? 24 ♘a3

24 b5 loses to 24...♘e4!.

24...♘h5 25 ♖e3 ♖g6+ 26 ♔f2 h6 27 ♖e5 ♕h3 28 ♔e3 ♘f6 29 ♕e2 ♖g2 0-1

A possible finish is 30 ♕e1 ♘g4+ 31 ♔d3 ♕xf3+ 32 ♖e3 ♘xe3 33 ♕xe3 ♕d1+ 34 ♔c3 ♕a1+ and mate next move.

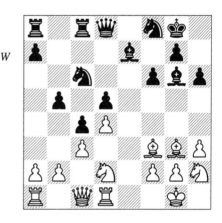

D. Janowski – S. Tarrasch
Ostend 1905

In this innocent-looking position, Janowski generates a powerful attack by pressurizing the fixed weakness on d5 and probing the weak squares around the black king.

23 ♖e1 b4 24 ♘df1!

The knight will come to e3; White's minor pieces are coordinating well.

24...bxc3 25 bxc3 ♕a5?!

The queen is needed for the defence of the kingside. 25...♕d7 is safer.

26 ♘e3 ♗f7

26...♖d8? allows the simple tactic 27 ♘xc4.

27 ♕d2

27 ♘xc4? is a mistake since after 27...dxc4 28 ♗xc6, Black hits back with 28...♗a3.

27...♗a3 28 ♖ab1 ♘d7?!

Intending ...♘b6, shoring up his position.

29 ♖b7!

This incursion is more than Black's fragile position can take.

29...♘b6 30 ♘f5 ♕a6

30...♗f8 31 ♘g4 piles on too much pressure, e.g. 31...♗g6 32 ♘fxh6+ gxh6 33 ♘xh6+ ♔h8 34 ♕f4 with a winning attack.

31 ♘xh6+!! gxh6 32 ♖xf7! ♔xf7 33 ♕xh6

Black is completely defenceless.

33...♔g8 34 ♕g6+ ♔h8 35 ♕xf6+ ♔g8 36 ♕g6+ ♔h8 37 ♖e5 1-0

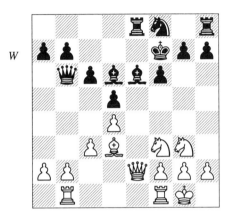

F. Marshall – M. Chigorin
Ostend 1905

14 ♘h4! ♗f5? 15 ♘hxf5!! ♖xe2 16 ♘xd6+ ♔e6

Black must pursue the knight; otherwise White gets too much material for the queen.

17 ♘c8 ♕c7 18 ♗xe2

The possibility of ♗g4+ preserves the c8-knight a little longer.

18...♔f7

18...g6 19 ♖fe1 saves the knight: 19...f5 20 ♗f3+ ♔f6 21 ♖e8. 18...♘d7 is a better defence, but 19 ♖fe1 ♕xc8 (19...♔f7? 20 ♗h5+ g6 21 ♖e7+) 20 ♗h5+ ♔d6 21 ♘f5+ ♔c7 22 ♘xg7 ♔b6 23 ♖e7 leaves White well in command.

19 ♘f5!

Now it's the fork on d6 that extends the knight's life-support.

19...♘e6 20 ♘fd6+ ♔g6 21 ♗d3+ ♔h5

Chigorin still hopes to round up the knights, but his king is now a major target.

22 ♖be1 ♘f4 23 ♖e7 ♕a5 24 ♗b1

24 ♖xg7 is simplest.

24...g6 25 g3 ♘h3+ 26 ♔g2 ♘g5 27 ♗d3 ♖xc8 28 ♘xc8 ♕d8 29 h4! ♕xc8 30 hxg5 1-0

Chess News in Brief

Janowski and Maroczy win the Barmen tournament, ahead of Marshall, O.Bernstein and Schlechter. The lower group, the *Hauptturnier*, is won by Duras and Rubinstein, ahead of Löwy and Vidmar.

Marshall wins the Scheveningen tournament.

Tarrasch scores a 12-5 match victory over Marshall at Nuremberg.

Marshall beats Janowski by 8 wins to 5 (4 draws not counting) in a match at Paris.

Isaac Kashdan [the leading USA player in the late 1920s and early 1930s] is born.

Sultan Khan [a natural talent from the Punjab who plays with remarkable success in Europe from 1929 to 1933] is born.

Carlos Torre [the first Mexican grandmaster] is born.

World News in Brief

The Japanese besiege Vladivostok. The Japanese navy achieves an annihilating victory over the Russian Baltic Fleet, which had sailed halfway around the world to assist their countrymen in the east. Unrest in Russia increases. The war ends, after heavy casualties on both sides, with Russia acquiescing to most of Japan's objectives.

An ongoing plague in India claims more than 1,000,000 lives.

More than 10,000 are killed by an earthquake in Lahore, India.

Norway declares its independence from Sweden.

German troops massacre thousands of the Herero people in Namibia in retaliation for an earlier uprising.

Albert Einstein publishes the Special Theory of Relativity. It links space and time in a new picture of our universe: a four-dimensional space-time. While it seems counter-intuitive, the new theory explains and predicts events that were hitherto incomprehensible. Its consequences include the idea that the speed of light is the theoretical maximum speed for anything to travel, and the famous mass-energy equation $E = mc^2$ (where E is energy, m is an object's rest-mass, and c is the speed of light).

1906

Pillsbury dies, leaving Marshall as the leading American player • Successes for Rubinstein

It is a year of few major chess events. There follow some interesting games.

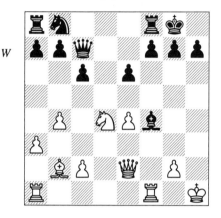

J. Mieses – J. Møller
Stockholm 1906

White has sacrificed two pawns in return for a vigorous attack.

17 ♕g4! e5

17...♗e5 allows 18 ♘xe6!, while after 17...♗h6 18 ♘xe6 ♕d7 19 ♗xg7 ♕xe6 20 ♕xe6 fxe6 21 ♖xf8+ ♔xg7 22 ♖af1, White's active rooks should bring him victory.

18 ♘f5 f6

18...g6? 19 ♕xf4 exf4 20 ♘h6#.

19 ♖xf4! exf4 20 ♖d1 ♔h8

20...♘a6? loses to 21 ♖d7.

21 e5! ♕f7

After the alternative 21...fxe5 22 ♖d6 ♘a6 23 ♗xe5 ♖f7 24 ♕h5 (threatening 25 ♖h6) 24...♔g8 25 ♖h6 ♖xf5 26 ♕xf5 Black must give up his queen.

22 e6?

22 exf6 gxf6 23 ♕g5 wins. The threat is 24 ♗xf6+ ♕xf6 25 ♕xf6+ ♖xf6 26 ♖d8+ ♖f8 27 ♖xf8#, while 23...♘a6 loses to 24 ♖d6 and 23...♘d7 to 24 ♖xd7.

22...♕g6

After 22...h5? 23 ♕xf4 ♕xe6 24 ♖d6 White's attack will crash through.

23 e7 ♖e8?

Now White forces a won ending. Instead, 23...♖g8 24 ♖d8 ♘a6 25 ♘d6 ♘c7 looks like a draw, as after 26 ♕d7 Black can give perpetual check.

24 ♕xg6 hxg6 25 ♖d8 ♘a6 26 ♘d6 ♖axd8 27 exd8♕ ♖xd8 28 ♘f7+ ♔g8 29 ♘xd8 c5 30 bxc5 ♘xc5 31 ♗d4 b6 32 ♗xc5 bxc5 33 ♔g1 g5 34 ♔f2 c4 35 ♔f3 ♔f8 36 ♘c6 a6 37 ♘b4 ♔e7 38 ♘xa6 ♔d6 39 ♔e4 ♔c6 40 ♔d4 g4 41 ♘b4+ ♔b5 42 ♘d5 g5 43 ♘xf6 g3 44 ♘e4 g4 45 ♘xg3 fxg3 46 c3 1-0

J. Mieses – M. Chigorin
Ostend 1906

1 e4 e5 2 ♘c3 ♘c6 3 ♗c4 ♗c5 4 ♕g4 ♕f6?! 5 ♘d5!

This has since become a well-known opening trap which has claimed many victims. It is surprising that the queen does so little on f2.

5...♕xf2+ 6 ♔d1 ♔f8 7 ♘h3 ♕d4 8 d3 d6

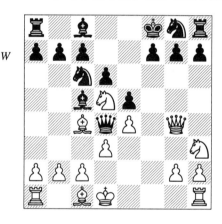

9 ♕h4 ♗xh3 10 ♕xh3 ♘a5 11 ♖f1 ♘xc4 12 ♕d7!

12 c3? ♘xb2+ 13 ♗xb2 ♕a4+ saves the queen.

12...f6 13 ♘xf6! ♕f2

13...gxf6 is mated by 14 ♖xf6+ ♘xf6 15 ♗h6+ ♔g8 16 ♕g7#.

14 ♖xf2 ♗xf2 15 ♘h5 1-0

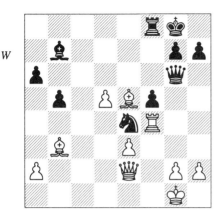

D. Janowski – G. Salwe
Ostend 1906

26 ♕c2

White now threatens 27 ♕xe4 fxe4 28 d6+. Black sees the idea, and parries it.

26...♘g5 27 ♖f1 h6 28 h4 ♘e4?

Salwe thinks it is now safe to put the knight on e4, as the king has a flight-square.

29 ♕xe4!

A rude awakening!

29...fxe4 30 d6+ ♔h7 31 ♖xf8 ♕g4 32 ♗g8+ ♔g6 33 ♗f7+ 1-0

33...♔h7 is met by 34 h5 and ♗g6+, winning.

Akiba Rubinstein wins a four-man triple-round tournament in Lodz with 6½/9, ahead of Chigorin (5½).

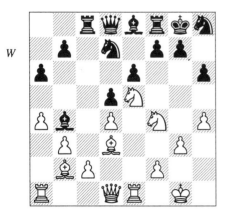

A. Rubinstein – M. Chigorin
Lodz 1906

Certain sources have erroneously given this game as Chigorin-Rubinstein.

White wins by methodical attacking play, interspersed with a few fine touches.

20 c3! ♗d6

20...♗xc3? loses to 21 ♕c2 ♘g6 22 ♘exg6.

21 ♕c2 g6 22 ♕d2 g5 23 ♘h3 ♘xe5 24 dxe5 ♗e7 25 hxg5 hxg5 26 ♕e2 ♘g6 27 ♕g4 ♔g7 28 ♖ad1 b5 29 axb5 axb5 30 c4!

It is time to open another front.

30...bxc4 31 bxc4 ♗c6 32 ♗c1 ♖h8 33 ♘xg5 ♕e8? 34 ♗xg6 fxg6 35 ♘xe6+ ♔g8 36 cxd5 ♗b7 37 ♗g5 ♗xg5 38 ♘xg5

Certainly not 38 ♕xg5? ♕xe6 39 dxe6?? ♖h1#.

38...♖c5 39 ♘e4 1-0

Chess News in Brief

Frank Marshall wins the German Open Championship with 12½/16 ahead of Duras (11), Forgacs and Schlechter (both 10½).

Georg Salwe wins the All-Russian Championship with 13/16, ahead of Blumenfeld and Rubinstein (both 12).

A large tournament at Ostend is won by Schlechter, ahead of Maroczy and Rubinstein.

Harry Nelson Pillsbury (born 1872) dies of syphilis, just four years before an effective cure is discovered.

Cecil Purdy [winner of the 1st Correspondence World Championship, 1950-3] is born.

Vera Menchik [Women's World Champion 1927-44 and the first woman to compete with any degree of success against the leading male players of the time] is born.

World News in Brief

Martial law is declared in Russia.

China grants Britain control of Tibet.

Britain and Japan both launch warships of unprecedented size and power.

A massive earthquake reduces much of San Francisco to rubble and kills about 700 people.

A typhoon in Tahiti kills more than 10,000 people.

A mining disaster claims 1,800 lives in France.

In Italy, Mount Vesuvius erupts; the town of Ottaviano is destroyed.

1907

Lasker outclasses Marshall to remain World Champion

Emanuel Lasker beats Frank Marshall by a large margin (11½-3½; 8 wins, 7 draws, no losses) to remain World Champion. The lopsided result seems surprising in view of Marshall's impressive tournament and match results, but he proves powerless against Lasker's all-round expertise and excellent psychology.

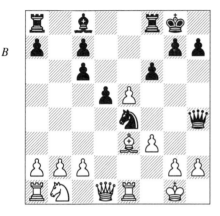

F. Marshall – Em. Lasker
World Ch match (game 1), New York 1907

13...fxe5!

This is a brave and correct sacrifice. It is also good psychology to play aggressively against a man whose natural flair is attacking play.

14 fxe4 d4 15 g3

White cannot yet cede the f2-square: 15 ♗d2? ♗g4! 16 ♕c1 ♖f2! with the decisive threats 17...♖xg2+ and 17...♗f3.

15...♕f6 16 ♗xd4?

Rather than grant Lasker an attack, Marshall opts for a difficult ending. However, he has underestimated the danger. 16 ♗d2 ♕f2+ 17 ♔h1 ♗h3 18 ♖g1 ♗f1! (18...h5? 19 ♘a3 ♗g4 20 ♖f1! defends) 19 ♗e1 ♕e3 20 ♘d2 ♗e2 21 ♕c1 ♗f3+ 22 ♘xf3 ♕xf3+ 23 ♖g2 ♕f1+ is a perpetual check, though White would need to have a lot of faith in his calculations to go into this line, where he is on the brink of disaster for several moves.

16...exd4 17 ♖f1 ♕xf1+ 18 ♕xf1 ♖xf1+ 19 ♔xf1 ♖b8! 20 b3 ♖b5!

Lasker's rook manoeuvre emphasizes that he has real winning chances in this ending.

21 c4?

21 ♘d2! is more satisfactory for White.

21...♖h5! 22 ♔g1

Not 22 h4? g5! 23 hxg5 ♖h1+, with a decisive pin on White's back rank.

22...c5 23 ♘d2 ♔f7 24 ♖f1+ ♔e7 25 a3?! ♖h6!

Preparing to attack the new weaknesses.

26 h4 ♖a6 27 ♖a1 ♗g4! 28 ♔f2 ♔e6 29 a4

29 ♘f3 ♗xf3 30 ♔xf3 ♔e5 is hopeless for White.

29...♔e5 30 ♔g2 ♖f6 31 ♖e1 d3 32 ♖f1 ♔d4

White has no counterplay, and can hardly even offer token resistance.

33 ♖xf6 gxf6 34 ♔f2 c6 35 a5 a6

White is in zugzwang.

36 ♘b1 ♔xe4 37 ♔e1 ♗e2 38 ♘d2+ ♔e3 39 ♘b1 f5 40 ♘d2 h5 41 ♘b1 ♔f3 42 ♘c3 ♔xg3 43 ♘a4 f4 44 ♘xc5 f3 45 ♘e4+ ♔f4 46 ♘d6 c5 47 b4 cxb4 48 c5 b3 49 ♘c4 ♔g3 0-1

A happier experience for Marshall:

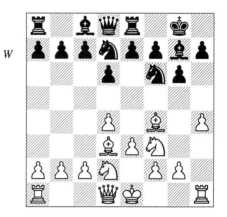

F. Marshall – A. Burn
Ostend 1907

8 h5!? ♘xh5 9 ♖xh5! gxh5 10 ♗xh7+! ♔xh7?

Maybe Burn genuinely didn't believe the sacrifice, or maybe the age of chivalry was not yet over. 10...♔f8 is necessary. White has good play for the exchange, but it is not clear that his attack will necessarily be decisive.

11 ♘g5+ ♔g6

11...♔g8 loses directly to 12 ♕xh5 ♘f6 13 ♕xf7+ ♔h8 14 0-0-0 and ♖h1+.

12 ♘df3! e5 13 ♘h4+ ♔f6

White now forces mate by a pretty dance with his knights.

14 ♘h7+ ♔e7 15 ♘f5+ ♔e6 16 ♘xg7+

16 d5+ ♔xf5 17 ♕xh5+ ♔e4 18 ♕f3+ ♔f5 19 g4+ ♔g6 20 ♕e4+ f5 21 ♕xf5# is a slightly quicker mate.

16...♔e7 17 ♘f5+ ♔e6 18 d5+ ♔xf5 19 ♕xh5+ ♔e4 20 0-0-0 1-0

Rising star Akiba Rubinstein plays a combination that will be admired for centuries to come:

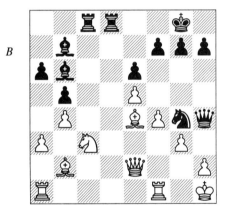

G. Rotlewi – A. Rubinstein
Lodz 1907/8

Here we see the finish of the 'Rubinstein Immortal'. It is clear that there is plenty wrong with the white position, but a lot of imagination is needed to find the best way to bring it crashing down.

22...♖xc3!!

The logic is to overload the white queen by the need to defend e4 and h2. However, the black queen is *en prise*, so many players would fail to look any deeper.

23 gxh4 ♖d2!

Now the overloading of the white queen proves decisive. There are several variations to analyse, but they are mostly short and end in mate to the white king.

24 ♕xd2

Or: 24 ♕xg4 ♗xe4+ 25 ♖f3 ♖xf3; 24 ♗xc3 ♗xe4+ 25 ♕xe4 ♖xh2#; 24 ♗xb7 ♖xe2 25 ♗g2 ♖h3 mating.

24...♗xe4+ 25 ♕g2 ♖h3! 0-1

White is defenceless: 26 ♖f2 ♖xh2+ 27 ♔g1 ♗xf2+ 28 ♔f1 ♗d3# or 26 ♖f3 ♗xf3 27 ♕xf3 ♖xh2#.

Chess News in Brief

Richard Teichmann wins the Berlin tournament.

Paul Leonhardt wins the Copenhagen tournament, ahead of Maroczy and Schlechter.

Akiba Rubinstein wins the Karlsbad tournament, ahead of Maroczy, Leonhardt, Nimzowitsch and Schlechter.

Siegbert Tarrasch wins a strong six-man tournament at Ostend, ahead of Schlechter, Marshall and Janowski.

Jacques Mieses wins the Vienna tournament, ahead of Duras and Tartakower.

England and the USA contest a cable match, resuming a yearly event.

Vladimirs Petrovs [the leading Latvian player in the 1930s] is born.

World News in Brief

Japan hands Manchuria back to China.

The USA puts its army in charge of building the Panama Canal.

Heavy rains and crop failures lead to millions of people starving in China.

There is widespread famine in Russia – the worst on record.

Oil is discovered in Persia.

In the British parliament, a bill to give women the vote is defeated.

New Zealand becomes a dominion.

In France, the Lumière brothers develop a way to project moving colour pictures.

In The Hague, a peace conference determines the conventions of war.

1908

Lasker comfortably fends off Tarrasch's challenge • Rubinstein and Schlechter achieve impressive results

Emanuel Lasker defends the World Championship against Siegbert Tarrasch, winning by 10½-5½ (8 wins, 5 draws, 3 losses). Tarrasch, while undoubtedly of World Champion calibre in the 1890s, proves unable to cope with Lasker's dynamism and energy. The following is perhaps the most significant game of the match.

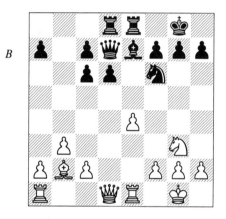

S. Tarrasch – Em. Lasker
World Ch match (game 2), Dusseldorf 1908

14...♘g4!?

Having misplayed the opening, Lasker decides that normal means will not suffice, and challenges Tarrasch to attack him. Although one may dispute whether this is the wisest policy (if Tarrasch had won the game, the decision would undoubtedly have been criticized), it is psychologically unpleasant for White, who may have been settling down to exploiting a pleasant advantage in a quiet position, without risk.

15 ♗xg7!

Otherwise Black can play ...♗f6.

15...♘xf2

15...♔xg7? 16 ♘f5+ is hopeless for Black.

16 ♔xf2

This must have been a difficult decision. 16 ♕d4! ♘g4 17 ♘f5 gives Black more problems.

16...♔xg7 17 ♘f5+ ♔h8 18 ♕d4+ f6 19 ♕xa7 ♗f8 20 ♕d4 ♖e5

White has won a pawn, but Black now has some potential advantages of his own.

21 ♖ad1 ♖de8 22 ♕c3 ♕f7 23 ♘g3?

This 'consolidating' move is all Black needs to gain counterplay. 23 ♕f3 is better.

23...♗h6 24 ♕f3

24 ♘f5, while probably best, would be an admission that the previous move was wrong.

24...d5 25 exd5 ♗e3+ 26 ♔f1 cxd5 27 ♖d3? ♕e6 28 ♖e2 f5

White has now got himself in serious trouble.

29 ♖d1 f4 30 ♘h1 d4 31 ♘f2 ♕a6

Threatening 32...♗xf2.

32 ♘d3 ♖g5 33 ♖a1 ♕h6 34 ♔e1 ♕xh2 35 ♔d1 ♕g1+ 36 ♘e1 ♖ge5 37 ♕c6 ♖5e6 38 ♕xc7 ♖8e7 39 ♕d8+?! ♔g7 40 a4?! f3 41 gxf3 ♗g5 0-1

Rubinstein wins a three-man match-tournament at Lodz, scoring 4½-3½ against his main rival, Marshall. Oddly enough, he also achieves the same score against Marshall in a later match, played at Warsaw. The following game is from the former event.

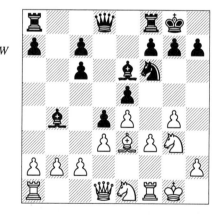

A. Rubinstein – F. Marshall
Match-tournament (game 2), Lodz 1908

Black has just played 13...d4?, which, by relaxing the pressure in the centre, gives White a freer hand on the kingside. Meanwhile, Black's doubled c-pawns cripple his queenside chances.

14 ♗d2 ♗e7 15 ♘g2 ♖b8 16 b3 c5 17 ♘f5 ♗xf5 18 gxf5 ♖b6 19 ♖f2 ♕d7 20 ♕e2 ♖fb8 21 f4 exf4 22 ♗xf4 c4

Rather a desperate measure, to try to change the course of the game.

23 bxc4

23 dxc4 ♗c5 24 ♕d3 ♘g4 25 ♖e2 f6 gives Black some compensation.

23...♖b1+ 24 ♖xb1 ♖xb1+ 25 ♖f1 ♖b2 26 e5 ♘e8 27 ♗g3 ♕a4 28 f6!

White can push ahead with his kingside attack. This sets up an exciting finish.

28...♗f8

After 28...gxf6 29 ♕g4+ ♚h8 30 e6 fxe6 31 ♕xe6 White regains the initiative, and should win.

29 ♕g4! g6

29...♕xc2 loses a piece to 30 ♘e1 followed by ♕c8.

30 e6! ♖xc2

30...♕xc2 31 exf7+ ♚h8 32 ♘h4! and White wins, e.g. 32...♘xf6 33 ♕g5!.

31 ♘e1! ♖xa2 32 exf7+ ♚xf7 33 ♘f3

The previously inactive knight has found a fast-track to the main battlefield.

33...♘xf6 34 ♘g5+ ♚g7 35 ♖xf6! ♚xf6 36 ♕f4+ ♚e7 37 ♕f7+ ♚d8 38 ♘e6+ 1-0

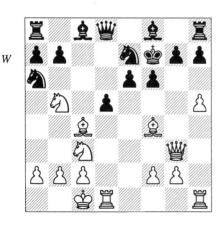

W

A. Bobrischev-Pushkin – N. Timofeev
Russia correspondence 1908-10

White has played an aggressive opening, sacrificing two pawns for a big lead in development. Black's last move, 14...♘c6-e7?, grossly underestimated the danger.

15 ♘d6+ ♚g8 16 ♘xd5!!

The threat of ♘xf6# forces the pace.

16...exd5

16...♘c6 loses to 17 ♘f5.

17 ♖xd5! ♗e6 18 ♘f5! ♘xf5 19 ♖xd8 ♗xc4 20 ♕c3 1-0

Chess News in Brief

Marshall wins the Dusseldorf tournament, ahead of Salwe and Spielmann.

Oldřich Duras and Carl Schlechter win the Prague tournament.

Maroczy, Schlechter and Duras share first place at the Vienna tournament; Richard Réti, making his international debut, is in last place with 1½/19.

Janowski scores a 6½-3½ match victory over Marshall at Suresnes.

Lasker tours Britain, the Netherlands and Germany.

Mikhail Chigorin (the leading Russian player in the late 19th century; World Championship challenger in 1889 and 1892) dies.

Vsevolod Rauzer [prominent Soviet theoretician in the inter-war years] is born.

Viacheslav Ragozin [winner of the 2nd Correspondence World Championship, 1956-8] is born.

World News in Brief

There is a crisis in the Balkans as Austria annexes Bosnia-Herzegovina. Bulgaria declares independence from the Ottomans.

In Portugal, a revolution fails; later the king and crown prince are assassinated.

The German Kaiser insults the British in an interview in the *Daily Telegraph*.

In Italy, an extremely violent earthquake destroys Messina.

The first Ford Model T is produced.

Ernest Rutherford wins a Nobel Prize for his work on radioactivity and the atom.

1909

Capablanca achieves an astonishing match victory over Marshall •
Lasker outclasses Janowski

José Raúl Capablanca creates a sensation by scoring an overwhelming match victory over Marshall at New York; his score of 8 wins, 14 draws and 1 loss is hardly less convincing than Lasker's victory over Marshall in his world title defence, yet at this time Capablanca is a virtually unknown player.

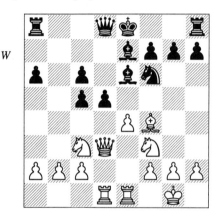

J. Capablanca – F. Marshall
Match (game 8), Wilkes-Barre 1909

Black is behind in development and his queenside pawns are weak. White must now decide how to exploit these circumstances.

14 ♘g5! d4

14...0-0? loses material: 15 e5 c4 16 ♘xe6 fxe6 17 ♕h3.

15 ♘xe6 fxe6 16 ♘a4

This disrupts Black's development, because 16...0-0? loses a pawn to 17 ♕c4.

16...♕a5 17 b3 ♖d8 18 ♘b2! ♘h5

18...♕xa2? 19 ♘c4 traps the queen.

19 ♗e5 0-0 20 ♘c4 ♕b4 21 ♕h3

Black has been outplayed, and must lose a pawn. He conceives a desperate plan of counterattack, but Capablanca ruthlessly stamps it out.

21...g6 22 ♕xe6+ ♖f7 23 g4 ♗h4

23...♘g7 24 ♗xg7 ♔xg7 25 ♘e5 picks off an exchange without ceding the initiative. 23...♘f6 24 ♗c7 and ♘e5 wins material.

24 gxh5 ♗xf2+ 25 ♔h1 ♕c3

25...♗xe1 loses to 26 hxg6 hxg6 27 ♕xg6+ ♔f8 28 ♘d6 ♖f1+ 29 ♔g2 ♖f2+ 30 ♔g1 ♗e7 31 ♘f5+ ♖xf5 32 exf5.

26 ♖e3!

The clearest way to repel Black's threats.

26...♕xc2

26...♗xe3 27 hxg6 hxg6 28 ♕xg6+ ♔f8 29 ♘d6 and White wins.

27 ♖ed3 ♕e2 28 ♘d6 ♖xd6 29 ♗xd6 ♗e1 30 ♕e8+ ♔g7 31 h6+ 1-0

Lasker and Rubinstein dominate the St Petersburg tournament, sharing first place.

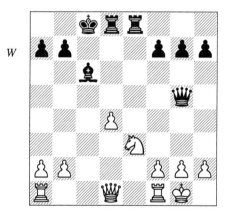

A. Rubinstein – Em. Lasker
St Petersburg 1909

White has won a pawn, but faces very dangerous counterplay. Some very precise play is needed to parry the threats without losing the advantage.

16 ♖c1!

Apparently ignoring Black's main threat, but there is a deep idea.

16...♖xe3

The slower 16...♔b8 allows White to solve his problem by 17 ♖c5!.

17 ♖xc6+ bxc6 18 ♕c1!!

This is the idea – White exploits the pin on the c1-h6 diagonal and the exposed black king.

18...♖xd4

18...♖e5!? 19 ♕xc6+ ♚b8 20 dxe5 ♕xe5 21 ♖c1 is hardly a better try.

19 fxe3 ♖d7 20 ♕xc6+ ♚d8 21 ♖f4!

Threatening 22 ♕a8+ ♚e7 23 ♖e4+ ♚d6 24 ♕f8+.

21...f5 22 ♕c5 ♕e7

Lasker seeks drawing chances in an unpleasant endgame, since 22...♖d1+ loses after 23 ♚f2 ♖d2+ 24 ♚e1 ♕xg2 25 ♕a5+ and 22...g6 23 ♕f8+ ♚c7 24 ♖c4+ ♚b6 25 ♕b4+ ♚a6 26 ♖c6# is no good either.

23 ♕xe7+ ♚xe7 24 ♖xf5 ♖d1+ 25 ♚f2!

Rubinstein gives up a pawn to activate his king. He realized his advantage in due course.

The players in the following extract are best known for a 'game' they most likely didn't play at all (Gibaud-Lazard: 1 d4 ♘f6 2 ♘d2 e5 3 dxe5 ♘g4 4 h3?? ♘e3 0-1).

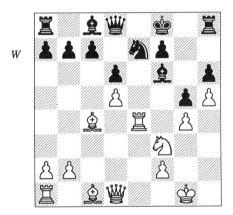

F. Lazard – A. Gibaud
Paris 1909

In this position, arising from a Giuoco Piano, Black has already made some unnecessary concessions, and so White now has rather dangerous play.

15 ♘d4 c6 16 ♕f3 ♘xd5 17 ♗d2 ♘c7

17...♘b6 looks sound.

18 ♖ae1

White threatens ♗a5, while it is difficult for Black to do anything constructive.

18...d5

This looks rather greedy, as Black is two pawns up, and should be looking to consolidate. However, 18...♚g7 doesn't fare any better after 19 ♖e7!.

19 ♗b4+ ♚g7

19...♚g8 20 ♗e7 ♕d7 (20...♗xg4 21 ♕xg4 ♗xe7 22 ♖xe7 dxc4 23 ♖d7 wins) 21 ♕xf6 ♘e8 keeps Black in the game, but his position remains constricted.

20 ♖e7! dxc4

20...♗xe7 21 ♖xe7 wins, as 21...♖f8 runs into the deadly 22 ♗c3 ♚g8 23 ♕f6. 20...♘e8 21 ♗c3 is very good for White, who threatens 22 ♘e6+.

21 ♘xc6! ♕d3

21...bxc6 22 ♕xf6+ ♚xf6 23 ♗c3+ mates.

22 ♖xf7+!

This move forces a speedy mate.

22...♚xf7 23 ♖e7+ ♚g8 24 ♕xf6 ♖h7 25 ♖e8+! 1-0

Chess News in Brief

Lasker easily defeats Janowski in a ten-game match.

An up-and-coming player, Alexander Alekhine, wins the All-Russian Championship.

World News in Brief

The Balkan crisis worsens, as Serbia and Austria argue over Bosnia-Herzegovina. An uneasy settlement is reached.

There are fears in Britain that Germany is preparing for war. The United States establishes a naval base at Pearl Harbor, Hawaii. France steps up military spending.

Indian nationalists turn to terrorism.

Moslems massacre at least 30,000 Armenians in the Ottoman Empire.

The Union of South Africa is formed.

Prohibition campaigners gain ground in parts of the United States, with many towns banning saloons.

Old Age Pensions are introduced in Britain.

Robert Peary is the first explorer to reach the North Pole.

Louis Blériot becomes the first man to fly an aeroplane across the English Channel.

1910

Lasker retains his world title through two (?) challenges

Emanuel Lasker and Carl Schlechter draw a match that has been the subject of much subsequent debate. It is unclear precisely what the regulations were and whether it was a World Championship match at all. Going into the tenth and final game, Schlechter led by one win to none, with eight draws. Schlechter played for a win, and ended up losing a dramatic game. Whether this was an act of some kind of chivalry, or whether he needed to win by more than one point to win the match, remains unclear.

There follow three interesting games from various events in 1910:

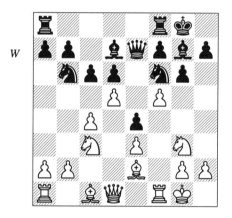

G. Rotlewi – E. Bogoljubow
Warsaw 1910

White now comes up with a forceful plan to keep the initiative.

13 a4 cxd5 14 a5 ♘xc4 15 ♘xd5 ♘xd5 16 ♕xd5 ♘xb2

16...♗xb2 17 ♗xb2 ♘xb2 might seem safer, but Bogoljubow's move stands up to scrutiny.

17 f6!?

The idea is to cut off the support for the b2-knight and to weaken Black's control of the dark squares around his king. However, White's position is also a little loose, which gives Black some chances of survival.

17...♗xf6 18 ♖xf6!? ♕xf6 19 ♘xe4 ♕g7

19...♕e5 20 ♕xe5 dxe5 21 ♘f6+ ♔g7 22 ♘xd7 leads to a winning ending for White.

20 ♕xd6 ♗e6

20...♘a4 21 ♘f6+ ♔h8 22 ♕xd7 ♘c3 23 ♕d2 ♖ac8 24 ♗b2 ♕xf6 (24...♖fd8 loses to 25 ♕xd8+! ♖xd8 26 ♗xc3) 25 ♖a3 wins material for White, while after 20...f5 21 ♕d5+ ♔h8 22 ♕xd7! ♕xd7 23 ♗xb2+ ♔f6 24 ♖d1 ♕e6 25 ♘xf6 White has a winning attack.

21 ♕e7 ♕e5

21...♘c4 loses to 22 ♘f6+ ♔h8 23 ♗xc4 ♗xc4 24 ♗b2. 21...♔h8 is also met by 22 ♘f6.

22 ♘f6+

22 ♕f6! is better.

22...♔g7?

22...♔h8 23 ♘g4 ♕c3 (23...♕g7 24 ♘f6 is the same as the note to Black's 21st move) is the only way to keep the game alive; now after 24 ♗d2 Black has the reply 24...♕g7, when after 25 ♘f6, the 'extra' tempo ♗d2 means that the b2-knight is not under attack.

23 ♘g4 ♖ae8

23...♕c3 loses to 24 ♗d2.

24 ♕xf8+ ♔xf8 25 ♘xe5 1-0

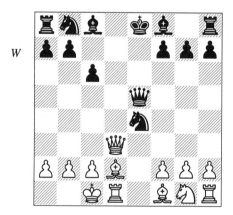

R. Réti – S. Tartakower
Vienna 1910

In this offhand game, Tartakower has just light-heartedly taken a knight. The mate that follows isn't at all deep, but is very pretty, and an important theme in quite a few opening variations.

9 ♕d8+! ♔xd8 10 ♗g5++ ♔c7

Or 10...♔e8 11 ♖d8#.

11 ♗d8# (1-0)

The king's bolt-hole on c7 turns out not to be very useful!

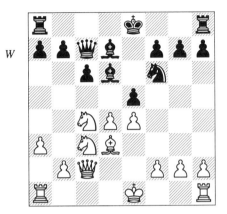

R. Spielmann – J. Mieses

Match (game 8), Regensburg 1910

It looks as if Black has managed to achieve the liberating ...e5 thrust just in time to avoid being suffocated, but Spielmann finds a way to keep the initiative.

14 f4!?

Black is frog-marched along a forcing line.

14...exd4 15 e5 ♗f8 16 exf6 dxc3 17 ♕e2+ ♔d8 18 0-0-0

White is more concerned with catching the black king in the centre than with defending his pawns.

18...♕xf4+ 19 ♔b1 ♔c7 20 ♖hf1 ♕g5 21 h4!

The queen is forced to a less active square.

21...♕c5 22 fxg7 ♗xg7 23 ♖xf7 ♗d4 24 ♖xd7+!?

One can hardly criticize this wonderful idea, but 24 bxc3 looks like a simpler win.

24...♔xd7 25 ♕g4+ ♔c7 26 ♕f4+ ♗e5 27 ♘xe5

Setting up an extremely powerful battery.

27...♖af8 28 ♕h2 ♕f2

Black goes for counterplay; the game is to have an exciting finish.

29 ♗c2 ♖hg8 30 ♖d7+

Spielmann again opts for the most spectacular continuation.

30...♔b6 31 ♘c4+

31 ♘d3 is also effective.

31...♔a6 32 ♕c7! ♕f1+ 33 ♔a2 ♕xc4+ 34 b3 ♕b5 35 a4! ♕b6 36 ♗d3+ ♔a5 37 ♕e5+ c5 38 ♖xb7! ♖xg2+ 39 ♔a3 ♖g4

39...♕b4+ doesn't quite work because after 40 ♖xb4 the c5-pawn is pinned.

40 ♖xb6 1-0

After 40...axb6, 41 ♕c7 forces mate.

Chess News in Brief

Lasker outclasses Janowski 9½-1½ in another challenge.

Schlechter wins the German Open Championship ahead of Duras and Nimzowitsch.

Moishe Mieczslaw (later Miguel) Najdorf [one of the world's strongest players around the middle of the 20th century] is born.

World News in Brief

Greece and Turkey come close to war over Crete, which two years earlier had declared itself part of Greece.

Russia and Britain intervene in Persia, where there is widespread unrest.

Japan annexes Korea.

In Britain, suffragette hunger-strikers force women's voting rights high on the political agenda.

Slavery is abolished in China.

Halley's Comet lights up the sky as it passes within 13 million miles of the Earth.

Thomas Edison demonstrates that it is possible to have talking motion pictures.

Bertrand Russell and A.N.Whitehead's *Principia Mathematica* is published. It seeks to provides a rigorous basis for fundamental mathematical concepts in formal logic.

1911

Another sensational result for Capablanca, who dominates a top-class tournament at San Sebastian

José Raúl Capablanca achieves a sensational result in the San Sebastian tournament, taking clear first place ahead of a world-class field (he scores 9½/14; Rubinstein and Vidmar share second place with 9 points). Before the tournament, several of the players objected to Capablanca's inclusion, on the basis that he had not sufficiently proved himself in the international arena. Capablanca's performance removes all doubts, and he is immediately seen as a potential World Champion. Lasker offers terms for a match that are generally seen as unfair, setting an unfortunate precedent of World Champions appearing to avoid their most dangerous rivals.

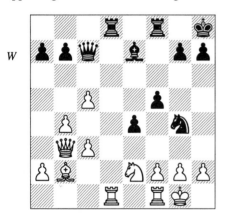

J. Capablanca – R. Spielmann
San Sebastian 1911

Capablanca has grabbed a fairly healthy pawn, but now appears to be coming under some pressure on the kingside, and needs to find some accurate moves.

20 ♘g3 f4 21 ♖xd8

21 ♘xe4 f3 22 g3 ♕e5 gives Black dangerous attacking chances.

21...♖xd8 22 ♕e6! fxg3 23 ♕xg4 gxh2+ 24 ♔h1

The white king is fairly safe here; the fact that it is a black pawn rather than a white pawn on h2 makes the king less prone to back-rank mates.

24...♕e5 25 ♖e1 ♖d2 26 ♖xe4! ♕c7 27 ♗c1! ♖xf2 28 ♗f4

Not only cutting off Black's threats, but starting a lightning-fast mating attack.

28...♕d8 29 ♖xe7! ♕f8 30 ♕xg7+! 1-0

30...♕xg7 31 ♖e8+ ♕g8 32 ♗e5+ ♖f6 33 ♗xf6#.

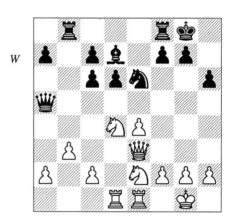

J. Capablanca – O. Bernstein
San Sebastian 1911

Black is establishing some threats on the queenside, so Capablanca decides to hit back with some vigorous kingside play.

18 ♘f5!? ♘c5

18...♕xa2 is an unwise pawn-grab since 19 ♕c3 gains time (by threatening ♖a1) to step up the threats to Black's kingside.

19 ♘ed4 ♔h7 20 g4

Securing the f5-knight and preparing to bring the other knight around to h5.

20...♖be8 21 f3 ♘e6 22 ♘e2 ♕xa2!?

This move, together with several of Black's previous decisions in this game, have come in for heavy criticism, but this does not appear to be justified. 22...♕b6 23 ♔g2 ♕xe3 24 ♘xe3 gives White a pleasant ending.

23 ♘eg3 ♕xc2!?

Again, an unjustly criticized move. Lasker advocated grim defence by 23...f6, but the text-move wrecks White's queenside and must be correct if White's attack does not crash through.

24 罝c1 豐b2 25 ♘h5 罝h8?

25...g5! would not only have saved Black, but given him definite winning chances. After Capablanca's intended 26 e5 (26 罝c3 f6 is a sturdy defence) there is the excellent reply 26...♘f4.

26 罝e2 豐e5 27 f4 豐b5 28 ♘fxg7

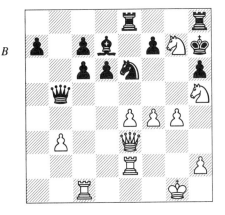

B

28...♘c5?

28...♘xg7 29 ♘f6+ ♔g6 30 ♘xd7 gives White a dominant position. Capablanca gave 30...f6 31 e5 ♔f7 32 ♘xf6 罝e7 33 ♘e4 as best play, and considered Black's position "untenable". 28...罝eg8 is best met by 29 罝g2; 28...♘xf4 29 豐xf4 豐xe2 30 ♘xe8 ♗xe8 31 ♘f6+, followed by 32 罝f1, wins for White.

The best defence is 28...罝d8 29 f5 ♘c5 (29...♘f8 30 g5 豐b6 31 gxh6 豐xe3+ 32 罝xe3 and the mate threats against the black king will decide the game, e.g. 32...♔xh6 33 ♔f2 罝g8 34 罝g1 ♘h7? 35 罝eg3 and mates) 30 g5 (30 豐d4 is most likely a draw), and now:

a) 30...豐d3 31 g6+ ♔g8 (31...fxg6 32 fxg6+ ♔g8 33 ♘f5 should win) 32 gxf7+ ♔xf7 33 e5 and, thanks to the overloaded d6-pawn, White's e-pawn runs through.

b) 30...♔g8 31 g6 is messy, but probably good for White, e.g. 31...fxg6 32 fxg6 ♘xe4 33 豐xe4 豐g5+ 34 ♔h1 豐xc1+ 35 罝e1.

29 ♘xe8 ♗xe8 30 豐c3 f6 31 ♘xf6+ ♔g6 32 ♘h5 罝g8 33 f5+ ♔g5 34 豐e3+ 1-0

Chess News in Brief

Richard Teichmann wins the Karlsbad tournament with 18/25, ahead of Rubinstein (17), Schlechter (17) and Rotlewi (16). Marshall and Nimzowitsch share fifth place with 15½, while future world champion Alexander Alekhine is down in joint eighth place.

Frank Marshall wins the New York tournament with 10/12, half a point ahead of Capablanca.

Tarrasch and Schlechter draw a match 8-8 in Cologne.

Mikhail Botvinnik [World Champion 1948-57, 58-60, 61-3] is born.

Samuel Reshevsky [Polish prodigy; later the leading American player from the mid-1930s to the late 1950s] is born.

Alberic O'Kelly de Galway [winner of the 3rd Correspondence World Championship, 1959-62] is born.

World News in Brief

Italy declares war on Turkey, and seizes Tripoli (Libya), which had previously been under Turkish rule. Towards the end of the year, Italy puts aeroplanes to military use against Turkish forces, and annexes further territory.

The President of Mexico is overthrown by a popular revolution. Shortly afterwards a massive earthquake hits Mexico City.

In China, 100,000 are killed by flooding along the Yangzi river. There is further loss of life in China in violent conflicts between Imperialists and Republicans.

France and Germany dispute briefly over Morocco.

In Britain, the National Insurance Bill is passed. It will provide support for the unemployed and sick.

Roald Amundsen becomes the first man to reach the South Pole. His expedition was far better prepared for the Antarctic weather than their British rivals, led by Captain Robert Scott.

Widespread strikes provoke riots and threaten famine in Britain.

Ernest Rutherford demonstrates that atoms have a tiny, extremely dense nucleus.

1912

A good year for Rubinstein

Rubinstein wins the San Sebastian tournament with 12½/19, ahead of Spielmann and Nimzowitsch, who both score 12. While it is not quite so strong as the previous year's event, Rubinstein's result, one of a string of successes, shows that he deserves a crack at Lasker. The most attractive game from the event, however, is one of Rubinstein's losses:

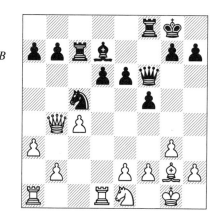

B

A. Rubinstein – R. Spielmann
San Sebastian 1912

Black has quite a pleasant position. He now launches an attack against the poorly defended f2-pawn.

17...f4! 18 ♘d3 fxg3 19 fxg3 ♘xd3 20 ♖xd3

White hopes that the weakness of e2 will be offset by Black's vulnerable pawns.

20...♕f2+ 21 ♔h1 ♗c6!?

A direct attack against the white king tips the balance in Black's favour.

22 e4

22 ♗xc6? loses to 22...♕xe2.

22...♖cf7 23 ♖e1

23 ♖xd6? is mated by 23...♗xe4! 24 ♗xe4 ♕e2 25 ♗g2 ♖f1+ 26 ♖xf1 ♖xf1+ 27 ♗xf1 ♕xf1#.

23...a5! 24 ♕c3 ♖c5 25 b4

It appears that White might be regaining the initiative. However...

25...♗xe4!

The threat is mate by 26...♖f1+.

26 ♖xe4

26 ♗xe4? ♖f1+ 27 ♖xf1 ♖xf1+ 28 ♔g2 ♖g1+ 29 ♔f3 ♕h5+ gives Black a very strong attack, but 26 ♖f3 ♕c6 27 b5 ♖xf3 28 ♕xf3 ♗xf3 29 bxc6 ♗xc6 30 ♗xc6 bxc6 31 ♖xe6 affords White some drawing chances.

26...♖f1+ 27 ♗xf1 ♖xf1+ 28 ♔g2 ♕f2+ 29 ♔h3 ♖h1 30 ♖f3 ♕xh2+ 31 ♔g4 ♕h5+ 32 ♔f4 ♕h6+ 33 ♔g4 g5!

The g-pawn participates in the mating attack, forcing White to return a rook.

34 ♖xe6 ♕xe6+ 35 ♖f5

35 ♔xg5 h6+ 36 ♔f4 h5 37 ♔g5 ♕g4+ 38 ♔h6 h4! and Black wins.

35...h6

Good enough, but 35...♕e4+! 36 ♔xg5 h6+ 37 ♔f6 ♕e8 forces mate.

36 ♕d3 ♔g7 37 ♔f3 ♖f1+! 38 ♕xf1 ♕xf5+ 39 ♔g2 ♕xf1+ 40 ♔xf1 axb4 41 axb4 ♔f6 42 ♔f2 h5 0-1

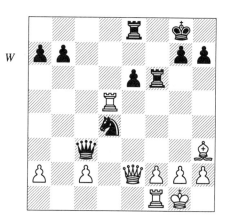

W

S. Levitsky – F. Marshall
German Open Ch, Breslau 1912

White now falls victim to an exquisite piece of tactics.

20 ♕h5? ♖ef8 21 ♖e5 ♖h6 22 ♕g5

Otherwise 22...♖xh3 simply wins material for Black.

22...♖xh3 23 ♖c5 ♕g3!!

A very pretty move to finish: 24 hxg3 ♘e2#; 24 ♕xg3 ♘e2+ 25 ♔h1 ♘xg3+, etc.; or 24 fxg3 ♘e2+ 25 ♔h1 ♖xf1#.

0-1

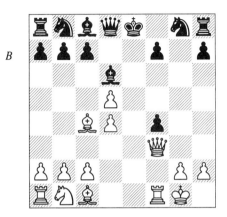

B

R. Réti – A. Flamberg
Gambit tournament, Opatija 1912

This position has resulted from a Muzio Gambit – a far cry from the flank openings that Réti was to develop later in his career!

8...♕f6?!

8...♘e7 is a better move. Now Réti develops a major initiative.

9 ♕e4+! ♕e7 10 ♘c3

Réti perceives that the exchange of queens will not deaden his attack.

10...♘d7 11 ♗xf4 ♕xe4 12 ♘xe4 ♗xf4 13 ♖xf4

Threatening 14 ♖e1.

13...f5 14 ♖xf5 ♘e7 15 ♖e1! ♘b6

15...♘xf5 16 ♘d6++ ♔f8 17 ♖e8+ ♔g7 18 ♘xf5+ ♔f6 19 ♖xh8 ♔xf5 is hopeless for Black.

16 ♗b5+ ♔d8?

16...♗d7 17 ♖e5 ♗xb5 18 d6 0-0-0 19 dxe7 ♖d5 20 ♘f6 ♖xe5 21 dxe5!? (21 ♖xe5 ♗e8 is quite solid) gives Black awkward problems.

17 ♖e5 ♘g6

17...♘bxd5? loses to 18 ♘g5!.

18 ♘g5! ♘xe5 19 ♖xe5 ♗d7 20 ♘f7+ ♔c8 21 ♘xh8 ♗xb5

Black has an extra piece, but is poorly developed, while White has plenty of mobile pawns.

22 ♖h5 ♗c4 23 ♖xh7 ♗xd5 24 h4 ♗e4 25 ♖g7 ♗xc2 26 h5 a5 27 h6 a4 28 h7 ♗xh7 29 ♖xh7 ♘c4

White must play accurately to meet his opponent's counterplay.

30 ♘f7 ♖a6 31 g4 ♘xb2 32 ♖h8+ ♔d7 33 ♘e5+ ♔e6 34 g5 ♘d1 35 ♖f8 ♘e3 36 ♔f2 ♘d5 37 g6 1-0

Chess News in Brief

Rubinstein dominates the Bad Pistyan tournament, scoring 14/17, ahead of Spielmann (11½) and Marshall (10½).

John O'Hanlon wins the Irish Championship for the first of nine times.

World News in Brief

Greece, Bulgaria, Montenegro and Serbia form an alliance to push the Ottomans out of the Balkans. This has considerable significance for European politics, as the break-up of the Ottoman Empire would leave a power vacuum that the great European powers would be eager to fill.

Germany and Britain step up military ship-building programmes, after Britain rejects a German proposal of a mutual guarantee of neutrality. Germany, Austria and Italy reconfirm their alliance.

China becomes a republic, as the Emperor is forced to step down. However, it is a hard-line general who takes control, rather than the leader of the Republicans.

British plans to grant home rule to Ireland are strongly opposed by the substantial Protestant minority in the north of Ireland.

The *Titanic* sinks after striking an iceberg in the North Atlantic. The luxury liner goes down quickly with the loss of more than 1,500 lives. The ship, considered 'unsinkable', does not have enough lifeboats.

An airmail service starts between London and Paris.

In America, Albert Berry makes the first parachute jump from an aeroplane.

Alfred Wegener publishes his theory of Continental Drift, which states that the continents are not fixed on the globe, but rather are moving, albeit very slowly.

1913

A mixed year for Capablanca • Alekhine shows his talent

Marshall wins the Havana tournament, half a point ahead of Capablanca.

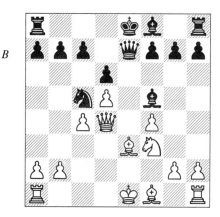

J. Corzo – J. Capablanca
Havana 1913

Here Capablanca is once again facing Corzo, against whom he played a match in 1901. Black has developed two minor pieces actively, while White's structure is defective. However, it is not clear how Black is to complete his kingside development, in view of the pressure on the a1-h8 diagonal. Capablanca finds an elegant solution:

10...g6! 11 ♔f2

11 ♕xh8? loses to 11...♕xe3+. 11 0-0-0 ♗g7 is good for Black: 12 ♕xg7 (or 12 ♕d2 ♕e4) 12...♕xe3+ and ...0-0-0.

11...♖g8 12 ♖e1 ♗g7 13 ♕d1 ♘e4+ 14 ♔g1 ♔f8 15 ♗d4 g5!

Capablanca makes good use of the rook on the g-file, which had seemingly gone there only to help the bishop develop. The game is sharpened considerably, and White is forced to play very accurately, which he does, up to a point.

16 ♗xg7+

16 fxg5 ♘xg5 17 ♗xg7+ ♖xg7 18 ♘xg5 ♕xg5 is only a little better for Black.

16...♖xg7 17 ♘d4 ♗d7 18 f5

More ambitious than 18 ♗d3 f5 19 ♗xe4 fxe4 20 f5 ♕e5 21 ♘e6+ ♗xe6 22 fxe6 c6 23 g3, which should be satisfactory for White.

18...♕e5 19 ♕d3 ♖e8 20 ♘e6+!

Otherwise White's position will crumble.

20...fxe6 21 fxe6 ♖xe6 22 dxe6 ♗c6

For the entombed rook on h1, Black has a centralized knight and threats against the white king. But is this enough?

23 ♕f3+ ♕f4 24 ♕e3!

Capablanca analysed 24 ♕xf4+ gxf4 25 h4 f3 26 ♖d1 f2+ 27 ♔h2 ♘g3 28 ♖d2 ♘xh1 29 ♔xh1 ♖xg2, winning.

24...♔e7 25 b4?

25 h4 is better, as 25...♘d2 26 hxg5 ♘f3+ 27 gxf3 ♖xg5+ fails to 28 ♗g2.

25...b6 26 b5 ♗b7 27 g3 ♘d2!

A highly attractive move.

28 ♕c3?

28 ♗g2 ♕xe3+ 29 ♖xe3 ♘xc4 30 ♖c3 ♗xg2 31 ♔xg2 d5 is a good ending for Black.

28...♘f3+ 29 ♔f2 ♕f8

Now Black is clearly winning.

30 c5 ♘e5+ 31 ♔g1 ♘f3+ 32 ♔f2 bxc5 33 ♕a5 ♘e5+ 34 ♔g1 ♕f3 35 ♕xc7+ ♔f6 36 ♕xd6 ♕xh1+ 37 ♔f2 ♕xh2+ 0-1

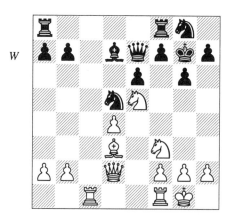

J. Capablanca – A. Alekhine
Exhibition game, St Petersburg 1913

This was the first game between these two men, who were subsequently to become great rivals.

18 ♗e4! ♗b5?!

This allows White to step up the pressure dramatically. 18...♘gf6 is more sound.

19 ♖fe1 ♕d6 20 ♗xd5 exd5 21 ♕a5 a6 22 ♕c7 ♕xc7 23 ♖xc7 h6

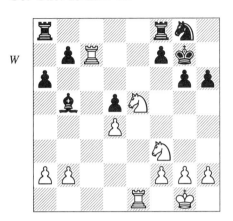

To prevent ♘g5, but this move weakens g6.

24 ♖xb7 ♖ac8

Alekhine hopes for counterplay on White's second rank, but his own king remains too vulnerable for this to work.

25 b3 ♖c2 26 a4 ♗e2 27 ♘h4! h5 28 ♘hxg6 ♖e8 29 ♖xf7+ ♔h6 30 f4

Capablanca constructs a mating net.

30...a5 31 ♘h4 ♖xe5 32 fxe5 ♔g5 33 g3 ♔g4 34 ♖g7+ ♔h3 35 ♘g2 1-0

de Rozynski – A. Alekhine
Paris 1913

1 e4 e5 2 ♘f3 ♘c6 3 ♗c4 d6 4 c3 ♗g4 5 ♕b3?!

The start of an over-ambitious plan to refute Black's opening.

5...♕d7 6 ♘g5

6 ♗xf7+ ♕xf7 7 ♕xb7 ♔d7! 8 ♕xa8 ♗xf3 9 gxf3 ♕xf3 10 ♖g1 ♕xe4+ is rather good for Black.

6...♘h6 7 ♗xf7+

7 ♕xb7 ♖b8 8 ♕a6 ♖b6 gives Black good compensation.

7...♘xf7 8 ♘xf7 ♕xf7 9 ♕xb7

White has won two pawns, but has neglected his development and king safety. Alekhine finds a wonderful way to exploit this.

9...♔d7! 10 ♕xa8 ♕c4

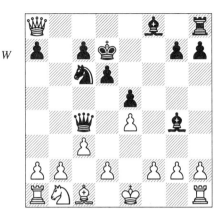

Now White's move c3 is seen only as weakening the light squares.

11 f3 ♗xf3! 12 gxf3 ♘d4! 13 d3?

13 cxd4 ♕xc1+ 14 ♔e2 ♕xh1 enables White to fight on, though his position is unpleasant.

13...♕xd3 14 cxd4 ♗e7! 15 ♕xh8 ♗h4# (0-1)

Chess News in Brief

Alekhine wins the Scheveningen tournament, ahead of Janowski.

Alexander Kotov [prominent Soviet grandmaster in the 1950s] is born.

World News in Brief

Turkish Nationalists seize power in the Ottoman Empire. Following a series of military defeats, the Ottomans agree to concede Macedonia, so ending the Balkan War. However, conflict almost immediately flares up between the victors, who cannot agree on the fate of Macedonia. A brief war ends with a change in the borders of Greece, Serbia, Montenegro, Bulgaria and Rumania. The greater size and power of Serbia is seen as a threat by Austria.

In the British House of Lords, a plan for Irish home rule is rejected.

In Britain, the suffragette movement has its first martyr.

Ford Model T's start rolling off assembly lines in Detroit.

The Panama Canal is opened.

1914

Lasker edges out Capablanca in the St Petersburg tournament • International chess is interrupted by the outbreak of war

The strongest tournament for many years is held at St Petersburg. Capablanca wins the Preliminary section with an impressive 8/10, which is 1½ points more than second-placed Lasker and Tarrasch. The tournament is of an unusual format, with the top five players competing in a Final section, in which Lasker is dominant, scoring 7/8, with Capablanca scoring 5. Lasker thus wins overall by half a point.

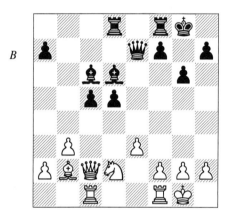

A. Nimzowitsch – S. Tarrasch
Preliminary event, St Petersburg 1914

Black has taken on the 'hanging pawns' (on c5 and d5, with no b- or e-pawns to support them). Here, Tarrasch can be very happy with the dynamic play that such positions can present.

18...d4!
Opening the diagonal for the c6-bishop and obstructing White's pieces.

19 exd4
19 ♘c4 also loses to 19...♗xh2+! 20 ♔xh2 ♕h4+ 21 ♔g1 ♗xg2.

19...♗xh2+! 20 ♔xh2 ♕h4+ 21 ♔g1 ♗xg2
This kind of double bishop sacrifice was first played by Lasker in 1889, and has been a standard attacking method ever since.

22 f3
Black wins without difficulties after 22 ♔xg2 ♕g4+ 23 ♔h1 ♖d5 24 ♕xc5 ♕h5+ 25 ♔g1 ♕g5+ 26 ♔h1 ♖xc5.

22...♖fe8!
Threatening 23...♖e2.

23 ♘e4 ♕h1+ 24 ♔f2 ♗xf1 25 d5
25 ♖xf1 ♕h2+ picks off the white queen. Nimzowitsch's actual move at least sets up an exciting finish, with some optical threats to the black king.

25...f5 26 ♕c3 ♕g2+ 27 ♔e3 ♖xe4+ 28 fxe4 f4+
Black has a quicker mate by 28...♕g3+ 29 ♔d2 ♕f2+ 30 ♔d1 ♕e2#.

29 ♔xf4 ♖f8+ 30 ♔e5 ♕h2+ 31 ♔e6 ♖e8+ 32 ♔d7 ♗b5# (0-1)

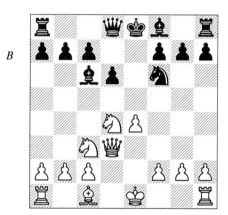

A. Nimzowitsch – J. Capablanca
Preliminary event, St Petersburg 1914

8...g6
This move allows White to win a pawn.

9 ♘xc6
Maybe 9 ♗g5 ♗g7 10 0-0-0 is a better choice.

9...bxc6 10 ♕a6 ♕d7 11 ♕b7 ♖c8 12 ♕xa7 ♗g7 13 0-0-0 0-0 14 ♕a6
Black has gained a few tempi for the pawn, but this in itself is unlikely to be sufficient compensation.

14...♖fe8 15 ♕d3?!
15 f3! is better, keeping the black queen tied to the defence of the c6-pawn, e.g. 15...d5 16

♕d3 dxe4 17 ♕xd7 ♘xd7 18 ♘xe4 ♗d4+ 19 ♔h1 ♗e5.

15...♕e6! 16 f3 ♘d7

Capablanca is now playing for advantage!

17 ♗d2?

17 b3 (intending ♗b2, when White is consolidating) 17...♘e5 18 ♕e3 ♘c4! 19 ♕d3 (19 bxc4 ♕xc4 regains the knight with advantage, since ...♗d4 is threatened) 19...♘e5 20 ♕d2 ♘c4! 21 ♕d3 (21 bxc4 ♕xc4 22 ♗b2 ♖b8 is very good for Black) 21...♘e5 is a draw.

17...♘e5 18 ♕e2 ♘c4

Black's queenside pressure provides ample compensation.

19 ♖ab1

19 b3? ♗d4+ 20 ♔h1 ♘xd2 21 ♕xd2 ♕f6 is very painful.

19...♖a8 20 a4?!

Nimzowitsch holds on to the pawn. A modern master would be looking for ways to relieve the pressure by returning it. 20 b3 ♘xd2 21 ♕xd2 ♖a3 ensures that Black will regain the pawn, but with only a small edge.

20...♘xd2! 21 ♕xd2 ♕c4! 22 ♖fd1 ♖eb8!

There is no need to take on c3 as yet – the a-pawn will not run away.

23 ♕e3 ♖b4

Again the threat of ...♗d4 comes into play.

24 ♕g5 ♗d4+ 25 ♔h1

Both White's king and queen are now further from the action. It is time for Black to cash in.

25...♖ab8

The threat is ...♗xc3; White's position crumbles.

26 ♖xd4

26 ♖bc1 ♖xb2 27 ♘b1 ♖xc2 exploits White's weak back rank.

26...♕xd4 27 ♖d1 ♕c4 28 h4 ♖xb2 29 ♕d2 ♕c5 30 ♖e1 ♕h5 31 ♖a1

31 ♕f2 is met by 31...♖xc2!.

31...♕xh4+ 32 ♔g1 ♕h5 33 a5 ♖a8 34 a6 ♕c5+ 35 ♔h1 ♕c4 36 a7 ♕c5 37 e5 ♕xe5 38 ♖a4 ♕h5+ 39 ♔g1 ♕c5+ 40 ♔h2 d5 41 ♖h4 ♖xa7 0-1

Chess News in Brief

Rudolf Spielmann wins the Baden tournament.

The Mannheim tournament (German Open Championship) is interrupted by the outbreak of World War I, and the Russian players are interned. Notable among them are Alekhine, who is released later in 1914, and Bogoljubow, who remains in Germany; others include Flamberg, Selezniev, I.Rabinovich and Romanovsky.

The outbreak of war also scuppers the Lasker-Rubinstein world championship match, planned for October.

World News in Brief

Ulster is close to civil war, as those who oppose home rule for Ireland step up their campaign.

Archduke Franz Ferdinand, the heir to the Austro-Hungarian Empire is assassinated in Sarajevo, Bosnia. Amid suspicions that this act was sanctioned by the Serbian authorities, Austria issues a drastic ultimatum to Serbia, and war subsequently breaks out. Serbia is supported by its ally Russia, and Austria by Germany. The system of alliances between the European powers causes the conflict to escalate dramatically. Germany declares war on Russia's ally France, perhaps perceiving their entry into the war as inevitable. The German invasion of Belgium brings Britain into the war; Britain is France's ally and is pledged to protect Belgium. Japan declares war on Germany and attacks the German port of Qingdao. The fact that the great colonial powers are involved in a war in Europe leads to conflicts in their dependencies and colonies around the world. The Ottomans enter the war by invading Armenia, leading to war with Russia and Britain.

On the Western Front, the German plan to encircle Paris is foiled, and intense fighting continues around the border of France and Belgium. On the Eastern Front, the advancing Russian forces suffer a major defeat at Tannenberg.

1915

No major tournaments due to the war

With the war ravaging Europe, there are few chess events in 1915; there is some minor activity in America, Russia and, oddly enough, in Germany, where the Russian internees contest a few tournaments.

N. Grigoriev – A. Alekhine
Moscow 1915

This game's main claim to fame is not what happened in the play itself, but an amazing 'fantasy' variation, which Alekhine dreamt up. He cited this as a game, with him playing White, and it became known as "Alekhine's five queens game". However, there is no evidence that the five queens line ever occurred, while Alekhine was notorious for such 'inventions'.

1 e4 e6 2 d4 d5 3 ♘c3 ♘f6 4 ♗g5 ♗b4 5 e5 h6 6 exf6 hxg5 7 fxg7 ♖g8 8 h4 gxh4 9 ♕g4 ♗e7 10 g3 c5

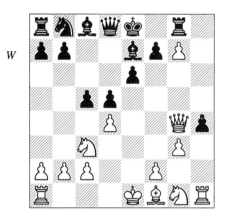

W

11 0-0-0

Alekhine's fantasy variation/game ran: 11 gxh4 cxd4 12 h5 dxc3 13 h6 cxb2 14 ♖b1 ♕a5+ 15 ♔e2 ♕xa2? 16 h7 ♕xb1 17 hxg8♕+ ♔d7 18 ♕xf7 ♕xc2+ 19 ♔f3 ♘c6 20 ♕gxe6+?! ♔c7 21 ♕f4+ ♔b6 22 ♕ee3+ ♗c5 23 g8♕ b1♕ 24 ♖h6!! ♕xf1? 25 ♕b4+ ♕b5 26 ♕d8+ ♔a6 27 ♕ea3+ '1-0'.

11...♘c6 12 dxc5 ♕a5 13 ♔b1 e5 14 ♕h5 ♗e6 15 ♘xd5?

This allows Black a devastating counterattack.

15...♗xd5 16 ♖xd5 ♘b4 17 ♖xe5 ♕xa2+ 18 ♔c1 0-0-0 19 ♗d3 ♕a1+ 20 ♔d2 ♕xb2 21 ♔e3 ♗f6! 22 ♕f5+ ♔b8 23 ♖e4 ♖xd3+ 24 cxd3 ♗d4+ 25 ♔f4 ♕xf2+ 0-1

Chess News in Brief

Four tournaments are contested at Triberg between the Russian internees; Bogoljubow comes out on top in all of them.

Capablanca wins a relatively weak tournament at New York; his score of 13/14 is one point more than Marshall.

World News in Brief

On the Western Front, the conflict becomes one of attrition, as both sides entrench their positions. This new form of combat – trench warfare – sees appalling suffering and huge loss of life over small territorial gains. Germany's use of poison gas adds a new dimension of horror.

Italy enters the war on the side of Britain, France and Russia, and declares war on Austria. Bulgaria enters the war on the side of Germany and Austria.

On the Eastern and Balkan Fronts, Germany and Austria make more gains, invading the Baltic provinces, and taking several major cities, including Warsaw, Brest-Litovsk and Belgrade.

The Allies' attempt to capture Istanbul, and so knock the Ottoman Empire out of the war, ends in failure.

Aircraft begin to play a greater role in the war.

A German submarine torpedoes the *Lusitania*, a passenger ship travelling between New York and Liverpool, which sinks with the loss of about 1,200 lives. This leads to increased pressure for the United States to abandon its policy of neutrality.

In central Italy, an earthquake kills 29,000 people.

The first transcontinental telephone call is made.

1916

The war rages on • New York hosts the only major events of the year

Capablanca wins the Rice memorial tournament in New York. He dominates the preliminary event, scoring 12/13, ahead of Janowski, Kostić and Kupchik on 8½; Janowski and Chajes have the satisfaction of winning the final group with 2½/4. A game from the event:

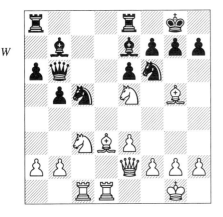

D. Janowski – O. Chajes
Rice memorial tournament, New York 1916

Janowski now decides to go for a sacrificial attack. Although it is not overwhelming, it is a reasonable idea, and puts great pressure on the opponent.

16 ♗xf6 ♗xf6 17 ♗xh7+!? ♔xh7 18 ♕h5+ ♔g8 19 ♕xf7+ ♔h7?

19...♔h8 is a better defence, when it is not clear whether White has more than a draw.

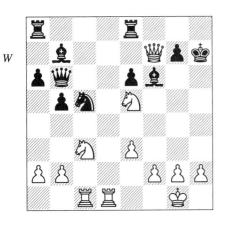

20 ♘d7! ♘xd7 21 ♖xd7
Black has no adequate defence.
21...♗c6 22 ♘e4!
22 ♘d5! is also good.
22...♗xb2
Now White forces mate.
23 ♘g5+ ♔h6 24 g4! g6 25 h4 ♖h8 26 ♕h7+! 1-0

Chess News in Brief

Ilia Rabinovich wins an internees tournament in Triberg.

Rubinstein wins the Warsaw city championship, after a play-off against Lowcki.

Paul Keres [the first world-class player from Estonia, and one of the world's leading players from the late 1930s to the late 1960s] is born.

World News in Brief

Conscription is introduced in Britain.

Two major battles on the Western Front claim colossal numbers of casualties, as the Germans launch a major offensive against the Verdun forts, and the British and French counterattack on the Somme. The battles rage for months, with very little territory being gained by either side, despite the Allies' use of tanks, for the first time, on the Somme.

On the Eastern Front, the Russians regain most of Galicia. Germany and Austria declare the independence of Poland. Japan and Russia make peace.

The Easter Rising, by Irish republicans, is put down by British forces.

Albert Einstein publishes the General Theory of Relativity. It extends his earlier Special Theory (1905) to incorporate gravity, not as a force between two objects whose strength depends on their masses, as in Newton's Theory, but rather as a curvature of space-time caused by the mass of objects. It explains and predicts phenomena that are otherwise incomprehensible, and represents a huge step forward in man's understanding of the universe.

1917

No major events

From the Warsaw Championship, a relatively strong tournament won by Rubinstein with 9/10:

Belsitzman – A. Rubinstein
Warsaw 1917

1 e4 e5 2 ♘f3 ♘c6 3 ♘c3 ♘f6 4 ♗b5 ♘d4

Rubinstein pioneered this move.

5 ♗c4 ♗c5 6 ♘xe5 ♕e7 7 ♘d3?! d5! 8 ♘xd5 ♕xe4+ 9 ♘e3 ♗d6 10 0-0?!

Castling into trouble, but the more circumspect 10 c3 ♘f5 11 ♕e2 0-0 still permits Black good play.

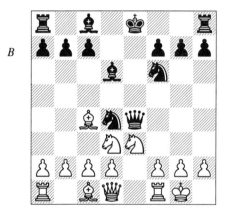

10...b5! 11 ♗b3 ♗b7 12 ♘e1 ♕h4 13 g3 ♕h3 14 c3 h5!

Black can ignore the attack on his knight, as the attack on the h-file is powerful.

15 cxd4 h4 16 ♕e2??

This allows a forced mate. 16 f3?? also loses, to 16...hxg3 17 ♕e2 gxh2+ 18 ♔h1 ♘h5.

However, the critical move, which has to my knowledge hitherto gone unmentioned, is 16 ♘f3!, when Black's best continuation seems to be 16...hxg3 17 fxg3 ♗xg3 18 ♕e2 ♗xf3 19 ♖xf3 ♗xh2+ 20 ♔f2 ♗g3+ 21 ♖xg3 ♘e4+. Now 22 ♔f3? loses in spectacular style: 22...♕xg3+! 23 ♔xe4 ♕g6+ 24 ♔f3 (24 ♘f5 loses to 24...0-0-0) 24...♖h3+ 25 ♔f4 ♗f8! 26 ♕g2 ♕h6+ 27 ♔e4 ♕h7+ 28 ♔d5 (or 28 ♔f4 ♖e8) 28...♖h5+ 29 ♔c6 ♕h6+ 30 ♔b7 ♖e8, etc. However, 22 ♔e1 ♕xg3+ 23 ♔d1 is far less clear.

16...♕xh2+! 17 ♔xh2 hxg3++ 18 ♔g1 ♖h1# (0-1)

Chess News in Brief

Laszlo Szabo [the leading Hungarian player during the 1940s and 1950s] is born.

World News in Brief

Germany adopts a policy of unrestricted submarine warfare, attacking ships from neutral states. Their sinking of several American merchant ships draws the USA into the war.

British forces achieve several victories over the Ottomans, capturing Baghdad and Jerusalem.

The Allies make gains on the Western Front. Germany pushes the Russians out of Riga. German forces drive deep into Italy.

In Russia, Tsar Nicholas II abdicates after liberals and moderate socialists take power and set up a provisional government. Subsequently, a bloodless coup brings the Bolsheviks, led by Lenin, to power. Finland declares its independence from Russia, as does the Ukraine. The Bolsheviks open peace talks with Germany and Austria.

China declares war on Germany and Austria.

Britain proposes making a Jewish national homeland in Palestine.

1918

International chess slowly resumes as the war ends

Strangely, two of the most interesting events of the year take place in Berlin, before the end of the war. Vidmar wins a strong four-man tournament in Berlin, scoring 4½/6, ahead of Schlechter on 3½. Lasker wins the second such event with 4½/6, ahead of Rubinstein on 4. The following game is from the first event.

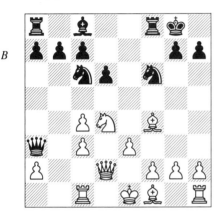

A. Rubinstein – M. Vidmar
Berlin 1918

This game was one of the first top-level tests of the Budapest Defence. White's last move, 13 e3?!, allows Black to develop a powerful initiative.

13...♘xd4 14 cxd4 ♘e4 15 ♕c2 ♕a5+ 16 ♔e2 ♖xf4! 17 exf4 ♗f5 18 ♕b2 ♖e8 19 ♔f3?

19 f3 is essential. Then 19...♘g3++ 20 ♔f2 ♘xh1+ 21 ♔g1 looks satisfactory for White, while 19...♘c3++ 20 ♔f2 ♘a4 21 ♕b5 ♕d2+ 22 ♔g3 ♖f8 23 ♗e2 ♘b2 is very unclear.

19...♘d2+

19...h5! is strong, e.g. 20 h3 (20 g4 ♗xg4+ 21 ♔g2 ♖f8 gives Black too powerful an attack) 20...h4 21 ♖d1 (21 g3 ♘d2+ 22 ♔g2 ♗e4 23 ♔h2 ♘f3+ wins for Black) 21...♘g5+! 22 fxg5 ♗e4+ 23 ♔f4 ♕f5+ and Black wins.

20 ♔g3 ♘e4+ 21 ♔h4?

Now White is mated by force. He should repeat the position by 21 ♔f3.

21...♖e6 22 ♗e2 ♖h6+ 23 ♗h5 ♖xh5+ 24 ♔xh5 ♗g6++ 0-1

Chess News in Brief

Capablanca wins the New York tournament, scoring 10½/12 ahead of the Serbian master Boris Kostić (9) and Marshall (7).

Rubinstein wins a match 3½-2½ against Schlechter in Berlin.

Carl Schlechter (born 1874) dies in Budapest, from pneumonia.

World News in Brief

Peace talks between Russia and Germany break down. After the Germans renew attacks, and Estonia declares its independence, the Bolsheviks adopt a policy of "peace at any price", surrendering large amounts of territory, including Poland, the Ukraine and the Baltic states, in return for an end to hostilities.

Germany is now able to devote more resources to the Western Front, and launches a massive offensive, gaining large amounts of territory, and nearly splitting the Allied forces. The Allies fight back, coordinating a ground offensive with artillery bombardment and support from the air. The German forces retreat.

There is civil war in Russia, as Armenia and Georgia declare their independence, while there is widespread anti-Bolshevism in the north and in Siberia. The Allies land at Arkhangelsk and Murmansk to support White Russian opposition to the Bolsheviks. The tsar and his family are slaughtered in Ekaterinburg.

The war ends in defeat for Germany and Austria. The Austrian Empire splits up: Hungary declares itself independent, and the new state of Czechoslovakia is formed. Yugoslavia is also created, a confederation of South Slavic peoples, including Serbia. Germany and Austria both become republics, as the German Kaiser and the Austrian emperor abdicate. Germany surrenders much of its military hardware.

An epidemic of "Spanish 'flu" claims more lives worldwide than the war had done.

Denmark grants independence to Iceland.

Married women over the age of 30 gain the vote in Britain.

1919

Good results for Spielmann, Bogoljubow and Capablanca, but few major tournaments

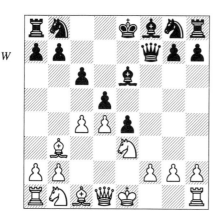

A. Nimzowitsch – C. Behting
Riga 1919

Nimzowitsch's e3-knight is an excellent blockader, while he has considerable pressure on Black's pawn-chain.

10 ♕e2 ♘f6 11 0-0 ♗b4

Black wishes to prevent ♘c3, which would put even more pressure on d5.

12 ♗d2 ♗xd2 13 ♘xd2 0-0 14 f4

Threatening f5, and so forcing Black to act. 14 f3 is also good.

14...dxc4 15 ♘dxc4 ♕e7 16 f5 ♗d5 17 ♘xd5 cxd5 18 ♘e3

The other knight reaches this ideal post. The pressure is unbearable.

18...♕d7? 19 ♘xd5! ♘xd5 20 ♕xe4 ♖d8 21 f6!

White wins by force.

21...gxf6 22 ♖f5 ♔h8 23 ♖xd5 ♖e8 24 ♖xd7 ♖xe4 25 ♖d8+ ♔g7 26 ♖g8+ ♔h6 27 ♖f1 1-0

Chess News in Brief

Capablanca beats Kostić 5-0 in a match, played in Havana. Capablanca also wins the Hastings tournament, scoring 10½/11 against a relatively weak field, with Kostić in second place. This is known as the Victory tournament, and only players from countries on the winning side in the war are invited.

Efim Bogoljubow wins a four-man tournament in Berlin.

Rudolf Spielmann wins a four-man tournament in Stockholm, ahead of Rubinstein, Bogoljubow and Réti.

Richard Réti tours the Netherlands.

World News in Brief

There is famine and widespread unrest in Germany. Notable amongst several uprisings is the brief formation of a 'soviet' republic in Bavaria; it is overthrown within a few months. There is also a communist revolt in Hungary, which is put down by Rumanian forces.

Negotiations over the formal agreements ending the First World War drag on for most of the year. Peace terms are finally agreed in the Treaty of Versailles. The demands, both financial and territorial, upon Germany are harsh, while the terms cause anti-Western sentiments in China, which refuses to sign.

The League of Nations is founded at the Paris peace conference.

The interned German fleet is scuttled at Scapa Flow by German seaman, fearful that the ships would have to be handed over to the Allies.

Britain grants Egypt a constitution.

Rutherford succeeds in 'splitting' the atom by bombarding nitrogen gas with alpha particles. The particles knocked out of the nuclei are given the name protons.

The first regular passenger air service starts, between London and Paris. The journey time is 3½ hours.

The first flight across the Atlantic (by a US Navy NC4 seaplane) is followed shortly by a non-stop trans-Atlantic flight, by Alcock and Brown; the 1,890 mile (3,040 km) flight takes 16 hours and 12 minutes.

During a solar eclipse in the Gulf of Guinea, scientists verify Einstein's General Theory of Relativity by observing the deflection of starlight around the sun.

1920

The hypermoderns make their mark –
good results for Réti and Breyer

Richard Réti wins the Gothenburg tournament with 9½/13, ahead of Rubinstein (9) and Bogoljubow (8). A game from the event:

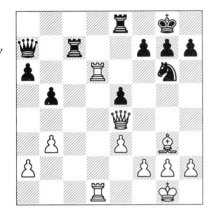

A. Rubinstein – G. Maroczy
Gothenburg 1920

Rubinstein has a firm grip on the position, but it is not obvious how he should make progress.

29 h4!
The idea of displacing the knight, and disrupting the black kingside by pushing the pawn all the way to h6, creates various threats.

29...f6 30 ♕d5+! ♔h8?
Black is definitely in trouble, but had more stubborn options. 30...♖f7 31 h5 ♘f8 32 h6 and 30...♔f8 31 ♕e4, intending h5, both favour White.

31 h5
This is good, but 31 ♖d8! wins instantly, and shows in full the value of White's h-pawn advance: 31...♖ce7 (or 31...♖f8 32 h5) 32 ♕c6 ♖f8 33 h5.

31...♘f8 32 h6 ♘g6?
This loses by force, but 32...♖ee7 will hardly be tenable in the long run.

33 ♕e6! ♖f8 34 ♖d7 gxh6 35 ♗h4! 1-0

After 35...♘xh4 (35...♖xd7 36 ♖xd7 wins the black queen) 36 ♕e7 mate is forced.

Chess News in Brief
Emanuel Lasker offers to resign the title of World Champion to Capablanca, but the chess-playing public naturally wants to see a match.

Gyula Breyer wins the Berlin tournament with 6½/9, ahead of Tartakower and Bogoljubow (both 5½).

Réti wins the Amsterdam tournament with 4½/6, ahead of Maroczy and Tartakower (both 4).

Alekhine wins what is now considered the 1st USSR Championship, though at the time it is called the All-Russian Chess Olympiad.

Lasker and Rubinstein both tour the Netherlands.

World News in Brief
In Russia, the Red Army achieves major victories over the opposition forces.

Tension is high in the demilitarized zone in Germany. French troops occupy Frankfurt, after German forces move in to oppose communists.

Several treaties redraw the map of the world, as the former territories of the Ottoman Empire are divided between the Allies, as are the former German colonies. There are further changes in the national borders in the Balkans, while Italy gains South Tirol from Austria.

The first session of the League of Nations opens, attended by representatives of 41 countries.

Martial law is declared in Ireland as the troubles escalate.

Women gain the vote in the USA.

Prohibition of the sale of alcohol is started in the USA.

Radio broadcasts begin in the USA.

1921

Capablanca finally becomes World Champion

José Raúl Capablanca beats Emanuel Lasker 9-5 (4 wins, 10 draws, no losses) to become World Champion.

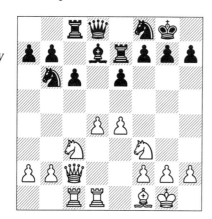

W

J. Capablanca – Em. Lasker
World Ch match (game 11), Havana 1921

It is clear that White has a pleasant spatial advantage. His next few moves make sure Black cannot free himself.

16 b4

White rules out ...c5; his plan is to play e5 and bring a knight to d6.

16...♗e8 17 ♕b3! ♖ec7 18 a4 ♘g6 19 a5 ♘d7 20 e5 b6 21 ♘e4 ♖b8 22 ♕c3?!

22 ♕a3 is better, since 22...♘f4 23 ♘d6 ♘d5 doesn't then gain a tempo on the white queen.

22...♘f4 23 ♘d6 ♘d5 24 ♕a3 f6 25 ♘xe8

Otherwise ...♗h5 would be annoying.

25...♕xe8 26 exf6 gxf6 27 b5

Capablanca's aim is to leave just one vulnerable black pawn on the queenside.

27...♖bc8 28 bxc6 ♖xc6 29 ♖xc6 ♖xc6 30 axb6 axb6 31 ♖e1

31 ♗b5 ♖c7 32 ♖e1 is another good way to keep the pressure on Black.

31...♕c8 32 ♘d2 ♘f8 33 ♘e4

White's knight is strong and Black's pawns are weak.

33...♕d8 34 h4 ♖c7?

Capablanca felt that 34...h6 was necessary, preparing ...f5.

35 ♕b3

White's aim is to exchange off the strong defensive knight on d5.

35...♖g7 36 g3 ♖a7 37 ♗c4 ♖a5 38 ♘c3 ♘xc3 39 ♕xc3 ♔f7 40 ♕e3 ♕d6 41 ♕e4 ♖a4

41...♖a7 is met by 42 d5.

42 ♕b7+ ♔g6

42...♕e7? 43 ♗xe6+!.

43 ♕c8 ♕b4 44 ♖c1 ♕e7

44...♖a3 45 ♗d3+ f5 46 ♕e8+ ♔h6 47 ♖c7 wins for White.

45 ♗d3+ ♔h6 46 ♖c7 ♖a1+ 47 ♔g2 ♕d6 48 ♕xf8+! 1-0

Alekhine wins the Budapest tournament with 8½/11, ahead of Ernst Grünfeld (8). It is at this tournament that he first uses the Alekhine Defence (1 e4 ♘f6).

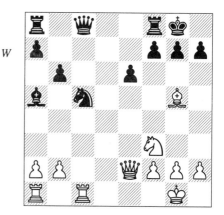

W

A. Alekhine – K. Sterk
Budapest 1921

White is a pawn down, but Black's queen-side pieces are in a tangle, while his kingside is short of defenders. Alekhine exploits these factors in a powerful, elegant manner.

21 ♖ab1

Threatening 22 b4.

21...♕a6

A neat response to the threat, but it takes the queen further away from the kingside.

22 ♖c4!

Walking into a pin is unnatural, but Alekhine has planned a devastating follow-up.

22...♘a4?!

22...♘b7 is a better defence.

23 ♗f6!

A neat way to switch over to a kingside attack.

23...♖fc8

After 23...h5, 24 ♖g4! ♕xe2? 25 ♖xg7+ ♔h8 26 ♘g5 forces mate. The text-move tries to turn the battery on the f1-a6 diagonal into a pin, but White can now play directly for mate.

24 ♕e5! ♖c5

24...♕xc4 25 ♕g5 ♔f8 26 ♕xg7+ ♔e8 27 ♕g8+ ♔d7 28 ♘e5+ wins; 24...♖xc4 25 ♕g5 ♖g4 26 ♕xg4 g6 27 ♕xa4 nets a piece.

25 ♕g3! g6 26 ♖xa4

White is a piece up and still has mating threats.

26...♕d3 27 ♖f1 ♖ac8 28 ♖d4 ♕f5 29 ♕f4 ♕c2 30 ♕h6 1-0

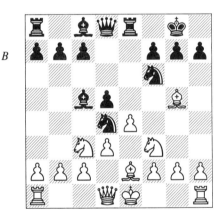

A. Nićifor – E. Kramer
Celje 1921

White has responded carelessly to a speculative gambit by Black, and as a result pays a heavy price.

9...♘xe4! 10 ♘xe4?

10 ♗xd8? ♘xf3+ wins back the queen with interest, since 11 gxf3? ♗xf2+ 12 ♔f1 ♗h3# is mate. 10 dxe4 is best.

10...dxe4! 11 ♗xd8 exf3

Already there is little hope for White.

12 ♗h4

After 12 ♔d2 ♖xe2+ (12...fxe2 13 ♕b1 isn't so clear) 13 ♕xe2 (if 13 ♔c1, then 13... fxg2 14 ♖g1 ♖xf2 wins for Black; 13 ♔c3 ♗e6 threatens 14...♘b5#) 13...♘xe2 the two pieces should prove better than the rook.

12...fxg2! 13 ♔d2 gxh1♕ 14 ♕xh1 ♖xe2+ 15 ♔d1 ♗g4 16 ♕xb7 ♖xc2+

16...♖ae8 is a somewhat faster win.

17 ♔e1 ♖e8+ 18 ♔f1 ♗h3+ 19 ♔g1 ♘e2+ 20 ♔h1 ♘c1 21 f4 ♖ee2 22 ♕b8+ ♗f8 23 ♗g3 ♖ed2 24 ♕xa7 ♖d1+ 25 ♕g1 ♗g2# (0-1)

Chess News in Brief

Alekhine wins a tournament at The Hague.

Max Euwe (born 1901) wins the Netherlands Championship for the first of 13 times (the last in 1955).

Vasily Smyslov [World Champion 1957-8] is born.

World News in Brief

The Russian civil war ends in victory for the Bolsheviks, confirming the nation as a communist state. After years of conflict, the new nation is beset by appalling famine. The USA sends 800,000 tons of food.

Allied troops occupy Ruhr towns, following German failures to pay war reparations. The threat of reoccupation forces the German government to acquiesce. The government later resigns in the face of a deepening economic crisis.

Britain agrees to the formation of an Irish Free State.

In response to growing unemployment, the USA sets quotas limiting immigration.

In Italy, Benito Mussolini, leader of the Fascists, unites right-wing groups against communism and gains support from the business community.

Mongolia declares its independence from China, becoming the world's second communist state.

In China, the first congress of the Communist Party is held.

Capital punishment is abolished in Sweden.

In France, a helicopter designed by Etienne Oehmichen is successfully tested.

1922

Another good year for Alekhine

Alexander Alekhine wins the Hastings tournament with 7½/10, ahead of Rubinstein (7), Bogoljubow and Thomas (4½). This is the critical last-round game:

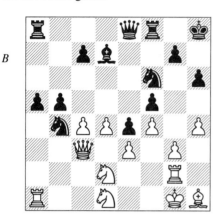

E. Bogoljubow – A. Alekhine
Hastings 1922

After some rather feeble play by White (just look at his ridiculous kingside set-up!), Alekhine has established a commanding position.

28...♘d3 29 ♖xa5 b4! 30 ♖xa8 bxc3!?

30...♛xa8 31 ♛b3 ♛a1 32 ♘f1 ♖a8 33 ♘b2 ♖a3 34 ♛d1 ♘g4 wins in more straightforward fashion.

31 ♖xe8 c2 32 ♖xf8+ ♚h7 33 ♘f2 c1♛+ 34 ♘f1

Alekhine has effectively exchanged two rooks for a queen. The white pieces are hopelessly uncoordinated, and Black's mate threats will win material.

34...♘e1 35 ♖h2 ♛xc4 36 ♖b8 ♗b5 37 ♖xb5 ♛xb5 38 g4 ♘f3+

38...♛e2 is also good.

39 ♗xf3 exf3 40 gxf5 ♛e2 41 d5 ♚g8

41...h5? 42 ♘h3 gives White some undeserved counterplay.

42 h5 ♚h7 43 e4 ♘xe4 44 ♘xe4 ♛xe4 45 d6 cxd6 46 f6 gxf6 47 ♖d2 ♛e2

Forcing a won king and pawn ending.

48 ♖xe2 fxe2 49 ♚f2 exf1♛+ 50 ♚xf1 ♚g7 51 ♚f2 ♚f7 52 ♚e3 ♚e6 53 ♚e4 d5+ 0-1

Richard Réti and Rudolf Spielmann share first place at Teplitz-Schönau. A sensational game from the event:

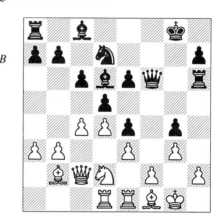

G. Maroczy – S. Tartakower
Teplitz-Schönau 1922

17...♖xh2!!

This sacrifice does not lead to a calculable short-term win, but gives Black a prolonged attack which will eventually cost White more than Black has sacrificed.

18 ♚xh2 ♛xf2+ 19 ♚h1

19 ♗g2 ♛xg3+ 20 ♚g1 ♛h2+ 21 ♚f2 ♗g3+ 22 ♚f1 b6 23 ♘xe4 ♗b7! is good for Black.

19...♘f6 20 ♖e2

20 ♖c1 ♘h5 21 ♘xe4 ♛xc2 22 ♘f6+ ♘xf6 23 ♖xc2 ♗xg3 24 ♖ee2 h5 gives Black more than enough for the exchange.

20...♛xg3 21 ♘b1

White is wriggling to get his pieces into the defence. 21 ♛c3 ♘h5 22 ♖g2 ♛h4+ 23 ♚g1 ♘g3 24 ♖h2 ♛g5 25 ♖f2 ♘f5 should be winning for Black.

21...♘h5 22 ♛d2 ♗d7

Calmly bringing his queenside pieces into play.

23 ♖f2 ♛h4+ 24 ♚g1?!

White had to try 24 ♖h2 ♗xh2 25 ♛xh2.

24...♗g3?!

24...♘g3! 25 ♖h2 ♛g5 26 ♖f2 ♘f5 followed by 27...♘h4 and ...♘f3+ leaves White helpless.

25 ♗c3?!

Again, White's best course was 25 ♖h2! ♗xh2+ 26 ♕xh2 ♕g5.

25...♗xf2+ 26 ♕xf2 g3 27 ♕g2 ♖f8

White now has no adequate defence against the threatened 28...♖f2 29 ♕h1 ♖h2.

28 ♗e1 ♖xf1+

Missing a quicker win by 28...e5! 29 ♖d2 ♕g5 30 ♖e2 ♗g4.

29 ♔xf1 e5 30 ♔g1 ♗g4 31 ♗xg3 ♘xg3 32 ♖e1 ♘f5 33 ♕f2 ♕g5 34 dxe5 ♗f3+ 35 ♔f1 ♘g3+ 0-1

Rubinstein wins the Vienna tournament.

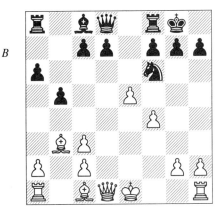

A. Alekhine – R. Réti
Vienna 1922

It appears that Alekhine is sweeping Réti from the board, but Black turns out to have considerable resources.

12...c5!

Black plans to blank out the b3-bishop.

13 ♗a3!

Now Black is obliged to sideline his queen.

13...♕a5 14 0-0 ♕xa3 15 exf6 c4 16 ♕d5 ♕a5

Getting the queen back into play and parrying the threat to the rook, since 17 ♕xa8? allows 17...♕b6+ and 18...♗b7.

17 fxg7 ♕b6+ 18 ♔h1 ♔xg7

Not 18...♖d8? 19 ♗xc4 bxc4 20 ♕xa8 ♗b7 21 ♖ab1.

19 ♗xc4

The bishop escapes, because 19...bxc4? 20 ♕xa8 ♗b7 fails to trap the queen due to 21 ♖ab1.

19...♗b7 20 ♕e5+ ♕f6 21 ♗d3 ♖fe8!

The best defence. White's combination has won him material, but at some positional cost.

22 ♕h5 h6 23 ♕g4+ ♔h8 24 ♕xd7 ♖e7 25 ♕d4 ♕xd4 26 cxd4 ♖d8

White would be happy to return a pawn to consolidate his position, but it is far from easy to do so.

27 f5 f6 28 ♖ae1

28 ♖f4 ♖g7 29 ♗f1 ♖c7 (or 29...♖c8 30 ♖f2) 30 ♖c1 may well be a better winning attempt.

28...♖g7! 29 ♗e4 ♖xd4 30 ♗xb7 ♖xb7 31 ♖e6 ♔g7 32 ♖xa6 ♖c4

Black will now reduce the deficit to one pawn. Alekhine did not manage to generate real winning chances from here, and the game was drawn on move 59.

Chess News in Brief

Bogoljubow wins the Bad Pistyan tournament, ahead of Spielmann and Alekhine.

Capablanca wins the London tournament, ahead of Alekhine, Vidmar and Rubinstein.

Alekhine tours Spain.

Yuri Averbakh [one of the world's leading players in the 1950s and a famous endgame theoretician] is born.

World News in Brief

Egypt declares its independence from Britain.

Benito Mussolini comes to power in Italy.

The Ottomans recover some territory that had been surrendered to Greece.

Soviet Russia renames itself as the Union of Soviet Socialist Republics (USSR).

The Irish Free State comes into being.

Britain makes an alliance with Iraq.

The British Broadcasting Company begins radio broadcasts.

Insulin is used for treatment of diabetes. It is a natural chemical that was isolated by Drs Banting and Best, working in Toronto.

Niels Bohr wins a Nobel Prize for his work on atomic structure.

1923

Successes for Alekhine and Nimzowitsch

Alekhine, Bogoljubow and Maroczy share first place with 11½/17 at the Karlsbad tournament. The following game was a setback for Alekhine though.

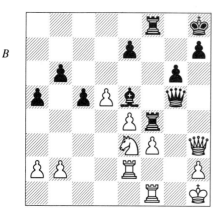

A. Alekhine – F. Yates
Karlsbad 1923

Yates, the leading British player of the day, has established a fine blockade on the dark squares, and must now decide how to make further progress.

31...♖h4

Forcing the queen away, and envisaging the forthcoming exchange sacrifice.

32 ♕e6 ♕h5

32...♗g3, threatening 33...♕h5 34 ♘g4 ♖xg4 35 fxg4 ♖xf1+ 36 ♔g2 ♕xh2+ 37 ♔xf1 ♕h1#, is also good.

33 ♘g4 ♖xg4!

This forces a position where Black has ♕+♗ vs ♕+♖, but White's pieces are uncoordinated and his king is on the run.

34 fxg4 ♖xf1+ 35 ♔g2 ♕xh2+ 36 ♔xf1 ♕h1+ 37 ♔f2 ♗d4+ 38 ♔g3 ♕g1+ 39 ♔h3 ♕f1+ 40 ♖g2 ♕h1+ 41 ♔g3

41 ♖h2 ♕f3+ 42 ♔h4 ♗f6+ wins for Black.

41...♕e1+ 42 ♔h3 g5! 43 ♖c2

White is compelled to move his rook away, but this gives Black an additional target.

43...♕f1+ 44 ♔h2 ♕g1+ 45 ♔h3 ♕h1+ 46 ♔g3 ♕d1!

White now faces mate or loss of his rook.

47 ♖c3

47 ♕f5 ♕d3+ 48 ♕f3 ♗e5+ picks off the rook with check.

47...♕g1+ 48 ♔h3 ♕f1+ 49 ♔g3 ♗f2+ 50 ♔f3 ♗g1+ 0-1

It is mate in two more moves: 51 ♔g3 ♕f2+ 52 ♔h3 ♕h2#.

Aron Nimzowitsch wins the Copenhagen tournament with 8/10, ahead of Sämisch and Tartakower (both 6).

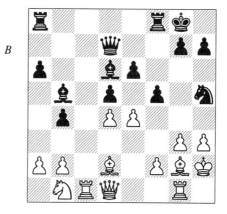

F. Sämisch – A. Nimzowitsch
Copenhagen 1923

White has just played 20 e2-e4?, discovering an attack on the h5-knight. However, Nimzowitsch has a fine reply ready.

20...fxe4! 21 ♕xh5 ♖xf2

Black has two pawns for the piece, and can make further inroads into White's badly organized position via the f-file.

22 ♕g5 ♖af8 23 ♔h1 ♖8f5 24 ♕e3 ♗d3

24...♖e2 25 ♕b3 ♗a4 also wins, but the text-move embodies a more beautiful idea.

25 ♖ce1 h6!! 0-1

Amazingly, White is in zugzwang – once he runs out of pawn moves on the queenside, any move he makes will involve a fatal concession. Moreover, by guarding g5, Black has created the threat of ...♖5f3.

Emanuel Lasker wins the Mährisch-Ostrau tournament with 10½/13, ahead of Réti (9½) and Grünfeld (8½).

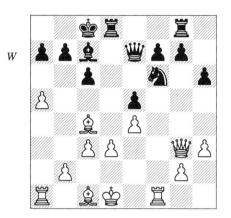

A. Rubinstein – K. Hromadka
Mährisch-Ostrau 1923

An aggressive opening, to which Black responded passively, has given White a useful advantage. He must now decide how to attack the black king.

18 ♗e3 ♔b8 19 ♔c2 ♔a8 20 ♖f3

Rubinstein perceives that Black will need to use his knight to defend his king, and so prepares to step up the pressure against f7. From the f2-square, the white queen will generate threats in two directions.

20...♘d5?!

Black goes in for an ingenious but flawed idea.

21 ♗g1

21 ♗xa7 is also good, but Rubinstein is after bigger game.

21...♘f4 22 ♕f2 ♗b8 23 g3!

Starting an impressive combination. Black's reply is forced.

23...♘xh3 24 ♖xf7 ♕d6

24...♘xf2 25 ♖xe7 ♗d6 26 ♖f7 is miserable for Black.

25 ♕b6! ♖d7

25...axb6 26 axb6+ ♗a7 27 ♖xa7+ ♔b8 28 ♖fxb7+ ♔c8 29 ♗c5 wins for White.

26 ♗c5!

The point. Black has no satisfactory move.

26...♖xf7 27 ♗xd6 ♖f2+ 28 ♕xf2 ♘xf2 29 ♗c5 1-0

Chess News in Brief

Romanovsky wins the 2nd USSR Championship.

Alekhine tours Britain and France.

Yakov Estrin [winner of the 7th Correspondence World Championship, 1972-5] is born.

Svetozar Gligorić [the leading Yugoslav player from the early 1950s to the mid-1970s] is born.

World News in Brief

French and Belgian troops occupy Essen, in response to German failures to make war reparations.

The economic crisis in Germany heightens dramatically, as hyperinflation renders German marks practically worthless. By the end of the year, the mark is worth about a billionth of its value at the start of the year – a British pound or American dollar would buy trillions of marks. This disaster is in part due to the German government printing large amounts of money to pay soldiers to oppose the threatened reoccupations.

The National Socialist (Nazi) Party, under the leadership of Adolf Hitler, attempts a coup in Munich. It fails completely, but gives Hitler a great deal of publicity.

Turkey, the heart of the old Ottoman Empire, declares itself a republic.

King George II of Greece is removed from office by a vote in the Greek parliament.

A massive earthquake destroys much of Tokyo, killing over 130,000 people and making more than a million homeless.

The first wireless broadcast is made between Britain and the USA.

1924

Lasker triumphs in the New York tournament – the strongest for a decade

Lasker wins the New York tournament, scoring a remarkable 16/20 against a world-class field, ahead of Capablanca (14½, after a poor start), Alekhine (12), Marshall (11) and Réti (10½).

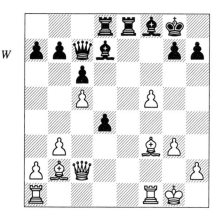

R. Réti – E. Bogoljubow
New York 1924

White's hypermodern opening (note the two fianchettoed bishops!) seems to have bemused his more classically-orientated opponent into some rather passive play. White has excellent control of the centre, and now goes onto the offensive, targeting the weakened black kingside.

19 ♗h5! ♖e5

Not a happy square for the rook, but 19...♖e7 20 ♗xd4 ♗xf5? (20...♗e8 21 ♕c4+) 21 ♖xf5 ♖xd4 22 ♖xf8+! ♔xf8 23 ♕xh7 is even worse.

20 ♗xd4 ♖xf5?

Black decides it is safe to re-establish material equality, but this turns out to be fatal. 20...♖d5 21 ♕c4 ♔h8 22 ♗g4! should be a technical win for White though.

21 ♖xf5 ♗xf5 22 ♕xf5 ♖xd4 23 ♖f1! ♖d8

There is no good defence; 23...♕e7 24 ♗f7+ ♔h8 25 ♗d5! cuts off the black rook from defending the back rank, and wins.

24 ♗f7+ ♔h8 25 ♗e8! 1-0

Suddenly f8 is threatened twice, and not defended at all.

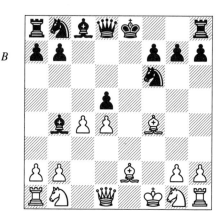

S. Tartakower – J. Capablanca
New York 1924

Capablanca now makes an uncompromising move, not deterred by an apparent problem.

8...dxc4! 9 ♗xb8?

Tartakower presumably thought he was winning a piece after 9...♖xb8? 10 ♕a4+. However, while Capablanca did occasionally make oversights, Tartakower really ought to have been more suspicious. White should prefer 9 ♗xc4.

9...♘d5!

Not only defending the b4-bishop, but also threatening ...♘e3+, so White cannot retrieve his bishop. The upshot is that White has ruined his own position for no good reason.

10 ♔f2

10 ♗f4 ♕f6! (not 10...♘xf4?? 11 ♕a4+) is the key point.

10...♖xb8 11 ♗xc4 0-0 12 ♘f3

12 ♗xd5 ♕xd5 13 ♘c3 is also fairly miserable for White.

12...♘f6 13 ♘c3 b5! 14 ♗d3

14 ♘xb5 ♘e4+ 15 ♔g1 a6 gives Black a powerful initiative.

14...♘g4+ 15 ♔g1 ♗b7 16 ♗f5 ♗xf3 17 gxf3 ♘e3!

There is no let-up for White.

18 ♗xh7+ ♔h8 19 ♕d3 ♗xc3

19...♘c4 is a very good alternative.

20 bxc3 ♘d5

20...♕g5+ 21 ♔f2 ♖be8 is favourable for Black.

21 ♗e4 ♘f4 22 ♕d2 ♕h4 23 ♔f1?

23 ♕e1 is a more resilient defence, but 23...♕h6 should be winning for Black.

23...f5 24 ♗c6 ♖f6 25 d5 ♖d8 26 ♖d1 ♖xc6 27 dxc6 ♖xd2 28 ♖xd2 ♘e6 29 ♖d6 ♕c4+ 30 ♔g2 ♕e2+ 0-1

Efim Bogoljubow wins the 3rd USSR Championship.

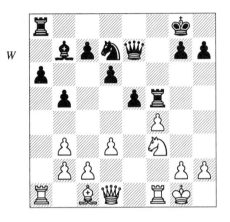

B. Verlinsky – G. Levenfish
USSR Ch, Moscow 1924

Black has achieved a good position with little difficulty. Rather than helping Black become even more active by taking on e5, White now decides to let Black take on f4, reckoning on regaining this pawn.

16 ♗d2 exf4 17 ♘d4 ♖g5

The threat against g2 forces White to step back.

18 ♘f3

Will Black be willing to repeat?

18...♖g4

No! White must act quickly; else Black will consolidate...

19 h3 ♖xg2+!!

A surprising sacrifice, based on the poor co-ordination of White's forces.

20 ♔xg2 ♕g5+ 21 ♔h1 ♘e5 22 ♕e2

Or 22 ♗e1 ♕h5 23 ♔g2 ♖e8, and Black wins.

22...♕g3 23 ♕g2 ♘xf3 24 ♗c3

24 ♕xg3 fxg3 leads to a hopeless ending for White.

24...♘d4! 25 ♕xb7

Now Black has a forced mate in five moves.

25...♕xh3+ 26 ♔g1 ♘e2+ 27 ♔f2 ♕e3+ 28 ♔e1 ♘xc3# (0-1)

Chess News in Brief

Ernst Grünfeld wins the Meran tournament with 10½/13, ahead of Spielmann (8½).

Alekhine tours the USA.

Fédération Internationale des Echecs (FIDE) is founded in Paris. There is an abortive attempt to hold a chess olympiad, also in Paris, but there are too few players. Hermannis Mattison makes the best score.

Joseph Blackburne (born 1841) dies. He was the leading British player from about 1870 to the turn of the century, and was still active at top level in 1914.

David Bronstein [World Championship challenger in 1951] is born.

Klaus Junge [German super-talent who died in 1945] is born.

World News in Brief

Lenin dies; Joseph Stalin is a member of the three-man council that succeeds him as leader of the USSR.

Mussolini's Fascists win the Italian election in an atmosphere of terror. There are allegations of widespread election fraud.

French and Belgian troops withdraw from the Ruhr after Germany agrees to a new package of war reparations.

Adolf Hitler is sentenced to five years' imprisonment for treason, but is freed later in the year.

Albania is declared a republic.

Clarence Birdseye develops the technique of quick-freezing foods.

The first Winter Olympics are held, at Chamonix, France.

1925

Efim Bogoljubow is the surprise winner of the strongest tournament of the year

Bogoljubow wins the Moscow tournament with 15½/20, ahead of Lasker (14), Capablanca (13½), Marshall (12½), Tartakower and Torre (both 12). For Carlos Torre, a little-known Mexican player, this is a sensational achievement.

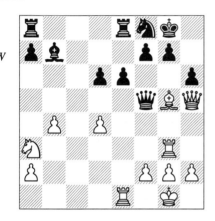

C. Torre – Em. Lasker
Moscow 1925

Torre's vigorous, though somewhat dubious, attacking play has just been rewarded with a few inaccuracies from his renowned opponent.

23 ♘c4! ♕d5?

After 23...hxg5 24 ♘xd6 ♕g6 25 ♕xg6 ♘xg6 26 ♘xb7 ♖eb8 27 ♘c5 ♖xb4 28 ♖xg5 a draw is probable, but Lasker must have overlooked the sensational queen sacrifice that awaits him.

24 ♘e3 ♕b5?

24...♕xd4 25 ♖d1 ♕e4 26 ♗xh6 ♘g6 27 ♗g5 is good for White.

25 ♗f6!!

In return for losing his queen, White sets up a deadly see-saw, which ultimately makes decisive material gains.

25...♕xh5 26 ♖xg7+ ♔h8 27 ♖xf7+ ♔g8 28 ♖g7+ ♔h8 29 ♖xb7+ ♔g8 30 ♖g7+ ♔h8 31 ♖g5+ ♔h7 32 ♖xh5 ♔g6 33 ♖h3 ♔xf6 34 ♖xh6+

White has collected three extra pawns.

34...♔g5 35 ♖h3 ♖eb8 36 ♖g3+ ♔f6 37 ♖f3+ ♔g6 38 a3 a5 39 bxa5 ♖xa5 40 ♘c4 ♖d5 41 ♖f4 ♘d7 42 ♖xe6+ ♔g5 43 g3 1-0

Alekhine wins the Baden-Baden tournament with 16/20, ahead of Rubinstein (14½) and Sämisch (13½).

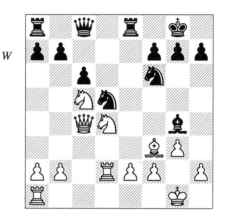

R. Réti – A. Alekhine
Baden-Baden 1925

Alekhine has just played 17...♗h3-g4!. By repeated offers to exchange bishops, he either forces a draw, or extracts a concession from White.

18 ♗g2 ♗h3 19 ♗f3 ♗g4

Réti avoids the repetition, and plays for the win.

20 ♗h1 h5 21 b4 a6 22 ♖c1 h4 23 a4 hxg3 24 hxg3 ♕c7 25 b5! axb5 26 axb5 ♖e3!

A fantastic idea, threatening 27...♖xg3+ and interfering with White's lines of communication. White must play very accurately.

27 ♘f3?

The critical line, as worked out by John Nunn, is 27 ♔h2! ♖aa3! 28 ♘d3! ♘h5 29 ♕xd5! ♘xg3 30 ♔g1 ♖xe2+ 31 ♘xe2 ♖xe2 32 ♕c5, when White is slightly better, but does not have real winning chances.

After the text-move, Black's lengthy combination runs like clockwork, with the rook on e3 generating all sorts of threats while remaining invulnerable.

27...cxb5 28 ♕xb5 ♘c3! 29 ♕xb7 ♕xb7 30 ♘xb7 ♘xe2+ 31 ♔h2

31 ♔f1 ♘xg3+ 32 fxg3 ♗xf3 33 ♗xf3 ♖xf3+ gives Black a winning attack.

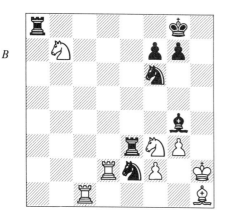

31...♘e4! 32 ♖c4

After 32 ♖d8+ ♖xd8 33 fxe3 ♖d5! 34 ♖c4 ♘2xg3 35 ♗g2 ♘f1+!! 36 ♔g1 ♖d1 37 ♗xf1 ♗xf3, the threat of 38...♘d2 is decisive.

32...♘xf2 33 ♗g2 ♗e6 34 ♖cc2 ♘g4+ 35 ♔h3 ♘e5+ 36 ♔h2 ♖xf3 37 ♖xe2 ♘g4+ 38 ♔h3 ♘e3+ 39 ♔h2 ♘xc2 40 ♗xf3 ♘d4 0-1

Nimzowitsch and Rubinstein share first place at the Marienbad tournament with 11/15, ahead of Marshall and Torre (both 10).

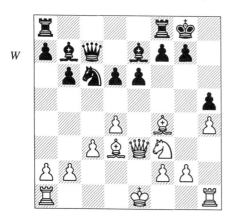

D. Janowski – F. Sämisch
Marienbad 1925

White has been trying by various means to get an attack moving, and now tries a rook-lift.

16 ♖h3!? e5

Black hits back in the centre – the standard method.

17 dxe5 ♘xe5 18 ♘xe5 dxe5?

This is fatal. Black could stay fully in the game by 18...♗f6, exploiting White's vulnerability on the e-file.

19 ♗xe5 ♗d6?

This loses on the spot, but there was nothing satisfactory.

20 ♕h6!! 1-0

20...f6 (20...gxh6 21 ♖g3#; 20...f5 21 ♗c4+ mates) 21 ♗h7+ ♔h8 22 ♕xh5 is a massacre.

Chess News in Brief

Alekhine wins a small tournament in Paris.

The first German edition of Nimzowitsch's *My System* is published.

Bogoljubow wins the 4th USSR Championship. Bogoljubow also wins the German Open Championship for the first time.

Efim Geller [strong Ukrainian grandmaster; runner-up in the 1962 Candidates tournament] is born.

Vladimir Zagorovsky [winner of the 4th Correspondence World Championship, 1962-5] is born.

World News in Brief

Famine in China claims three million lives.

In Turkey, a Kurdish uprising is put down.

In the USA, the first national congress of the Ku Klux Klan opens. The organization claims more than a million members.

The Nazi *Schutzstaffel* (SS) is founded. Hitler's book *Mein Kampf* is published. In it, amongst other things, he blames Germany's defeat in the First World War on the Jews and communists.

In South Africa, a law is passed that excludes Blacks, Coloureds and Indians from skilled jobs.

Australia encourages large-scale immigration.

Henry Souttar performs the first surgical operation inside the heart.

1926

A sensational result for Nimzowitsch • Alekhine achieves consistently good results

Nimzowitsch dominates the Dresden tournament, scoring 8½/9, with Alekhine in second place on 7.

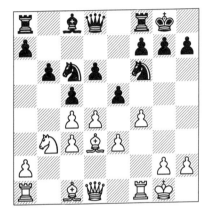

P. Johner – A. Nimzowitsch
Dresden 1926

This game is famous for Nimzowitsch's queen manoeuvre, which starts a subtle plan of restraining White's kingside.

11...e4! 12 ♗e2 ♕d7!!

Nimzowitsch perceives that he must prevent White expanding on the kingside. The queen move prevents g4, and is part of a further plan of restraint. Instead, 12...♘e8 13 g4 f5 14 d5 ♘e7 15 g5 is rather drawish – Nimzo is already playing for more.

13 h3?!

White should play 13 ♗d2 ♘e7 14 ♗e1 ♗a6!? 15 ♘h4 ♘f5 16 ♗xf6 ♘xe3 17 ♕c1 ♘xf1 18 ♗h4 ♘xh2 19 ♔xh2.

13...♘e7 14 ♕e1?

Considering what follows, 14 g4!? is worth trying.

14...h5!

Now Black can clamp down on the kingside.

15 ♗d2 ♕f5! 16 ♔h2 ♕h7!

Black's queen manoeuvre is completed. On h7, the queen is ideally placed not only to prevent kingside play by White, but also to support Black's own activity.

17 a4 ♘f5

17...a5! is more accurate, as after the text-move, White could play 18 a5.

18 g3 a5!

Sealing up the queenside. Black will now build up an overwhelming kingside attack at his leisure.

19 ♖g1 ♘h6 20 ♗f1 ♗d7 21 ♗c1 ♖ac8 22 d5 ♔h8 23 ♘d2 ♖g8 24 ♗g2 g5 25 ♘f1 ♖g7 26 ♖a2 ♘f5 27 ♗h1 ♖cg8 28 ♕d1 gxf4! 29 exf4 ♗c8 30 ♕b3 ♗a6 31 ♖e2

Or 31 ♗d2 ♖g6! 32 ♖e1 ♘g4+ 33 hxg4 hxg4+ 34 ♔g2 ♗xc4! 35 ♕xc4 e3.

31...♘h4! 32 ♖e3 ♗c8 33 ♕c2 ♗xh3! 34 ♗xe4 ♗f5

With the eventual idea of ...h4.

35 ♗xf5 ♘xf5 36 ♖e2 h4 37 ♖gg2 hxg3+ 38 ♔g1 ♕h3 39 ♘e3 ♘h4 40 ♔f1 ♖e8! 0-1

Efim Bogoljubow wins the Berlin tournament with 7/9, ahead of Rubinstein (6). A game from the event:

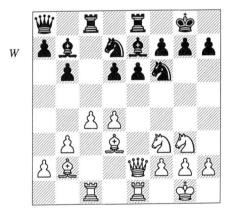

E. Colle – E. Grünfeld
Berlin 1926

At first sight this position looks rather quiet, but f7 and e6 are somewhat weak, and Black's queen is too far away to provide support.

16 ♘g5

Pretty much forced, to avoid ...♗xf3.

16...g6?

Black guards h7, which wasn't really under attack, and allows White's main idea. 16...♗f8 or 16...♘f8 is necessary.

17 ♘xf7! ♔xf7 18 ♕xe6+ ♔g7

18...♔f8 19 d5 ♘c5 20 ♕e3 ♘xd3 21 ♕xd3 gives White a very strong attack.

19 d5 ♘c5

19...♘e5 20 ♘f5+! gxf5 21 ♕xf5 is good for White, while 19...♘f8? loses to 20 ♕xe7+ ♖xe7 21 ♖xe7+.

20 ♘f5+! ♔f8

Or 20...gxf5 21 ♕xf5, and Black's position falls apart.

21 ♕e3 gxf5

21...♘g4 22 ♕f3 wins; for example, 22...♗f6 23 ♗xf6 ♘xd3 24 ♗e7+.

22 ♕h6+ ♔f7 23 ♗xf5 ♗xd5 24 ♖xe7+ ♖xe7 25 ♕xf6+ ♔e8 26 ♕h8+ ♔f7 27 ♗xc8 1-0

Spielmann wins the Semmering tournament with 13/17, ahead of Alekhine (12½), Vidmar (12), Nimzowitsch and Tartakower (both 11½).

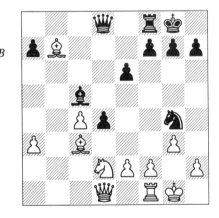

A. Rubinstein – A. Alekhine
Semmering 1926

Alekhine shows his talent for sensing when it is worth looking beyond the obvious moves.

18...♘xf2!

Stronger than 18...dxc3, although this is also good: 19 ♘e4 ♘e3!, e.g. 20 ♕xd8 ♖xd8 21 fxe3 ♗xe3+ 22 ♔g2 c2 23 ♘c3 ♖b8!.

19 ♔xf2

Other moves are no better: 19 ♖xf2 dxc3, 19 ♗a5 ♘xd1 20 ♗xd8 d3+ and 19 ♕a1 dxc3 20 ♘b3 ♗e3! 21 ♔g2 ♕b6 are all winning for Black.

19...dxc3+ 20 e3

20 ♔e1 loses to 20...cxd2+ 21 ♕xd2 ♕b6.

20...cxd2

Black is winning easily.

21 ♔e2 ♕b8 22 ♗f3 ♖d8 23 ♕b1 ♕d6 24 a4 f5 25 ♖d1 ♗b4 26 ♕c2 ♕c5 27 ♔f2 a5 28 ♗e2 g5 29 ♗d3 f4 0-1

Chess News in Brief

Ernst Grünfeld and Mario Monticelli share first place in the Budapest tournament with 9½/15.

Capablanca wins the Lake Hopatcong tournament with 6/8, ahead of Kupchik (5).

The so-called 'Little Olympiad' is played in Budapest, with just four countries taking part. Hungary captures first place, ahead of Yugoslavia.

World News in Brief

The General Strike brings Britain to a virtual standstill; the police and army are brought in to break the strike.

British troops pull out of the Rhineland, ending seven years of occupation.

A Nazi rally is held in Nuremberg.

Mussolini bans all opposition in Italy.

Moslem-Hindu riots break out in Calcutta.

A military coup brings Josef Pilsudski to power in Poland.

An international team makes the first flight over the North Pole in an airship.

In London, the Scottish engineer John Logie Baird successfully demonstrates a procedure for the wireless transmission of moving images, which becomes known as television. Baird believes that one day there will be a television in every home.

In the USA, Robert Goddard develops multistage rockets to study the upper atmosphere.

An anti-tetanus serum is discovered at the Pasteur Institute in Paris.

1927

Capablanca loses World Championship to Alekhine •
The first Olympiad • Botvinnik impresses in the USSR

Capablanca dominates the New York tournament (scoring 14/20 vs Alekhine, Nimzowitsch, Vidmar, Spielmann and Marshall), but loses the subsequent World Championship match to Alekhine. The score is Alekhine 6 wins to Capablanca's 3, with 25 draws. This is one of Capablanca's wins:

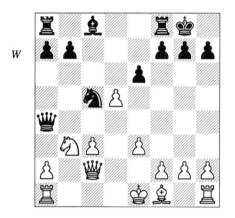

J. Capablanca – A. Alekhine
World Ch (game 7), Buenos Aires 1927

Alekhine has used a lot of time on his clock to reach this dubious position. There are plenty of ways for White to keep an extra pawn, but Capablanca now displays great accuracy in choosing the one that gives Black the least counterplay.

15 Rd1!
15 dxe6? Âxe6 is good for Black.
15...exd5 16 Rxd5 Ãxb3?!
16...b6 makes White's task more difficult.
17 axb3 Wc6 18 Rd4 Re8
Otherwise White could untangle his kingside by f3 and Êf2.
19 Âd3!
Capablanca decides to play for an attack against the black king.
19...Wxg2 20 Âxh7+ Êf8
20...Êh8 leaves the black king more exposed.
21 Âe4 Wh3

21...Âf5 22 Âxg2 Âxc2 is a hopeless ending for Black.
22 Wd2 Âe6 23 c4 a5 24 Rg1 Wxh2?!
Black now goes down in flames, but otherwise he remains a pawn down and all White's pieces are active.
25 Rh1 Wc7 26 Wb2
Threatening 27 Wa3+ Êg8 28 Âh7+!.
26...Wc5 27 Âd5!
The threat is now 28 Âxe6.
27...Ra6 28 Re4 Rd6 29 Rh7!
Now Black must lose further material.
29...Êe7 30 Wxg7 Êd8 31 Âxe6 fxe6 32 Wxb7 Wb4+ 33 Wxb4 axb4 34 c5 Rc6 35 Rxb4 Rxc5 36 Ra7 1-0

Bogatyrchuk and Romanovsky share the 5th USSR Championship; the 16-year-old Botvinnik comes joint 5th.

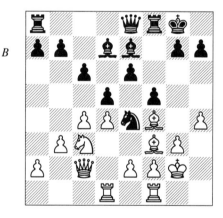

I. Rabinovich – M. Botvinnik
USSR Ch, Moscow 1927

Botvinnik's Dutch Defence has worked well. He has a firm grip on e4 and White's kingside has been weakened.
16...Âb4!? 17 Âxe4?!
It is probably a lesser evil to retreat by 17 Ãb1!? planning a3 and b4.
17...fxe4
Now Black can attack on the f-file.

18 ♖h1 ♕h5 19 f3

Trying to dissolve Black's pawn phalanx.

19...♕g6

Threatening 20...exf3+.

20 ♔f1 e5! 21 dxe5?

Now White succumbs to a direct attack. 21 h5 ♕f5 22 dxe5 exf3 is pleasant for Black.

21...♖xf4! 22 gxf4 ♕g3 23 ♘xe4

23 cxd5? loses the queen to 23...♗h3+ 24 ♖xh3 ♕xh3+ 25 ♔f2 ♗c5+ 26 e3 ♕h2+.

23...dxe4 24 ♖xd7

24 ♕xe4 ♗c5 25 e3 ♗f5! wins for Black.

24...♗c5

Not 24...e3?? 25 ♖xg7+!.

25 e3 ♕xf3+ 26 ♕f2 ♕xh1+ 27 ♔e2 ♕h3 28 f5 ♕g4+ 29 ♔d2 ♖f8 30 e6 ♕xf5

Botvinnik avoids another snare: 30...♖xf5? 31 ♖d8+ ♗f8 32 ♕xf5! ♕xf5 33 e7.

31 ♕xf5 ♖xf5 32 ♖xb7 ♖f2+ 33 ♔e1 ♖f6 34 b4 ♗xe3 35 ♔e2 ♗g1 36 e7 ♔f7 37 e8♕+ ♔xe8 38 ♖xg7 ♖g6 39 ♖xh7 ♗d4 40 c5 ♖g2+ 41 ♔f1 ♖f2+ 42 ♔e1 e3 0-1

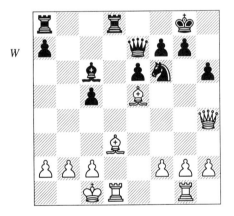

R. Spielmann – R. L'Hermet
Magdeburg 1927

Black's poor play has allowed White a powerful position. The finish is attractive.

20 g4! c4 21 g5! ♘d7 22 ♕xh6! gxh6 23 gxh6+ ♔f8 24 ♖g8+! 1-0

White's advanced pawn, which stands on its original square in the diagram, will promote with mate.

Chess News in Brief

The first Olympiad is played in London. 16 nations compete. Hungary wins, with 40/60, ahead of Denmark (38½) and British Empire (36½). Réti makes the best score on top board.

Also in London, Vera Menchik becomes the first Women's World Champion. Menchik is far stronger than other women players of the day, and is the first woman to play with some success against the top masters. She is to remain Women's World Champion for the rest of her life by winning the tournaments held alongside the Olympiads and through a privately-arranged challenge match against the German player Sonja Graf.

Robert Byrne [strong American grandmaster who reached the Candidates matches in 1973] is born.

World News in Brief

Political tension between Britain and the USSR heightens, amid allegations of espionage.

In China, the Communists, led by Mao Zedong, attempt to overthrow the government, but suffer setbacks, and are driven into rural areas.

Germany and Poland sign a trade pact.

Oil is discovered in Iraq.

Malcolm Campbell sets a new land speed record: 174.2 miles per hour (280.5 km/h); it is broken later in the year by Henry Segrave: 203.8 miles per hour (328.2 km/h).

Charles Lindbergh flies solo across the Atlantic.

The British Broadcasting Corporation (BBC) comes into being.

In England, Paul Dirac proposes the existence of anti-particles.

In Germany, Werner Heisenberg puts forward the 'Heisenberg Uncertainty Principle'. It is one of the foundations of a completely new way of looking at matter and energy – Quantum Theory. It states that there are certain paired variables for a particle, such as position and momentum, that cannot be measured simultaneously without a minimum degree of uncertainty.

1928

An excellent year for Capablanca

Bogoljubow wins the Bad Kissingen tournament with 8/11, ahead of Capablanca (7) and Euwe and Rubinstein (both 6½).

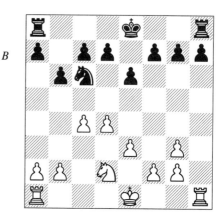

E. Bogoljubow – J. Capablanca
Bad Kissingen 1928

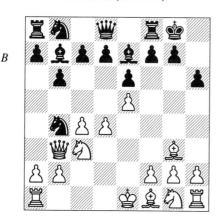

A. Nimzowitsch – F. Marshall
Bad Kissingen 1928

This is the type of opening Nimzowitsch might have played as Black: White's pawns have been lured forward, and Black, with a few well-aimed blows from his pawns, puts his oddly-placed pieces to good use.

10...d5! 11 exd6 ♗xd6 12 0-0-0

The white king is exposed on the queenside, but a better plan for White is not obvious.

12...♘8c6! 13 ♗xd6 ♕xd6 14 a3 ♘xd4! 15 ♖xd4?!

15 ♕xb4 c5 16 ♕a4 ♗c6 17 ♕a6 ♕f4+ 18 ♔b1 ♕xf2 19 ♘ge2 ♖fd8 is rather good for Black.

15...♕xd4 16 axb4 ♕xf2

Black is material up and threatens both to gain more material and to attack the white king.

17 ♕d1

17 ♘h3 ♕e3+ 18 ♔b1 ♗e4+ 19 ♔a2 a5 20 b5 a4 gives Black an overwhelming attack.

17...♖fd8 18 ♕e2 ♕f4+ 19 ♔c2 a5!

Black will keep pushing this pawn until lines are opened.

20 bxa5 ♖xa5 21 ♘f3 ♖a1 22 ♔b3 b5 23 ♕e5 bxc4+ 24 ♔b4 ♕c1 25 ♘b5 c5+ 0-1

Bogoljubow is happy with a draw due to the tournament situation. However, his play shows some indecision as his desire to avoid complications interferes with his natural inclination to find the best moves.

14...♔e7 15 g4 h6

Stopping any h-file pressure.

16 a3 a6

With ideas of ...b5.

17 ♔e2 ♖hb8 18 ♘e4?! b5 19 c5 d5!

Black breaks open lines one way or another.

20 cxd6+ cxd6 21 f4?!

21 ♖hc1 ♔d7 22 ♖c2 ♖a7 23 ♖ac1 is better.

21...♖c8 22 f5?

This gives Black too much leeway on the queenside.

22...♘a5 23 ♔d3 ♘c4 24 ♖ab1

24 b3 ♘a5 25 ♘d2 ♖c7 gives Black the c-file.

24...d5! 25 ♘c3

25 ♘c5 allows 25...e5.

25...♖c6 26 fxe6 fxe6 27 g5 hxg5 28 ♖h5 ♔f6 29 ♖h3 ♖ac8

Threatening 30...♘xb2+.

30 ♘a2 a5 31 ♖f3+ ♔g6 32 g4 ♘d6 33 ♘c3 b4 34 axb4 axb4 35 ♘d1 ♖c2 36 ♖f2 b3

Black is also constructing a mating net around the white king.

37 ♖a1 ♘e4 38 ♖e2

38 ♖xc2 ♖xc2 and 39...♖d2#.
38...♖8c6 39 ♖b1
39 ♘c3 ♖6xc3+ 40 bxc3 ♖xc3#.
39...e5! 40 ♖a1 ♖6c4 41 ♖a5 ♘c5+! 0-1
There follows 42...e4#.

Capablanca wins a strong double-round tournament in Berlin with 8½/12, ahead of Nimzowitsch (7) and Spielmann (6½).

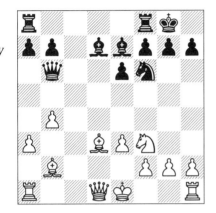

A. Rubinstein – J. Capablanca
Berlin 1928

Capablanca's opening play has been none too successful; he has nothing to make up for White's more harmonious development and kingside attacking chances.
13 ♗d4 ♕c6!?
A brave move, at least forcing White to play precisely, rather than the meek 13...♕d8.
14 0-0 ♕d5 15 ♕e2 ♖fc8 16 ♖ad1
White will now win a pawn, but Capablanca finds a way to complicate.
16...♕b3 17 ♗xf6 ♗xf6 18 ♗xh7+ ♔xh7
19 ♖xd7 ♔g8 20 h4
20 ♖xb7 ♕xa3 21 ♕b5, with possibilities of either ♕d7 or ♕h5, may well be White's best try for advantage.
20...♕xa3 21 ♘g5
Threatening 22 ♕h5.
21...♗xg5 22 hxg5 ♕xb4 23 ♕f3
It looks as if the attack by queen, rook(s) and g-pawn must now prove decisive.
23...♕f8 24 ♖xb7 a5
The a-pawn is Black's only counterplay, but it turns out to be sufficient.

25 ♖d1 a4 26 ♖dd7 a3! 27 ♖xf7 a2 28 ♖xg7+
Not 28 ♖xf8+? ♖xf8, when Black wins.
28...♕xg7 29 ♖xg7+ ♔xg7
The a-pawn is too strong, so White must give perpetual check.
30 ♕f6+ ♔g8 31 ♕g6+ ♔f8 32 ♕f6+ ½-½

Chess News in Brief
Capablanca wins the Budapest tournament with 7/9 ahead of Marshall (6).

Réti wins the Vienna tournament with 10½/13, two points clear of the field.

Bogoljubow scores a 5½-4½ match victory over Euwe.

The Hague Olympiad is convincingly won by Hungary with 44/64, ahead of the USA (39½) and Poland (37). Isaac Kashdan emerges as a new American star, scoring 13/15 on top board.

Lothar Schmid [a strong German grandmaster, who was also a leading correspondence player and the chief arbiter at several world championship matches] is born.

World News in Brief
Stalin cracks down on his rivals and former colleagues. He exiles about 30 leading Bolsheviks. They include Leon Trotsky, one of the intellectuals behind communism, and Zinoviev and Kamenev, his fellow members of the ruling council. Stalin subsequently introduces his five-year plan, which is intended to revitalize the Soviet economy by means of rapid industrialization.

In the Far East, there is conflict between Japan and China.

A separatist parliament is set up in Croatia.

There are signs of financial turbulence, as panic selling hits Wall Street.

Women over the age of 21 gain the vote in Britain.

In London, the River Thames bursts its banks, causing flooding in low-lying areas of the city.

The 'flying doctors' begin operation in Australia.

Alexander Fleming discovers the medical use of penicillium mould.

1929

Alekhine retains the World Title in a one-sided match against Bogoljubow • Good results for Nimzowitsch and Capablanca

Nimzowitsch wins the Karlsbad tournament with 15/21, ahead of Capablanca and Spielmann (both 14½).

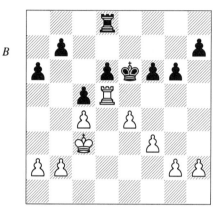

B

H. Mattison – A. Rubinstein
Karlsbad 1929

Clearly, Black cannot be better here. However, Rubinstein is able to exploit a number of innocent-looking inaccuracies by his opponent, and win the game.

23...f5!? 24 exf5+

24 ⌖d3 fxe4+ 25 ⌖xe4 ⌖b8 followed by ...b5 gives Black counterplay.

24...gxf5 25 ⌖d2

25 g4 fxg4 26 fxg4 ⌖f8 27 ⌖h5 and White should survive.

25...b5 26 b3

This passive reply lets Black's initiative grow. 26 b4 is likely to liquidate the queenside pawns.

26...h5

Black wants to target the g2-pawn.

27 g3 f4!

Rubinstein keeps giving his opponent awkward decisions.

28 ⌖e2+

28 g4 hxg4 29 fxg4 ⌖h8 keeps the white pawns immobile, while the black f-pawn will be free to advance.

28...⌖f5 29 ⌖e4 fxg3 30 hxg3 ⌖g8 31 ⌖f4+

31 g4+ hxg4 32 ⌖xg4 and now 32...⌖h8 (32...b4+ 33 ⌖d3 ⌖xg4 34 fxg4+ ⌖f4 35 g5 ⌖xg5 36 ⌖e4 ⌖f6 37 ⌖d5 ⌖e7 38 ⌖c6 ⌖e6 39 ⌖b6 is a draw; 32...⌖xg4? 33 fxg4+ ⌖xg4 34 cxb5 axb5 35 a4 and White wins) leaves White with some problems to solve.

31...⌖e6 32 ⌖e4+

32 g4 is met by 32...h4.

32...⌖d7 33 g4 ⌖f8! 34 ⌖e3 h4! 35 a4 bxa4 36 bxa4 ⌖e8 37 ⌖d2?

37 ⌖d3 is a better try.

37...⌖xe3 38 ⌖xe3 d5! 0-1

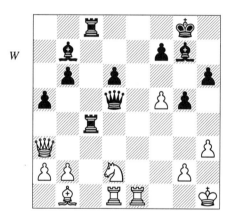

W

M. Vidmar – M. Euwe
Karlsbad 1929

Black has just chosen the wrong way to grab a loose white pawn on d5.

29 ⌖e4! ⌖xe4 30 ⌖xe4 ⌖xf5

Black was doubtless intending this as an exchange sacrifice to exploit the poorly defended white king. However, there is a snag.

31 ⌖xd6! ⌖xg2+ 32 ⌖xg2 ⌖c2+ 33 ⌖h1 ⌖f4

So, how does White prevent mate on h2? Answer: by giving mate himself!

34 ⌖e8+ ⌖f8

34...⌖h7 35 ⌖d3+ picks off the black rook.

35 ⌖xf8+! ⌖xf8 36 ⌖f5+ 1-0

36...⌖g8 37 ⌖f8+ ⌖xf8 38 ⌖d8#.

Alekhine wins the Bradley Beach tournament with 8½/9, ahead of L.Steiner (7).

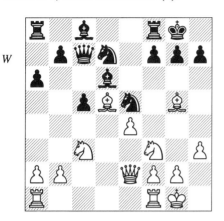

A. Alekhine – H. Steiner
Bradley Beach 1929

Here we see a Queen's Gambit Accepted gone somewhat wrong for Black. Alekhine now attacks mercilessly.

14 ♘h4

With two ideas: ♘f5 and f4.

14...♘b6 15 f4 ♘c6 16 f5!

A very concrete move – typical of Alekhine's style. He perceives that the threat of f6 and control of e6 are more significant than the weakening of the dark squares.

16...♘e5 17 ♕h5

Threatening 18 f6.

17...♖e8 18 ♖f4

While this move carries no immediate threat, it calmly brings another piece nearer the black king and prepares to bring the other rook into the battle. Black now makes an unsuccessful attempt to defuse the situation.

18...♗e7? 19 f6! ♗f8

19...g6, which would have been the answer to f6 if White had played it earlier, now fails to the combination 20 ♘xg6! hxg6 21 ♗xf7+! ♔xf7 22 fxe7+.

20 fxg7 ♗xg7 21 ♖af1 ♗e6 22 ♘f5

The attack is now overwhelming.

22...♗xd5 23 ♘xg7 ♘g6 24 ♘xe8 ♖xe8 25 ♘xd5 1-0

Chess News in Brief

Alekhine comfortably defends the World Championship against Bogoljubow, winning the match 15½-9½.

Capablanca wins the Budapest tournament with 10½/13 ahead of Rubinstein (9½) and Tartakower (8).

Rubinstein wins the Rogaška Slatina tournament with 11½/15, ahead of Flohr (10½).

Verlinsky wins the 6th USSR Championship.

Sultan Khan wins the British Championship.

Alekhine makes an extensive tour of America.

Richard Réti dies.

Tigran Petrosian [World Champion 1963-9] is born.

Hans Berliner [winner of the 5th Correspondence World Championship, 1965-8] is born.

World News in Brief

The Wall Street Crash marks the beginning of the Great Depression, which brings about an industrial slump and widespread poverty, first in the United States, and consequently around the world over the following years.

Following a deal between Mussolini and the Catholic Church, the Vatican state is founded in Rome.

Conflict between China and Russia flares up on the Manchurian border.

Britain declares martial law in Jerusalem following fighting between Jews and Arabs.

There are skirmishes on the USA-Mexico border.

The All-Indian National Council demands independence for India.

There is civil unrest in Berlin.

Trotsky is refused asylum in both France and Britain.

In Britain, Frank Whittle proposes the use of a jet engine for propelling aeroplanes.

1930

Alekhine dominant at San Remo

Alekhine dominates the San Remo tournament, scoring 14/15, ahead of Nimzowitsch (10½), Rubinstein (10) and Bogoljubow (9½) – one of the best tournament performances ever.

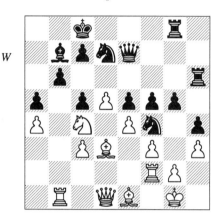

W

E. Bogoljubow – M. Monticelli
San Remo 1930

This position arose from a modern-looking Queen's/Nimzo-Indian hybrid. Bogoljubow's next move smacks of impatience.

23 d6?

23 ♘e3 is more natural, and better.

23...♖xd6! 24 ♘xd6+ ♕xd6

Black's exchange sacrifice would come very naturally to a modern master, but the pre-war masters tended to overvalue the rook relative to a minor piece.

25 ♗c4 ♖f8 26 exf5 ♖xf5 27 ♖d2 ♕e7 28 ♕b3 ♖f8 29 ♗d3 e4!?

29...♘xd3 30 ♖xd3 e4 is also highly effective.

30 ♗xe4 ♗xe4 31 fxe4 ♕xe4

White's pieces are poorly placed either to attack or to defend.

32 ♕c2 ♕c6 33 c4 g4! 34 ♗xh4 gxh3 35 g3 ♘e5! 36 ♖b3

36 gxf4 ♘f3+ 37 ♔f2 ♘xd2 38 ♕xd2 ♕g2+ 39 ♔e3 ♖e8+ 40 ♔d3 ♕e4+ 41 ♔c3 ♕xb1 wins for Black.

After Bogoljubow's actual move, Black has an attractive forced mate.

36...♘e2+! 37 ♖xe2 ♖f1+ 38 ♔xf1 ♕h1+ 39 ♔f2 ♘g4# (0-1)

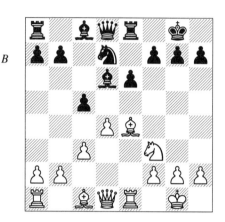

B

E. Colle – J. O'Hanlon
Nice 1930

Black has responded to White's play – an opening that became known as the Colle System – rather inaccurately. His next move invites White to launch a sacrificial attack.

11...cxd4 12 ♗xh7+!?

This type of sacrifice is normally clearly good or clearly bad. This is one of the rare borderline cases.

12...♔xh7 13 ♘g5+ ♔g6?

13...♔g8 is the critical line: 14 ♕h5 ♕f6 15 ♕h7+ ♔f8 16 ♘e4 ♕e5 17 f4 (17 cxd4 ♕xh2+ escapes to a roughly equal ending) 17...♕d5 18 c4 ♕c6 19 f5!? (19 ♕h8+ ♔e7 20 ♕xg7 is unclear) 19...♘f6 20 ♘xf6 gxf6 21 ♗g5!? ♔e7 22 ♗xf6+ ♔xf6 23 ♕h4+ ♔g7 24 f6+ ♔g6 25 ♖e4 gives White dangerous threats, but he has sacrificed a great deal of material. After 25...♗xh2+ 26 ♔xh2 e5 27 ♖f1 ♖h8 28 ♕xh8 ♕xe4 29 ♕g7+ ♔h5 30 ♕xf7+ ♔g6 a draw is the most likely result.

14 h4!

The threat of 15 h5+ is very powerful.

14...♖h8?

Now Black loses by force. 14...f5 15 h5+ ♔f6 16 ♕xd4+ ♗e5 17 ♕h4! is very good for White;

the threat is 18 ♗f4, while 17...♕a5 18 b4 enables him to regain the piece with advantage.

15 ♖xe6+! ♘f6

15...fxe6 16 ♕d3+ forces mate.

16 h5+ ♔h6

16...♖xh5 17 ♕d3+ ♔h6 18 ♘xf7#.

17 ♖xd6 ♕a5 18 ♘xf7+ ♔h7 19 ♘g5+ ♔g8 20 ♕b3+ 1-0

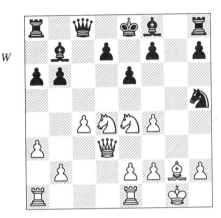

A. Lilienthal – M. Romih
Paris 1930

Black has misplayed a Queen's Indian – quite a novel opening at the time – and now falls victim to some powerful tactics.

19 ♕f3

Hitting the loose pieces on h5 and b7.

19...♖g8 20 ♔f1

Side-stepping Black's tactical defence. Now the g8-rook is an additional target.

20...♕xc4 21 ♖ed1 ♕d5

Threatening ...♖xg2, and inviting more tactics.

22 ♕xh5! ♕xh5 23 ♘f6+ ♔d8 24 ♘xe6+!

This is the point of White's queen sacrifice.

24...♔e7

Otherwise White safely recoups his investment: 24...fxe6 25 ♖xd7+ ♔c8 26 ♗xb7+ ♔b8 27 ♘xh5.

25 ♘xg8+ ♔xe6 26 ♗xb7

White has a rook and piece for the queen, and a mating attack in which the apparently vulnerable g8-knight plays a vital role.

26...♖d8 27 ♗d5+ ♔f5 28 ♗f3

28 ♗e4+ also wins.

28...♕h3+

28...♕g6 29 ♖d5+ ♔xf4 30 ♗h5 wins for White.

29 ♗g2 ♕xh2

Now White forces mate.

30 ♖d5+ ♔e6 31 f5# (1-0)

Chess News in Brief

Nimzowitsch wins the Frankfurt tournament, ahead of Kashdan.

Colle wins the Scarborough tournament.

The Hamburg Olympiad ends in victory for Poland with 48½/68, ahead of Hungary (47) and Germany (44½). Rubinstein makes the best score on top board (15/17); Alekhine scores 100%, but only plays 9 games.

Vladimirs Petrovs wins the Latvian Championship for the first time (1930/1).

Horst Rittner [winner of the 6th Correspondence World Championship, 1968-71] is born.

World News in Brief

Stalin decrees that all farms in the USSR shall become collectives. Stalin's agents are reported to be murdering about 40 *kulaks* (rich peasants) a day. It is the kulaks who are most likely to oppose the reforms.

In elections in Germany, the Nazi Party gains the second largest share of the vote. Their promise is to make Germany great again, and their campaign plays on the electorate's fears of economic chaos and social unrest.

Socialists win the Austrian parliamentary election.

Britain recognizes Iraq as an independent country.

Famine in China claims millions of lives. Communist armies attack Hankow.

France pulls its troops out of the Rhineland; later France decides to build a line of defences along its border with Germany.

Turkey and Greece sign a treaty of friendship.

Clyde Tombaugh discovers Pluto, the outermost planet of the solar system. It is a tiny planet, with an eccentric orbit.

1931

A great result for Alekhine

Alekhine dominates the Bled tournament; his score of 20½/26 puts him 5½ points clear of second-placed Bogoljubow.

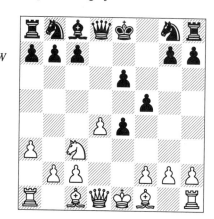

A. Alekhine – A. Nimzowitsch
Bled 1931

Nimzowitsch has made the risky decision to cling on to a gambit pawn by 6...f7-f5?!. Alekhine now attacks ferociously.

7 f3!? exf3 8 ♕xf3 ♕xd4

8...♕h4+ 9 g3 ♕xd4 is also precarious for Black after 10 ♘b5!? or 10 ♗f4.

9 ♕g3!

The main threats are 10 ♘b5 and 10 ♗f4.

9...♘f6!?

9...♘e7 10 ♗e3! ♕f6 11 0-0-0 favours White.

10 ♕xg7 ♕e5+

Black uses a tempo to cover the c7-pawn. 10...♖g8!? 11 ♕xc7 ♘c6 12 ♗f4 ♘e4 13 ♗e2 gives White dangerous play, but is unclear.

11 ♗e2 ♖g8 12 ♕h6 ♖g6 13 ♕h4 ♗d7?!

13...♖xg2?! 14 ♗f4 is good for White, but 13...♖g4!? could be tried.

14 ♗g5! ♗c6?

This leads to trouble, but 14...♘c6 15 0-0-0 0-0-0 16 ♖he1 is awkward for Black.

15 0-0-0 ♗xg2

Or 15...♘bd7 16 ♖he1 with a decisive attack.

16 ♖he1 ♗e4 17 ♗h5 ♘xh5 18 ♖d8+ ♔f7 19 ♕xh5 1-0

Black is defenceless; one threat is 20 ♘xe4.

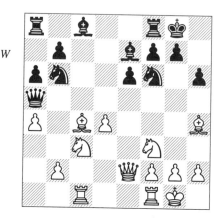

A. Alekhine – G. Maroczy
Bled 1931

15 ♗d3! ♗d7 16 ♘e5 ♖fd8!

16...♗xa4 is strongly met by 17 ♘g6!.

17 f4!?

17 ♕f3 is a simpler method; White has an edge after 17...♗c6 18 ♘xc6 bxc6 19 ♖fd1.

17...♗e8 18 ♘g4 ♖xd4 19 ♗xf6 ♗xf6 20 ♘xf6+ gxf6 21 ♘e4 ♖ad8?!

Better is 21...f5! 22 ♘f6+ ♔f8, when White has no immediate way to smash through.

22 ♘xf6+ ♔f8 23 ♘h7+! ♔e7

23...♔g7 24 ♕g4+ ♔h8 25 ♕h4! ♖xd3 26 ♕xh6 leaves Black with no adequate defence.

24 f5 ♖8d6 25 b4!

This surprising blow on the queenside disrupts the coordination of the black pieces.

25...♕xb4

25...♖xb4 26 ♕h5 e5 27 f6+ ♔d8 28 ♕xh6 ♖xd3 29 ♕f8 gives White a winning attack.

26 ♕e5 ♘d7 27 ♕h8! ♖xd3?

27...♖c6! 28 ♖xc6 bxc6 29 fxe6 fxe6 30 ♘f6 leaves White with some advantage, but it is not necessarily decisive.

28 f6+ 1-0

Capablanca wins the New York tournament (scoring 10/11), ahead of Kashdan. However, Capablanca's fabled invincibility may have been a factor in the following episode.

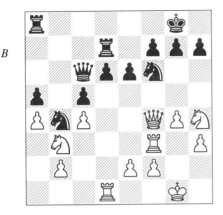

F. Marshall – J. Capablanca
New York 1931

21...♕xa4?!

This move is based on a faulty combination.

22 ♖xd6 ♘bd5?? 23 ♕e5??

Marshall misses a golden opportunity to swindle Capablanca. 23 ♖a6! exploits Black's weak back rank, and wins, e.g. 23...♘xf4 24 ♖xa8+ ♖d8 25 ♖xd8+ ♘e8 26 ♖xf4 with too much material for the queen. One can only presume that Marshall thought that Capablanca would never allow such a thing, and so wasn't even looking.

23...♖xd6 24 ♕xd6 ♘e4 25 ♕e5 ♕xc4

From here, Capablanca went on to win easily.

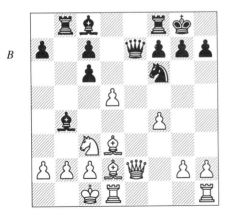

S. Slonim – N. Riumin
Moscow Ch 1931

White has handled the opening carelessly, giving insufficient attention to his king's defences.

13...♗a3!! 14 ♘a4

Or 14 ♕xe7 ♗xb2+ 15 ♔b1 ♗xc3+ 16 ♔c1 ♗b2+ 17 ♔b1 ♗a3+, and Black emerges a piece up.

14...♗xb2+! 15 ♘xb2 ♕a3 16 ♕e5 ♖e8 17 ♕d4 c5! 18 ♕c3 ♕xa2 19 ♗e1

This allows a forced mate, but 19 ♗e3 is also terrible for White.

19...♖e2!! 20 ♗xe2 ♘e4 0-1

Chess News in Brief

Capablanca scores a 6-4 match victory over Euwe in Amsterdam.

Sultan Khan beats Tartakower 6½-5½ in a match at Semmering.

The Prague Olympiad ends in victory for the USA, with 48/72, ahead of Poland (47) and Czechoslovakia (46½). Only four points separate the top nine teams (from a total of 19). Alekhine makes the best score on top board.

Botvinnik wins the 7th USSR Championship.

Viktor Korchnoi [Candidates Finalist in 1974; World Championship Challenger in 1978 and 1981] is born.

World News in Brief

Canada gains independence from Britain.

War breaks out between China and Japan, as Japanese forces occupy Shenyang in Manchuria.

In Germany, nearly five million people are unemployed.

In Spain, republicans gain a large majority in parliament; King Alfonso XIII abdicates.

The effects of the Great Depression hit Europe. Britain and other countries abandon the gold standard.

In New York, the Empire State Building is opened. At 1,245 feet (379 metres), it is the world's tallest building.

Ernst Ruska invents the electron microscope.

In the USA, radio telescopes are developed by Karl Jansky.

1932

With the Great Depression at its height, it is a year of few major tournaments

Alekhine wins the London tournament with 9/11 ahead of Flohr (8), Kashdan and Sultan Khan (both 7½).

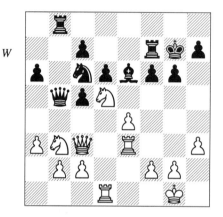

W

A. Alekhine – G. Koltanowski
London 1932

Black has just passed up an opportunity to exchange off White's d5-knight. He does not get another chance.

22 ♘xc7!?

This sacrifice is the start of a very complicated combination.

22...♖xc7 23 ♖xd6 ♗c4?

Also bad is 23...♔f7? 24 ♖f3 ♔e7 25 ♖xe6+! (25 a4 ♕xb3 is less clear) 25...♔xe6 26 ♘xc5+ ♔d6 27 b4 and White wins, e.g. 27...♖f7 28 ♖xf6+ ♖xf6 29 ♕xf6+ ♔c7 30 ♕f7+ ♔b6 31 c4 ♘e5 32 ♕e6+ ♕c6 33 ♕xe5 with four pawns for an exchange.

Black should play 23...♖e8! 24 ♘xc5 ♘d4 (not 24...♘d8? 25 b4 ♖c6 26 e5! ♖xd6 27 exd6, when White's powerful passed pawn and threats to the black king prove too much, e.g. 27...♕b6 28 ♘d7! ♗xd7 29 ♖xe8 ♗xe8 30 ♕c7+! or 27...♗d5 28 d7 ♖f8 29 ♕d4 leaves Black with no real counterplay) 25 ♕xd4 and now:

a) 25...♕xc5? 26 ♖c3! ♕a7 27 ♖cc6! ♔f7 and now the simplest win is by 28 ♕xa7 (28 e5!? is good too) 28...♖xa7 29 ♖xa6, with four pawns for a piece.

b) 25...♖xc5 looks like Black's best defence. The game is unclear, since 26 ♖f3 ♖e5 27 ♖xf6 ♔xf6 28 f4 will result in the black king being well centralized in the ending.

24 a4! ♕xa4 25 ♘xc5 ♕b5 26 ♕xf6+ ♔g8 27 ♘d7!

From here the knight can help generate threats against the black king.

27...♖d8 28 ♖f3

Threatening 29 ♘e5.

28...♕b4

28...♖dc8 29 b3 runs the bishop out of squares: 29...♗e2 30 ♕e6+ ♔h8 31 ♖f7 ♕g5 32 f4 ♕h6 33 ♘e5 and Black's position collapses.

29 c3 ♕b5 30 ♘e5 ♖dc8 31 ♘xc6 1-0

Alekhine wins the Berne tournament with 12½/15, ahead of Euwe and Flohr (both 11½), and Sultan Khan (11).

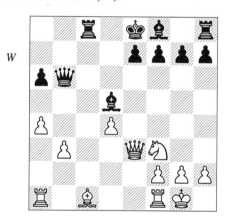

W

A. Alekhine – Sultan Khan
Berne 1932

Black has given up a pawn for a considerable amount of positional compensation.

17 ♗d2!

Alekhine is not interested in clinging on to his extra pawn if it means Black completing his development in an harmonious way.

17...e6

17...♛xb3 18 ♖fc1 ♖xc1+ 19 ♖xc1 intensifies White's development advantage, simplification notwithstanding.

18 ♖fc1 ♖b8 19 ♘e5 f6?!

19...♝e7 20 ♘c4 ♛xb3 21 ♛xb3 ♖xb3 22 ♘d6+ gives White a good ending.

20 ♘c6! ♖a8 21 ♘a5

Not only defending b3, but also threatening 22 ♖c6.

21...♚f7 22 ♘c4 ♛b7 23 ♛g3 ♝e7 24 a5 ♖ad8 25 ♘b6

With the knight planted on b6, White can infiltrate on the c-file.

25...♝c6 26 ♖c4 ♖he8

26...e5 27 ♖ac1 ♖xd4 28 ♖xc6 ♖xd2 29 ♛g4 ♖hd8 30 ♛e6+ ♚f8 31 h3 gives White a very strong position.

27 ♖ac1 ♝b5 28 ♖c7 ♛e4 29 d5! ♚g8?

Black would be losing in any case after 29...exd5 30 ♖e1 ♝e2 31 ♘a4! followed by ♘c5.

30 ♖e1 ♛f5 31 ♝b4 ♖d7 32 ♖xd7 ♝xd7 33 ♝xe7 exd5 34 ♛d6 1-0

Spielmann scores a 4½-1½ match victory over Stoltz. However, in the following game his aggressive style got him into trouble:

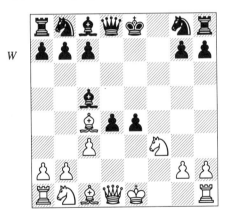

G. Stoltz – R. Spielmann
Match, Stockholm 1932

This position comes from a sharp line of the King's Gambit.

8 ♘e5 ♘f6?! 9 ♘f7 ♛e7 10 ♘xh8 d3

Other moves are not considered any better. 10...♘c6 11 ♝g5 ♘e5 12 ♝xf6 gxf6 13 ♛h5+ ♚f8 14 ♘g6+! ♘xg6 15 ♛d5 was analysed as good for White by Keres.

11 ♝g5 ♝f2+!? 12 ♚xf2 ♛c5+ 13 ♝e3! ♛xc4 14 h3! ♝e6 15 ♘d2 ♛d5 16 g4!

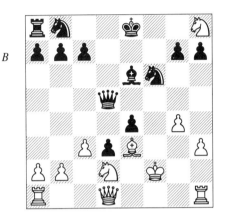

White has ideas both of playing g5 followed by ♛h5+, and ♛b3, offering an exchange of queens.

16...♘c6 17 c4 ♛d7 18 g5 ♝g4 19 ♛f1! ♝e2 20 ♛g2 ♛f5+ 21 ♚g1 ♘d7 22 ♛xe4+ ♛xe4 23 ♘xe4 ♚e7

23...♝f3 24 ♘c3! ♝xh1 25 ♚xh1 ♘de5 26 ♖f1! is good for White, as Black cannot trap the h8-knight.

24 ♘g3 ♖xh8 25 ♘xe2 dxe2 26 ♖h2 ♚f7 27 ♖xe2 ♖e8 28 ♖d1 ♘de5 29 ♝f4 ♖e6 30 ♚f1 ♚g6 31 ♖d5 ♚f5 32 ♝g3 ♖e7 33 b4 1-0

World News in Brief

Japanese forces take Shanghai, and set up a puppet regime in Manchuria.

Adolf Hitler is granted German citizenship. The Nazis become the largest party in the German parliament. Germany prepares to rearm.

In the USSR, Stalin purges his political rivals.

Worldwide, more than 20% of the workforce is unemployed.

Sydney Harbour Bridge, the world's largest single-span bridge, is completed.

1933

Botvinnik shows his class

Botvinnik wins the 8th USSR Championship with 14/19.

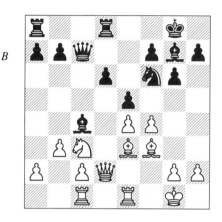

B

V. Rauzer – M. Botvinnik
USSR Ch, Leningrad 1933

16...d5!!

Very thematic. Black blasts open the centre, creating all manner of threats.

17 exd5!

Best. Instead, 17 fxe5 ♘xe4! 18 ♗xe4 dxe4 19 ♕f2 ♗xe5 20 ♘xe4 f5 is good for Black.

17...e4! 18 bxc4

White should play 18 ♘xe4! ♘xd5 19 ♔h1 ♘xe3 20 ♕xe3 ♗d4 21 ♕d2 ♗e6 22 ♖cd1 ♗e5 23 ♕b4!?, which isn't too bad for him.

18...exf3 19 c5 ♕a5

Threatening 20...♘xd5.

20 ♖ed1?!

The critical line is 20 ♕d3! b6!, which breaks up White's pawns.

20...♘g4! 21 ♗d4 f2+ 22 ♔f1

22 ♔h1 loses to 22...♖xd5! 23 ♘xd5 f1♕+!.

22...♕a6+ 23 ♕e2 ♗xd4 24 ♖xd4

Black wins after 24 ♕xa6? ♘e3+ 25 ♔e2 (25 ♔xf2? ♘xd1++) 25...f1♕+! 26 ♖xf1 bxa6.

24...♕f6! 25 ♖cd1

Or: 25 ♕d2 ♕h4!; 25 ♕d3 ♖e8! 26 g3 ♖e3 27 ♘e4 ♕f5 28 ♕c4 ♕h5! 29 h4 ♘h2+ 30 ♔g2 ♕f3+ 31 ♔xh2 ♖e1 32 ♕f1 ♖xc1! winning.

25...♕h4 26 ♕d3 ♖e8 27 ♖e4 f5 28 ♖e6 ♘xh2+ 29 ♔e2 ♕xf4 0-1

The USA wins the Folkestone Olympiad, scoring 39/56, ahead of Czechoslovakia (37½) and Sweden, Poland and Hungary (all 34). Only 15 teams compete. The low turn-out is partly due to the organizers refusing to consider late entries, and partly due to withdrawals. The German Chess Federation, now under Nazi influence, is in open conflict with FIDE, and does not send a team. Alekhine makes the best percentage score on top board, while Kashdan's 10/14 is almost as good, and a major ingredient in the USA's success.

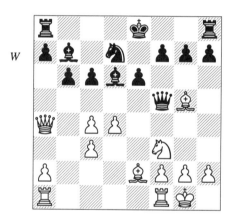

W

S. Flohr – I. Kashdan
Folkestone Olympiad 1933

Flohr has played a line of the English Opening now known as the Flohr-Mikenas Attack. He secures the advantage with a pawn sacrifice.

13 c5! bxc5 14 dxc5 ♕xc5

14...♗xc5 15 ♖fd1 and 14...♘xc5 15 ♕d4 both offer White good play.

15 ♖fd1 ♗e7 16 ♖xd7! ♔xd7 17 ♗e3 ♕a3 18 ♕d4+ ♔e8 19 ♕xg7

Now White's attack is decisive.

19...♖f8 20 ♘g5 ♖d8 21 ♗h5 ♗xg5 22 ♗xg5 ♖d5 23 c4 ♖xg5 24 ♕xg5 ♔d7 25 ♖d1+ ♔c8 26 ♗xf7 ♔b8 27 ♗xe6 ♕xa2 28 ♖d8+??

28 ♕c5 should win without incident.

28...♔c7??

28...♗c8! leaves White struggling.

29 ♕e7+ ♔b6 30 c5+ 1-0

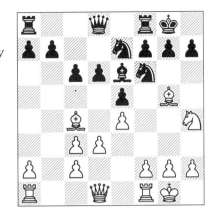

J. Capablanca – H. Steiner

Exhibition game, Los Angeles 1933

11 ♗xf6! gxf6 12 ♗xe6 fxe6 13 ♕g4+ ♔f7
14 f4! ♖g8 15 ♕h5+ ♔g7 16 fxe5 dxe5 17
♖xf6!

Black's king is given no respite.

17...♔xf6 18 ♖f1+ ♘f5

Black's only hope is to evacuate his king to
the queenside. 18...♔g7? allows 19 ♖f7+ ♔h8
20 ♕xh7#.

19 ♘xf5! exf5 20 ♖xf5+ ♔e7

The king is at the mercy of White's queen
and rook. Capablanca finds a neat way to finish.

**21 ♕f7+ ♔d6 22 ♖f6+ ♔c5 23 ♕xb7! ♕b6
24 ♖xc6+! ♕xc6 25 ♕b4# (1-0)**

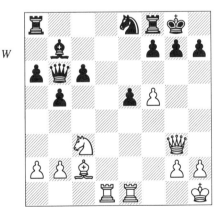

A. Taube – Hennig

Altona 1933

White has already given up two pawns, but
his attack proves strong enough.

22 f6! ♘xf6 23 ♖d6 ♘h5

After 23...♘e8 24 ♘d5 ♕a5 25 ♗xh7+ ♔h8
26 b4 Black must give up his queen or be mated.
23...♔h8 loses a piece to 24 ♖xf6, as 24...gxf6
25 ♕h4 forces mate.

24 ♕h4 g6 25 ♖xe5 ♖ad8

25...♖fe8 26 ♘d5 ♕a7 (26...♕a5 27 ♘e7+
♔f8 28 ♗xg6! ♕a4 29 ♕xh5 ♕f4 30 ♖d1 ♖xe7
31 ♖xe7 ♔xe7 32 ♕c5+ ♔f6 33 ♗d3 gives
White a decisive attack) 27 ♘e7+ ♖xe7 (worse
is 27...♔f8 28 ♖d7) 28 ♖xe7 is good for White.

**26 ♘d5! ♖xd6 27 ♘xb6 c5 28 ♖xh5 gxh5
29 ♕g5+ ♖g6 30 ♗xg6 hxg6 31 h3 1-0**

Chess News in Brief

A match between Botvinnik and Flohr
(played in Moscow and Leningrad) is drawn
6-6. This is seen in the USSR as a demonstration that Soviet chess is in no way inferior to
that of the rest of the world.

Salo Flohr wins the Hastings tournament
(1933/4) with 7/9, ahead of Alekhine and Lilienthal (both 6½).

Alekhine tours the Far East, South-East Asia
and Central Europe.

World News in Brief

The Chinese-Japanese War ends in victory
for Japan.

Adolf Hitler becomes German Chancellor
and, following the *Reichstag* building being destroyed by fire, he assumes dictatorial powers.
The Nazis open a concentration camp at Dachau.
Hitler orders a boycott of Jewish shops and proposes eugenic laws, banning mixed Jewish and
Aryan marriages.

War breaks out between Paraguay and Bolivia over ownership of the Chaco Boreal, a strategically important piece of wasteland that has
been the subject of dispute between the two
countries since 1825.

In the USA, the prohibition of alcohol ends.
President Roosevelt embarks on a major plan of
public spending to revitalize the economy.

1934

Alekhine remains Champion • Capablanca and Lasker return to competitive chess

Alekhine comfortably defends the World Championship against Bogoljubow (for a second time) with a score of 15½-10½.

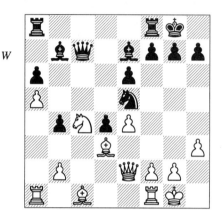

W

A. Alekhine – E. Bogoljubow
World Ch match (2), Baden-Baden 1934

After some speculative opening play, and some inaccuracies by his opponent, Alekhine has achieved excellent attacking chances in return for a pawn.

19 ♗f4! ♗d6

19...f6 20 ♖fc1 gives White excellent play.

20 ♗xe5 ♗xe5 21 ♘b6

The knight is very strongly placed here.

21...♖a7

21...♖ad8 is best met by 22 ♖fd1 followed by taking the a6-pawn.

22 ♖ac1

White has several plans, including advancing his f-pawn and attacking the black b-pawn.

22...♛d6 23 ♖c4 f5?

Opening the position proves to be disastrous. 23...♗f4 24 ♖d1 e5 25 ♛e1 is pleasant for White. 23...♗f6!, with ideas of ...♗d8 or ...e5, looks best.

24 exf5 exf5 25 ♖e1!

Black's position is now untenable. A hand-to-hand fight has begun, and Black's a7-rook is in no position to take part.

25...♛g6

25...♗f6 is no good due to 26 ♗xf5, while 25...♗f4 26 ♛e6+ will give White a winning endgame.

26 f3 ♖e8

There is nothing better. 26...♗f4 27 ♖xd4 (e.g. 27...♛g3? 28 ♗c4+ ♔h8 29 ♛e7) and 26...♗g3 27 ♛e6+ are both very good for White.

27 f4 ♛g3 28 fxe5 ♖xe5 29 ♖c8+!

The rook is untouchable as the black bishop must not take its eye off g2. Black faces mate or ruinous loss of material.

29...♔f7 30 ♛h5+ g6 31 ♛xh7+ ♔f6 32 ♖f8+ ♔g5 33 h4+ ♔f4 34 ♛h6+ g5 35 ♖xf5+ ♖xf5 36 ♛d6+ ♔g4 37 ♗xf5+ 1-0

Alekhine wins the Zurich tournament with 13/15, ahead of Euwe and Flohr (both 12), Bogoljubow (11½) and Lasker (10).

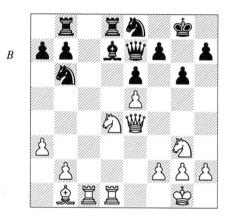

B

M. Euwe – Em. Lasker
Zurich 1934

It looks as if White has some initiative, but in fact he may already have overpressed a little. Black's game is very solid, and he now goes about loosening White's position.

21...♗a4! 22 b3

White would do better to move his rook.

22...♗d7 23 a4 ♘d5

The c3-square beckons.

24 ♗d3 ♖bc8 25 ♗c4 ♗c6! 26 ♘xc6 bxc6

Black's queenside pawns look a little loose, but they cannot really be attacked, while the d5-knight is very strong, and White's backward b-pawn is sensitive.

27 ♖d3?!

White tries to attack on the kingside, but this is an over-ambitious plan.

27...♘b4 28 ♖f3 ♖c7 29 h4 ♖cd7 30 h5 ♕g5 31 ♖e1 ♖d4 32 hxg6 hxg6

Black should not consider 32...♖xe4? 33 gxf7+ ♔f8 34 fxe8♕++ ♔xe8 35 ♘xe4.

33 ♕e2 ♖d2 34 ♕f1?! ♘c2 35 ♘e4

White has realized his plan, but by now Black has a radical answer ready.

35...♕xe5 36 ♘f6+ ♕xf6 37 ♖xf6 ♘xf6 38 ♖c1

38 ♖e2 ♖d1 39 ♖xc2 is a better try.

38...♘e4 39 ♗e2 ♘d4 40 ♗f3 ♘xf2 41 ♕c4 ♘d3 42 ♖f1 ♘e5

Black's pieces are coordinating wonderfully.

43 ♕b4 ♘exf3+ 44 gxf3 ♘e2+ 45 ♔h2 ♘f4+ 46 ♔h1 ♖2d4 47 ♕e7 ♔g7 48 ♕c7 ♖8d5 49 ♖e1 ♖g5 50 ♕xc6 ♖d8 0-1

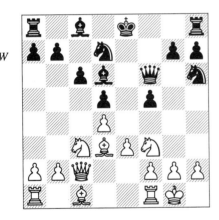

G. Grohmann – L. Engels
German Ch, Aachen 1934

It looks as if a phase of positional manoeuvring lies ahead, but White can exploit Black's backward development and exposed king by a dramatic tactical blow.

10 e4!! fxe4

10...dxe4 11 ♗xe4 0-0 is a more prudent course.

11 ♗xe4 dxe4 12 ♘xe4 ♕f8

Other queen moves are no better, as they let White's minor pieces advance with tempo.

13 ♖e1 ♔d8 14 d5! c5

14...cxd5 15 ♘d4 ♘f6 16 ♘g5 ♕g8 17 ♘ge6+ ♗xe6 18 ♘xe6+ ♔d7 19 ♕a4+ ♔c8 20 ♗f4 gives White a winning attack.

15 b4! ♘g4

15...cxb4 16 ♘xd6 ♕xd6 17 ♖e6 wins.

16 ♗g5+ ♘gf6 17 ♖ac1 b6 18 ♘d4! ♘e5

18...cxd4 loses to 19 ♕c6.

19 ♘xd6 ♕xd6 20 ♖xe5 cxd4 21 ♗f4 d3 22 ♕d2 ♕d7 23 d6! ♖e8 24 ♖c7 ♕g4 25 f3

25 ♖xe8+! is also good.

25...♕g6 26 ♖g5 ♖e2 27 ♖xg6 ♖xd2 28 ♖gxg7 ♖c2

Or 28...♖d1+ 29 ♔f2 d2 30 ♗g5 ♖f1+ 31 ♔e3 d1♕ 32 ♖g8#.

29 ♖cf7 ♔e8 30 ♖xf6 d2 31 ♖e7+ ♔d8 32 ♖f8# (1-0)

Chess News in Brief

Lilienthal wins the Ujpest tournament with 11/15, ahead of Pirc (10½).

Levenfish and I.Rabinovich win the 9th USSR Championship (1934/5).

Max Euwe, Sir George Thomas and Salo Flohr share first place at the Hastings tournament (1934/5) with 6½/9, ahead of Capablanca (5½), Lilienthal and Botvinnik (both 5).

Paul Keres (born 1916) wins the Estonian Championship (1934/5) for the first time.

Siegbert Tarrasch dies.

Lev Polugaevsky is born.

Leonid Stein is born.

World News in Brief

Martial law is declared in Spain.

In the 'Night of the Long Knives' in Germany, about a hundred senior Nazi Storm Troopers are massacred. The SS takes over many of the Storm Troopers' functions.

Stalin renews a policy of terror, purging 'Trotskyists' in the communist party.

In China, following the encirclement of the Xiangxi Soviet Republic, Mao Zedong leads his followers on the Long March, heading eastwards in search of a safe place.

Fascists seize power in Bulgaria.

A Nazi *coup d'état* fails in Austria.

1935

Alekhine loses the world title to Euwe •
More success for Botvinnik

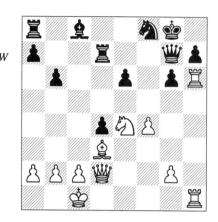

K. Baranov – Y. Rokhlin
USSR correspondence 1935-6

White has been attacking vigorously from the opening, and must now decide how to make further progress.

20 f5!? exf5

20...gxf5 allows 21 ♘f6+.

21 ♗c4+ ♔h8 22 ♘g5 ♕f6 23 ♕f4

Threatening 24 ♕h4, when h7 would collapse.

23...a5

So that Black can support h7 by playing ...♖aa7.

24 g4! b5

Trying to divert the bishop and open the b-file. 24...♖aa7 25 ♘xh7 ♖xh7 (25...♘xh7 also loses to 26 g5) 26 g5 ♕g7 27 ♕d6! leaves Black defenceless against the threat of 28 ♖xh7+, e.g. 27...♖d7 28 ♖xh7+ ♘xh7 29 ♖xh7+ forcing mate.

25 ♘xh7!

White's threats are potent enough that he can ignore Black's last move.

25...♖xh7 26 ♖xh7+ ♘xh7 27 ♖xh7+ ♔xh7 28 g5

White's queen, bishop and g-pawn prove a powerful mating force; Black must give up his queen, but the material losses will not end there.

28...♕xg5 29 ♕xg5 bxc4 30 ♕g2! ♖a7 31 ♕h2+ ♔g7 32 ♕b8 ♖f7 33 ♕xc8 f4 34 ♕xc4 f3 35 ♕xd4+ ♔h6 36 ♕h4+ ♔g7 37 ♕f2 g5 38 ♔d2 ♔g6 39 ♔e3 ♖f4 40 ♕xf3 1-0

Flohr and Botvinnik share first place at the Moscow tournament with 13/19, ahead of Lasker (12½), Capablanca (12) and Spielmann (11).

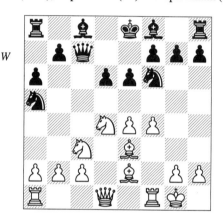

Em. Lasker – V. Pirc
Moscow 1935

In a normal Sicilian position, Black has just played 9...♘c6-a5?!. While the aim of this move is laudable, it costs too much time.

10 f5! ♘c4 11 ♗xc4 ♕xc4 12 fxe6 fxe6

12...♗xe6 13 ♘xe6 ♕xe6 14 ♗g5 ♗e7 15 ♘d5 puts Black in a horrible mess.

13 ♖xf6! gxf6 14 ♕h5+ ♔d8

14...♔e7 loses to 15 ♘f5+!, and 14...♔d7 to 15 ♕f7+ ♗e7 16 ♘f5.

15 ♕f7 ♗d7

15...♗e7 16 ♘f5 (again the pin on the g8-a2 diagonal proves vital) 16...♕c7 17 ♘a4! ♖f8 18 ♕xh7 leaves Black defenceless.

16 ♕xf6+ ♔c7 17 ♕xh8 ♗h6 18 ♘xe6+!

An important desperado.

18...♕xe6 19 ♕xa8 ♗xe3+ 20 ♔h1 1-0

The Warsaw Olympiad ends in victory for the USA with 54/76, ahead of Sweden (52½) and Poland (52). The American success is mostly due to the phenomenal scores made on the lower boards by Dake and Horowitz. The best score on top board is made by Flohr, but the sensation of the Olympiad is the Estonian, Paul Keres (born 1916) who scores 12½/19 on top board, playing direct attacking chess.

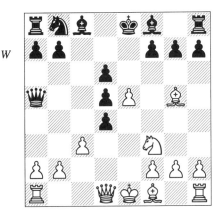

W

P. Keres – W. Winter
Warsaw Olympiad 1935

In keeping with his style at the time, Keres interprets this position in gambit style.

9 ♗d3!? dxc3 10 0-0 cxb2?!

10...♘c6 is more cautious.

11 ♖b1 dxe5?

Keres regarded 11...♘c6 12 ♖e1 ♗e6 as necessary, and later played a correspondence game from this position, winning as follows: 13 ♖xb2 ♕c7 14 ♕a4 dxe5 15 ♘xe5 ♗d6 16 ♖be2 ♗xe5 17 ♖xe5 ♕d7 18 ♖5e3 0-0 19 ♗xh7+! ♔xh7 20 ♕h4+ ♔g8 21 ♗f6 ♗f5 22 g4 1-0. However, the assessment of the whole line looks very unclear.

12 ♘xe5 ♗d6

12...♗e6 can be met by 13 ♖e1 with the point that 13...♗b4 14 ♘xf7! ♗xe1 15 ♘xh8 gives White a massive attack.

13 ♘xf7!

This piece sacrifice shatters Black's king position.

13...♔xf7 14 ♕h5+ g6

14...♔f8 15 ♖fe1 ♗d7 16 ♖e3 ♔g8 17 ♖f3 ♗xh2+ 18 ♔h1! and White forces mate.

15 ♗xg6+! hxg6 16 ♕xh8 ♗f5

16...♘d7 loses to 17 ♕h7+.

17 ♖fe1 ♗e4 18 ♖xe4! dxe4 19 ♕f6+ 1-0

19...♔g8 20 ♕xg6+ ♔f8 21 ♕xd6+ leads shortly to mate.

Chess News in Brief

Alekhine loses the World Championship to Euwe (the score is 15½-14½ in Euwe's favour), though Alekhine's fondness for alcohol is undoubtedly a factor.

Samuel Reshevsky wins the Margate tournament with 7½/9, ahead of Capablanca (7).

Reuben Fine wins the Hastings tournament (1935/6) with 7½/9, ahead of Flohr (6½).

Laszlo Szabo (born 1917) wins the Hungarian Championship for the first time.

Aron Nimzowitsch (born 1886) dies of pneumonia.

Bent Larsen [one of the world's top players during the 1960s and 1970s] is born.

Fritz Baumbach [winner of the 11th Correspondence World Championship, 1983-8] is born.

Grigory Sanakoev [winner of the 12th Correspondence World Championship, 1984-91] is born.

World News in Brief

Italy invades Ethiopia.

The German air force, the *Luftwaffe*, is created. Germany introduces conscription, to international condemnation.

Britain announces plans to treble the size of its air force. Britain, France and Italy form a united front against German rearmament.

The war between Bolivia and Paraguay ends.

Radar is developed in Britain by Robert Watson-Watt and A.F. Wilkins, following on from an observation that passing aircraft distort radio reception.

In Utah, Malcolm Campbell sets a new land speed record of 301.3 miles per hour (485.2 km/h).

An artificial material, later named Nylon, is invented. It is the first of a new type of material – polymers – which consist of long chains of repeating units of relatively simple chemical composition.

1936

Vintage performances by Capablanca

Botvinnik and Capablanca share first place in the very strong Nottingham tournament with 10/14, ahead of Fine, Reshevsky and Euwe (all 9½), Alekhine (9), and Flohr and Lasker (both 8½).

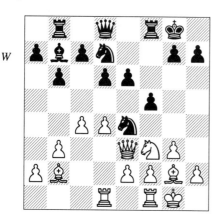

W

A. Alekhine – C. Alexander
Nottingham 1936

White is ready to attack on the light squares.
13 d5!
This thematic blow is a constant menace in positions of this type.
13...exd5
13...e5 14 ♘h4! undermines the e4-knight, and with it Black's whole set-up.
14 cxd5 ♘df6
Black appears to have counterplay against the d5-pawn, but Alekhine has calculated that the pawn is untouchable.
15 ♘h4 ♕d7
15...♘xd5? loses to 16 ♖xd5 ♗xd5 17 ♕d4.
16 ♗h3 g6
Now the pin on the h3-c8 diagonal means that 16...♘xd5?? loses to 17 ♕xe4.
17 f3 ♘c5 18 ♕g5 ♕g7
Black must walk into another pin – it is the only response to the threats to f5 and f6.
19 b4 ♘cd7 20 e4! ♘xe4 21 ♕c1!
Alekhine is a step ahead again. The knight must go back into its pin, giving White time for the final attack.

21...♘ef6 22 ♗xf5! ♔h8
22...gxf5 23 ♘xf5 ♕h8 (otherwise the queen is lost) 24 ♘h6+ ♔g7 25 ♕g5#.
23 ♗e6 ♗a6 24 ♖fe1 ♘e5 25 f4 ♘d3 26 ♖xd3! ♗xd3 27 g4 1-0

Capablanca wins the double-round Moscow tournament without losing a game (scoring 13/18) – one of the best results of the later stages of his career. The tournament is also a triumph for second-placed Botvinnik (12), who is 2½ points clear of third-placed Flohr (9½).

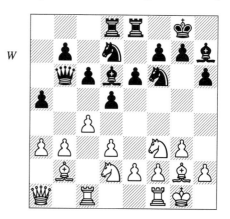

W

J. Capablanca – A. Lilienthal
Moscow 1936

Capablanca has started the game *à la* Réti. Black is now intending ...e5.
21 ♘e5 ♗xe5 22 ♗xe5 ♘xe5 23 ♕xe5 ♘d7 24 ♕b2
White's pressure on d5 keeps Black under restraint.
24...♘f6 25 b4
White will remorselessly attack the black pawns on the h1-a8 diagonal.
25...axb4 26 ♕xb4 ♕xb4 27 axb4 ♖a8 28 ♖a1 ♘d7 29 ♘b3 ♔f8 30 ♖a5 dxc4?!
There is no easy solution to Black's problems, but giving up his main bastion on the long diagonal can hardly help.
31 dxc4 ♘b6 32 ♖xa8 ♖xa8 33 ♘a5 ♖a7 34 ♖d1

White's rook threatens to penetrate, and there are tactical threats against c6 and b7.

34...♔e8

34...♔e7 35 ♗xc6 ♘xc4 36 ♘xb7 gives White an extra pawn.

35 ♘xb7! ♖xb7 36 ♗xc6+ ♖d7 37 c5 ♔e7

37...♘d5 38 b5 ♔e7 39 ♗xd7 ♔xd7 40 ♖a1 and the rook shepherds the pawns forward.

38 ♗xd7 ♘xd7 39 c6 ♘b6 40 c7 ♗f5 41 ♖d8 e5

Black's pieces can stop White queening, but only by neglecting the kingside pawns.

42 ♖b8 ♘c8 43 b5 ♔d6 44 b6 ♘e7 45 ♖f8 ♗c8 46 ♖xf7 ♘d5 47 ♖xg7 ♘xb6 48 ♖h7 ♘d5 49 ♖xh6+ ♔xc7 50 e4 ♘e7 51 f3 ♔d7 52 h4 ♔e8 53 ♖f6 ♘g8 54 ♖c6 1-0

Keres and Alekhine share first place at the Bad Nauheim tournament, with 6½/9.

G. Ståhlberg – P. Keres
Bad Nauheim 1936

Keres now opens the position to the benefit of his active pieces.

15...d4! 16 exd4 cxd4 17 ♖xe8+ ♕xe8 18 cxd4 ♘xd4 19 ♗a4 ♕e5

Threatening 20...♘xf3+ or 20...♘e2+.

20 ♖b1 ♘d5! 21 ♗b2 ♘c3 22 ♗xc3 ♖xc3 23 ♔h1 h5! 24 ♗d7 ♖d3?

24...h4! wins, e.g. 25 ♘e4?! ♗e2.

25 ♕a4 ♗b7 26 ♘e4?

26 ♕c4 ♖b3 27 ♖d1 ♖e3 is equal.

26...♗xe4 27 fxe4 ♘f3! 0-1

Mate is forced.

Chess News in Brief

Fine wins the Zandvoort tournament with 8½/11, ahead of Euwe (7½), Tartakower and Keres (both 6½).

Flohr wins the Podebrady tournament with 13/17, ahead of Alekhine (12½).

Alekhine wins the Dresden tournament with 6½/9; Keres's lowly placing, with just 3½ points, is surprising.

Euwe and Fine share first place in a small tournament in Amsterdam, with 5/7, ahead of Alekhine (4½).

Alekhine wins the Hastings tournament (1936/7) with 8/9, ahead of Fine (7½).

An unofficial Olympiad is held in Munich (hosted by the Great German Chess Federation, not a member of FIDE), at the same time as the Nottingham tournament. It is a major event, with 21 teams of eight players competing. Hungary wins, with 110½/160, ahead of Poland (108) and Germany (106½). England and the USA do not take part.

Samuel Reshevsky wins the United States Championship for the first of six times.

Mikhail Tal [World Champion 1960-1] is born.

Eduard Gufeld [Ukrainian grandmaster and trainer] is born.

World News in Brief

German forces return to the Rhineland, breaking the treaties of Versailles and Locarno.

Civil war breaks out in Spain, as Franco's Nationalist forces invade from Morocco. Opposing the Nationalists are two groups of republicans: those who support the constitution and those who want social revolution. The government appeals for foreign help. Hitler and Mussolini support Franco.

Mussolini makes an anti-communist 'Axis' with Germany, and urges France and Britain to join. Germany and Japan agree to protect the world from Bolshevism.

Paraguay sets up a fascist regime.

In Palestine, there is conflict between Arabs and British troops.

In the USA, the Boulder Dam (later renamed the Hoover Dam) is completed.

1937

Alekhine regains the world title • Successes for Keres, Fine and Reshevsky

Alekhine regains the World Championship in a convincing 15½-9½ victory over Euwe.

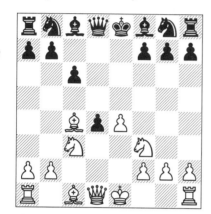

A. Alekhine – M. Euwe
World Ch match (6), Haarlem 1937

Alekhine has chosen a somewhat over-impetuous opening. However, it forces Black to calculate some intricate variations, and Euwe immediately falters.

6...b5?

The correct response was worked out some years later. Black should take the piece: 6...dxc3! 7 ♗xf7+ ♔e7 8 ♕b3 cxb2! 9 ♗xb2 ♕b6! 10 ♗a3+ (10 ♗xg8 ♖xg8 11 ♕xg8 ♕b4+ 12 ♘d2 ♕xb2 13 ♖b1 ♕c2 is good for Black) 10...c5 11 ♗xg8 ♖xg8 12 ♗xc5+ (12 ♕xg8 ♕a5+ picks up the a3-bishop) 12...♕xc5 13 0-0 ♕h5! is good for Black, since 14 ♕xg8 ♗e6 sidelines the white queen.

7 ♘xb5!

Euwe had overlooked this move.

7...♗a6 8 ♕b3! ♕e7

8...♗xb5? loses to 9 ♗xf7+ ♔d7 10 ♘xd4!.

9 0-0 ♗xb5 10 ♗xb5 ♘f6

10...cxb5? 11 ♕d5 wins the a8-rook.

11 ♗c4

White's gamble has paid off – his position is completely overwhelming.

11...♘bd7 12 ♘xd4!?

12 e5 is also good.

12...♖b8 13 ♕c2 ♕c5 14 ♘f5

Not 14 ♘xc6? ♖c8.

14...♘e5 15 ♗f4! ♘h5 16 ♗xf7+! ♔xf7 17 ♕xc5 ♗xc5 18 ♗xe5 ♖b5 19 ♘d6 ♗b6 20 b4! ♖d8 21 ♖ad1 c5 22 bxc5 ♗xc5 23 ♖d5 1-0

Keres wins the Semmering-Baden tournament with 9/14, confirming his status as one of the world's elite. Fine is second with 8 points, ahead of Capablanca and Reshevsky (both 7½).

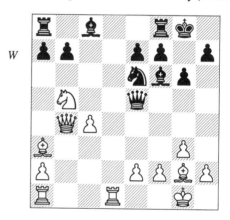

P. Keres – S. Flohr
Semmering-Baden 1937

White has strong pressure against Black's queenside, but needs to play accurately to keep his pieces coordinated.

17 ♖ac1!

Parrying Black's threat of ...a6, and rightly ignoring the possibility of ...♕xe2.

17...♖d8

17...♕xe2 18 ♘c3 ♕e5 (taking the knight with the f6-bishop would leave Black terribly exposed; 18...a5 19 ♕b1 does not fundamentally change anything) 19 ♘d5 wins back the pawn with advantage.

18 ♖d5!? ♖xd5

18...♕xe2 19 ♘c3 is very good for White.

19 cxd5 a6 20 ♘a7!

This very strong and surprising move effectively ends the game.

20...♘d4

20...♖xa7 21 ♖xc8+ ♘f8 22 ♕b6 wins.

21 ♖xc8+ ♖xc8 22 ♘xc8 ♕xe2 23 h4 ♘f5 24 ♕e4 1-0

Levenfish wins the 10th USSR Championship.

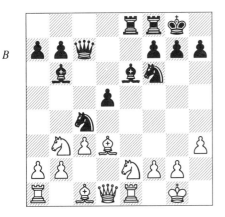

V. Panov – I. Bondarevsky
USSR Ch, Tbilisi 1937

White has just played 16 ♘d4-e2, believing he has time to rearrange his knights around the d4-square. However, this gives Black enough leeway to detonate the white kingside.

16...♗xh3! 17 ♗f4

17 gxh3 walks into 17...♖xe2!. Then 18 ♕xe2 ♕g3+ 19 ♔f1 ♕xh3+ 20 ♔g1 ♘g4 wins.

17...♕d7 18 gxh3

18 ♗xc4 ♕g4 19 ♗xd5 ♘xd5 20 ♕xd5 ♖xe2 21 ♖xe2 ♕xe2 22 ♗g3 ♖d8 is good for Black.

18...♕xh3 19 ♗xc4 ♕g4+ 20 ♔f1

20 ♗g3 ♖xe2 21 ♖xe2 ♕xg3+ is winning for Black.

20...♗xf2!?

20...♕f3! 21 ♘bd4 ♗xd4 22 ♕xd4 ♖xe2 is a somewhat clearer win.

21 ♔xf2 ♘e4+ 22 ♔f1 ♕f3+ 23 ♔g1 ♕f2+ 24 ♔h1 ♖e6 25 ♗xd5?!

25 ♗xd5? ♖g6 is terminal. 25 ♕d3 dxc4 26 ♕e3 cxb3 27 axb3 ♕h4+ 28 ♔g2 ♕g4+ 29 ♘g3 ♘g5 should be a win for Black.

25...♕f3+ 26 ♔h2 ♖g6 27 ♗xf7+ ♖xf7 28 ♕d8+ ♖f8 29 ♕d5+ ♔h8 30 ♘g3 ♕f2+ 0-1

Mate is forced.

Chess News in Brief

Reshevsky, Petrovs and Flohr share first place at the Kemeri tournament with 12/17, ahead of Alekhine and Keres (both 11½).

Fine and Keres win the Margate tournament with 7½/9, ahead of Alekhine (6).

Paul Schmidt wins the Pärnu tournament with 5½/7, ahead of Ståhlberg, Keres and Flohr (all 4½).

Grob, Keres and Fine share first place at the Ostend tournament.

Euwe wins a four-man tournament in Germany with 4/6, ahead of Alekhine and Bogoljubow (both 3½).

Reshevsky wins the Hastings tournament (1937/8) with 7/9, ahead of Alexander and Keres (both 6½), and Fine and Flohr (both 6).

The Stockholm Olympiad is convincingly won by the USA with 54½/72, ahead of Hungary (48½), Poland and Argentina (both 47). Flohr makes the best score on top board. 19 countries compete.

A match between Botvinnik and Levenfish is drawn 6½-6½.

Boris Spassky [World Champion 1969-72] is born.

Lajos Portisch [Hungarian grandmaster; a Candidate eight times] is born.

World News in Brief

War breaks out between Japan and China, as the Japanese occupy Beijing and seize Nanjing.

In Britain, the government take measures to suppress fascism.

Hitler offers to stop intervention in Spain if other countries follow suit, but the USSR continues aid for the republican rebels. The German air force bombs Guernica, causing devastation and thousands of civilian casualties.

India gains a constitution, and Burma is separated.

Britain announces a plan to partition Palestine.

The German airship *Hindenberg* explodes over New Jersey. 36 people die; many survive by leaping from the burning airship.

Amelia Earhart vanishes over the Pacific Ocean during an attempted round-the-world flight via the equator.

1938

The AVRO tournament – a triumph for Keres and Fine

The idea of the AVRO tournament is to bring together the eight best players in the world, with the winner (or the runner-up if Alekhine wins) earning the right to challenge Alekhine for the World Championship. The format of the event, with each round played in a different Dutch city, does not favour the older players. Keres and Fine share first place with 8½/14. Botvinnik is in third place with 7½, ahead of Euwe, Reshevsky and Alekhine (all 7), Capablanca (6 – the only time in his career when he failed to make a plus-score in a tournament) and Flohr, in last place with 4½.

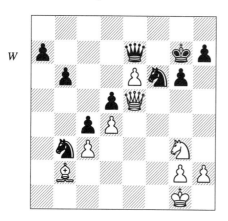

M. Botvinnik – J. Capablanca
AVRO tournament, Rotterdam 1938

Following a classic attacking build-up in the centre, it is time for Botvinnik to find a way through.

30 ♗a3!!

Drawing the queen away from defending the f6-knight and lifting the blockade on the white e-pawn.

30...♕xa3

After 30...♕e8 31 ♕c7+ ♔g8 32 ♗e7 White makes easy progress.

31 ♘h5+! gxh5

31...♔h6 loses to 32 ♘xf6 ♕c1+ 33 ♔f2 ♕d2+ 34 ♔g3 ♕xc3+ 35 ♔h4 ♕xd4+ 36 ♘g4+.

32 ♕g5+ ♔f8 33 ♕xf6+ ♔g8 34 e7!

White is still a piece down, but his pawn is now unstoppable. Black's only hope is perpetual check, but it isn't quite there.

34...♕c1+ 35 ♔f2 ♕c2+ 36 ♔g3 ♕d3+ 37 ♔h4 ♕e4+ 38 ♔xh5 ♕e2+

After 38...♕g6+ 39 ♕xg6+ hxg6+ 40 ♔xg6 the white king joins the attack.

39 ♔h4 ♕e4+ 40 g4 ♕e1+ 41 ♔h5 1-0

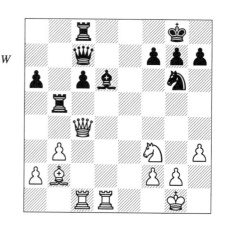

P. Keres – J. Capablanca
AVRO tournament, Haarlem 1938

Black's queenside pawns are weak, but that in itself may not be enough for White to win.

21 ♘d4!

Stopping the black rook coming to d5 as 21...♖d5? would now lose a pawn to 22 ♘xc6! ♖xd1+ 23 ♖xd1 ♕xc6 24 ♖xd6.

21...♖b6 22 ♘e6! ♕b8! 23 ♘g5

The point of Black's last move is shown by 23 ♘xg7?! ♗e5.

23...♖b7 24 ♕g4 ♗f4 25 ♖c4 ♖b5?!

This allows White's attack to flare up anew. However, 25...♗xg5 26 ♕xg5 is also very unpleasant for Black.

26 ♘xf7!?

There is a more clear-cut win by 26 ♖xf4! ♖xg5 27 ♕xg5 ♕xf4 28 ♖d8+ ♖xd8 29 ♕xd8+ ♘f8 30 ♗a3 c5 31 ♕c8!.

26...♖e8 27 g3 ♕c8?! 28 ♖xf4! ♕xg4 29 ♖xg4 ♗xf7 30 ♖d7+ ♖e7 31 ♖xe7+ ♔xe7 32

♗xg7 ♖a5 33 a4 ♖c5 34 ♖b4 ♔e6 35 ♔g2 h5 36 ♖c4 ♖xc4 37 bxc4 ♔d6 38 f4 1-0

Alekhine wins the Margate tournament with 7/9, ahead of Spielmann (6) and Petrovs (5½).

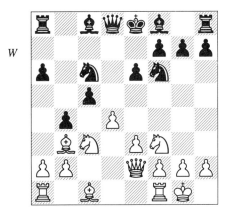

A. Alekhine – E. Böök
Margate 1938

Böök has handled the opening in an extremely ambitious manner.

10 d5 ♘a5

10...exd5 11 ♘xd5! ♘xd5 12 ♖d1 is very pleasant for White.

11 ♗a4+ ♗d7 12 dxe6 fxe6 13 ♖d1?!

This leads to amazing complications, but White has a strong alternative in 13 ♘e5!.

13...bxc3 14 ♖xd7! ♘xd7 15 ♘e5 ♖a7 16 bxc3

This critical position is extremely unclear, though the odds in a practical game heavily favour Black slipping up. 16 ♕h5+ g6 17 ♘xg6 hxg6 18 ♕xh8?! (18 ♕xg6+ is a draw) 18...♔f7 gives Black the initiative.

16...♔e7?

Black should try one of the following:

a) 16...g6 17 ♕f3!? (17 ♕d3, as analysed by Alekhine, is unconvincing) 17...♕h4 (17...♕g5 18 ♘xd7 ♖xd7 19 e4 ♕d8 20 ♗g5 ♕xg5 21 ♖d1 ♗e7 22 ♗xd7+ ♔d8 23 ♕d3 c4 24 ♕d4 is winning for White) 18 ♕f7+ ♔d8 19 ♗xd7 and White seems to have more than enough for the exchange after 19...♕e7 20 ♗xe6 or 19...♗d6 20 ♕xe6.

b) 16...♕b8 17 ♘xd7 ♖xd7 18 ♕xa6 ♕d6!? (following 18...♕c7 19 ♕xe6+ ♔d8 20 e4 the

introduction of the dark-squared bishop makes the attack decisive) 19 ♕b5 ♔e7 20 ♗a3 ♘b7 leads to an odd position, where Black is tied up, but White remains a rook down.

17 e4! ♘f6 18 ♗g5 ♕c7

18...♕c8 19 ♖d1 threatens 20 ♕h5, while 18...♖b7 loses material to 19 ♕h5 g6 20 ♘xg6+ ♔f7 21 ♘xh8++ ♔g8 22 ♕h3.

19 ♗f4

19 ♕h5! is a more clear-cut win.

19...♕b6 20 ♖d1 g6 21 ♗g5 ♗g7 22 ♘d7 ♖xd7 23 ♖xd7+ ♔f8 24 ♗xf6 ♗xf6 25 e5 1-0

Chess News in Brief

Erich Eliskases wins the Noordwijk tournament with 7½/9, ahead of Keres (6½), Pirc (5½) and Euwe (5).

Vasja Pirc wins the Lodz tournament with 11½/15, ahead of Tartakower (10).

Kostić wins the Ljubljana tournament with 10½/15, ahead of Szabo (10).

Szabo wins the Hastings tournament (1938/9) with 7½/9, ahead of Euwe (6½).

Eliskases, from recently annexed Austria, wins the German Championship by a margin of 2½ points.

World News in Brief

Pro-Nazis gain power in Austria, and Germany is invited to invade the country. Within days, Germany has annexed Austria, and within weeks leading Austrian Jews are being sent to concentration camps.

Britain and France agrees to defend Czechoslovakia. Sudetenland, a predominantly German-speaking part of Czechoslovakia, is offered self-government. France and England acquiesce, in an attempt to avoid war, to Sudetenland being ceded to Germany. On 9th November, which becomes known as *Kristallnacht*, Jews and Jewish property across Germany are subjected to violent attacks.

Stalin's purges continue, with executions of high-ranking Soviet figures.

War rages on in China.

Franco gains decisive victories in the Spanish Civil War.

Mexico nationalizes all US and British oil companies.

1939

World War II throws international chess into chaos

The Buenos Aires Olympiad is disrupted by the outbreak of World War II, which occurs just after the completion of the preliminaries. The England team returns home immediately. Three of the English players, Stuart Milner-Barry, Harry Golombek and Hugh Alexander, are to work at the top-secret code-breaking station at Bletchley Park. Remarkably, the final goes ahead, but with the French, Polish and Palestinian teams refusing, for obvious reasons, to play against Germany (a team strengthened by the inclusion of Austrian players). The organizers decide that unplayed matches will be scored as 2-2 draws. Germany wins the final, with 36/56 ahead of Poland (35½) and Estonia (33½). The 'Czecho-Moravian Protectorate' is sixth, with 32 points. Three of Germany's matches, including what would have been the critical last-round match against Poland, are unplayed. High scorers on top board include Alekhine and Capablanca, but they do not play each other.

Yanofsky (born 1925) creates a sensation, scoring 13½/16 on second board for Canada.

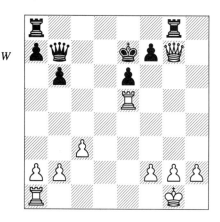

D. Yanofsky – A. Dulanto
Buenos Aires Olympiad prelims 1939

22 Rxe6+!! Kxe6 23 Re1+ Kd6
Black has no good defence.
24 Wf6+ Kc5 25 Re5+ Kc4
White can now force mate in 7 moves.
26 b3+ Kd3

26...Kxc3 27 Rc5++ Kb4 28 Rc4+ mates.
27 Wd6+ Kc2 28 Re2+ 1-0

Many European players remain in Argentina after the Olympiad, and settle in South America, rather than returning to war-torn Europe. These include most of the Polish team, led by Najdorf, and, ironically after the political machinations, the whole German team (Eliskases and Becker from Austria; and Engels, Michel and Reinhardt). Ståhlberg (Sweden) also remains in South America. This influx of talent has a considerable positive impact on South American chess.

Keres wins a match against Euwe (Netherlands 1939/40) by the score 7½-6½.

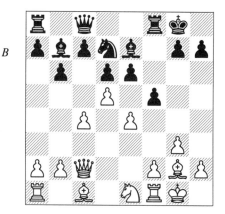

M. Euwe – P. Keres
Match (game 9), Netherlands 1939/40

Euwe is trying to block out the b7-bishop, but his position is too shaky for this plan to succeed.

13...fxe4! 14 Wxe4 Nc5 15 We2 Bf6 16 Bh3 Re8!
Black's threat of 17...exd5 denies White the time to bring another piece to bear on e6, or to oust the black knight from c5.
17 Be3 Wd8 18 Bxc5 exd5! 19 Be6+?
19 Be3 d4 20 Bg2 is safer.
19...Kh8 20 Rd1

20 &a3 ♕e7 21 ♘g2 ♕xe6 22 ♕xe6 ♖xe6 23 ♘f4 gives White a little more play.

20...dxc5 21 ♘g2

21 cxd5 is no good in view of, for example, 21...&xd5 22 ♖xd5 ♕e7.

21...d4 22 f4 d3! 23 ♖xd3 ♕xd3!

This queen sacrifice gives Black's rooks and bishops immense scope.

24 ♕xd3 &d4+ 25 ♖f2

Or 25 ♔h1 ♖xe6 intending ...♖ae8 followed by ...♖e2.

25...♖xe6 26 ♔f1 ♖ae8 27 f5

27 ♖d2 &e4 28 ♕a3 &f5! 29 ♕f3 &h3 30 ♕d1 ♖e4, intending ...g5, is very good for Black.

27...♖e5 28 f6 gxf6 29 ♖d2 &c8 30 ♘f4 ♖e3!? 31 ♕b1 ♖f3+ 32 ♔g2 ♖xf4! 33 gxf4 ♖g8+ 34 ♔f3 &g4+ 0-1

White is mated or loses his queen.

Botvinnik wins the 11th USSR Championship with 12½/17, a point ahead of Alexander Kotov, for whom it is an impressive debut in the USSR Championship.

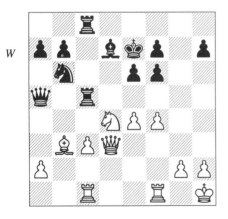

A. Kotov – M. Yudovich
USSR Ch, Leningrad 1939

Black's position would be quite attractive if his king had a safe refuge.

20 c4 &e8 21 e5

The threat of 22 ♘f5+ forces lines open.

21...fxe5 22 fxe5 ♖xe5 23 ♖cd1!

Threatening 24 ♘b5.

23...♕c5 24 ♕g3! ♖e4

24...♖h5 loses to 25 ♘xe6!, e.g. 25...♔xe6 26 ♖fe1+ ♖e5 27 ♖xe5+ ♕xe5 28 c5+.

25 ♖f5! exf5

25...♕xd4 26 ♖xd4 ♖xd4 prolongs the resistance, but will not save the game.

26 ♘xf5+! ♔f6 27 ♖d6+ ♔xf5 28 ♕f3+ ♖f4 29 ♕h5+ ♔e4 30 &c2+ ♔e3 31 ♖d3+ 1-0

Chess News in Brief

Vera Menchik retains the Women's World Championship in a tournament held alongside the Olympiad. She scores 18/19, two points ahead of the German, Sonja Graf, who has been the only player to threaten Menchik's hold on the world title. Graf opts to remain in South America after the tournament.

Flohr wins a strong training tournament, played in Leningrad and Moscow, with 12/17, ahead of Reshevsky (10½). Well down the field are Keres and Smyslov (both 8).

Keres wins the Margate tournament with 7½/9, ahead of Capablanca and Flohr (6½).

Flohr wins the Kemeri tournament with 12/15, ahead of Ståhlberg and Szabo (11).

Eliskases scores a 11½-8½ match victory over Bogoljubow.

World News in Brief

Franco takes Barcelona and Madrid, ending the Spanish civil war.

Germany invades Czechoslovakia. Britain and France sign an mutual assistance pact with Poland. Italian forces move into Albania. Hitler and Mussolini sign a military alliance. Britain fails to achieve an alliance with the Soviet Union; Hitler and Stalin sign a non-aggression pact. Germany invades Poland, starting World War II. Britain and France declare war on Germany. The USA declares its neutrality. Soviet troops invade Poland from the east. Turkey signs a mutual assistance pact with Britain and France. Hostilities break out between the USSR and Finland.

Frank Whittle succeeds in building a prototype of a jet engine, the concept that he had devised in 1929. However, the German engineer Dr Hans von Ohain has already used a jet engine to power a Heinkel aeroplane.

Igor Sikorsky invents the single-rotor helicopter.

Work on nuclear fission proceeds in the USA.

1940

Chess continues in the USSR and Germany

Bondarevsky and Lilienthal share first place in the 12th USSR Championship (with 13½/19), an event strengthened by the USSR's annexation of the Baltic states and occupation of parts of Poland. Smyslov finishes third with 13 points. Keres (4th place) and Botvinnik (joint 5th-6th) have disappointing results. Botvinnik, not satisfied with the conditions at the tournament, or that the event has determined which of the Soviet players ought to challenge for the world title, pushes for a further event between the top six players. He has the support of a new sports official, Snegiriov, and an 'Absolute Championship' is scheduled for 1941!

For the sacrificed pawn, White now dominates the dark squares.

18...♘xb4

18...♗e6, trying to keep the long diagonal closed, fails to 19 ♖hg1, when White will crash through brutally on g6.

19 e6! ♘d5

19...♘xd3+ 20 cxd3 fxe6 21 ♖df1 ♖f5 22 ♖hg1 wins – the black king is just too exposed.

20 exf7+ ♖xf7 21 ♗c4!

An attractive move, even though the variations are simple enough.

21...c6 22 ♖xd5 ♕xc4 23 ♕e8+ 1-0

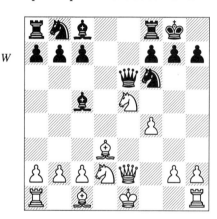

W

P. Keres – V. Petrovs
USSR Ch, Moscow 1940

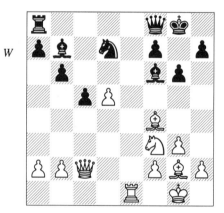

W

I. Bondarevsky – G. Lisitsyn
USSR Ch, Moscow 1940

White has a development advantage, but the position of his pawn on f4, and the consequent weakening of the g1-a7 diagonal, could count against him if he fails to press home his initiative.

10 ♘e4 ♘xe4 11 ♕xe4 g6 12 b4!

Very logical: White gains time to put his bishop on the long diagonal, which Black's last move weakened.

12...♗e7 13 ♗b2 ♗f6 14 0-0-0! ♘c6 15 h4 h5

15...♘xe5 16 fxe5 ♗g7 17 h5 also gives White a very strong attack.

16 g4! ♗xe5 17 fxe5 ♕xg4 18 ♕e3

White has an excellent game here, and with a few accurate blows manages to shatter Black's position.

19 ♕a4! ♕d8 20 ♘d2!

The threat of bringing the knight to d6 causes an immediate crisis.

20...g5?

Black's only chance is 20...♗xb2 21 ♘c4 ♗c3, although 22 ♖e3 (22 ♖c1 ♗h8! is not at all clear) 22...♗d4 23 ♘d6 ♗xe3 24 ♘xb7 ♗xf2+ 25 ♔xf2 should be good for White.

21 ♘e4! ♗xd5

21...gxf4 loses to 22 ♕xd7!.

22 ♖d1 ♗d4 23 ♗xg5 f6

23...♕e8 loses to 24 ♘d6, and 23...♕c7 to 24 ♖xd4 cxd4 25 ♕xd7.

24 ♗xf6 ♕xf6

24...♘xf6 25 ♘xf6+ exploits the various pins and forks to win material.

25 ♘xf6+ ♘xf6 26 ♗xd5+ ♘xd5 27 ♖xd4 cxd4 28 ♕xd4 ♖d8 29 h4 ♔f7 30 h5 ♖d7 31 g4 ♘f6 32 ♕f4 ♔g7 33 h6+ 1-0

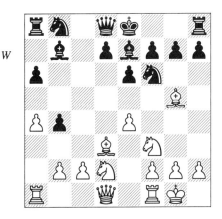

E. Bogoljubow – L. Rellstab
Krakow 1940

Black has allowed White too much ground in the centre.

11 e5 ♘d5 12 ♗xe7 ♘xe7 13 ♘c4

The d6-square is a horrible weakness.

13...♘c8 14 ♖e1 d5

This loses by force, but after 14...0-0 15 ♗e4 ♘c6 16 ♕d3, followed by ♖ad1, Black's game is untenable anyway.

15 exd6 ♘xd6 16 ♗g6!!

The threat of ♖xe6+ denies Black the time to rescue his d6-knight.

16...hxg6

16...♘xc4 loses the queen to 17 ♖xe6+; 16...♔e7 is no good due to the threat to the f7-pawn: 17 ♘xd6 ♕xd6 18 ♕xd6+ ♔xd6 19 ♗xf7.

17 ♘xd6+ ♔e7 18 ♘xb7 ♕c7

The only matter now to be resolved is whether White can extricate his knight.

19 ♕d5 ♖h5 20 ♕e4 ♘c6 21 g4!

Mission accomplished: the black rook must release its guard on White's 5th rank.

1-0

Chess News in Brief

Euwe wins a six-man tournament in Budapest with 4½/5, ahead of Vidmar (3½).

Reshevsky wins the USA Championship with 13/16, ahead of Fine (12½) and Kashdan (10½).

World News in Brief

Germany occupies Denmark, Norway, Belgium, the Netherlands, and much of France, including Paris. On land, the German *blitzkrieg* (lightning war) is effective, while at sea, their 'U-boat' submarines are devastating. At Dunkirk, Britain manages to evacuate most of its Expeditionary Force from France. A massive attack on Britain by the German *Luftwaffe* is thwarted by the Royal Air Force at the Battle of Britain. There is heavy bombing of British cities by the *Luftwaffe*. The Royal Navy sinks the French and Italian fleets, with heavy loss of life.

Rumania falls to Germany and Italy; Slovakia joins the Axis.

Finland surrenders a large part of its territory to the USSR, in return for peace. The USSR annexes the Baltic states of Estonia, Latvia and Lithuania.

Greece repels an attempted invasion by Italian forces.

In Africa, Italian forces advance into British Somaliland.

In China, Mao Zedong's Red Army fights back against the Japanese.

Japan signs a ten-year pact with Germany and Italy, putting pressure on the USSR and giving an effective warning to the USA that entering the war in Europe may mean a war in the Pacific.

Britain occupies the strategically important Faeroes and Iceland.

1941

Botvinnik proves his 'Absolute' superiority

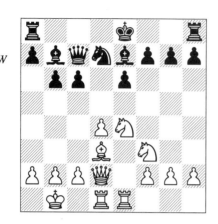

P. Schmidt – H. Nowarra
Warsaw 1941

White storms Black's somewhat passive set-up with a remarkable series of sacrifices.

13 ♘eg5!? h6 14 ♘xf7!? ♔xf7 15 ♖xe6! ♔xe6 16 ♗c4+ ♔f6 17 ♖e1!?

17 ♕e3 ♕d6 18 ♘e5 ♘xe5 19 ♕f4+ ♔g6 20 ♕e4+ gives White a draw.

17...♘f8

17...♕d6? loses to 18 ♕c3 b5 (18...g5 19 d5+ ♔g6 20 ♖e6+ ♕xe6 21 dxe6 ♘c5 22 ♘e5+ is very good for White) 19 ♘e5 (19 ♘h4 is also effective) 19...c5 20 ♕d3, e.g. 20...♘f8 21 ♘g4+ ♔g5 22 ♖e5+ ♕xe5 23 h4+!.

18 ♕c3 ♔g6?

After 18...♗c8 19 ♘e5 White has a very strong attack, but Black retains chances of survival.

19 ♕d3+ ♔f6 20 ♘e5! ♗c8 21 ♕f3+ ♗f5 22 g4 ♕c8

22...g6 loses to 23 ♘xg6.

23 gxf5 h5 24 ♘g6 ♗b4

Now White can force mate in 6.

25 ♖e6+! ♘xe6 26 fxe6+ ♔xg6 27 ♗d3+ 1-0

Botvinnik wins the 'Absolute Championship of the USSR' (a six-man, quadruple-round event) with 13½/20, ahead of Keres (11), Smyslov (10), Boleslavsky (9), Lilienthal (8½)

and Bondarevsky (8). It turns out to be a one-off event; there are no further 'Absolute Championships'.

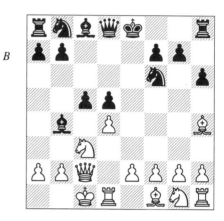

P. Keres – M. Botvinnik
Absolute USSR Ch, Moscow/Leningrad 1941

8...♗xc3! 9 ♕xc3?!

9 ♗xf6 is a better try.

9...g5! 10 ♗g3 cxd4! 11 ♕xd4 ♘c6 12 ♕a4 ♗f5

Black's active pieces and open lines against the white king are far more relevant than White's theoretical advantages (the bishop-pair and superior pawn structure).

13 e3 ♖c8 14 ♗d3

14 ♘e2 a6 15 ♘c3 b5 16 ♕xa6 b4 17 e4 ♗xe4 18 ♗b5 0-0 19 ♗xc6 bxc3 20 f3 cxb2+ 21 ♔xb2 ♕e7 also leads to a strong attack for Black.

14...♕d7 15 ♔b1 ♗xd3+ 16 ♖xd3 ♕f5

The pin on the h7-b1 diagonal is deadly.

17 e4 ♘xe4 18 ♔a1 0-0

By delaying castling until now, Botvinnik has maximized his initiative – indeed castling is itself now an attacking move.

19 ♖d1 b5!

The idea is to get the d4-square for the knight.

20 ♕xb5 ♘d4 21 ♕d3 ♘c2+ 22 ♔b1 ♘b4 0-1

White loses his queen – for a start.

I. Boleslavsky – A. Lilienthal
Absolute USSR Ch, Leningrad/Moscow 1941

1 e4 e5 2 ♘f3 d5?!

It is surprising that this dubious gambit should occur in such a high-level game.

3 ♘xe5?! ♕e7?! 4 d4 f6 5 ♘d3! dxe4 6 ♘f4

The knight is well placed on f4.

6...♕f7?

As the white bishop does manage to reach c4, this move must be considered a failure.

7 ♘d2 ♗f5

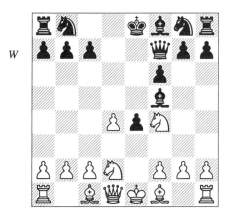

W

8 g4! ♗g6 9 ♗c4 ♕d7 10 ♕e2 ♕xd4 11 ♘e6 ♕b6

11...♕e5 is met by 12 ♘b3 with the killing threat of 13 ♗f4.

12 ♘xe4 ♘d7 13 ♗f4

There is no reason for White to get embroiled in 13 ♘xf6+ ♘gxf6 14 ♘xc7++ ♔d8 15 ♘xa8.

13...♘e5 14 0-0-0 ♗f7 15 ♘4g5! fxg5 16 ♗xe5 ♗xe6 17 ♗xc7 1-0

Chess News in Brief

Gösta Stoltz (from Sweden, a neutral country in the war) wins the Munich tournament with 12/15, ahead of Alekhine and Lundin (both 10½).

Gideon Ståhlberg wins the Mar del Plata tournament with 13/17, ahead of Najdorf (12½) and Eliskases (11½).

Jan Foltys wins a modest tournament in Trenčianske Teplice with the impressive score 10/11.

Ståhlberg and Najdorf share first place at Buenos Aires with 11/14.

Klaus Junge (born 1924) finishes joint first in the German Championship, but loses the play-off to P.Schmidt.

Daniel Abraham (Abe) Yanofsky (born 1925) wins the Canadian Championship for the first time.

A radio match is contested between clubs in Moscow and Leningrad.

Emanuel Lasker (World Champion 1894-1921) dies. He had fled from Germany in 1933, and all his property had been confiscated. He lived from 1937 onwards in the USA.

Vsevolod Rauzer (prominent Soviet theoretician) dies.

Tõnu Õim [winner of the 9th and 14th Correspondence World Championships, 1977-83 and 1994-9 respectively] is born.

Vytas Palciauskas [winner of the 10th Correspondence World Championship, 1978-84] is born.

World News in Brief

Allied forces, principally British and Australian, take control of Italy's colonies in North Africa.

Germany occupies Bulgaria, Yugoslavia and Greece.

Stalin signs a neutrality pact with Japan.

The USA sends forces to Greenland and Iceland to secure supply lines to Britain and protect against German invasion. In spite of its formal neutrality, the USA has been selling arms to Britain and agrees to a deferment of payment until the cessation of hostilities. The Atlantic Charter with Britain brings the USA a step closer to war.

Germany, together with Finnish, Rumanian and Hungarian forces, invades the USSR, bringing the USSR into the war on the side of the Allies. Germany makes rapid gains, including Minsk and Kiev. Leningrad is besieged. Britain declares war on Finland, Rumania and Hungary.

Japan attacks Pearl Harbor, bringing the USA into the war on the side of the Allies. Japan, bogged down in its war in China, attacks British, French and Dutch colonies in the Far East, making rapid progress towards India and Australia.

1942

Alekhine and Keres fight it out in Nazi tournaments

Junge and Alekhine share first place at a tournament in Prague celebrating the 60th birthday of Oldřich Duras, with 8½/11, ahead of Foltys (7).

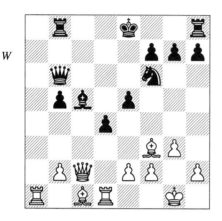

A. Alekhine – K. Junge
Prague 1942

Alekhine has sacrificed a pawn; his compensation consists of Black's somewhat shaky position and uncastled king.

18 罝a6! 豐xa6 19 豐xc5

White's further sacrifice keeps the black king in the centre and makes it hard for Black to protect his weak pawns.

19...豐e6

He cannot afford to lose his e-pawn, while 19...②d7? 20 ②c6 is a slaughter.

20 ②c6+ ②d7

20...②d8? loses to 21 ②d2 b4 22 豐a5+ ②e7 23 豐c7+ ②d7 24 ②xd7 豐xd7 25 豐xe5+ 豐e6 26 豐xg7.

21 ②xd7+ ②xd7 22 豐a7+ ②c6?!

22...②d6! is best: 23 ②f4 (23 f4 豐d7 24 fxe5+ ②e6 is messy) 23...exf4 24 罝xd4+ ②c6 25 罝d1 will lead to perpetual check, e.g. 25...罝hc8 26 罝c1+ ②d5 27 罝d1+ ②c6, etc.

23 ②d2 罝hc8! 24 e4 豐b3?

This loses immediately, but 24...b4 25 罝a1 ②b5 26 b3 豐b6 27 豐a4+ ②c5 28 豐d7 豐b5 29 豐xf7 ②b6 30 罝a4 also looks unpleasant for Black.

25 罝a1 b4 26 罝a6+ ②b5 27 罝a5+ ②c6 28 豐c5+ ②d7 29 罝a7+ 1-0

Alekhine wins the Munich tournament with 8½/11 ahead of Keres (7½).

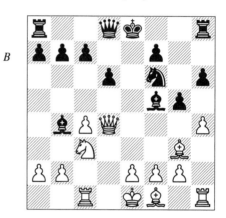

P. Keres – K. Richter
Munich 1942

Keres has just played 11 h2-h4?, which looks like an effective way to break up the kingside, but rebounds on White after Black's sensational reply.

11...②d7!!

Black simultaneously unpins the f6-knight and the h6-pawn, nullifying White's play and threatening ...②e4.

12 罝d1

Rattled, Keres keeps playing for the attack rather than trying to minimize the damage.

12 ②e5 is met by 12...②c5!, but 12 f3 looks best.

12...②e4 13 豐e5 ②xc3+ 14 bxc3 ②xg3 15 fxg3

15 豐xg3 b6! gives White nothing.

15...②g6! 16 hxg5

16 c5 豐e7 and 16 h5 ②c2 17 豐b5+ ②c8 18 罝d2 ②e4 are both good for Black.

16...豐xg5! 17 豐f4 罝ae8 18 罝d5 豐xf4 19 gxf4 b6!

Black is now clearly better, and won on move 59.

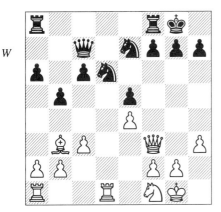

A. Alekhine – K. Junge
Krakow 1942

This position arose from a Ruy Lopez. It might look innocent enough, but Alekhine has preserved his Lopez bishop on the a2-f7 diagonal, while his knight is on an ideal circuit.

18 a4!

Prising open the a-file will add to Black's worries.

18...Rad8 19 Ng3 Nec8 20 axb5 axb5 21 Nf5

A pawn on f5 would be a powerful battering-ram against the black king.

21...Nb6

21...Kh8 enables Black to meet 22 Qe3 with 22...Nxf5 23 exf5 f6, but this is clearly very pleasant for White.

22 Qe3! Nxf5

22...Nbc4 23 Bxc4 Nxc4 24 Qc5 is hopeless for Black in view of his back-rank problems and the possible knight invasion on e7. For example, 24...Nxb2 25 Rxd8 Rxd8 26 Ra7, winning.

23 exf5 c5

After 23...Nd5 Alekhine intended the simple 24 Qf3.

24 f6 gxf6 25 Qh6 f5 26 Bxf7+! Qxf7 27 Rxd8 Na4 28 b3 1-0

Chess News in Brief

Alekhine wins a strong double-round tournament in Salzburg with 7½/10, ahead of Keres (6), Junge and P.Schmidt (5), Bogoljubow (3½) and Stoltz (3). Alekhine achieves two wins against Keres, but loses a game to the German teenager Klaus Junge.

Smyslov wins the Moscow Championship with 12/15, ahead of Boleslavsky (11), and Kotov and Lilienthal (both 10½).

Boleslavsky wins the Kuibyshev tournament with 9/11, ahead of Smyslov (8).

Najdorf wins the Mar del Plata tournament with 13½/17, ahead of Pilnik and Ståhlberg.

José Raúl Capablanca (born 1888; World Champion 1921-7) dies, in New York, from a stroke.

Rudolf Spielmann (born 1883) dies, in Sweden, where he had fled in the face of Nazi persecution.

Ilia Rabinovich (born 1891) dies as a result of malnutrition suffered during the siege of Leningrad.

World News in Brief

Japan seizes the Philippines, Singapore and Java, and makes inroads into Burma. US planes bomb Tokyo. The US Navy scores a major victory over the Japanese at Midway. The Japanese shell Australian cities, including Sydney. Japanese ground forces are forced to pull back in both New Guinea and Burma.

Germany sets in motion a plan to exterminate the 11 million Jews in Europe, starting the deportation of Jews to the Auschwitz concentration camp.

The Royal Air Force begins a heavy bombing campaign against German munitions factories.

Germany makes gains on the Russian Front, and advances on Stalingrad. After lengthy and intense fighting, Soviet forces start to gain the upper hand.

A German-led offensive in Egypt is effectively ended by the Allies' decisive victory at El Alamein.

In the USA, Enrico Fermi builds the first nuclear reactor.

In Germany, Wernher von Braun invents the rocket-propelled missile.

1943

Sverdlovsk becomes the centre of chess activity in the USSR

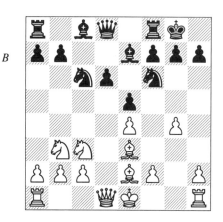

Vinogradov – I. Boleslavsky
Sverdlovsk Ch 1943

This position has arisen from a line of the Sicilian that was to become known as the Boleslavsky Variation. White has just played the aggressive thrust 9 g2-g4?!, but this does not turn out well.

9...a5! 10 g5

10 a4 ♘b4 gives Black good control of d5.

10...♘e8 11 ♘d5

Effectively forcing a swap of White's g-pawn for the black a-pawn. Instead, 11 h4 a4 12 ♘d2 a3 13 b3 ♘b4 affords Black excellent play.

11...♗xg5 12 ♗b6 ♕d7 13 ♖g1 f6 14 ♗g4 ♕f7 15 ♗xc8 ♖xc8 16 ♘xa5

It looks as if White has been forcibly achieving his strategic objectives. However, White's position is rather loose: his pieces are scattered and his king is exposed.

16...♘e7!

This move immediately solves the problem of the backward d-pawn.

17 c4

17 ♘c3 d5 was Boleslavsky's intention, e.g. 18 exd5 (or 18 ♘xd5 ♘xd5 19 exd5 ♘d6) 18...♘d6 with good counterplay.

17...♘xd5 18 ♕xd5 ♕xd5 19 exd5 ♗f4 20 b4

Black is intending to advance his kingside majority, so it is natural for White to try to do

likewise on the queenside, but his pawns will not be well enough supported. Otherwise, however, Black would play 20...f5 and 21...♘f6, and White will find it hard to advance his pawns at all.

20...f5 21 c5 dxc5 22 bxc5 ♘f6

The white pawns will now be broken up.

23 ♖d1 ♘d7 24 ♘xb7 ♖b8 25 ♘d8!?

25 c6 ♘xb6 26 d6 e4 is no good for White.

25...♘xc5! 26 ♗xc5 ♖fxd8 27 ♗e7 ♖d7 28 ♗g5 ♗xh2 29 ♖h1 ♗f4 30 ♗xf4 exf4

This ending holds no prospects for White; Black's kingside pawns are too strong.

31 ♖h3 ♖a8 32 a3 ♖a5 33 ♖hd3 ♔f7 34 ♔e2 h5 35 d6 ♖a6 36 ♖d4 g5 37 ♖c1 ♖dxd6 38 ♖c7+ ♔f6 39 ♖h7 ♔g6 40 ♖xd6+ ♖xd6 41 ♖h8 h4 42 a4 ♖e6+ 43 ♔f1 f3 44 a5 ♖a6 0-1

A strong double-round tournament in Sverdlovsk is won by Botvinnik with 10½/14, ahead of Makogonov (9), Smyslov and Kan (both 8).

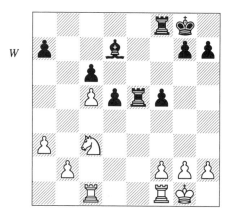

M. Botvinnik – A. Konstantinopolsky
Sverdlovsk 1943

It is impressive how skilfully Botvinnik keeps Black's bishop bad.

20 f4! ♖e7 21 ♖fe1 ♖fe8 22 ♖xe7 ♖xe7 23 ♔f2 ♔f7 24 ♖d1 ♖e8 25 ♖d2 h6 26 ♖e2 ♖b8 27 ♔e3 ♖b3 28 ♔d4

The king is ideally placed here, and frees the rook for action.

28...♔f6 29 ♘a2 ♖b8 30 b4 g5 31 g3 gxf4 32 gxf4 a6 33 ♘c3 ♖g8 34 a4 ♖g4 35 ♖f2 ♗e6 36 b5 axb5 37 axb5 cxb5 38 ♘xb5 ♖g1 39 ♘c3 ♔f7 40 ♖b2 ♖f1 41 ♘e2 ♖e1 42 ♔e5 d4 43 ♔xd4 ♔g6 44 ♘c3 ♔h5 45 ♖e2 ♖xe2 46 ♘xe2 ♔g4 47 ♔e5 ♗c8 48 ♘d4 h5 49 ♘xf5! ♗d7 50 ♘g7 ♗a4 51 f5 ♔g5 52 ♘e6+ 1-0

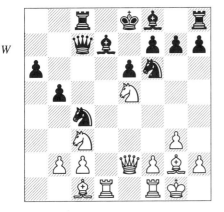

G. Ravinsky – V. Panov
Moscow Ch 1943/4

Black has grabbed a pawn at the cost of development and central control.

17 ♘xd7 ♘xd7 18 ♘d5 ♕a7 19 ♘f4

The threat of 20 ♘xe6 is quite hard to meet.

19...♘ce5 20 ♖xd7! ♘xd7 21 ♘xe6! fxe6 22 ♕xe6+ ♗e7 23 ♖e1 ♕c5

Black's last few moves have all been forced. White must now find a way to force the pace. He would like to play ♗g5, so...

24 b4! ♘f8 25 ♕g4!

The black queen cannot simultaneously defend c8, e7 and g7, so something has to give.

25...♕c3 26 ♖xe7+!

The start of a brutal king-hunt.

26...♔xe7 27 ♗g5+ ♔d6 28 ♕d1+ ♔c7 29 ♗f4+ ♔b6 30 ♕d6+ ♔a7 31 ♕e7+ ♖c7 32 ♗xc7

32 ♗e3+ ♔b8 33 ♕d8+ ♖c8 34 ♕b6# is a quicker mate.

32...♕a1+ 33 ♗f1 ♘g6 34 ♕c5+ ♔b7 35 ♗a5 ♖f8 36 ♕b6+ 1-0

Chess News in Brief

Keres and Alekhine dominate a six-man double-round tournament at Salzburg, both scoring 7½/10.

Alekhine wins the Prague tournament with 17/19, ahead of Keres (14½) and Katetov (13).

Najdorf wins the Mar del Plata tournament with 11/13, ahead of Ståhlberg (10½).

Keres wins a relatively weak tournament in Madrid, scoring 13/14.

Vladimirs Petrovs (born 1908) dies in the Vorkuta *Gulag*, after being denounced for allegedly making derogatory comments about conditions in Soviet Latvia.

Robert (Bobby) Fischer [World Champion 1972-5] is born.

Lubomir (Lubosh) Kavalek [a leading Czech, and later US, player and trainer] is born.

World News in Brief

The Soviets break the 16-month siege of Leningrad, and complete a decisive victory at Stalingrad. It is the key turning point in the fighting on the Russian Front. Soviet forces subsequently regain much of their lost territory, including Kiev.

The Allies complete their victory in North Africa, and advance upon Italy. Mussolini falls from power, and Italy signs a secret armistice with the Allies. German troops occupy Rome; meanwhile the Allies take Naples. Italy declares war on Germany, and assists Tito's partisans in their fight against the Germans in Yugoslavia.

An Allied bombing campaign causes devastation in the Ruhr, Germany's main industrial area, and saturation bombing razes a substantial part of Hamburg.

Work begins on constructing Colossus, the world's first electronic computer, at Bletchley Park (see page 82), in England. It is to be used to crack the secret codes used by the Germans. Work at Bletchley Park has already provided priceless information about German plans, enabling shipping convoys to be better protected, and shedding light on German troop movements.

1944

Less chess as the war escalates

Botvinnik wins the 13th USSR Championship, scoring 12½/16, two points ahead of second-placed Smyslov.

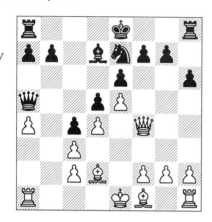

V. Smyslov – M. Botvinnik
USSR Ch, Moscow 1944

Black can be happy with his prospects. The a4-pawn will inevitably fall, while White's kingside play is not sufficient compensation.

15 h4 ♗xa4! 16 h5 ♕b5!

The threat of 17...♗xc2 disrupts White's play.

17 ♔d1 ♖c8! 18 ♗c1

White cannot ignore Black's queenside play: 18 ♗e2 ♖c6 19 g4? loses to 19...♗xc2+ 20 ♔xc2 ♕b3+ 21 ♔c1 ♖b6.

18...♖c6 19 ♗e2?!

19 g4 ♖a6 20 ♖a2 is better.

19...♖a6 20 ♔d2

White is forced to cut off his own bishop's action on the c1-h6 diagonal.

20...0-0?!

Black should simplify by 20...♕d7 21 g4 ♗b5.

21 g4!

Threatening 22 g5.

21...f6 22 exf6 ♖xf6 23 ♕c7

The queen causes a surprising amount of chaos in the black position.

23...♖f7 24 ♕d8+ ♔h7 25 f4! ♕a5?!

Very risky, as White only needs a little time to drum up a deadly initiative by g5. It is time

for Black to bail out by 25...♕d7 26 ♕xd7 ♗xd7 27 ♖xa6 bxa6 with a likely draw.

26 ♕b8 ♘c6 27 ♕e8 ♖e7

27...♖xf4? loses to 28 g5 hxg5 29 ♕g6+.

28 ♕g6+?

28 ♕f8! ♕d8 (otherwise 29 g5 wins material) 29 ♕xd8 ♘xd8 30 g5 is good for White.

28...♔g8 29 ♗a3

29 g5 ♘xd4! is no good for White.

29...e5?!

29...♕c7! 30 ♖hf1 ♘b4!, threatening 31...♗e8 and 31...♗xc2, leaves Black in command.

30 fxe5?

30 dxe5 is better, as 30...♘d4 would not then come with the capture of a white pawn.

30...♘xd4! 31 ♗b4 ♕d8 32 ♕xa6

32 cxd4 ♖xg6 33 hxg6 c3+ works well for Black.

32...bxa6 33 cxd4 ♖b7! 34 ♖xa4 ♕g5+ 35 ♔d1 a5

35...c3! forces mate: 36 ♔e1 ♖f7 37 ♗xc3 ♕c1+ 38 ♗d1 ♕e3+ 39 ♗e2 ♖f2, etc.

36 ♗f3 ♖xb4 37 ♗xd5+ ♔f8 38 ♖f1+ ♔e8 39 ♗c6+ ♔e7 40 ♖xb4 ♕xg4+ 0-1

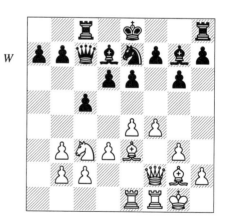

R. Kofman – E. Kogan
Kiev 1944

White has a good position, and turns this to account by vigorous kingside play.

16 f5! gxf5?!

16...exf5 17 exf5 ♗xf5 18 g4 ♗e6 19 ♘e4 gives White good play for the pawn.

17 exf5 ♘xf5 18 g4! ♗xc3 19 bxc3 ♗c6

19...♖g8 20 ♗d2 e5 (20...♖xg4? 21 ♕xf5) 21 gxf5 ♗c6 22 ♖e4 is no good for Black.

20 ♗xc6+

20 gxf5? allows Black's idea: 20...♖g8.

20...♕xc6 21 ♗g5! ♔d7 22 ♕xf5!

This queen sacrifice starts a 'see-saw'.

22...exf5 23 ♖e7+ ♔d8 24 ♖xf7+ ♔e8 25 ♖e7+ ♔d8

Or 25...♔f8 26 ♖xf5+ ♔g8 27 ♗h6, with unavoidable mate.

26 ♖xb7+ ♔e8 27 ♖e1+ ♔f8 28 ♗h6+ ♔g8 29 ♖g7+ 1-0

It is forced mate: 29...♔f8 30 ♖g5+ ♔f7 31 ♖xf5+ ♔g8 32 ♖e7.

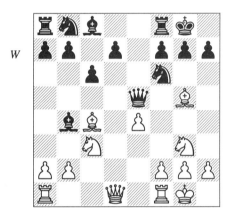

E. Rojahn – G. Klavestad
Correspondence 1944-5

10 f4! ♕c5+ 11 ♔h1 ♕xc4 12 ♗xf6 gxf6 13 ♖c1

White's ideas include ♘d5, ♘f5 and ♕g4+.

13...♕e6

13...♗xc3 14 ♘f5 ♔h8 15 ♖xc3 ♕b5 16 ♖h3 and White wins.

14 ♘d5! ♘a6

14...cxd5 15 ♘f5 forces Black to give up his queen, as 15...♔h8 16 ♕g4 ♖g8 17 ♖xc8 mates.

15 ♘f5 ♔h8 16 ♕h5

White intends ♖f3-h3; there is no adequate defence.

16...♖g8 17 ♖f3 ♖g6 18 ♖h3 ♔g8 19 ♕xh7+ ♔f8 20 ♕h8+ ♖g8 21 ♘xf6 1-0

Chess News in Brief

Pilnik and Najdorf win the Mar del Plata tournament with 12/15.

Alekhine wins a tournament at Gijon with 7½/8; the draw is against Arturo Pomar (born 1931).

Frank Marshall (born 1877) dies. He was a stalwart of American chess for decades, and among the world's top ten from 1904 to the mid-1920s. He played for and captained the American team in five Olympiads, earning a gold medal four times.

Vera Menchik (born 1906) dies, a civilian casualty of the German bombing of London. She was Women's World Champion from 1927, when the title was introduced, until the time of her death. Menchik's overall score in FIDE-organized Women's Championships was 78 wins, 4 draws and 1 loss: 80/83, or 96.4%. She was the first woman to perform with any degree of success in top-level 'male' tournaments, scoring victories over such players as Euwe, Reshevsky, Sultan Khan, Colle and Becker.

Vlastimil Hort [leading Czechoslovakian grandmaster] is born

Jørn Sloth [winner of the 8th Correspondence World Championship, 1975-80] is born.

World News in Brief

Germany occupies Hungary, and starts deporting Jews. Soviet forces move into Rumania. The Germans are forced out of the Crimea. Soviet forces recapture Minsk and the Baltic states, and later move into Hungary, Rumania, Poland and Yugoslavia.

The Allies capture Rome.

German V1 flying bombs cause devastation in London.

US planes bomb mainland Japan. Japan launches a major attack on China. US warships land in the Philippines.

The Normandy landings by the Allies (principally British, American and Canadian) mark the start of the invasion of Europe. Later, a large Allied force lands on France's Mediterranean coast. The Allies, including the Free French under General de Gaulle, liberate Paris. Allied forces push on into Belgium and the Netherlands.

1945

The USSR dominates the first post-war chess matches

Botvinnik routs the opposition at the 14th USSR Championship, scoring 15/17, three points clear of second-placed Boleslavsky, who is in turn two points clear of Bronstein. Keres is barred from playing because he had been in enemy territory during the war.

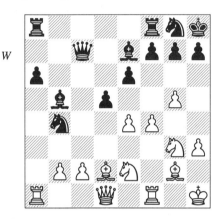

W

A. Tolush – A. Kotov
USSR Ch, Moscow 1945

Tolush, a feared attacking player, spots the vulnerability of the g7-square, and targets it consistently over the forthcoming moves.

20 ♗c3! dxe4 21 ♘h5 f6 22 ♘xg7!

This sacrifice is the type that can hardly be decided upon by analysis alone; Tolush's intuitive feel for the attack must have told him that he would get more than enough compensation for the piece.

22...♗xe2

22...♔xg7 23 ♘d4 ♗c4 24 ♗xe4 and 25 ♕h5 gives White a strong attack.

22...♖ad8 23 ♘d4 ♖xd4 24 ♕xd4 ♗xf1 25 ♘xe6 ♗xg2+ 26 ♔xg2 is awkward for Black.

23 ♕xe2 ♔xg7 24 ♗xe4 ♘d5 25 ♕h5

White's pieces coordinate superbly, leaving Black defenceless.

25...♖fd8 26 ♖g1!? ♗c5 27 gxf6++ ♔f8 28 ♖xg8+ ♔xg8 29 ♗xh7+ ♔f8

29...♕xh7 30 f7+ ♕xf7 31 ♕h8#.

30 ♕g6 ♘xf6 31 ♕xf6+ ♕f7 32 ♕h6+ ♔e7 33 ♕g5+ ♔d7 34 ♕xc5 ♕xh7 35 ♖d1+ ♔e8

36 ♕c6+ ♔f8 37 ♗b4+ ♔f7 38 ♕c7+ ♔g6 39 f5+!

Forcing mate.

39...♔h6 40 ♕f4+ ♔g7 41 ♕g5+ 1-0

The USA-USSR radio match (1st-4th September) is the first international sporting event after the end of the war. The USSR scores a decisive 15½-4½ victory. This is one of the Americans' few successes:

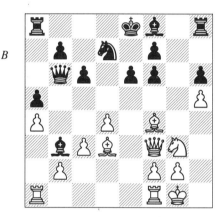

B

I. Horowitz – S. Flohr
USA-USSR radio match 1945

Flohr has followed up an uncharacteristically aggressive opening with some slightly passive play, and is now in trouble. His next move, lashing out, does not help.

16...e5?! 17 ♗e3 ♗d5 18 ♗e4 ♕b3 19 dxe5 fxe5 20 ♖ad1 ♗xe4 21 ♕xe4 ♕e6 22 ♖d2 ♘f6 23 ♕f3 ♖g8

Black has to some extent stabilized the position, but the problem of his exposed king and ragged pawns remains.

24 ♖fd1 ♖g4?!

This allows some crisp blows..

25 ♘f5! e4 26 ♗b6!

The mate threat on d8 seals matters.

26...♖xg2+

26...♗e7 27 ♕xg4 ♘xg4 28 ♘g7+ wins.

27 ♕xg2 ♕xf5 28 ♖d8+ ♖xd8 29 ♖xd8+ ♔e7 30 ♕g3 ♘d7 31 ♗c7 ♕d5 32 c4 ♕g5 33

♕xg5+ hxg5 34 ♖a8 ♔e6 35 ♗xa5 f5 36 ♗c3 f4 37 a5 g4 38 b4 f3 39 ♗d2 ♔f7 40 ♖a7 g3 41 ♖xb7 1-0

Reshevsky wins the Pan American tournament in Hollywood, with 10½/12, ahead of Fine (9) and Pilnik (8½).

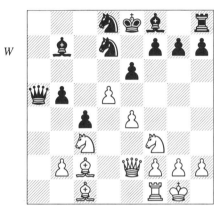

R. Fine – H. Steiner
Pan American, Hollywood 1945

White now plays forcefully to drive home his obvious advantage.

16 ♘d4 b4

16...♗a6 17 dxe6 is very good for White, since 17...fxe6? allows 18 ♘dxb5.

17 ♘cb5 e5 18 ♕xc4! exd4 19 ♘c7+ ♔e7 20 e5! ♘xe5?!

20...♘c5 puts up better resistance.

21 ♖e1 f6 22 d6+! ♔xd6 23 ♘b5+ ♕xb5

23...♔e7 24 ♖xe5+! fxe5 25 ♗g5+ mates.

24 ♕xb5 ♔c7 25 ♕a5+ 1-0

Chess News in Brief

Emil Richter wins the Prague tournament with 7/10, ahead of Opočensky and Pachman (both 6½).

Smyslov becomes Moscow Champion, scoring 13/16, ahead of Ragozin (11) and Lilienthal (10½).

Klaus Junge (born 1924) is killed in action, three weeks before fighting ceases. He had been born in Chile, but his parents decided to bring their three sons to Germany, in the hope that they would receive a better education. All three perished in the war.

World News in Brief

Budapest and Warsaw are taken by the advancing Red Army. Subsequently Auschwitz is taken, and the scale of the Nazi atrocities becomes clear to the world.

The Allies carry out a massive air strike on Dresden. 40,000-80,000 people die as a firestorm engulfs the city.

The USA recapture the Philippines and British forces make gains in Burma. Vietnam and Cambodia declare their independence.

Allied forces advance into Germany from the west.

Mussolini is executed and Hitler commits suicide. Germany surrenders. The victorious Allies intend to partition Germany into four districts, to be controlled by Britain, France, the USA and the USSR. The German capital, Berlin, is to be partitioned likewise. The USSR is set to dominate Eastern Europe.

The United Nations Organization is formed.

In the USA, atomic bombs are tested. Subsequently, atomic bombs are dropped on two Japanese cities, Hiroshima and Nagasaki. Japan surrenders. World War II is over. The USSR reoccupies territory in Manchuria, and Korea is divided between the USA and the USSR.

The Allies fail to reach agreement on the new borders for Germany. The USSR aims to make its own atom bomb. The situation in Europe remains tense.

Britain grants Syria and Lebanon independence, and agrees to make India independent.

In the USA, an electronic computer is built. At the time, it is regarded as the world's first computer, since the Colossus machine (see page 91) was dismantled on the orders of Churchill once its work was completed, and the world is not to know of its existence, or that of the code-breaking station, until the 1970s.

1946

Alekhine dies • Botvinnik wins the first major international tournament since the 1930s

The first major post-war international tournament takes place at Groningen. Botvinnik wins with 14½/19, ahead of Euwe (14), Smyslov (12½), and Najdorf and Szabo (both 11½). This is one of Botvinnik's losses:

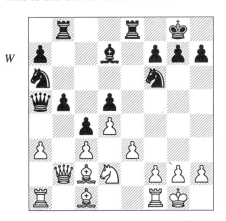

W

M. Najdorf – M. Botvinnik
Groningen 1946

White's position appears rather passive, but he has long-term chances due to his central majority and bishop-pair.

18 ♘f3!

Avoiding 18 f3 ♖xe3 19 ♘e4 ♘xe4! 20 ♗xe3 ♘xc3, which is good for Black.

18...♕c7 19 ♘e5 ♗e6 20 f3

The centre pawns rumble forwards.

20...♘c5 21 ♗d2 ♘a4?!

This is all strongly reminiscent of the game Botvinnik-Capablanca, AVRO 1938 (the finish of which is on page 80). 21...♘cd7 22 ♘xd7 ♗xd7 23 ♖ae1 ♗c6 24 ♕b1 ♕b7 is more solid, but then 25 ♖e2, with ideas of g4 or ♗e1-h4, is promising for White.

22 ♕b1 ♖b6 23 ♕e1 ♘d7 24 ♕h4 ♘f8 25 e4! f6 26 ♘g4 ♘g6 27 ♕h5 ♕f7 28 ♖ae1 ♖bb8 29 ♘e3 ♘e7?

29...♘b6!? is a better way to support d5.

30 ♕h4

Threatening 31 exd5.

30...f5

Hoping to block the position, but Najdorf is having none of it.

31 g4! f4

31...g6 fails since after 32 exf5 gxf5 33 gxf5 the d5-pawn is too weak.

32 exd5!

Now Black loses material.

32...♘g6 33 dxe6 ♖xe6 34 ♗xg6 hxg6 35 ♘g2 ♖be8 36 ♖xe6 ♖xe6 37 ♘xf4 ♖f6 38 ♕g5 ♘xc3 39 ♗xc3 ♖xf4 40 ♔g2 1-0

A further USA-USSR match (this time played over the board, in Moscow) again confirms the Soviets' superiority, though the margin of victory is reduced to 12½-7½ – with hindsight quite a success for the USA.

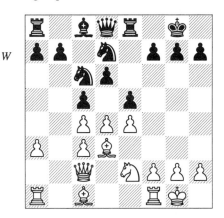

W

A. Denker – V. Smyslov
USSR-USA team match, Moscow 1946

Structurally, Black is doing well, but White has kingside chances.

12 f4 b6 13 ♗e3

13 d5 ♘a5 14 f5 b5! gives Black excellent counterplay.

13...♗a6 14 fxe5

This exchange gives Black's knights the d6-square in the long run, but after 14 d5 ♘a5 Black will gain the e5-square by ...exf4.

14...dxe5 15 d5 ♘a5 16 ♕a2 ♘f8 17 ♘g3 ♘g6

For now, this knight patrols the kingside, but its long-term sights are on the d6-square.

18 ♕e2 ♘b7 19 ♘f5 ♘d6 20 g3

Planning to attack by pushing the h-pawn.

20...f6 21 ♘xd6

21 h4 ♘xf5 22 ♖xf5 ♘h8 23 h5 h6 24 ♖af1 ♘f7 stabilizes the kingside, and Black will soon exploit White's weak pawns.

21...♕xd6 22 h4 ♘e7 23 a4 ♗c8 24 ♔h2

White wants to prevent ...♗h3 and ...♕d7.

24...a5! 25 ♕g2?! ♗g4 26 ♗e2 ♗xe2 27 ♕xe2

White has traded his 'bad' bishop, but now Black's minor piece is far better than White's.

27...♖ad8 28 ♖ab1 ♘c8! 29 h5 ♖f8 30 ♖f2 ♖f7 31 h6 g6 32 ♖bf1 ♕e7 33 ♕g4 ♘d6

The culmination of Black's strategy.

34 ♕e6 ♘xe4 35 ♕xb6 f5! 36 ♖b2 f4

While White has been regaining pawns, Black has whipped up a fierce kingside attack.

37 ♕e6 fxe3 38 ♖xf7 ♕xf7 39 ♕xe5 ♘f6 40 ♖b8 ♘g4+ 41 ♔h3 ♘xe5 42 ♖xd8+ ♕f8 43 ♖xf8+ ♔xf8 0-1

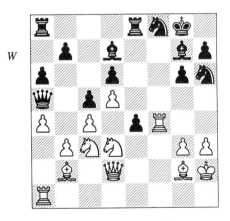

V. Ragozin – I. Solin
Helsinki 1946

20 b4! e3

20...cxb4 21 ♘xe4 is very good for White as the g7-bishop will be exchanged off.

21 ♕c1 ♕c7 22 ♘e4 ♗f5 23 bxc5 ♗xe4

23...dxc5 24 d6 ♕f7 25 ♘g5 ♕d7 26 ♗d5+ ♔h8 27 ♕c3! ♗xc3 28 ♗xc3+ ♕g7 29 ♗xg7+ ♔xg7 30 ♘xc5 is very good for White.

24 cxd6 ♗xb2 25 ♕xb2! ♕xc4 26 ♖c1 ♕xd5

26...♕xd3 loses to 27 ♖c7.

27 ♖c7 ♘e6 28 ♖xe4 ♕xd6

28...♘f5? 29 ♖xh7 costs Black his queen.

29 ♖xb7 ♘f5

This sets up an exciting finish.

30 ♕f6 ♕xg3+ 31 ♔h1 ♘eg7 32 ♖g4 ♕d6

32...♖f8 33 ♕xg7+ ♘xg7 34 ♖xg3 should be winning for White.

33 ♖xg7+ ♔h8 34 ♖h4! ♘xh4

34...♘g3+ does White no real harm: 35 ♔h2 ♘f1+ 36 ♔g1 ♕h2+ 37 ♔xf1 e2+ 38 ♔f2.

35 ♕xd6?! 1-0

Chess News in Brief

Najdorf dominates the Mar del Plata tournament, scoring 16/18.

Najdorf wins the Barcelona tournament with 11½/13, ahead of Yanofsky (9½).

Tigran Petrosian wins a match against the great study composer Genrikh Kasparian by a score of 8-6.

A radio match is contested between the UK and the USSR. The British perform surprisingly well, losing only by 6-18.

Alekhine (born 1892) dies in Estoril, Portugal. This scuppers a planned match against Botvinnik, and raises the question of how the World Championship should be decided.

Arturo Pomar (born 1931) is Spanish Champion for the first of seven times.

World News in Brief

Churchill introduces the term 'Iron Curtain' for the frontier across Europe, separating the capitalist West from the Soviet-dominated, communist East.

In Japan, Emperor Hirohito declares his divinity to be a "false conception", opening the way for a more modern method of government.

China moves towards all-out civil war between the Communists and the Nationalists.

Fighting between Hindus and Moslems leaves 3,000 dead in Calcutta.

France declares martial law in Vietnam.

A British crackdown on the illegal immigration of Jews to Palestine sparks terrorist attacks from Zionist groups.

A new type of pen, named after its inventor, Laszlo Biro, becomes available.

1947

FIDE organizes new World Championship

Keres (now 'rehabilitated') wins the 15th USSR Championship with 14/19, ahead of Boleslavsky (13), Bondarevsky and Smyslov (both 12). Botvinnik does not play.

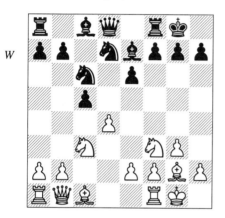

W

P. Keres – G. Levenfish
USSR Ch, Leningrad 1947

Black has spent several tempi trying to create counterplay, and while he manages to dissolve White's centre, the time spent takes its toll.
  11 dxc5 ♘xc5
  11...♗xc5 12 ♘g5! is good for White, as after 12...♗f6?, 13 ♗xc6! bxc6 14 ♘ce4 wins material.
  12 ♖d1 ♕a5 13 ♗d2 ♘d7
  Black blocks his own development in order to meet the threat of 14 ♘d5.
  14 ♘e4 ♕f5 15 ♗c3
  White has control of both long diagonals.
  15...♖d8
  15...♘b6 16 ♘d4 ♘xd4 17 ♗xd4 ♘d5 18 ♕c1! keeps Black under pressure.
  16 ♘d4 ♘xd4 17 ♖xd4 ♘b6 18 ♖xd8+ ♗xd8
  The exchanges have not eased Black's problems.
  19 ♕d1
  19 ♘d6, inviting further exchanges, is a simpler way to make progress.
  19...♗e7 20 ♕d4 ♕g6 21 ♘c5 ♘d5!? 22 ♖d1 b6

Allowing a combination, but there was nothing better.
  23 ♘xe6! ♗xe6
  23...fxe6? 24 ♗xd5 exd5 25 ♕xd5+ wins the black rook.
  24 ♗xd5 ♖d8 25 e4 ♗g4 26 ♖d3 ♔h8
  Black is hoping for some sort of miracle.
  27 ♕e5! ♗f6
  White also wins after 27...♗d6 28 ♗b3! h5 29 ♖xd6 ♖xd6 30 ♕e8+ ♔h7 31 ♗xf7.
  28 ♕c7 ♖d7 29 ♕c6 ♗h3 30 ♗e6! 1-0

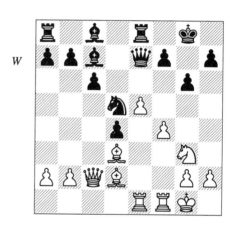

W

A. Tolush – V. Alatortsev
USSR Ch, Leningrad 1947

White has excellent play for the sacrificed pawn, and he pushes home his advantage in exemplary fashion.
  19 f5! ♗xe5 20 fxg6 f6
  Either recapture is met by 21 ♗xg6.
  21 ♗h6!
  The threat is 22 g7, followed by ♗xh7+.
  21...♘e3
  21...hxg6 22 ♗xg6 ♖d8 exposes Black to a strong attack, but may be the best chance. After 21...♘b4 22 ♗c4+ ♘d5 23 ♘h5 f5 24 ♗f4 ♕d6 25 ♗xd5+ cxd5 26 ♕a4 White wins material.
  22 ♖xe3! dxe3 23 g7
  Black has no adequate defence.
  23...f5 24 ♘xf5!

Avoiding 24 ♗c4+? ♗e6 25 ♘xf5 ♕d7 26 ♗xe6+ ♖xe6 27 ♘e7+?? ♕xe7 28 ♖f8+ ♖xf8 29 gxf8♕+ ♕xf8 30 ♗xf8 e2!, when White loses.

24...♗xf5 25 ♖xf5! ♗xg7

Otherwise, a check on the a2-g8 diagonal is instantly decisive.

26 ♖g5 e2 27 ♗xe2 ♕e3+ 28 ♔h1 ♕xg5 29 ♗xg5 ♔h8 30 h4 ♖e5 31 ♗f4 ♖a5 32 ♕e4 ♖f8 33 ♗d3 ♖h5 34 ♗g5 ♗xb2 35 g4 1-0

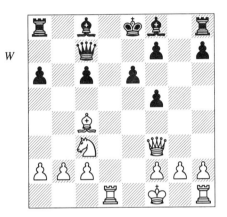

R. Nezhmetdinov – A. Suetin
Russian Ch, Kuibyshev 1947

Black's position is rather loose, but White's king is not ideally placed. Nezhmetdinov decides to attack without further ado. This has its risks but a slower approach would give Black time to organize his counterplay.

15 g4!? fxg4 16 ♕xg4 ♗b7

Risky, but not necessarily bad.

17 ♗xe6!?

17 ♕h5 and 17 ♕d4 are less dramatic, but may give better chances of advantage.

17...fxe6 18 ♕xe6+ ♗e7?

This loses. Black should play 18...♕e7 19 ♕f5 ♗c8 exploiting the looseness of White's kingside. Then 20 ♕h5+ (20 ♕f3 ♕c5 is unclear) 20...♕f7 21 ♕e5+ ♕e7 22 ♕h5+ repeats (not, however, 22 ♕xh8?? ♗h3+ 23 ♔g1 ♕g5#).

19 ♘e4 ♗c8 20 ♘f6+ ♔f8 21 ♖d7?

21 ♘d7+! ♔e8 22 ♖g1 wins: 22...♗xd7 23 ♖g8+ ♖xg8 24 ♕xg8+ ♗f8 25 ♖e1+ ♗e6 26 ♖xe6+, etc.

21...♗xd7?

21...♕d6! gives Black a fighting chance, e.g. 22 ♕xd6 ♗xd6 23 ♘xh7+ (23 ♖xd6? ♔e7 gives Black the better of it after 24 ♘e4 ♗h3+ or 24 ♖xc6 ♗h3+) 23...♖xh7 24 ♖xh7 ♗e6.

22 ♘xd7+ ♔e8 23 ♘f6+ ♔d8

23...♔f8 loses to 24 ♖g1.

24 ♔e2 ♕d6 25 ♖d1 ♕xd1+ 26 ♔xd1 ♗xf6 27 ♕xf6+ ♔c7 28 ♕e7+ ♔b6 29 c4 1-0

Chess News in Brief

The USSR joins FIDE, enabling the latter to organize a credible World Championship and a cycle of qualifying events.

Botvinnik wins the Chigorin Memorial tournament in Moscow, with 11/15, ahead of Ragozin (10½), and Boleslavsky and Smyslov (both 10).

Svetozar Gligorić wins the Warsaw tournament with 8/9, ahead of Boleslavsky, Pachman, Smyslov and Sajtar (all 6).

Ståhlberg wins a six-man double-round tournament at Buenos Aires and La Plata, with 8/10, ahead of Najdorf (6½) and Eliskases (5½).

Keres wins a strong tournament in Pärnu with 9½/13, ahead of Kotov (9) and Lilienthal (8½).

The first zonal tournaments are played, in FIDE's new World Championship cycle.

Gligorić wins the Yugoslav Championship for the first of 11 times.

World News in Brief

India is granted independence as two separate states, India and Pakistan. The latter is a Moslem state, but the partitioning, and consequent mass migration, prompts widespread violence, in which about 400,000 people are killed.

In the USA, plutonium fission is discovered, paving the way for the generation of nuclear power.

Bell Laboratories develop the transistor, to replace the vacuum tubes that hitherto have been used in electronic devices. The transistor, a solid-state electronic component, is faster, lighter and far smaller.

In the USA, a manned aircraft breaks the sound barrier for the first time. The supersonic aircraft, a Bell X-1 rocketplane, is piloted by Chuck Yeager.

1948

Botvinnik convincingly wins the World Championship

After much wrangling about the format and composition of an event to determine the World Champion, a quintuple-round match-tournament is played in the Hague and Moscow. Mikhail Botvinnik wins convincingly with 14/20, ahead of Smyslov (11), Keres, Reshevsky (both 10½) and Euwe (4). Botvinnik's large margin of victory is largely due to his 4-1 score against Keres. The tournament was intended to have six players, but Fine withdrew, apparently amid dissatisfaction with the event's organization, and, in particular, the fact that half the tournament would be played in the USSR.

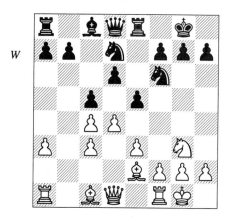

W

M. Botvinnik – P. Keres
World Ch, The Hague/Moscow 1948

This game has attracted considerable attention from those who argue that Keres was under orders to let Botvinnik win the world title. However, Keres's much-criticized plan of opening the position in search of good posts for his knights is one that had brought him considerable success in similar positions against lesser players. However, Botvinnik handles the position very well, and Black is crushed.

11 f3!
Preparing e4, as Black's knight being on d7 (rather than c6) reduces the pressure on d4.
11...cxd4?!
This does not work out, but Black's game was already difficult.

12 cxd4 ♞b6 13 ♗b2 exd4?!
13...♗e6, trying to keep the centre blocked, is a possible improvement.
14 e4!
This excellent move stops Black playing ...d5 and keeps the a1-h8 diagonal open. Black will have grave difficulty defending g7.
14...♗e6 15 ♖c1 ♖e7
15...♖c8 16 ♕xd4 ♞a4 17 ♗a1 ♞c5 gives Black slightly more of a grip on the position.
16 ♕xd4 ♕c7 17 c5! dxc5 18 ♖xc5 ♕f4
Or 18...♕d8 19 ♕e3 with powerful threats.
19 ♗c1 ♕b8 20 ♖g5! ♞bd7
20...♞e8 21 ♞h5 brings intolerable pressure to bear on g7.
21 ♖xg7+! ♔xg7 22 ♞h5+ ♔g6 23 ♕e3 1-0

The first Interzonal tournament is played, at Saltsjöbaden. This being the first such event, many of the players are nominated, rather than qualifying via zonal events. David Bronstein wins with 13½/19, ahead of Szabo (12½) and Boleslavsky (12). There are later disagreements about how many players should qualify for the Candidates tournament.

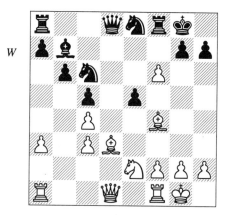

W

A. Lilienthal – M. Najdorf
Interzonal tournament, Saltsjöbaden 1948

Black has just played the highly ambitious 14...e6-e5?, which meets with a stunning tactical rejoinder.

15 fxg7! ☐xf4 16 ᘀxf4 exf4 17 ♗xh7+ ♚xh7 18 ♕h5+ ♚xg7 19 ☐ad1

It is surprising that Black, with three pieces for a rook, has no adequate defence here.

19...♕f6

Black returns a piece immediately, but to no avail. There was nothing significantly better: 19...♕c8 20 ☐fe1 ♚g8 21 ♕d5+ ♚f8 22 ☐e4; 19...♕c7 20 ♕g4+ and ☐d7.

20 ☐d7+ ♚f8 21 ☐xb7 ᘀd8 22 ☐d7 ᘀf7 23 ♕d5 ☐b8?

23...ᘀe5 24 ♕xa8 ᘀxd7 25 ☐e1 keeps Black tied up.

24 ☐e1 f3? 25 ☐e3 1-0

Szabo wins the Budapest tournament with 12/15, ahead of Gligorić (10½).

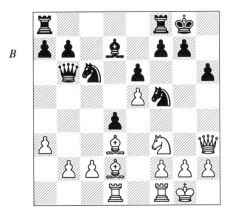

L. Steiner – G. Füster
Budapest 1948

Black is under pressure on the kingside, and tries to change the course of the game by a little tactical trick.

15...ᘀe3!? 16 ♗c1! ᘀxd1 17 ♗xh6!

A resolute response: White goes for mate.

17...f5 18 exf6 ☐xf6 19 ♗g5 ☐f5 20 ☐xd1

White is winning. He can easily recoup his material, and still has a powerful attack.

20...☐af8 21 g4! ☐5f6 22 ♕h7+ ♚f7 23 ♗xf6 ♚xf6 24 ♕h4+ 1-0

Najdorf wins the Venice tournament with 11½/13. Euwe is in 4th place.

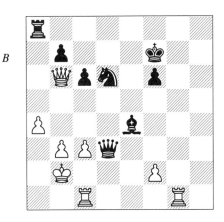

S. Tartakower – M. Euwe
Venice 1948

38...♕d2+ 39 ♚a3 ᘀc4+! 40 bxc4 ☐xa4+! 41 ♚xa4 ♕a2+ 42 ♚b4 ♕b2+ 0-1

Chess News in Brief

Bronstein and Kotov share the 16th USSR Championship, scoring 12/18, ahead of Furman (11).

Pal Benko (born 1928) wins the Hungarian Championship for the first time.

Chess is being encouraged in Argentina during the Peron era.

World News in Brief

Israel is created, and is immediately attacked by its Arab neighbours.

There is a rift in relations between Yugoslavia and the USSR, as Tito's regime adopts a more liberal form of communism.

Communists seize power in Czechoslovakia.

Mahatma Gandhi, the man whose policy of peaceful protest helped India towards independence, is assassinated.

A Soviet blockade on the sectors of Berlin under the control of the Western Allies (West Berlin) forces the Western powers to fly in massive amounts of food and other essential supplies.

North Korea declares its independence.

In Britain, the National Health Service, which offers free health care to the public, is started by the Labour government.

1949

David Bronstein emerges as a new star

Bronstein and Smyslov share the 17th USSR Championship, scoring 13/19, ahead of Geller and Taimanov (12½). Keres finishes a disappointing 8th, while Petrosian has a rough debut, including a 13-move loss to Kotov in the first round. A game from the event:

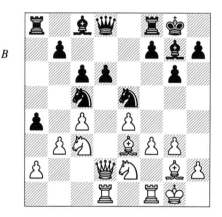

A. Kotov – E. Geller
USSR Ch, Moscow 1949

White has threats against c5 and d6, so it is the moment of truth for Black – he must sacrifice.

15...axb3! 16 ♗xc5 ♘xc4 17 ♕c1 bxa2

Bronstein suggested the interesting queen sacrifice 17...b2 18 ♕c2 dxc5 19 ♖xd8 ♖xd8.

18 ♘xa2 ♕a5 19 ♕xc4 ♗e6 20 ♕c1 dxc5

Black has just two pawns for the piece, but they will become a queenside avalanche.

21 ♘ac3 b5 22 ♘b1

White should strive for activity with 22 f4, as after the meek text-move, Black's pawns become too powerful.

22...b4 23 ♘f4 ♗b3 24 ♖d6?! c4! 25 ♖xc6 c3

The pawns cannot be eliminated even at the cost of a piece.

26 ♘d5 ♗xd5 27 exd5 ♕xd5 28 f4

White has freed his position, but his pieces are uncoordinated and his king exposed.

28...♕d4+ 29 ♔h1 ♖a2! 30 ♗f3 ♖b2 31 f5 ♗e5 32 ♕e1 ♖d8 33 ♗e4

Black has no objection to 33 ♕e4 ♕xe4 34 ♗xe4 ♖d4, when his pawns will decide.

33...♔g7!?

White can do nothing constructive, so Black improves his position.

34 f6+ ♔g8

Now Black has the clear plan of advancing his h-pawn.

35 ♖a6 h5

35...c2 also wins.

36 ♖a5 h4 37 ♗xg6 ♖xh2+!? 38 ♔xh2 ♗xg3+ 39 ♕xg3 hxg3+ 40 ♔h3 fxg6 0-1

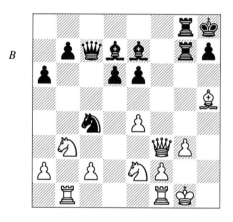

A. Fuderer – S. Gligorić
Yugoslav Ch, Zagreb 1949

Black has an excellent position, and now finds a way to break open more lines toward the white king.

25...d5! 26 exd5 ♗d6!

An instructive move – Black goes for maximum activity.

27 ♔h1

27 dxe6 ♗xe6 28 ♕f6 might, despite its greedy appearance, be a better way to cause Black inconvenience.

27...exd5 28 ♕c3 ♗e5 29 ♘bd4 ♗h3 30 ♖fe1 ♕d6 31 ♗f3 ♕h6 32 ♔g1 ♘d2 33 ♖bd1 ♘e4 34 ♗xe4 dxe4 35 ♕d2 ♕h4!

Now Black wins by force.

36 ♔h1 ♗xg3

36...♗f1+ 37 ♔g1 ♗xg3 and 36...♗g2++ 37 ♔xg2 ♗xg3 are also clear wins.

37 fxg3 ♖xg3 38 ♘xg3 ♖xg3 39 ♖e2

39 ♕h2 ♗g2+ 40 ♔g1 ♗f3+ wins.

39...♗g2++ 40 ♔g1 ♗f3+ 41 ♔f2 ♖g2++
0-1

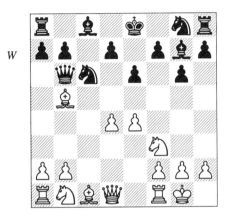

N. Rossolimo – A. O'Kelly de Galway
Oldenburg 1949

White solves the problem of his loose d4-pawn by sacrificing it, to exploit his better development and Black's weak dark squares.

8 ♘a3! ♘xd4 9 ♘c4 ♘xf3+ 10 ♕xf3 ♕c7 11 ♗f4 e5 12 ♘xe5!

White can already begin the decisive combination.

12...♗xe5 13 ♖ac1 ♕b8

After 13...♕d6 14 ♖fd1 ♕e6 15 ♗xe5 ♕xe5 16 ♖xc8+ ♖xc8 17 ♗xd7+ White emerges material up.

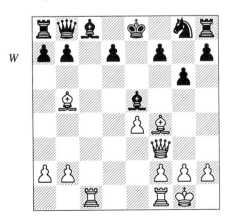

14 ♖xc8+! ♕xc8 15 ♗xe5 f6 16 ♗xf6 ♘xf6 17 ♕xf6 ♖f8 18 ♕e5+

18 ♕e6+ ♔d8 19 ♖d1 is even better.

18...♔d8

18...♔f7 19 ♗a4 and ♗b3+.

19 ♕g5+ ♔e8 20 ♖c1 ♕d8

20...♕b8 is a little more robust, but White still wins as he pleases.

21 ♕e5+ ♕e7 22 ♗xd7+! ♔f7 23 ♗e6+ ♔e8 24 ♖c7 1-0

Chess News in Brief

Szabo wins the Venice tournament with 11½/15, ahead of Rossolimo (10½) and Prins (10).

Ståhlberg wins the Trenčianske Teplice tournament with 14/19, ahead of Szabo and Pachman (both 13½).

Hector Rossetto wins the Mar del Plata tournament with 13/17 ahead of Guimard and Eliskases (both 12).

Szabo and Rossolimo dominate the Hastings tournament (1949/50), scoring 8/9 and 7½ respectively, ahead of Euwe (5½) and Evans (5).

World News in Brief

The Federal Republic of Germany is created. It comprises the British, French and American sectors of Germany. A Soviet proposal to re-unify Germany is rejected by the Western Allies. The Soviet sector becomes a communist state, the German Democratic Republic (East Germany).

The Communists take control of China. The defeated Nationalists establish their capital on the island of Formosa (Taiwan).

The USSR develops its own atomic bomb.

The North Atlantic Treaty Organization (NATO) is formed. It is comprised of the USA and several Western European nations, and is a defensive military alliance to protect against the perceived threat from the USSR.

A system for broadcasting colour television is devised.

The first non-stop round-the-world flight is made by Captain James Gallagher in a Boeing B-50A. During the 23,453 mile (37,743 km) journey, which takes 94 hours, the plane is refuelled four times in flight.

1950

Chess and Politics mix • Bronstein edges out Boleslavsky in Candidates play-off

The first Candidates tournament is held in Budapest. The Americans, Reshevsky and Fine, are refused permission by the State Department to travel to Hungary. The tournament, a double-round ten-player event, ends in a tie between David Bronstein and Isaak Boleslavsky with 12/18, ahead of Smyslov (10) and Keres (9½). The Bronstein-Boleslavsky play-off (held in Moscow) is won by Bronstein (7½-6½), who thus becomes Botvinnik's challenger.

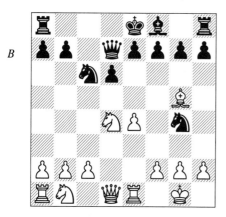

B

A. Lilienthal – M. Najdorf
Candidates tournament, Budapest 1950

Najdorf now embarks on an interesting plan of counterattack.

9...h6 10 ♗h4 g5!? 11 ♗g3 h5 12 ♘xc6

12 f3? h4 is good for Black.

12...bxc6 13 h3 h4 14 ♗xd6

It looks as if White is now winning a pawn, but Black has a cunning reply.

14...♘xf2! 15 ♔xf2?

This gets White into trouble. After 15 ♕d4 ♘xh3+ 16 gxh3 ♕xd6 17 ♕xh8 ♕g3+ Black gives perpetual check.

15...exd6 16 ♘d2 0-0-0 17 ♕g4

White's king is too exposed on the dark squares, so he now removes the queens. 17 ♕f3 is met by 17...♗g7 followed by ...f5.

17...♕xg4 18 hxg4 ♗g7 19 c3 ♗e5 20 ♔f3 ♖h6 21 ♖f1 ♖e8

White's king is under heavy attack.

22 ♘b3

22 ♔e2 ♗f4 23 ♔d3 ♖he6 ties White up.

22...d5! 23 ♔e2

23 exd5 loses material after 23...♗xc3.

23...♗f4 24 ♔d3 ♖xe4 25 ♖ae1 ♖he6 26 ♖xe4 ♖xe4 27 ♖f3 ♖e1 28 ♖f2 ♖e3+ 29 ♔c2 ♖g3 30 ♘d4 ♗e3! 31 ♖xf7 ♗xd4 32 cxd4 ♖xg2+ 33 ♔c3 ♖xg4 34 ♔b4 ♖xd4+ 35 ♔c5 ♖c4+ 36 ♔d6 h3 37 b3 ♖h4 0-1

Paul Keres wins the 18th USSR Championship with 11½/17, ahead of Aronin, Lipnitsky and Tolush (all 11). Smyslov, Boleslavsky and Geller are further down the field.

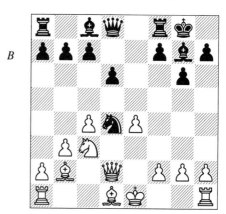

B

V. Alatortsev – I. Boleslavsky
USSR Ch, Moscow 1950

Black is ahead in development and has a more harmonious position.

13...f5 14 exf5 ♗xf5 15 ♘e2?

Now White's king gets caught in the centre.

15...♘xe2! 16 ♗xe2

16 ♗xg7 is strongly met by 16...♘f4!.

16...♗xb2 17 ♕xb2 ♕g5! 18 g3 ♖ae8! 19 0-0

White finally manages to castle, but only into a massive attack.

19...♗h3 20 f4

If the f1-rook moves, 20...♖xf2 is decisive.

20...♗xf1!! 21 fxg5 ♖xe2 22 ♕c3 ♗g2!
Threatening ...♗c6.

23 ♕d3
23 ♖e1 ♗h3 24 g4 ♖f3 25 ♕a1 ♖ef2 is winning for Black.

23...♗f3 24 ♖f1 ♖g2+ 25 ♔h1 ♗c6! 26 ♖xf8+ ♔xf8 27 ♕f1+ ♖f2+ 0-1

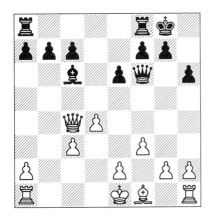

M. Beilin – I. Lipnitsky
Dzintari 1950

White's position looks suspect, but he only needs a few moves to seize the centre by e4 and consolidate.

13...e5! 14 d5?!
This is asking too much of White's position.

14...♗d7 15 ♕xc7 e4!
Ruling out White's ideas of e4 and opening lines for the black queen.

16 ♖c1 ♖ac8! 17 ♕xd7 e3
Directly targeting the white king.

18 ♕a4
Or 18 ♕b5 ♖xc3 19 ♖d1 ♖fc8 20 ♕b2 ♕a6, and White's king is caught.

18...♖xc3 19 ♖d1 ♖fc8 20 g3 ♖c1 21 ♗h3 ♕c3+ 22 ♔f1 ♖xd1+ 23 ♕xd1 ♕d2 24 ♔g2 ♖c1! 0-1

Chess News in Brief
With the Cold War in full swing, there is very little interaction between players from East and West.

Kotov wins the Venice tournament with 12½/15 ahead of Smyslov (12) and Rossolimo (10).

Keres wins the Szczawno Zdroj tournament with 14½/19 ahead of Szabo, Barcza and Taimanov (13½). One of Keres's games, Keres-Arlamowski, goes 1 e4 c6 2 ♘c3 d5 3 ♘f3 dxe4 4 ♘xe4 ♘f6 5 ♕e2 ♘bd7?? 6 ♘d6# (1-0).

Najdorf wins the Amsterdam tournament with 15/19, ahead of Reshevsky (14) and Ståhlberg (13½).

The first post-war Olympiad takes place in Dubrovnik, but is blighted by a boycott by the USSR and the rest of the Eastern bloc in view of the rift between Stalin and Tito. A solid team performance sees Yugoslavia taking first place with 45½/60, ahead of Argentina (43½), West Germany (40½) and the USA (40). The top scorers on first board are Najdorf and Unzicker. 16 teams compete.

Liudmilla Rudenko becomes the Women's World Champion after winning a tournament in Moscow (1949/50) to determine the fate of the title, vacant since Menchik's death in 1944.

FIDE introduces the Grandmaster and International Master titles, and awards them to players deemed, by general consent, to be worthy of them. Criteria are introduced by which players can earn these titles by means of their tournament results. Similar titles are already in common use, but hitherto there has been no formal mechanism by which they are awarded.

Ljubomir Ljubojević [Yugoslav grandmaster] is born.

World News in Brief
War breaks out in Korea, between North Korea, supported by China, and South Korea, backed by United Nations forces.

China and the USSR sign a mutual defence treaty. China occupies Tibet.

There is tension in Vietnam, as the Western nations recognize Emperor Bao Dai as leader, while communist nations recognize a rival communist regime, led by Ho Chi Minh.

Egypt demands that Britain pulls out of the Suez Canal Zone.

Anti-communist 'witch-hunts' begin in the USA, led by Senator Joseph McCarthy.

New racial legislation marks the start of Apartheid in South Africa.

An air crash in Wales kills 80 people.

1951

A rusty Botvinnik survives Bronstein's challenge

Botvinnik remains World Champion by drawing a match against Bronstein 12-12. Since winning the world title in 1948, Botvinnik has been largely inactive; to what extent his rustiness is a factor in the match is not clear. Bronstein was the better-prepared player going into the match, but Botvinnik's more practical approach pays dividends. Bronstein squanders some points, such as the famous ending in game 6. Game 9 is also remarkable: Botvinnik wins a rook, but the game is drawn.

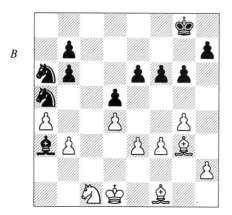

M. Botvinnik – D. Bronstein
World Ch match (game 23), Moscow 1951

Botvinnik, in a must-win situation (trailing 10½-11½ with two games to play), has so far been none too successful in generating winning chances.

35...♗xc1?

This pawn-grab gives Black no winning chances, and only serves to activate White's bishops.

36 ♔xc1 ♘xb3+ 37 ♔c2 ♘a5 38 ♔c3 ♔f7 39 e4 f5 40 gxf5 gxf5 41 ♗d3 ♔g6 42 ♗d6?!

The sealed move, but an error. White's plan is to put his bishops on b1 and d6, exchange on d5 and to play ♗a2, but this is the wrong move-order. Botvinnik preferred 42 ♗b1 fxe4 (42...♘c6 43 exd5 exd5 44 ♗a2 ♘e7 45 ♗h4) 43 fxe4 dxe4 44 ♗xe4+.

42...♘c6 43 ♗b1 ♔f6

43...♘a7! 44 exd5 exd5 45 ♗a2 b5 46 a5 b4+! enables Black to defend.

44 ♗g3!

Now Black has no constructive moves.

44...fxe4

44...♘ab4 is met by 45 ♗e5+! ♔g6 46 ♗d6.

45 fxe4 h6 46 ♗f4 h5 47 exd5 exd5 48 h4 ♘ab8 49 ♗g5+ ♔f7 50 ♗f5 ♘a7

Black's only hope of counterplay is ...b5.

51 ♗f4 ♘bc6 52 ♗d3 ♘c8 53 ♗e2 ♔g6 54 ♗d3+ ♔f6 55 ♗e2 ♔g6 56 ♗f3 ♘6e7 57 ♗g5 1-0

Black is in zugzwang, e.g. 57...♘c6 58 ♗xd5 ♘d6 59 ♗f3 ♔f5 60 ♗c1!.

Keres wins the 19th USSR Championship with 12/17, ahead of Geller and Petrosian (both 11½). Botvinnik is a disappointing 5th, and Bronstein is joint 6th. Consequently, Botvinnik is left out of the team for the 1952 Olympiad, a decision that irritates him greatly.

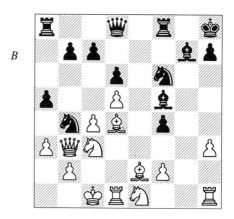

O. Moiseev – V. Simagin
USSR Ch, Moscow 1951

18...c5!!

Black is prepared to give up a piece in return for an open a-file and enhanced dark-square control.

19 ♗xf6

19 dxc6 ♘xc6 is good for Black.

19...♕xf6 20 axb4 axb4 21 ♘b5

21 ♘a2 f3! 22 ♗d3 ♗d7 and ...♗a4 traps the white queen. After 21 ♘b1 f3! 22 ♗d3 (22 ♘xf3 ♖a1) 22...♗d7 23 ♖d2 ♗a4 24 ♕a2 ♗c2! Black wins a lot of material.

21...♖a1+

21...f3 22 ♗d3 ♖a1+ 23 ♔c2 ♖xd1 24 ♔xd1 ♖a8 is also good.

22 ♔d2 f3!

The white king comes under attack from all angles.

23 ♘c2

23 ♗xf3 ♖e8 24 ♘c2 ♖xd1+ 25 ♖xd1 ♗h6+ 26 ♘e3 ♗e4 27 ♗e2 ♕xf2 28 ♖f1 ♕g3 29 ♘c7 ♗d3 is good for Black, as is 23 ♖xa1 ♗h6+ 24 ♔d1 fxe2+ 25 ♔xe2 ♗g6! 26 f3 ♖e8+.

23...♗xc2! 24 ♔xc2 fxe2 25 ♖xa1 ♕g6+! 26 ♔d2

26 ♕d3 e1♘+ and 27...♖xf2+.

26...♗h6+ 27 ♕e3 ♖xf2 28 ♖he1 ♗xe3+ 29 ♔xe3 ♕g3+ 30 ♔d2 ♕f4+ 0-1

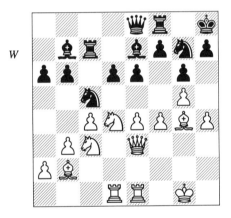

W

E. Gereben – O. Troianescu
Sopot 1951

White now exploits the awkwardly placed knight on g7 and the loose rook on c7.

27 e5!

Threatening 28 exd6 ♗xd6 29 ♘xe6 (or 29 ♘db5), so Black has little choice.

27...dxe5?

27...d5 28 cxd5 exd5 is necessary, but clearly unpleasant for Black.

28 ♕xe5

Now Black cannot avoid a calamity on the a1-h8 diagonal. The fact that the b2-bishop is obstructed by two knights is just a minor inconvenience.

28...♕b8 29 ♘d5! ♖fc8 30 ♘xe6! ♘xe6 31 ♗xe6 ♗c5+ 32 ♔h2 fxe6

Black has managed to defend c7 and g7, but there are more tactics on the way.

33 ♘xc7 ♖xc7

33...♕xc7 34 ♕xc7 ♖xc7 35 ♖d8+ ♗f8 36 ♖xf8#.

34 ♖d7 ♗d4 35 ♗xd4 1-0

Chess News in Brief

Gligorić wins the Staunton memorial tournament, played in Cheltenham, Leamington and Birmingham.

The first World Junior Championship is held, in Coventry and Birmingham. The new event is to be played every alternate year, and is open to national representatives under the age of 20. The winner of the inaugural event is Borislav Ivkov (born 1933). Notable among the contestants are Bent Larsen and Fridrik Olafsson [future World Championship Candidates] and Arnold Eikrem [organizer of many tournaments in Norway]. The USSR does not send a representative, apparently because the Swiss system is used for the pairings.

Ortvin Sarapu (who was born in Estonia in 1924) wins the New Zealand Championship (1951/2) for the first of 16 times.

Geza Maroczy dies.

Anatoly Karpov [World Champion 1975-85] is born.

Jan Timman [Dutch grandmaster] is born.

Ulf Andersson [Swedish grandmaster] is born.

Rafael Vaganian [Armenian grandmaster] is born.

Eugenio Torre [Filipino grandmaster] is born.

World News in Brief

The world's first thermonuclear device – a hydrogen bomb – is tested by the USA.

The Iranian government nationalizes the Anglo-Iranian Oil Company's oil fields.

British troops occupy the Suez Canal Zone.

Libya declares its independence from Italy.

Flooding leaves half a million homeless in Missouri.

1952

Excellent performances by Botvinnik, Keres and Kotov

Alexander Kotov wins the Stockholm/Saltsjöbaden Interzonal with a remarkable score of 16½/20, ahead of Petrosian, Taimanov (both 13½, and, like Kotov, undefeated) and Geller (13). Averbakh also qualifies on tie-break, ahead of Gligorić, Szabo and Ståhlberg, but all four get a place in the Candidates tournament when it is later decided to increase the number of players.

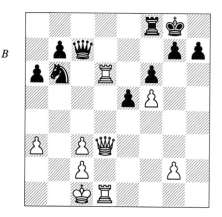

L. Szabo – T. Petrosian
Interzonal tournament, Saltsjöbaden 1952

26...♛c5!

Now the a-pawn falls, and with it the safety of the white king.

27 ♖d8 ♛xa3+ 28 ♔b1 h5!

Black creates the threat of 29...♘a4 and dislocates White's f5-pawn.

29 ♖xf8+ ♛xf8 30 ♛e4 ♛e7 31 ♛b4 ♛c7 32 ♛d6? ♛xd6 33 ♖xd6 ♘c4!

The ending is very good for Black, whose knight proves remarkably dextrous.

34 ♖d7 b5 35 ♖a7 ♘e3 36 ♖xa6 ♘xg2

White cannot cope with the h-pawn and the e-pawn, ably supported by the knight.

37 ♔c1

37 ♖b6 h4 38 ♖xb5 h3 39 ♔a2 (or 39 ♖d5 e4 40 ♔c1 e3) 39...e4 40 c4 e3 41 c5 e2 42 ♖b1 e1♛ 43 ♖xe1 ♘xe1 44 c6 h2 45 c7 h1♛ 46 c8♛+ ♔h7 is a straightforward win for Black.

37...h4 38 ♔d2 h3 39 ♖a1

White halts the h-pawn, but has failed to activate his own pawns.

39...♘h4 40 c4 bxc4 41 ♖h1

Or 41 ♔c3 ♘xf5 42 ♔xc4 ♘g3, and the h-pawn runs through.

41...♘xf5 42 ♔c3 ♘d6 43 ♖xh3 ♔f7 44 ♖h7 f5 45 ♔b4 f4 46 ♔c5 f3! 47 ♖h1

After 47 ♔xd6 f2 48 ♖h1 e4 49 ♖f1 e3 50 ♔d5 ♔g8! the pawns overpower the rook.

47...e4 0-1

Botvinnik and Taimanov are joint first in the 20th USSR Championship with 13½/19; Botvinnik wins a play-off held in early 1953. The rules for this event ban draws under 30 moves. In his notes to victories against members of the Olympiad team, Botvinnik makes clear his annoyance at not being a part of that team.

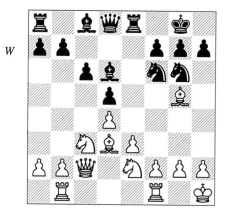

M. Botvinnik – P. Keres
USSR Ch, Moscow 1952

Botvinnik plays a model game in an Exchange Queen's Gambit.

13 f3!

Since it is difficult for Black to unpin his f6-knight in any convenient way, a central build-up is the right strategy for White.

13...♗e7 14 ♖be1 ♘d7 15 ♗xe7 ♖xe7 16 ♘g3 ♘f6 17 ♛f2

White prepares the e3-e4 advance by covering d4 and eyeing f7.

17...♗e6 18 ♘f5 ♗xf5

After 18...♖e8 19 g4 White's game starts to play itself.

19 ♗xf5 ♕b6 20 e4 dxe4

Keres decides to open the game immediately, but White is better prepared for this.

21 fxe4 ♖d8 22 e5 ♘d5 23 ♘e4 ♘f8

23...♘c7 24 ♘d6 ♘e8 loses to 25 ♗xg6 hxg6 26 ♘xf7.

24 ♘d6

Threatening 25 ♘c8 and 25 ♘xf7.

24...♕c7 25 ♗e4 ♘e6 26 ♕h4 g6 27 ♗xd5 cxd5 28 ♖c1 ♕d7 29 ♖c3

White has all manner of threats, while Black has no counterplay.

29...♖f8 30 ♘f5! ♖fe8 31 ♘h6+ ♔f8 32 ♕f6 ♘g7 33 ♖cf3 ♖c8 34 ♘xf7 ♖e6 35 ♕g5 ♘f5 36 ♘h6 ♕g7 37 g4 1-0

Keres wins a very strong tournament in Budapest with 12½/17, ahead of Geller (12), Botvinnik, Ståhlberg and Smyslov (all 11½).

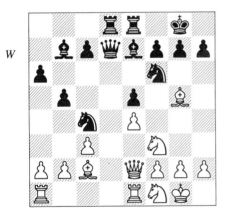

P. Keres – E. Geller
Budapest 1952

16 ♘e3!

Keres wants to evict the knight without making any concessions.

16...♘xb2?

This allows White a combination that exploits Black's vulnerability on the a2-g8 diagonal. 16...♘xe3 17 ♕xe3 ♘g4 should bring Black equality.

17 ♘xe5 ♕e6 18 ♘xf7! ♕xf7 19 ♗b3 ♘c4 20 ♘xc4 bxc4 21 ♗xc4 ♘d5 22 ♗xe7 ♕xe7

After 22...♖xe7 23 ♕d2 White will also emerge a pawn up.

23 exd5 ♕xe2 24 ♖xe2 ♖xe2 25 ♗xe2 ♗xd5 26 a4!

White has an extra pawn, while Black has problems with his a6-pawn and on the d-file. Keres went on to win.

Chess News in Brief

The Helsinki Olympiad is won by the USSR, playing in an Olympiad for the first time. Their team, despite Botvinnik's absence, is so strong as to make the result seem a foregone conclusion, although the margin of victory is surprisingly small. 25 teams compete, so there are preliminaries followed by finals. The USSR scores 21/32 in the A-final, ahead of Argentina (19½) and Yugoslavia (19). The top scorer on board 1 is Najdorf.

Vladimir Zagorovsky wins the Moscow Championship with 10/15, ahead of Kotov, Antoshin and Simagin (all 9½). World Championship Candidate Averbakh is in 13th place.

Gligorić wins the Hollywood tournament with 7½/9, ahead of Pomar (7).

Reshevsky and Najdorf win the Havana tournament with 16½/20, ahead of Gligorić (15).

A student tournament in Liverpool ends with Bronstein and Taimanov tying for first.

Fridrik Olafsson (born 1935) wins the Icelandic Championship for the first time.

Elizaveta Bykova wins the first women's candidates tournament.

Efim Bogoljubow dies.

Mikhail Umansky [winner of the 13th Correspondence World Championship, 1989-95] is born.

World News in Brief

In Vietnam, French troops come under 'guerrilla' attacks from Communist forces.

Britain develops its own atom bomb.

The US Air Force accomplishes the first trans-Atlantic helicopter flight.

The first jet-powered passenger service begins.

Surgeons in the USA pioneer the use of a mechanical heart to maintain a patient's blood flow during an operation.

1953

Smyslov triumphs at Zurich

Smyslov qualifies as Botvinnik's next challenger by convincingly winning the Zurich Candidates tournament, scoring 18/28 in the 15-player, double-round event. Bronstein, Keres and Reshevsky share second place with 16 points, followed by Petrosian (15). The tournament features many fine games, and is the subject of a famous book by Bronstein. However, such a large tournament is expensive to organize, prompting FIDE to reduce the number of competitors for the next Candidates tournament.

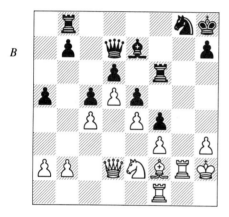

Y. Averbakh – A. Kotov
Candidates tournament, Zurich 1953

White has failed to attend sufficiently to his king safety, allowing Black to start a spectacular king-hunt.

30...♕xh3+!! 31 ♔xh3 ♖h6+ 32 ♔g4 ♘f6+ 33 ♔f5

It is not so easy to finish off the white king, since Black has poor light-square control, and White can afford to give back a lot of material.

33...♘d7

33...♘g4! is a quicker win. Black threatens 34...♖f8+ 35 ♔xg4 ♖g8+ 36 ♔f5 ♖f6# but also stops White playing ♖g5. 34 ♘xf4 ♖g8! 35 ♘h5 ♖hg6 36 ♕g5 ♗xg5 37 ♔xg4 ♗f4+ 38 ♔h3 ♖xg2 39 ♘xf4 exf4 is a straightforward win.

34 ♖g5 ♖f8+ 35 ♔g4 ♘f6+ 36 ♔f5 ♘g8+ 37 ♔g4 ♘f6+

Kotov, short of time, repeats the position. 37...♗xg5 is a more efficient way to win.

38 ♔f5 ♘xd5+

Black doesn't want to take this pawn, but it is necessary to avoid a draw by repetition.

39 ♔g4 ♘f6+ 40 ♔f5 ♘g8+ 41 ♔g4 ♘f6+ 42 ♔f5 ♘g8+ 43 ♔g4 ♗xg5! 44 ♔xg5 ♖f7

The threat is 45...♖g7+.

45 ♗h4 ♖g6+

45...♖g7+ 46 ♔f5 ♖hg6 is ineffective due to 47 ♕xd6! – the consequence of taking the d5-pawn.

46 ♔h5 ♖fg7 47 ♗g5 ♖xg5+ 48 ♔h4 ♘f6 49 ♘g3 ♖xg3 50 ♕xd6 ♖3g6 51 ♕f8+ ♖g8 0-1

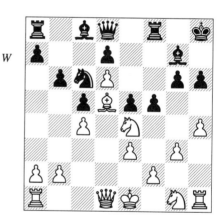

M. Euwe – M. Najdorf
Candidates tournament, Zurich 1953

14 ♘g5

It seems that White will eventually be forced into retreat, but he has some remarkable resources.

14...♗b7 15 g4! e4

Black opens the long diagonal at the cost of giving White the f4-square. Instead, 15...♕f6!? 16 ♘f7+ ♖xf7 17 g5 ♕xd6 18 ♗xf7 doesn't give Black enough compensation.

16 ♘e2 ♗xb2 17 ♘f4 ♕f6

Black cannot take the rook immediately, because 17...♗xa1 18 gxf5 ♗c3+ 19 ♔f1 ♖xf5 20 ♘xg6+ ♔g7 21 ♘xe4 ♖xd5 22 ♕xd5 ♘a5 23

♕f5 ♗xe4 24 ♕xe4 gives White a decisive attack.

18 gxf5!? ♗xa1

18...gxf5 19 ♖b1 ♗e5 20 ♕h5 ♗xf4 21 exf4 ♘d8 may be a better chance.

19 ♘xg6+ ♔g7 20 ♘xe4

Bronstein recommended instead 20 ♘f4, e.g. 20...♕c3+ 21 ♔f1.

20...♗c3+ 21 ♔f1 ♕xf5 22 ♘f4

Threatening 23 ♘g3 followed by 24 ♕g4+.

22...♔h8! 23 ♘xc3 ♖ae8 24 ♘ce2 ♖g8

Black should try 24...♗a6.

25 h5 ♖g5 26 ♘g3 ♖xg3 27 fxg3 ♖xe3 28 ♔f2 ♖e8

28...♖c3 29 ♖e1 ♕c2+ 30 ♕xc2 ♖xc2+ 31 ♔g1 ♖xa2 32 ♖e7! is a win for White.

29 ♖e1 ♖xe1 30 ♕xe1 ♔g7 31 ♕e8 ♕c2+ 32 ♔g1 ♕d1+ 33 ♔h2 ♕c2+ 34 ♘g2 ♕f5 35 ♕g8+ ♔f6 36 ♕h8+ ♔g5 37 ♕g7+ 1-0

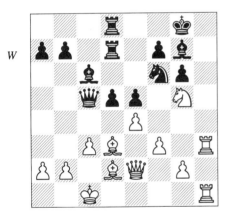

L. Schmid – M. Udovčić
Venice 1953

White now stakes everything on an h-file offensive.

24 g4!? dxe4 25 fxe4 ♔f8

25...♘xg4 loses to 26 ♘e6! fxe6 27 ♕xg4 with decisive threats.

26 ♖f1!

White focuses his attention on the f-file.

26...♔g8 27 ♗e3 ♕a5 28 ♗c4 b5 29 ♗b3 ♕c7 30 ♕h2 ♗xe4

Allowing White a decisive combination, but there was nothing better.

31 ♖xf6! ♕c4

A nice try, but White's mates come first.

32 ♖h8+ ♗xh8 33 ♕h7+ ♔f8 34 ♗c5+! 1-0

Chess News in Brief

Following Stalin's death, there is more scope for Soviet players to compete abroad.

Smyslov wins a training tournament at Garga with 6½/9, ahead of Petrosian (6) and Boleslavsky (5½).

Gligorić wins the Mar del Plata tournament with 16/19, ahead of Najdorf (14½).

Tolush wins the Bucharest tournament with 14/19, ahead of Petrosian (13), Smyslov (12½), Boleslavsky, Spassky and Szabo (all 12).

Abe Yanofsky wins the British Championship.

The veteran Tartakower wins the French Championship.

There is a combined German Championship, comprising players from East and West (which is won by Unzicker); this is not to be repeated until Germany is reunified in 1990.

Mikhail Tal (born 1936) wins the Latvian Championship for the first time.

Oscar Panno wins the World Junior Championship, on tie-break from Klaus Darga.

Cecil Purdy wins the 1st Correspondence World Championship (1950-3).

Alexander Beliavsky [Ukrainian grandmaster] is born.

World News in Brief

The Korean War ends, with victory for neither side. The situation in the Korean peninsula remains tense.

Stalin dies after a stroke. Nikita Khrushchev is elected first secretary of the Communist Party.

Anti-Communist rioting breaks out in East Berlin. The authorities declare martial law, enforced by Soviet tanks.

Egypt declares itself a republic.

Tensing Norgay and Edmund Hillary climb Mount Everest.

At the Cavendish Laboratory in Cambridge, Drs Watson and Crick work out the structure of deoxyribonucleic acid (DNA) – it is a double helix.

The Polio virus is identified, and photographed. A vaccine is tested.

1954

Botvinnik hangs on in another drawn World Championship match

Botvinnik retains the world title by drawing his match with Smyslov 12-12, with each player scoring seven wins.

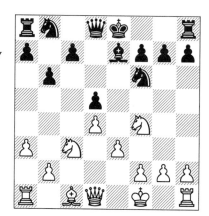

M. Botvinnik – V. Smyslov
World Ch match (game 2), Moscow 1954

In many games, Botvinnik showed a very fine sense of when it was safe to advance pawns in front of his own king. This is a case in point.

10 g4! c6?!

10...g5 11 ♘h5 ♘xh5 12 gxh5 ♕d7 13 ♕f3 c6 14 e4 gives White excellent play.

11 g5 ♘fd7

After 11...♘e4 12 ♘xe4 dxe4 13 h4 Black's e-pawn is too weak.

12 h4 ♗d6 13 e4!

Another surprise: White opens the centre.

13...dxe4 14 ♘xe4 ♗xf4 15 ♗xf4 0-0 16 h5!

White threatens to cause a huge hole in Black's kingside by 17 h6. Meanwhile, Black isn't active enough to exploit the looseness in White's position.

16...♖e8 17 ♘d6 ♖e6 18 d5! ♖xd6

18...cxd5 loses to 19 ♕xd5 ♘a6 20 g6.

19 ♗xd6 ♕xg5 20 ♕f3 ♕xd5

The alternative 20...cxd5 21 ♖g1 is also hopeless for Black.

21 ♕xd5 cxd5 22 ♖c1 ♘a6 23 b4 h6 24 ♖h3 ♔h7 25 ♖d3 ♘f6 26 b5 ♘c5 27 ♗xc5 bxc5 28 ♖xc5 ♖b8 29 a4 ♖b7 30 ♖dc3 1-0

Letelier wins the Montevideo tournament with 14½/17, ahead of O.Bernstein and Najdorf (both 14).

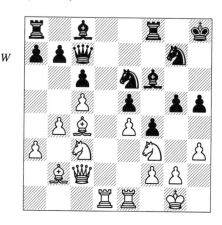

O. Bernstein – M. Najdorf
Montevideo 1954

It looks as if Black is making rapid progress on the kingside, while White's queenside attack will take a long time to yield anything – in particular his knights are a long way from the d6-square. However, White has a far more radical way to play:

21 ♘d5! cxd5

Otherwise White wins the e5-pawn.

22 exd5 ♘d4

22...♘d8 23 ♘xe5 is a disaster for Black.

23 ♘xd4 exd4 24 d6 ♕d7

24...♕d8 loses to 25 ♕g6! ♗f5 26 ♕h6+ ♗h7 27 ♗d3, and 24...♕c6 to 25 ♕g6 ♘f5 26 ♕xh5+ ♔g7 27 ♖xd4.

25 ♖xd4! f3

25...♗xd4 loses to 26 ♗xd4, since 26...♖e8 27 ♕g6 forces mate.

26 ♖de4?

What a shame White didn't find 26 ♖e7!!, winning brilliantly: 26...♗xe7 (26...♕f5 27 ♗d3 wins Black's queen; 26...♕d8 27 ♕g6 forces mate) 27 ♕g6 ♖f6 (27...♕f5 28 dxe7! ♖g8 29 ♕xg7+!? ♔xg7 30 ♖d6+ wins everything) 28 ♖h4!! forces mate in sensational fashion.

26...♕f5?

Black must play 26...fxg2!? 27 ♗xf6 ♖xf6 28 ♖e7 ♕f5!, with a very unclear position.

27 g4! hxg4 28 hxg4

The black queen has no good square.

28...♕g6 29 ♖e8! ♗f5

29...♕xc2 loses to 30 ♖xf8+ ♔h7 31 ♗g8+, while after 29...♖xe8 30 ♕xg6 ♖xe1+ 31 ♔h2 Black will be mated.

30 ♖xa8 ♖xa8

30...♗xc2 31 ♖xf8+ ♔h7 32 ♗g8+ ♔h6 33 ♖xf6 is killing.

31 gxf5 ♕h5 32 ♖e4

Not 32 ♗xf6?? ♕g4+ 33 ♔h2 ♕g2#.

32...♕h3 33 ♗f1 ♕xf5 34 ♖h4+! gxh4 35 ♕xf5 ♘xf5 36 ♗xf6+ ♔g8 37 d7 1-0

Yuri Averbakh wins the 21st USSR Championship with 14½/19, ahead of Taimanov, Korchnoi (both 13), Lisitsyn and Petrosian (both 12½).

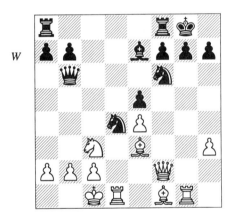

V. Korchnoi – E. Geller
USSR Ch, Kiev 1954

17 ♖xd4! exd4 18 ♗xd4 ♕d8

18...♕e6 seems more secure. Then 19 ♘d5 ♘e8 20 ♗c4 ♕h6+ 21 ♔b1 ♗h4 22 ♕f5 gives White enough play for the exchange.

19 ♘d5 ♘e8

19...♔h8? loses to 20 ♘xe7 ♕xe7 21 ♖xg7!.

20 ♕g3 f6?

20...♗h4 21 ♕xg7+ ♘xg7 22 ♖xg7+ ♔h8 23 ♖xf7+ ♔g8 24 ♖g7+ ♔h8 25 ♖g6+ ♗f6 26 ♖xf6 ♔g8 27 ♗c4 ♖f7 28 ♖f4 ♖c8 (28...♕d6 29 ♖g4+ ♔f8 30 e5 ♕c6 31 e6 ♕xc4 32 ♗g7+ ♖xg7 33 ♖xc4 is good for White) 29 ♘f6+

♕xf6 30 ♗xf6 ♖xc4 gives White some winning chances.

21 ♗c4 ♖f7 22 ♘f4 ♗d6 23 ♗xf7+ ♔xf7 24 ♕b3+ ♔e7 25 ♗xf6+ 1-0

Chess News in Brief

Korchnoi wins the Bucharest tournament with 13/17, ahead of Nezhmetdinov (12½), Kholmov and Filip (both 11).

Bronstein wins the Belgrade tournament with 13½/19, ahead of Matanović (13), Trifunović (12½), Ivkov and Petrosian (both 11½).

Smyslov and Keres share first place in the Hastings tournament (1954/5) with 7/9.

The Amsterdam Olympiad is dominated by the USSR, which wins the final by 7 clear points, scoring 34/44, ahead of Argentina (27) and Yugoslavia (26½). Botvinnik makes the best score on top board, while Keres massacres the opposition on board 4, scoring 13½/14. Bent Larsen makes an excellent score on top board for Denmark, albeit playing in the B-final. 26 teams compete.

The first World Student Team Championship ('Student Olympiad') is held in Oslo. It is to be a yearly event, organized by the International Student Union, for students under the age of 27. Ten nations compete, with Czechoslovakia edging out the USSR.

Bent Larsen (born 1935) wins the Danish Championship for the first time.

World News in Brief

There is unrest in Cyprus, as Greeks demand self-determination.

The French suffer a major defeat in Vietnam, and agree to the Communists controlling the north of the country.

France agrees to give Morocco and Tunisia self-rule. There are riots in Algeria as nationalists protest against French rule.

Roger Bannister runs the first sub-four-minute mile.

IBM plans to market an electronic calculating machine for use by businesses.

Observations of over 800 galaxies support the Big Bang Theory, which proposes that the universe originated from a single point, and in its early stages was extremely hot and dense.

1955

Bronstein's brilliant result • Spassky shows his talent

David Bronstein wins the Gothenburg Interzonal, scoring 15/20 without losing a game. Keres is second with 13½, ahead of Panno (13) and Petrosian (12½).

B. Spassky – H. Pilnik
Interzonal tournament, Gothenburg 1955

1 e4 c5 2 ♘f3 d6 3 d4 cxd4 4 ♘xd4 ♘f6 5 ♘c3 a6 6 ♗g5 e6 7 f4

This move was quite new in 1955.

7...♗e7

In an earlier round, Panno had tried the Poisoned Pawn, 7...♛b6, against Keres, but without success.

8 ♛f3 h6 9 ♗h4 g5!?

This has become known as the Gothenburg Variation. It was introduced simultaneously by three Argentines who, by coincidence, all had Black against Soviet players in the same round of this tournament. White won all three games, using the same spectacular sacrificial sequence, worked out over the board!

10 fxg5 ♘fd7 11 ♘xe6!?

Geller was the first of the trio to play this move.

11...fxe6 12 ♛h5+ ♚f8

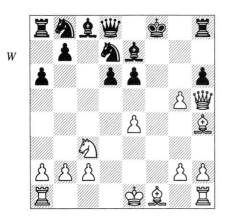

W

13 ♗b5!

An extraordinary move, 'pinning' the 'ghost' of a knight. White wants to be able to eliminate a black knight from e5 by ♗g3xe5, and so

makes sure it cannot be supported by the other knight.

13...♚g7?

13...♘e5? 14 ♗g3 ♗xg5 15 0-0+ ♚e7 16 ♗xe5 led to a quick win for White in Geller-Panno. 13...♖h7! is the critical defence.

14 0-0 ♘e5

14...♛g8 15 g6 ♗xh4 16 ♛xh4 gives White a strong attack.

15 ♗g3 ♘g6 16 gxh6+ ♖xh6 17 ♖f7+! ♚xf7 18 ♛xh6 axb5

18...♛h8 loses to 19 ♖f1+ ♗f6 20 ♗e8+!.

19 ♖f1+ ♚e8 20 ♛xg6+ ♚d7 21 ♖f7 ♘c6

21...b4 is strongly met by 22 ♘d5, while 21...♚c6 loses to 22 ♛h5!.

22 ♘d5! ♖xa2

22...exd5 23 ♛xd6+ ♚e8 24 ♛g6 leaves Black defenceless.

23 h3

23 h4 ♛h8 24 ♘xe7 ♘xe7 25 ♛g5 1-0 was the finish of Keres-Najdorf.

23...♛h8

23...exd5 24 ♛xd6+ ♚e8 25 ♛g6 ♗e6 26 ♛xe6 and White wins.

24 ♘xe7 ♘xe7 25 ♛g5 ♖a1+ 26 ♚h2 ♛d8 27 ♛xb5+ ♚c7 28 ♛c5+ ♚b8 29 ♗xd6+ ♚a8 30 ♗xe7 ♖a5 31 ♛b4 1-0

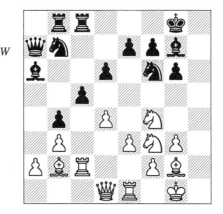

W

G. Idigoras – O. Panno
Mar del Plata 1955

In this seemingly quiet position, White targets the poorly-defended black king.

21 ♗h3 ♖f8 22 ♘g5!? ♗h6

22...♕b6 23 ♘xg6!? fxg6 24 ♗e6+ ♔h8 25 f4 ♗h6 26 ♖h2 ♔g7 27 d5 is similar to the game.

23 ♘xg6!?

This sacrifice leads to very dangerous play.

23...fxg6 24 ♗e6+ ♔g7 25 f4 ♘d8 26 d5

White's pin on the f6-knight enables his queen to approach the black king, and opens up ideas of winning back the sacrificed piece.

26...♗c8 27 ♖h2 ♗xe6 28 dxe6 ♕a6

28...♖h8 is a reasonable defensive try.

29 ♕g4 ♖h8 30 ♘f3 ♕d3 31 e4 c4 32 bxc4 ♕xc4 33 f5 g5 34 ♕h5 ♔f8 35 ♕g6 ♗g7 36 ♖xh8+ ♗xh8 37 ♘xg5 ♗g7?

Now White forces mate, but there was no adequate defence.

38 ♘h7+ ♔g8 39 ♗xf6 exf6 40 ♘xf6+ ♔f8 41 ♕e8# (1-0)

Efim Geller wins the 22nd USSR Championship after a play-off against Smyslov. Geller and Smyslov score 12/19, ahead of Botvinnik, Ilivitsky, Petrosian and Spassky (all 11½). The previous year's runner-up, Korchnoi, finishes in 19th place, illustrating the strength in depth of these Championships.

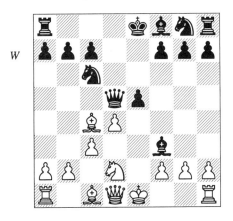

W

P. Keres – M. Botvinnik
USSR Ch, Moscow 1955

Botvinnik has handled the opening carelessly, and is caught with a nasty piece of tactics.

8 ♕b3! ♘a5?!

Even the superior continuation 8...♕d7 9 ♘xf3 exd4 leaves White substantially better.

9 ♕a4+! ♕d7 10 ♗xf7+! ♔d8 11 ♕xd7+ ♔xd7 12 ♘xf3 exd4 13 ♘xd4

A good pawn up, Keres won easily.

Chess News in Brief

Smyslov wins the Zagreb tournament with 14½/19, ahead of Matanović and Ivkov (12½).

Ivkov wins the Mar del Plata tournament with 11½/15, ahead of Najdorf (11) and Gligorić (10).

Viktor Korchnoi and Fridrik Olafsson share first place at the Hastings tournament (1955/6).

Ivkov wins the Buenos Aires tournament with 13/17, ahead of Gligorić (12½) and Pilnik (12).

Wolfgang Uhlmann wins the East German Championship for the first time.

Boris Spassky wins the World Junior Championship. Other notable competitors include Lajos Portisch and Joop van Oosterom [top-level correspondence player and generous chess patron].

John Nunn [British grandmaster and writer] is born.

Tony Miles [the first British over-the-board grandmaster] is born.

World News in Brief

The Warsaw Pact is formed. It is a military alliance between the USSR and the other communist nations of eastern Europe. Yugoslavia is not a signatory, though Khrushchev manages to improve relations with Tito.

The USSR tests a hydrogen bomb.

Rival factions vie for power in South Vietnam.

Juan Peron is overthrown in Argentina.

The bus boycott in the USA marks the beginning of a campaign of peaceful protest against racist regulations. The publicity campaign is led by the Rev Martin Luther King Jr.

Albert Einstein dies.

Flooding in Australia kills 200 people and 300,000 sheep.

Eighty-five spectators are killed in accidents at the Le Mans 24-hour motor race.

In France, Tefal develops non-stick pans.

1956

Smyslov is the Challenger again • Fischer's 'Game of the Century'

Robert (Bobby) Fischer (born 1943) wins the USA Junior Championship. Fischer's result in his first adult master event, the Rosenwald Trophy, is modest (4½/11; Reshevsky is first, with 9/11), but one of his games causes a sensation.

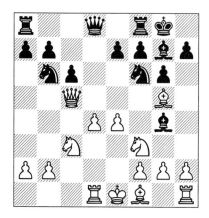

D. Byrne – R. Fischer
Rosenwald Trophy, New York 1956/7

White's position is a little loose and under-developed, but it is surprising that the punishment is so severe.

11...♘a4!! 12 ♕a3

12 ♘xa4 is met by 12...♘xe4.

12...♘xc3 13 bxc3 ♘xe4!

Fischer is willing to sacrifice an exchange, given the open e-file he will gain against the white king.

14 ♗xe7 ♕b6 15 ♗c4

Byrne, not content with 15 ♗xf8 ♗xf8 16 ♕b3 ♘xc3!, tries to find a tactical solution.

15...♘xc3! 16 ♗c5 ♖fe8+ 17 ♔f1 ♗e6!!

To foresee this spectacular queen sacrifice several moves in advance – as Fischer must have done – is extraordinary.

18 ♗xb6

18 ♗xe6 ♕b5+ 19 ♔g1 ♘e2+ 20 ♔f1 ♘g3++ 21 ♔g1 ♕f1+! 22 ♖xf1 ♘e2# is a beautiful smothered mate.

18...♗xc4+ 19 ♔g1 ♘e2+ 20 ♔f1 ♘xd4+ 21 ♔g1 ♘e2+ 22 ♔f1 ♘c3+ 23 ♔g1 axb6 24 ♕b4 ♖a4 25 ♕xb6 ♘xd1

Black has more than enough material for his queen, and White's position is still a mess. Fischer went on to win without difficulty.

Mark Taimanov wins the 23rd USSR Championship (after a play-off against Averbakh and Spassky). These three players score 11½/17, ahead of Korchnoi (11). Mikhail Tal, in his first USSR Championship, is joint fifth, with 10½ points. In a few games Tal was able to demonstrate his flair for combinative play.

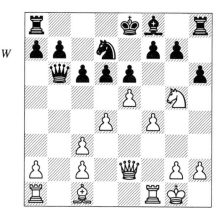

M. Tal – V. Simagin
USSR Ch, Leningrad 1956

Following a rather risky opening, Simagin has just chosen to provoke Tal into sacrificing, by playing 11...h6?.

12 ♘xf7! ♔xf7 13 f5 dxe5

13...♔g8 14 fxe6 ♘xe5 15 ♔h1 ♘g6 16 ♕h5 is very good for White.

14 fxe6++ ♔xe6 15 ♖b1! ♕xb1 16 ♕c4+ ♔d6 17 ♗a3+ ♔c7 18 ♖xb1 ♗xa3 19 ♕b3 ♗e7 20 ♕xb7+ ♔d6 21 dxe5+?!

21 ♖d1! is a clear win, e.g. 21...e4 22 d5!.

21...♘xe5 22 ♖d1+ ♔e6 23 ♕b3+ ♔f5 24 ♖f1+ ♔e4 25 ♖e1+ ♔f5 26 g4+

The pawn provides a vital extra ingredient for White's attack.

26...♔f6 27 ♖f1+ ♔g6 28 ♕e6+ ♔h7 29 ♕xe5 ♖he8 30 ♖f7 ♗f8 31 ♕f5+ ♔g8 32 ♔f2?!

Yes, Tal really is intending to bring his king up to g6 to mate its opposite number!

32...♗c5+ 33 ♔g3 ♖e3+ 34 ♔h4 ♖ae8! 35 ♖xg7+ ♔xg7 36 ♕xc5 ♖8e6 37 ♕xa7+ ♔g6 38 ♕a8 ♔f6 39 a4

Despite the slight misadventure with his king, the ending remains very good for White.

39...♔e5 40 a5 ♔d5 41 ♕d8+ ♔e4 42 a6 ♔f3 43 a7 ♖e2 44 ♕d3+ ♖6e3 45 ♕xe3+ 1-0

The Moscow Olympiad is dominated by the USSR, though they lose one match, to Hungary. The USSR's score of 31/44 in the A-final is ahead of Yugoslavia, Hungary (both 26½) and Argentina (23). The best score on top board is made by Bent Larsen (14/18), while Keres, Bronstein and Geller achieve the best scores on their respective boards. 34 teams compete.

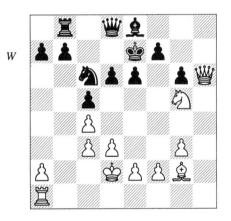

M. Botvinnik – S. Gligorić
Moscow Olympiad 1956

17 ♕g7 ♔d7 18 f4 ♕e7 19 ♖h1 ♘d8 20 ♘e4 ♔c7 21 ♖h8 ♗c6 22 ♘f6 ♔b6

22...♗xg2 23 ♖e8 traps the queen.

23 ♗xc6 ♘xc6 24 ♖h7 ♘d8

24...♖f8?? loses to 25 ♕xf8.

25 ♕xg6 ♔a6

This king move is to prepare ...b5, which would give Black a glimmer of counterplay.

26 a4 ♔a5

To win back the pawn, but it is amusing that Black's king is being 'hunted' up the board even though White's pieces are on the other wing.

27 ♕g5 ♔xa4 28 ♖h1 ♔b3

Alas, there is no way back: 28...♔a5 29 ♖a1+ ♔b6 30 ♘d5+ wins the queen.

29 ♕h4 ♔b2 30 g4 1-0

Next will come 31 ♕e1.

Chess News in Brief

Vasily Smyslov wins the Amsterdam/Leeuwarden Candidates tournament, a double-round ten-player event, with 11½/18, ahead of Keres (10) and five players on 9½ (Bronstein, Geller, Petrosian, Spassky and Szabo). Astonishingly, there had been a ruling that the unsuccessful challenger from the previous cycle (i.e. Smyslov) did not have the right to take part, but this was overturned.

Botvinnik and Smyslov share first place in the Alekhine Memorial tournament in Moscow with 11/15, ahead of Taimanov (10½), Gligorić (10), Bronstein (9½), Najdorf (9), Keres and Pachman (8½). It is noteworthy that, just ten years after his death, Alekhine, formerly reviled as a Nazi collaborator, has been 'rehabilitated' as a Soviet hero.

Olga Rubtsova defeats Bykova and Rudenko in a triangular match to become Women's World Champion.

Savielly Tartakower dies.

World News in Brief

Nikita Khrushchev denounces Joseph Stalin as a deranged torturer who committed appalling acts of mass-murder during his reign of terror.

A popular anti-Soviet uprising in Hungary is brutally crushed as Soviet tanks move in. It is a clear indication that the USSR intends to allow no dissent against communist rule in its Warsaw Pact 'allies'.

In Egypt, President Nasser nationalizes the Suez Canal Company, which had been under Anglo-French control. Britain, France and Israel take military action against Egypt, but fail to obtain backing from the USA, and are obliged to make a humiliating climb-down.

Martial law is declared in Poland after civil unrest and demonstrations against Soviet domination.

Morocco is given independence from France.

A prototype video recorder is demonstrated.

Velcro is developed.

1957

Smyslov is the new World Champion • Tal and Fischer win their first national championships

Tal wins the 24th USSR Championship. His daring, sacrificial style of play causes a sensation, and a certain indignation amongst some of his colleagues. Tal scores 14/21, ahead of Bronstein, Keres (both 13½), Spassky and Tolush (both 13).

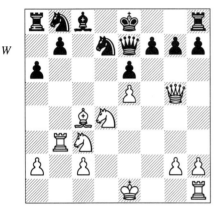

P. Keres – A. Tolush
USSR Ch, Moscow 1957

In a sharp line of the Najdorf Poisoned Pawn, Black has just played 14...♕a3-e7?. Modern theory has established that the queen should instead go to c5. Keres's punishment of Black's error is ruthless.

15 ♕xg7 ♕f8 16 ♕g5 ♖g8 17 ♕f4 ♘c5 18 0-0! ♕g7 19 ♖f2 ♘bd7

19...♘xb3 20 ♗xb3 followed by ♘e4 wins for White. 19...♘c6 loses to 20 ♘xc6 ♘xb3 21 ♘e4.

20 ♘d5! ♘xb3

20...exd5 21 ♗xd5 wins for White since 21...♘xb3 is met by 22 ♗xf7+.

21 ♘c7+ ♔e7 22 ♗xb3 ♕xe5

22...♖b8 loses to 23 ♘dxe6!.

23 ♕xf7+ ♔d6 24 ♘dxe6 ♘f6?!

24...♖f8 25 ♘xf8 ♔xc7 26 ♗e6 wins material.

25 ♖xf6 ♕e1+ 26 ♖f1 ♕e3+ 27 ♔h1 ♗xe6 28 ♘xe6 ♖ac8 29 ♕xb7 1-0

29 ♘d8 is even more destructive.

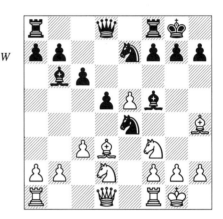

L. Aronin – Y. Estrin
USSR correspondence Ch 1957

Black's position appears quite healthy, apart from his slight vulnerability on the b1-h7 and h4-d8 diagonals. White is quick to exploit this.

14 ♕c2 ♘xd2 15 ♗xf5! ♘xf1 16 ♗xh7+ ♔h8 17 ♖xf1

White has, in effect, sacrificed an exchange for a pawn and attacking chances against the black king. Note that White has no intention of withdrawing his bishop from h7; instead it will be the cornerstone of a winning attack.

17...♕e8

Black cannot trap the white bishop by 17...g6 since White then wins by 18 ♗f6+ ♔xh7 19 ♘g5+ ♔g8 20 ♕d3.

18 ♖e1 ♗d8

18...g6 19 ♗f6+ ♔xh7 20 ♘g5+ ♔g8 21 ♕d3 ♕d7 22 ♕g3 ♕f5 23 ♖f1 leaves Black defenceless.

19 ♗f6! ♕d7

19...gxf6 20 exf6 ♕d7 21 ♖e3! gives White a decisive attack.

20 e6 ♕d6 21 ♕d2! fxe6 22 ♗e5 ♕d7 23 ♕h6 ♘g8 24 ♕h5 ♗f6 25 ♗c2+ ♘h6 26 ♕g6 ♔g8 27 ♕h7+ ♔f7 28 ♗xf6 ♔xf6 29 ♕g6+ ♔e7 30 ♕xg7+ ♘f7 31 ♘e5 ♕e8 32 ♗g6 ♖d8 33 f4 1-0

White wins a piece by pushing his f-pawn.

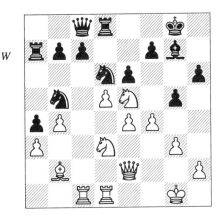

G. Barcza – P. Keres
Team match, Tallinn 1957

White now breaks through.
28 fxg5 hxg5 29 ♖f1 exd5 30 exd5 ♕h3 31 ♘xf7! ♘xf7 32 ♖xf7! ♔xf7

32...♗xb2 33 ♘xb2 ♔xf7 34 ♖f1+ ♔g8 35 ♕e7 wins for White.

33 ♖f1+ ♔g8 34 ♗xg7 ♕d7 35 ♗f6

The main threat is ♕h5.

35...♕e8 36 ♕g4

36 ♘e5 is also strong.

36...♖xd5

36...♕e3+ 37 ♖f2 ♖xd5 38 ♕c8+ wins.

37 ♘e5 ♖xe5 38 ♗xe5 ♕xe5 39 ♕c8+ ♔h7 40 ♖f7+ ♔g6 41 ♕g8+ 1-0

Chess News in Brief

Vasily Smyslov becomes World Champion, winning his match against Botvinnik by the impressive score of 12½-9½. However, Botvinnik has the right to a return match in 1958.

Gligorić and Reshevsky share first place at the Dallas tournament with 8½/14, where the young Larsen makes another good showing (equal third with Szabo, on 7½ points).

Keres wins the Mar del Plata tournament with 15/17, ahead of Najdorf (14).

Bobby Fischer wins the United States Championship (1957/8) for the first of eight times. He scores 10½/13, without loss, a point ahead of Reshevsky, whom he catches with the beautiful opening trap 1 e4 c5 2 ♘f3 ♘c6 3 d4 cxd4 4 ♘xd4 g6 5 ♘c3 ♗g7 6 ♗e3 ♘f6 7 ♗c4 0-0 8 ♗b3 ♘a5? 9 e5 ♘e8 10 ♗xf7+! ♔xf7 11 ♘e6!.

The final of the first European Team Championship is contested at Vienna/Baden, between four qualifying teams of ten players. The USSR wins the double-round event with 41/60, ahead of Yugoslavia (34); the only sensation is that the USSR loses one match to Yugoslavia.

William Lombardy becomes World Junior Champion, with a perfect score: 11/11.

The first Women's Olympiad is played at Emmen. Hitherto there had simply been too few women players for such an event to be contemplated. Teams of two from 21 countries take part. The USSR wins on tie-break from Romania.

World News in Brief

The USSR launches *Sputnik 1*, the first artificial satellite. It weighs 84 kilograms (184 pounds), and is a 56 centimetre (22 inch) sphere. It orbits the Earth every 95 minutes, transmitting continuous signals. The satellite has no direct military purpose, but the USA is stunned that its superpower rival has won the first 'round' of the space 'race'. The effect is to galvanize the US space programme into more urgent action. Subsequently the USSR launches *Sputnik 2*, which carries a dog named Laika. The dog is alive and well throughout the journey, suggesting that manned space travel may be possible. However, there is no way for the animal to return to Earth, and it is put to sleep.

The Treaty of Rome, setting up the European Economic Community, lays the foundation for closer links between the nations of western Europe.

The governor of Arkansas calls in the National Guard to prevent negro children from entering a 'white' high school in Little Rock. Only the intervention of President Eisenhower enables integration plans to be enforced.

A committee of medical experts in the USA provides evidence of a link between smoking and cancer.

The first US atomic power plant opens in Shippingport, Pennsylvania.

1958

Botvinnik regains the world title • Tal and Fischer achieve sensational results

Tal achieves a repeat victory at the 25th USSR Championship. His score of 12½/18 (after scoring 8 points from his last 9 games) places him ahead of Petrosian (12), Bronstein (11½) and Averbakh (11). The Championship doubles as a zonal tournament.

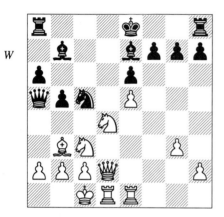

B. Spassky – L. Polugaevsky
USSR Ch, Riga 1958

In a normal-looking Sicilian position, Spassky exploits the poorly-defended black king.

17 ♗xe6! 0-0

17...fxe6 18 ♘xe6 wins: 18...♘xe6 19 ♕d7+ ♔f7 20 ♖f1+ or 18...♖d8 19 ♘xg7+ ♔f7 20 ♕h6.

18 ♗b3 ♖ad8

White has won a pawn, but this is just part of the battle. Black has the bishop-pair and a considerable amount of activity. Meanwhile, the extra pawn is isolated and could easily become weak if White lost the initiative.

19 ♕f4 b4 20 ♘a4!

The key move, exchanging Black's active knight – but isn't the white knight *en prise*?

20...h6

White needed to take into account this move, which intends ...♗g5. Instead, 20...♘xa4 loses to 21 ♘f5 ♖xd1+ 22 ♖xd1 ♗d8 (or 22...♗c5 23 ♕g5 g6 24 ♘h6+ ♔g7 25 ♘g4) 23 ♗xa4 ♕xa4 24 ♖xd8 ♖xd8 25 ♕g5.

21 ♘xc5 ♕xc5

21...♗g5 22 ♘xb7 ♗xf4+ 23 gxf4 gives White far too much material for the queen.

22 h4 ♗d5 23 ♘f5 ♗xb3 24 axb3 ♖xd1+ 25 ♖xd1 ♖c8 26 ♕e4 ♗f8 27 e6 fxe6 28 ♕xe6+ ♔h8 29 ♕e4

Black now has no real compensation for the pawn, and Spassky wins efficiently.

29...♕c6 30 ♕d3 ♖e8 31 h5 ♗e7 32 ♘xe7 ♖xe7 33 ♕g6 ♕e8 34 g4 ♖e1 35 ♕xe8+ ♖xe8 36 ♖d4 a5 37 ♔d2 ♖e5 38 c4 bxc3+ 39 bxc3 ♖g5 40 c4 ♔g8 41 ♖f4 g6

Sealed; Polugaevsky resigned without resuming.

1-0

Tal wins the Portorož Interzonal with 13½/20, ahead of Gligorić (13), Benko, Petrosian (both 12½), Fischer and Olafsson (both 12). The 15-year-old Fischer's result is sensational, earning him a place in the Candidates, and making him the youngest grandmaster to date. The record is to stand until 1991.

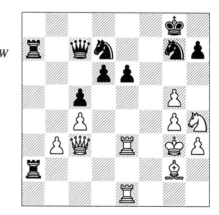

H. Rossetto – R. Cardoso
Interzonal tournament, Portorož 1958

40 ♗d5!

A marvellous idea. Black responds innocently.

40...exd5?

Overlooking a brilliant queen sacrifice that wins by force. 40...♘e5 41 ♖xe5 dxe5 42 ♗e4 gives White good compensation, but is far from clear.

41 ♕xg7+!! ♚xg7 42 ♘f5+ ♚g6

42...♚g8 43 ♘h6+ ♚g7 44 ♖e7+ ♚g6 45 ♖1e6+ ♘f6 46 ♖xf6+ ♚xg5 47 ♖ee6 and mate by h4# is inevitable.

43 ♖e6+ ♘f6 44 ♖xf6+ ♚xg5 45 ♖ee6 ♖g2+ 46 ♚xg2 ♕d8 47 ♘e7 1-0

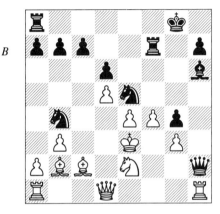

L. Polugaevsky – R. Nezhmetdinov
RSFSR Ch, Sochi 1958

Black has been attacking vigorously since the opening, and crowns his offensive with a magnificent queen sacrifice.

24...♖xf4!!

The white king will be dragged all over the board to its doom.

25 ♖xh2

White cannot instead take the rook: 25 gxf4 ♗xf4+ 26 ♘xf4 ♘xc2+ and 25 ♘xf4 ♘xc2+ are both winning for Black.

25...♖f3+ 26 ♚d4 ♗g7!

Threatening the remarkably calm 27...b5 and 28...♘ec6#.

27 a4

There is no good option here. The following sample lines are all winning for Black: 27 ♘g1 ♖xg3 28 ♘e2 ♖f3 29 ♘g1 ♘ed3+ 30 ♚c4 ♘xb2+ 31 ♚b4 ♗c3+ 32 ♚a3 b5! 33 b4 a5 34 bxa5 ♘c4+ 35 ♚b3 ♘xa5+ 36 ♚a3 ♘c4+ 37 ♚b3 ♖a3#; 27 ♖f2 c5+ 28 dxc6 ♘ed3+ 29 ♚c4 b5+ 30 ♚xb5 ♖b8+ 31 ♚a4 ♘xb2+ 32 ♚a3

♘xd1 33 ♖xf3 ♘xc2+ 34 ♚a4 ♘b2+ 35 ♚a5 gxf3; or 27 ♘c3 ♘ed3+ 28 e5 ♖xe5+ 29 ♚c4 ♘xb2+ 30 ♚xb4 ♗xc3+ 31 ♚a3 ♘xd1 32 ♖xd1 ♖xg3 33 ♖xh7 ♖g2.

27...c5+ 28 dxc6 bxc6 29 ♗d3 ♘exd3+ 30 ♚c4

Or 30 e5 ♗xe5+ 31 ♚c4 d5#.

30...d5+ 31 exd5 cxd5+ 32 ♚b5 ♖b8+ 33 ♚a5 ♘c6+ 0-1

Mate is forced.

Chess News in Brief

Botvinnik wins the return match against Smyslov 12½-10½ to regain the World Championship.

Bent Larsen wins the Mar del Plata tournament with 12/15, ahead of Lombardy (11).

The Munich Olympiad is won by the USSR, who score 34½/44 in the A-final, ahead of Yugoslavia (29), Argentina (25½) and the USA (24). The best score on top board is made by Gligorić (12/15), while Tal is rampant as first reserve, scoring 13½/15. 36 teams compete.

Jonathan Penrose wins the British Championship – the first of six consecutive victories, and of ten in total.

Lajos Portisch (born 1937) wins the Hungarian Championship for the first time.

Bykova regains the Women's World Championship.

Viacheslav Ragozin wins the 2nd Correspondence World Championship (1956-8).

Computers start to play chess.

World News in Brief

The USA launches its first space satellite, *Explorer 1*.

The pro-Western regime in Iraq is overthrown in a bloody *coup d'état*.

Thousands of babies are born in Europe with severe birth defects, which are attributed to the drug thalidomide, which had been introduced to counteract morning sickness.

The US nuclear submarine *Nautilus* makes the first undersea journey beneath the Arctic Polar ice cap.

Britain and Iceland dispute over fishing rights.

The integrated circuit is invented.

1959

Tal is to challenge Botvinnik – Keres is second yet again

Mikhail Tal dominates the Candidates tournament, played at Bled, Zagreb and Belgrade. It is a quadruple-round eight-man event. Tal's score of 20/28 (including a 4-0 result against Fischer) puts him ahead of Keres, whose total of 18½ is also a magnificent achievement. Petrosian is third, with 15½ points, ahead of Smyslov (15), Fischer, Gligorić (both 12½), Olafsson (10) and Benko (8).

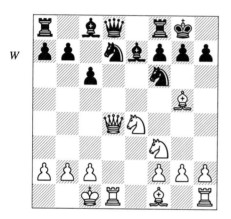

W

M. Tal – V. Smyslov
Candidates tournament, Bled 1959

This game is a fine example of Tal's tactical brinkmanship. He keeps giving Smyslov problems, and is eventually rewarded with a blunder.

10 ♘d6!?

Embarking upon a daring attacking scheme.

10...♛a5 11 ♗c4

There is no time for 11 ♔b1 due to 11...♗xd6 12 ♛xd6 ♘e4.

11...b5

Black's best response is counterattack.

12 ♗d2!

A useful repositioning of this piece, freeing g5 for a knight.

12...♛a6

12...♛a4 13 ♘xc8 ♖axc8 14 ♗b3 ♛xd4 15 ♘xd4 and 12...♛c7 13 ♗xf7+ ♖xf7 14 ♘xf7 ♔xf7 15 ♘g5+ ♔g8 16 ♖he1 both give White strong pressure.

13 ♘f5 ♗d8

13...♗c5? 14 ♛h4 bxc4 15 ♗c3 ♛xa2 16 ♖xd7 ♗b4 (16...♗xd7? is mated by force: 17 ♘h6+ ♔h8 18 ♛xf6) doesn't quite save Black: 17 ♘h6+ ♔h8 18 ♗xb4 (18 ♛xf6 ♛a1+ 19 ♔d2 gxf6 is Black's idea) 18...♗xd7 (18...♛a1+ 19 ♔d2 ♛xh1 20 ♘xf7+ ♔g8 21 ♘h6+ ♔h8 22 ♗xf8 ♗xd7 23 ♗xg7+ ♔xg7 24 ♛g5+ ♔f8 25 ♛xf6+ ♔e8 26 ♘g8 forces mate) 19 ♗c3 ♛a1+ 20 ♔d2 ♛xh1 21 ♛xf6 ♛xg2 22 ♘g5 ♛d5+ 23 ♔e3 ♖ae8+ 24 ♔f4 ♛d2+ 25 ♔g3 and Black must give up his queen.

14 ♛h4!?

Tal sacrifices a piece, going directly for the attack.

14...bxc4

14...♘e5? loses to 15 ♘h6+ gxh6 16 ♘xe5!, e.g. 16...♘g4 17 ♗xf7+ ♖xf7 18 ♛xd8+ ♖f8 19 ♗xh6! ♖xh6 20 ♛g5+.

15 ♛g5 ♘h5

After 15...g6 16 ♘h6+ ♔g7 White can take a draw by 17 ♘f5+, whereas Tal's intended 17 ♗c3 is not at all clear.

15...♘e8 is well met by 16 ♛xd8 ♛xa2 17 ♗c3: 17...♘ef6 18 ♖xd7 ♛a1+ (18...♗xd7 19 ♘h6+ ♔h8 20 ♛xf6 forces mate) 19 ♔d2 ♘e4+ 20 ♔e3 ♗xd7 21 ♘e7+ and White emerges material up; while 17...♘c5 18 ♘e7+ ♔h8 19 ♘g5 ♗b7 20 ♛d4 is good for White.

16 ♘h6+ ♔h8 17 ♛xh5 ♛xa2

17...♘f6 18 ♛c5 ♘d7 19 ♛d6 gives White good play, but 17...♗f6 18 ♗c3?! (18 ♘xf7+ ♔g8 19 ♘7g5 h6 20 ♘e4 ♛xa2 21 ♘xf6+ ♘xf6 22 ♛a5 ♛xa5 23 ♗xa5 is likely to lead to a draw) 18...♗xc3 (for 18...♛xa2, see 17...♛xa2 18 ♗c3 ♗f6) 19 ♘g5 ♗xb2+! is at least satisfactory for Black.

18 ♗c3 ♘f6?

Missing White's queen sacrifice. Black can still hold on by 18...♗f6; for example, 19 ♘xf7+ ♔g8 20 ♘3g5 ♛a1+ 21 ♔d2 ♗xc3+ 22 bxc3 ♘f6.

19 ♛xf7! ♛a1+ 20 ♔d2 ♖xf7 21 ♘xf7+ ♔g8 22 ♖xa1 ♔xf7 23 ♘e5+ ♔e6 24 ♘xc6 ♘e4+ 25 ♔e3 ♗b6+ 26 ♗d4 1-0

Tigran Petrosian wins the 26th USSR Championship with 13½/19, ahead of Spassky and Tal (both 12½).

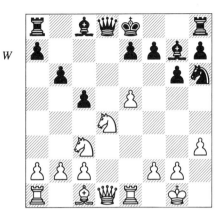

R. Kholmov – P. Keres
USSR Ch, Tbilisi 1959

Keres may have been expecting an easy time here: the knight retreats, the queens come off, and nothing is wrong with Black's position. However, Kholmov had a daring reply ready.

12 ᐃc6!!

This seems like madness, as the knight has no escape, but the move is based on concrete considerations.

12...♕d7

12...♕xd1 13 ♖xd1 ♗f5 (after 13...♗d7 14 ᐃd5 ♗xc6 15 ᐃc7+ ♔f8 16 ᐃxa8 the knight escapes) 14 ᐃb5 ♔f8 15 ᐃc7 ♖c8 16 ᐃxa7 ♖b8 17 c3 and White keeps an extra pawn.

13 ᐃxe7!!

A second surprise.

13...♔xe7

There was nothing better: 13...♕xd1 14 ♖xd1 ♔xe7 15 ♗g5+! ♔e6 16 ♖d6+ ♔f5 17 f4 ♗xe5 18 ♖d5 f6 19 ♗xh6 ♗b7 20 fxe5 ♗xd5 21 ᐃxd5 is winning for White; 13...♕xe7 14 ᐃd5 ♕d8 15 ᐃf6+ ♗xf6 (15...♔e7 16 ♗g5! ♕xd1 17 ♖axd1 ♗e6 18 ᐃh5+ ♔f8 19 ᐃxg7 ♔xg7 20 ♗f6+ ♔g8 21 g4 leaves Black in a comical mess) 16 exf6+ ♗e6 17 ♗xh6 ♕xf6 18 c3 and White will win by a direct attack.

14 ♗xh6!

White finds the quickest way to bring all his pieces into the attack, while affording the defender no respite.

14...♗xh6 15 ♕f3 ♗g7 16 ᐃd5+! ♔d8

After 16...♖e8 17 ᐃf6+ ♗xf6 18 exf6+ it is safe for White to take the a8-rook.

17 ♖ad1 ♗b7

If 17...♕b7, then White wins by 18 e6! fxe6 19 ᐃb4+.

18 ♕b3!

Black is defenceless. He cannot get more than a rook for his queen.

18...♗c6 19 ᐃxb6 axb6 20 ♕xf7! ♗xe5 21 ♖xd7+ ♗xd7 22 ♖xe5 ♔c7 23 ♖e7 ♖ad8 24 a4 g5 25 ♕d5 ♖he8 26 ♖xh7 g4 27 a5 gxh3 28 axb6+ ♔xb6 29 ♖xd7 1-0

Chess News in Brief

Bronstein, Smyslov and Spassky share first place at the Alekhine memorial tournament in Moscow with 7/11.

Tal wins the Zurich tournament with 11½/15, ahead of Gligorić (11), Fischer and Keres (both 10½).

Spassky wins the Riga tournament with 11½/13, ahead of Mikenas (11), Tolush (9½) and Tal (9).

World News in Brief

A revolution in Cuba brings Fidel Castro to power. The USA immediately recognizes the new regime, which promises to honour international agreements. However, Castro's subsequent confiscation of property, including much under foreign ownership, alarms the US.

The first weather satellite, *Vanguard 2*, is deployed by the USA.

The European Free Trade Association (EFTA) is formed. It comprises seven non-Common Market countries, including Britain.

Cyprus votes to become a republic, but tensions between Greek and Turkish Cypriots remain.

NASA names the astronauts for its manned Mercury space programme. Two monkeys are safely brought back to Earth following a spaceflight. One of the monkeys later dies during an operation to remove a cerebral electrode.

An unmanned soviet craft, *Luna 3*, photographs the dark side of the moon.

Iceland uses live ammunition in its fishing dispute with Britain.

1960

Tal becomes World Champion • Fischer has a mixed year

Viktor Korchnoi wins the 27th USSR Championship with 14/19, ahead of Geller and Petrosian (both 13½). Korchnoi's triumph is despite him blundering away a good position against Bagirov by picking up the wrong piece. Keres does not play, as he is in Cuba as part of a cultural delegation from Estonia.

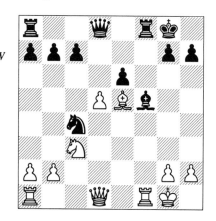

E. Geller – V. Korchnoi
USSR Ch, Leningrad 1960

The Four Pawns Attack in the Alekhine Defence has led to a tactically charged position.

17 ♗xg7! ♘e3!

Far better than 17...♔xg7? 18 ♕d4+.

18 ♕e2 ♘xf1 19 ♗xf8 ♘xh2! 20 ♗c5!

20 ♔xh2 ♕xf8 21 dxe6 ♕h6+ is good for Black.

20...♘g4 21 dxe6

White has a powerful passed pawn, but his king is exposed.

21...♕h4 22 e7 ♕h2+ 23 ♔f1 ♕f4+ 24 ♔g1

24 ♔e1 ♖e8!? 25 ♘d5 ♕h2! (not 25...♕g3+? 26 ♔d2 intending ♖f1) 26 ♘xc7 (26 ♔d2 ♕h6+ 27 ♔c3?! ♘f6!) 26...♖xe7 draws: 27 ♗xe7 ♕g1+ 28 ♔d2 ♕d4+ 29 ♔e1 (29 ♔c1? ♕f4+) 29...♕g1+ 30 ♕f1 ♕e3+, etc., or 27 ♕xe7 ♕g3+ 28 ♔d2 ♕d3+ 29 ♔e1 ♕g3+.

24...♖e8 25 ♕f3

25 ♘d5?! ♕h2+ 26 ♔f1 c6 27 ♕c4? ♕h1+ 28 ♗g1 ♗e6! 29 ♘f6+ ♔f7 and Black wins. 25 ♖d1 b6 26 ♖d8 ♔f7 is good for Black.

25...♕h2+ 26 ♔f1 ♕h5!

Black's intentions include 27...♘h2+ and 27...♗d3+, as exchanging bishops removes the defence from the e7-pawn.

27 ♕d5+

After 27 ♔g1! Black should repeat the position by 27...♕h2+ since 27...b6 28 ♕d5+ and 27...♔g7 28 ♕f4 are good for White.

27...♔g7 28 ♕d4+?

White's safest course is 28 ♖e1! ♗d3+ 29 ♕xd3 ♕xc5 30 ♕g3 h5 31 ♕f4 ♖xe7 32 ♖xe7+ ♕xe7 33 ♘d5, with a likely draw.

28...♔g6 29 ♘e2

29 ♕d8 ♕h1+ 30 ♔e2 (30 ♗g1? loses to 30...♘e3+ 31 ♔f2 ♕xg2+ 32 ♔xe3 ♕g5+!) 30...♕xg2+ 31 ♔e1 ♘f6 is good for Black.

29...♕h1+ 30 ♘g1?

Now Black wins. 30 ♕g1 ♕xg1+ (30...♕h4 31 g3! keeps White in the game) 31 ♔xg1 b6 32 ♗a3 c5 is difficult, but not hopeless, for White.

30...b6! 31 ♕d8

Or 31 ♗a3 ♕h4.

31...♘f6 32 ♗a3 ♗e4 33 ♕d2 c5 34 b4 c4 35 b5 ♗d3+ 0-1

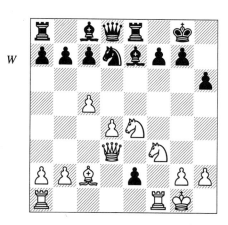

B. Spassky – D. Bronstein
USSR Ch, Leningrad 1960

Spassky's next move is both memorable and spectacular.

15 ♘d6!? ♘f8?

This does not work, as White can continue to put to good use the time he has gained by ignoring the black pawn on e2. The critical line is 15...♗xd6! 16 ♕h7+ ♔f8 17 cxd6 exf1♕+ 18 ♖xf1 cxd6 19 ♕h8+ ♔e7 20 ♖e1+ ♘e5 21 ♕xg7 ♖g8 22 ♕xh6 ♕b6 23 ♔h1 ♗e6 24 dxe5 d5 with an unclear position.

16 ♘xf7! exf1♕+ 17 ♖xf1 ♗f5

Or 17...♕d5 18 ♗b3 ♕xf7 19 ♗xf7+ ♔xf7 20 ♕c4+ ♔g6 21 ♕g8! ♗f6 22 ♘h4+ ♗xh4 23 ♕f7+ ♔h7 24 ♕xe8, and White wins.

18 ♕xf5 ♕d7 19 ♕f4 ♗f6 20 ♘3e5 ♕e7

After 20...♗xe5 21 ♘xe5 ♕e7 22 ♕e4, Black has no good defence to the threats of 23 ♖xf8+ and 23 ♗b3+.

21 ♗b3 ♗xe5 22 ♘xe5+ ♔h7 23 ♕e4+ 1-0

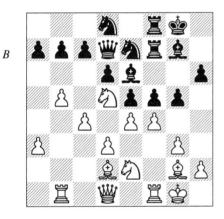

W. Uhlmann – R. Kholmov
Moscow 1960

Black has manoeuvred well, and is ready for the opening of the position.

16...gxf4 17 gxf4 ♘g6 18 fxe5 ♘xe5 19 ♘df4 fxe4! 20 ♗xe4 c6!

Instructive: Black plays in the centre rather than immediately targeting the white king.

21 bxc6 bxc6 22 ♔h1 ♗h3 23 ♖f2 d5! 24 cxd5 cxd5 25 ♗xd5

25 ♗f3 ♘xd3 is no good for White either.

25...♕xd5+!! 26 ♘xd5 ♖xf2

Black has several threats, including 27...♘f3.

27 ♗f4 ♘f3

Threatening 28...♗g2#, while after 28 ♘e3 ♖xf4, h2 collapses anyway.

0-1

Chess News in Brief

Tal beats Botvinnik 12½-8½ and so becomes the youngest World Champion to date. Botvinnik has the right to a return match in 1961.

Spassky and Fischer share first place at the Mar del Plata tournament with 13½/15, ahead of Bronstein (11½) and Olafsson (10½).

Korchnoi and Reshevsky share first place at the Buenos Aires tournament with 13/19, ahead of Szabo (12). Fischer has a disastrous result, finishing joint 13th with 8½ points.

Petrosian wins the Nimzowitsch memorial tournament in Copenhagen with 11½/13, ahead of Geller (10½).

The Leipzig Olympiad is won by the USSR, who score 34/44 in the A-final, winning all their matches and only losing one individual game (when Penrose defeats Tal in the last round). The USA finishes second with 29 points, ahead of Yugoslavia (27). The best score on top board is made by Robatsch of Austria (playing in the B-final). Of the top-board players in the A-final, Tal scores 11/15 and Fischer 13/18. The best score of the Olympiad is made by Petrosian, who achieves 12/13 as second reserve. 40 teams compete.

Artur Yusupov [Russian grandmaster] is born.

World News in Brief

Large numbers of East Berliners seek refuge in West Berlin.

An American U-2 spy plane is shot down over the USSR. Its pilot, Gary Powers, is captured and put on trial. It is a diplomatic catastrophe for the USA and its allies.

In South Africa, police fire upon demonstrators at Sharpeville, killing 56.

Castro nationalizes US businesses in Cuba.

The Congo is granted independence from Belgium. Within two weeks, civil war is brewing, and within three months, a military coup brings Joseph-Desire Mobutu to power.

Nigeria gains independence from Britain.

In Egypt, work starts on the Aswan High Dam.

Lasers are developed for use in precision cutting and surgery.

1961

Tal becomes the youngest Ex-World Champion

There are two Soviet Championships this year, due to a change in the scheduling of the event. Petrosian wins the 28th USSR Championship (played in Moscow in Jan-Feb) with 13½/19, ahead of Korchnoi (13), Geller and Stein (both 12). Spassky wins the 29th USSR Championship (played in Baku in Nov-Dec) with 14½/20, ahead of Polugaevsky (14), Bronstein (12½), Vasiukov and Tal (both 12). Here we see Tal succumbing in spectacular style to a player whose attacking skills have become legendary.

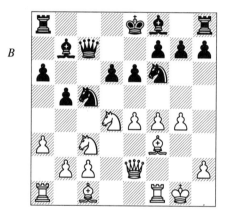

B

R. Nezhmetdinov – M. Tal
USSR Ch, Baku 1961

Tal decides it is time to take action in the centre, but Nezhmetdinov comes up with a surprising response.

12...e5 13 ♘f5 g6 14 fxe5! dxe5 15 ♘h6!

This move is heavily committal, but the disruption of Black's kingside and the pressure on f7 turn out to be highly effective.

15...♘e6 16 ♗g2 ♗g7

16...♘f4 17 ♗xf4 exf4 18 e5 works well for White.

17 ♖xf6!

This powerful sacrifice sets Black up for a series of forceful blows.

17...♗xf6 18 ♘d5 ♕d8

18...♗xd5 19 exd5 ♘d4 20 ♕f2 gives White too many threats.

19 ♕f2 ♘f4 20 ♗xf4 exf4

20...♗xd5 21 exd5 exf4 22 ♕xf4 is hardly better; if Black wants to evacuate his king, the only way is 22...♕b6+ 23 ♔h1 0-0-0, but then f7 collapses.

21 e5! ♗xe5

21...♘h4 22 ♕d4 ♖f8 23 ♖d1 is no good for Black, e.g. 23...♖c8 24 ♕a7 ♗xd5 25 ♗xd5 ♕c7 26 ♕xa6.

22 ♖e1 f6 23 ♘xf6+! ♕xf6 24 ♕d4 ♔f8 25 ♖xe5 ♕d8

25...♖d8 loses to 26 ♖e8+.

26 ♖f5+ gxf5 27 ♕xh8+ ♔e7 28 ♕g7+ ♔e6 29 gxf5+ 1-0

Another example of Nezhmetdinov's skills:

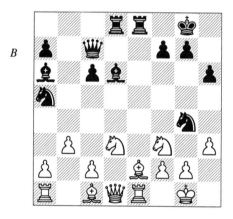

B

L. Belov – R. Nezhmetdinov
Russian Ch, Omsk 1961

White's opening play has involved winning a pawn at the cost of the initiative. Consequently, Nezhmetdinov is in his element...

18...♘xf2! 19 ♔xf2 ♕b6+ 20 ♔f1 ♗g3

The threats are by no means subtle.

21 ♕d2 c5!

Intending 22...c4.

22 c4 ♗xe1 23 ♔xe1 ♘xc4! 24 bxc4 ♗xc4

White has three pieces for a rook, but too many of them are pinned and attacked.

25 ♔f2

25 ♔f1 ♖xe2! 26 ♗xe2 ♖xd3 27 ♕xd3 ♗xd3+ 28 ♔xd3 ♕f6! wins.

25...♗xd3 26 ♗xd3 c4+ 27 ♔g3 ♖xd3 28 ♕b2 ♕g6+ 29 ♔f2 ♕e4 30 ♗d2 ♖xf3+ 31 gxf3 ♕h4+ 0-1

The final of the second European Team Championship is played at Oberhausen, and features six teams of ten players. The USSR dominates the double-round event, scoring 74½/100 (their smallest margin of victory in any match is 6½-3½), ahead of Yugoslavia (58½) and Hungary (53).

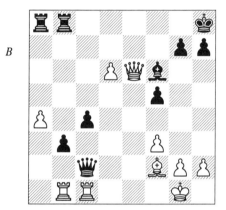

B

V. Hort – P. Keres
European Team Ch, Oberhausen 1961

White is poised to round up Black's c-pawn. However, Black is prepared to sacrifice to keep his two connected passed pawns.

35...♕xc1+! 36 ♖xc1 b2 37 ♖b1 c3 38 ♕e2!

38 ♕xf5 ♖xa4 followed by ...♖a1 would paralyse White.

38...♖xa4 39 d7 h6?

Keres preferred 39...♖g8, intending 40...♖a1.

40 ♕e8+ ♔h7 41 d8♕?

41 ♕xb8 c2 42 ♕xb2 ♗xb2 43 ♖f1 ♖a8 44 ♗b6 ♖a1 45 d8♕ ♖xf1+ 46 ♔xf1 c1♕+ 47 ♔f2 should probably hold the draw.

41...♖xd8! 42 ♕xa4 ♖d2!

White, a queen up, has no good way to cope with the threat of 43...c2.

43 ♖xb2

43 ♕b5 c2 44 ♕f1 ♖d5!, with ideas, amongst others, of ...♖a5-a1, wins for Black.

43...cxb2 44 ♕b3 ♖d8

The plan is ...♖a8-a1.

45 ♕c2 ♖b8 46 ♕b1

46 ♕xf5+ loses to 46...g6!.

46...g6

46...♖a8 is also good enough, e.g. 47 ♕xf5+ g6 48 ♕d7+ ♔h8.

47 g4 ♖a8 48 ♔g2 ♖a1 49 ♕c2 b1♕ 50 ♕c7+ ♗g7 51 ♗d4 ♕f1+ 52 ♔g3 f4+ 53 ♔xf4 ♕c1+ 0-1

Chess News in Brief

Botvinnik wins the return match 13-8 to regain the World Championship. Tal's poor health is a factor, but so also is Botvinnik's excellent preparation and steely determination.

A few months after losing the world title, Tal is back in form, winning the Bled tournament with 14½/19; Fischer is a point behind with 13½, undefeated, having beaten Tal in their individual game. Third place is shared by Petrosian, Keres and Gligorić (all 12½).

Keres wins the Zurich tournament with 9/11, ahead of Petrosian (8½).

Smyslov and Vasiukov share first place in the Moscow tournament.

Korchnoi wins the Maroczy memorial tournament in Budapest.

Botvinnik wins the Hastings tournament (1961/2).

Akiba Rubinstein dies.

World News in Brief

The communists build the Berlin Wall, which physically splits the city in two. The Wall surrounds West Berlin, but its main purpose is to prevent East Berliners fleeing to West Berlin.

Yuri Gagarin becomes the first man in space. His *Vostok 1* spacecraft makes one orbit of the Earth before he is parachuted safely back to the ground. Within a month, Alan Shepard becomes the first American in space, though he does not make an orbit before returning to Earth. President Kennedy announces a programme aimed at putting an American on the moon.

The US-backed 'Bay of Pigs' attempt to invade Cuba fails disastrously. President Kennedy accepts responsibility.

South Vietnam receives military assistance from the USA to oppose infiltration by the Viet Cong.

1962

Both glory and agony for Fischer

Fischer dominates the Stockholm Interzonal, scoring 17½/22, ahead of Geller, Petrosian (both 15), Filip and Korchnoi (both 14). Leonid Stein is one of three players on 13½, but fails to qualify for the Candidates due to a ruling that no more than three players from one country can qualify from the Interzonal.

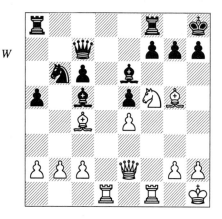

L. Stein – L. Portisch
Interzonal tournament, Stockholm 1962

White now smashes through with a far from obvious combination.

19 ♘xg7! ♗xc4

19...♔xg7 20 ♗f6+ leads to mate, while after 19...♘xc4 20 ♗f6 the mate threats are decisive.

20 ♗f6! ♗e7

20...♗xe2 21 ♘f5+ ♔g8 22 ♘h6#.

21 ♕f3 1-0

After 21...♔g8 White has a choice of mates.

The Varna Olympiad ends in victory for the USSR, though the margin of victory is a little smaller than usual. They score 31½/44 in the A-final, ahead of Yugoslavia (28), Argentina (26) and the USA (25). The best score on top board is made by Olafsson, albeit in the B-final. Najdorf scores very well for Argentina, while Penrose's 12½/17 helps England to a joint first place in the B-final. For Keres, it is his fifth consecutive Olympiad without a defeat. The

Olympiad features the one and only game between Botvinnik and Fischer, in which Fischer refutes Botvinnik's opening preparation, but is eventually held to a draw. 37 teams compete.

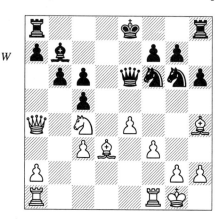

M. Tal – H.-J. Hecht
Varna Olympiad 1962

We are about to see a 'Tal special': a series of astonishing moves, involving a number of sacrifices, posing the opponent immense problems.

18 e5! b5!

Black must go after the white queen, since 18...♘xh4 19 ♘d6+ ♔f8 20 ♖ae1 is pleasant for White.

19 exf6!

A remarkable queen sacrifice, based on the activity of White's minor pieces.

19...bxa4?!

It is of course natural to take the queen, but after this Black seems to be worse. The critical line, from a mass of possibilities, is 19...0-0! 20 ♖ae1 ♕xe1 21 ♖xe1 bxa4 22 ♗xg6 fxg6 23 ♖e7 g5 24 ♖xg7+ ♔h8 25 ♗g3 ♗a6 26 ♗e5! ♗xc4 27 f7 h5 28 g4! hxg4 29 fxg4 ♖ad8 30 h4 ♖d1+, with a draw. Black will keep checking on the d-file until the white king moves to the f-file; then ...♗xf7 draws.

20 fxg7 ♖g8 21 ♗f5!!

It seems like sheer witchcraft that this move works. Instead, 21 ♗xg6 fxg6 22 ♖fe1 ♗c8! is good for Black.

1 Emanuel Lasker, World Champion 1894-1921.

2 Siegbert Tarrasch, Challenger in 1908.

3 Harry Nelson Pillsbury, the leading American player at the start of the 20th century.

4 Akiba Rubinstein, whose World Championship challenge in 1914 was cancelled due the outbreak of the First World War.

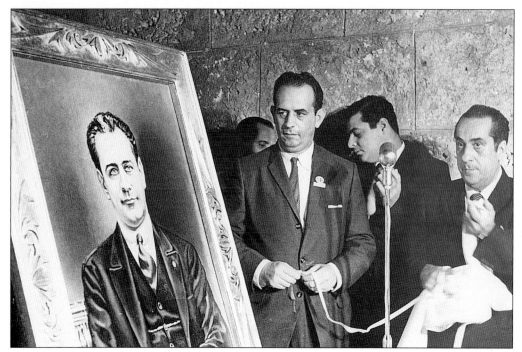

5 Portrait of José Raúl Capablanca.

6 Richard Réti, a leading Hypermodern.

7 Aron Nimzowitsch, author of *My System*, and a leading player in the 1920s.

8 Efim Bogoljubow, Challenger in 1929 and 1934.

9 Max Euwe, World Champion 1935-7.

10 Mikhail Botvinnik, 'Patriarch' of Soviet chess.

11 Paul Keres, one of the best players never to become World Champion.

12 Laszlo Szabo gives a simultaneous display.

13 David Bronstein, Challenger in 1951.

14 Vasily Smyslov inspects a king.

15 Viktor Korchnoi, among the world's top players for more than three decades.

16 Mikhail Tal, about to beat Krogius at the 1962 USSR Championship.

17 Tigran Petrosian strolls while Boris Spassky considers his move.

18 Tigran Petrosian, World Champion 1963-9.

19 Bobby Fischer, American chess superstar.

20 Anatoly Karpov at the 1971 Alekhine Memorial Tournament.

21 Round 4 of the 1979 Keres Memorial Tournament in Tallinn. Paul Keres became a national hero in Estonia.

22 Efim Geller (left) and Vasily Smyslov.

23 Nigel Short in 1982.

24 Sweden's Pia Cramling, who became the highest rated woman in the world in 1983.

25 A young Garry Kasparov.

26 The tempestuous press conference at the termination of the 1984/5 Karpov-Kasparov World Championship match.

27 The USA's Yasser Seirawan (left) playing Hungary's Lajos Portisch.

28 Ukrainian grandmaster Alexander Beliavsky, one of the top players of the 1980s and 1990s.

29 Zsofia Polgar, who achieved a sensational result at Rome 1989.

30 The Fischer-Spassky return match in 1992.

31 Judit Polgar: a teenage girl playing on top board for Hungary.

32 Peter Leko, who broke his compatriot Judit Polgar's record to become the youngest grandmaster in history.

33 Vladimir Kramnik (left) and Peter Svidler enjoy a beer with friends.

34 Game 14 of the Kasparov-Anand PCA World Championship match in 1995. Is Garry impressed by Vishy's opening?

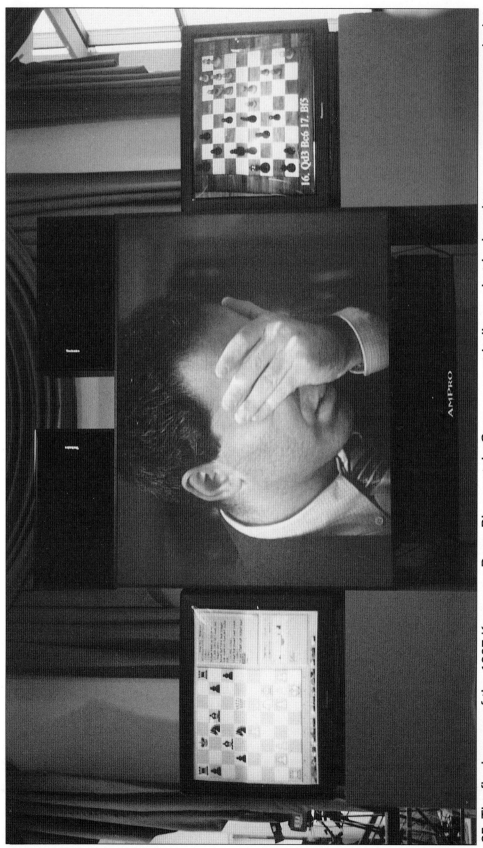

16. Qd3 Bc6 17. Bf5

35 The final game of the 1997 Kasparov-Deep Blue match. Garry cannot believe what he has done – nor can anyone else!

37 Irina Krush, the greatest talent in US women's chess. Her detailed and helpful advice in the 1999 Kasparov vs World Internet match has earned her many fans.

36 Alexei Shirov: WCC Challenger in 1998, or then again, maybe not.

39 Alexander Khalifman, the surprising winner of the 1999 FIDE World Championship.

38 The Ukrainian Ruslan Ponomariov, the youngest player ever to get the grandmaster title.

21...♘xh4

No better is 21...♕xf5 22 ♘d6+ ♔d7 23 ♘xf5 ♘xh4 24 ♖ad1+ ♔c7 25 ♘xh4 ♖xg7 26 ♖fe1 or 21...♗a6 22 ♗xe6 fxe6 23 ♘d6+ ♔d7 24 ♘e4. In either case Black gets an unpleasant ending.

22 ♗xe6 ♗a6 23 ♘d6+ ♔e7 24 ♗c4

White's pieces are linked by an invisible thread. The overall result of this prolonged and violent combination has been a significant weakening of Black's pawn structure.

24...♖xg7 25 g3 ♔xd6 26 ♗xa6 ♘f5 27 ♖ab1 f6 28 ♖fd1+ ♔e7 29 ♖e1+ ♔d6 30 ♔f2

From here, Tal realized his endgame advantage without undue difficulty.

Gufeld has cited the following game as a great influence on him, describing Kavalek as having "a moment of inspiration".

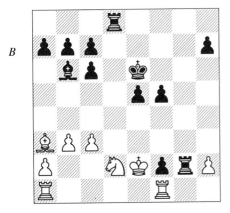

E. Gufeld – L. Kavalek
Student Olympiad, Marianske Lazne 1962

23...♖xd2+!!

Black wants to maintain his flock of pawns, and, to do so, needs to keep his powerful dark-squared bishop. In this light, the exchange sacrifice makes perfect sense. However, it demands a great deal of foresight to believe that the pawns will be worth more than White's extra rook.

24 ♔xd2 e4 25 ♗f8

25 c4, intending to blank out the black bishop directly, fails in view of 25...♗d4 26 ♖ad1 f4 27 ♔c2 ♔e5 28 ♗c1 c5!.

25...f4 26 b4! ♖g5! 27 ♗c5?

The idea of exchanging bishops is logical, but fails to Black's remorselessly consistent reply.

After 27 c4 ♗e3+ 28 ♔c2 ♖g2 29 ♗c5 ♗xc5 30 bxc5 ♔f5 31 ♔d2 e3+ 32 ♔d3 ♖xh2 33 ♖ab1 b6 34 cxb6 cxb6 White is paralysed.

27...♖xc5! 28 bxc5 ♗xc5

Believe it or not, the bishop and pawns will beat the two rooks!

29 ♖ab1 f3 30 ♖b4 ♔f5 31 ♖d4 ♗xd4 32 cxd4 ♔f4 0-1

Chess News in Brief

Petrosian wins the Curaçao Candidates tournament with 17½/27 (undefeated), ahead of Geller and Keres (both 17). Fischer's 4th place (14 points, with 7 losses) is disappointing after his Interzonal success, and he reacts badly to it, accusing the Soviet players of "team play at individual tournaments". Tal withdraws three-quarters of the way through the tournament to have urgent surgery on his ailing kidney.

Najdorf wins the Capablanca memorial tournament in Havana with 16½/21, ahead of Spassky and Polugaevsky (both 16).

Korchnoi wins the 30th USSR Championship with 14/19, ahead of Taimanov, Tal (both 13½) and Kholmov (13).

Nona Gaprindashvili scores a crushing victory over Bykova to become Women's World Champion; this heralds the start of a long period of Georgian domination of women's chess.

Alberic O'Kelly de Galway wins the 3rd Correspondence World Championship (1959-62).

Ernst Grünfeld dies.

World News in Brief

The Cuban missile crisis takes the world to the brink of nuclear war. The matter is resolved when Khrushchev agrees to remove the USSR's missiles from Cuban soil in return for an American undertaking not to invade Cuba.

There is fighting on the border between India and China.

Algeria gains independence from France.

In South Africa, Nelson Mandela is jailed.

The first active communications satellite, *Telstar*, is put into orbit.

A passenger hovercraft service opens on the Dee estuary in Britain.

1963

Petrosian defeats Botvinnik • Fischer's 'exhibition'

Fischer makes a clean sweep at the US Championship (1963/4) scoring 11/11, including some beautiful games.

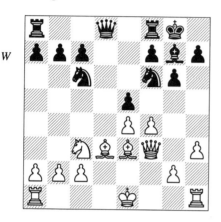

W

R. Fischer – P. Benko
USA Ch, New York 1963/4

White has chosen the aggressive Austrian Attack against his opponent's Pirc Defence, and now plays directly for a kingside attack.

11 f5

White's intended follow-up is g4-g5, so Black must react.

11...gxf5

11...♘d4 is the alternative, but then 12 ♕f2 gxf5 13 exf5 is good for White.

12 ♕xf5

Not 12 exf5?! e4!.

12...♘d4 13 ♕f2

Fischer was tempted by the queen sacrifice 13 ♕xe5 ♘g4 14 ♕xg7+!? ♔xg7 15 hxg4, but rejected it on account of 15...♘c6.

13...♘e8 14 0-0 ♘d6 15 ♕g3! ♔h8

15...f5 16 ♗h6 ♕f6 17 ♗xg7 ♕xg7 18 ♕xg7+ ♔xg7 19 exf5 gives White a pleasant positional advantage.

16 ♕g4 c6?!

16...c5 gives Black more play.

17 ♕h5

The threat is 18 ♗xd4 exd5 19 e5. Black's next move responds to this, but is brilliantly refuted.

17...♕e8?

17...♘e6 avoids instant loss.

18 ♗xd4 exd4 19 ♖f6!!

This sensational move makes sure the black f-pawn remains immobile just long enough for White to execute his e5 idea.

19...♔g8

19...dxc3 20 e5 and 19...♗xf6 20 e5 both see Black mated.

20 e5 h6 21 ♘e2! 1-0

The f6-rook remains invulnerable, while the d6-knight is lost (21...♘b5 22 ♕f5 mates).

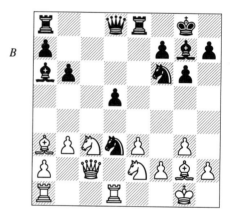

B

R. Byrne – R. Fischer
USA Ch, New York 1963/4

Black has taken on an isolated queen's pawn, relying on his piece activity. This is the crunch moment: he must either retreat or sacrifice.

15...♘xf2!! 16 ♔xf2 ♘g4+ 17 ♔g1

17 ♔f3 loses to 17...♖xe3+ 18 ♔xg4 h5+, forcing mate.

17...♘xe3 18 ♕d2 ♘xg2!

This surprising move strips the white king of its best defender, though it is as yet far from obvious that this is enough for Black.

19 ♔xg2 d4!

Opening the long diagonal.

20 ♘xd4 ♗b7+ 21 ♔f1

Other moves are no better. For instance, 21 ♔f2 ♕d7! 22 ♖ac1 ♕h3 23 ♘f3 ♗h6 24 ♕d3

♗e3+ 25 ♕xe3 ♖xe3 26 ♔xe3 ♖e8+ 27 ♔f2 ♕f5! picks up the f3-knight.

21...♕d7! 0-1

The key point is the beautiful 22 ♕f2 ♕h3+ 23 ♔g1 ♖e1+!! 24 ♖xe1 ♗xd4, forcing mate.

Smyslov wins the Alekhine memorial tournament in Moscow with 11½/15, ahead of Tal (10½) and Gligorić (10).

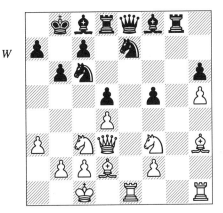

W

M. Tal – N. Padevsky
Alekhine memorial, Moscow 1963

Tal notices that the c7-pawn is extremely vulnerable.

21 ♗f4 ♕xh5 22 ♘b5 ♖d7 23 ♕c3!

The threat is 24 ♘xc7 ♖xc7 24 ♖xe7 ♗xe7 25 ♕xc6.

23...♗b7 24 ♘e5 ♘xe5 25 dxe5

Now White intends 26 e6, but seems to have allowed Black a strong counterblow...

25...d4 26 e6!! dxc3 27 exd7 ♗g7 28 ♘xc7

Black has a queen for a rook, but there is no satisfactory answer to White's idea of playing ♘e8+ followed by d8♕. For example, 28...♕f3 29 ♘d5+ ♔a8 30 ♗g2! ♕xg2 31 ♘c7+ ♔b8 32 ♘e8+, winning, or 28...♗e4 29 ♘e8+ ♔b7 30 ♗g2, when White wins material.

1-0

Chess News in Brief

Petrosian beats Botvinnik 12½-9½ to become World Champion. This time Botvinnik has no right to a return match (the result of a decision at the 1958 FIDE Congress), and decides not to compete for the World Championship any more.

Keres and Petrosian share first place with 8½/14 in the First Piatigorsky Cup in Los Angeles. Despite the organizers' best efforts, Fischer does not play.

Jan Hein Donner wins the Beverwijk tournament with 12/17, ahead of Bronstein (11½).

Korchnoi wins the Capablanca memorial tournament in Havana with 16½/21, ahead of Tal, Geller and Pachman (all 16).

Leonid Stein wins the 31st USSR Championship after a play-off (in early 1964) with Spassky and Kholmov. This trio score 12/19, ahead of Bronstein, Geller and Suetin (all 11½). The top six qualify for the Soviet zonal, to be played in 1964.

Garry Kasparov [World Champion from 1985 onwards] is born.

Johann Hjartarson [Icelandic grandmaster] is born.

The Women's Olympiad, held in Split, is won by the USSR with 25/28, ahead of Yugoslavia (24½).

World News in Brief

President John F. Kennedy of the United States is assassinated in Dallas. The man arrested for the murder, Lee Harvey Oswald, is himself shot dead two days later.

The USSR, USA and Britain sign a treaty banning atmospheric tests of nuclear weapons.

A telephone hotline, linking the White House and the Kremlin, comes into operation. The intention is to improve communication, and so lessen the likelihood of misunderstandings escalating into conflict.

Valentina Tereshkova becomes the first woman in space.

There is a major scandal in British politics, as the war minister John Profumo resigns after lying to Parliament about his relationship with a 'good-time girl', Christine Keeler, who was concurrently having an affair with a Soviet naval officer.

The greatest train robbery in history takes place in Britain, as a dozen robbers make off with more than a million pounds in cash and jewellery.

An earthquake devastates the Yugoslav city of Skopje.

1964

Spassky becomes a Candidate

The Amsterdam Interzonal ends in a four-way tie for first between Smyslov, Larsen, Spassky and Tal on 17/23. Due to the rule preventing more than three players from one country qualifying, 5th and 6th placed Stein and Bronstein fail to qualify for the Candidates matches, their places going to Ivkov and Portisch (the latter after a play-off against Reshevsky), who finished with 1½ points less.

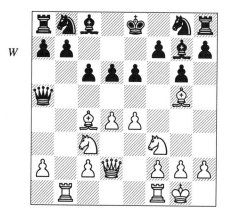

M. Tal – G. Tringov
Interzonal tournament, Amsterdam 1964

Tringov has grabbed a 'hot' pawn, inviting Tal to launch an all-out attack.

10 ♖fe1! a6 11 ♗f4 e5?! 12 dxe5 dxe5 13 ♕d6! ♕xc3

13...♕d8? loses to the obvious 14 ♗xf7+, while 13...exf4 14 ♘d5! is devastating.

14 ♖ed1 ♘d7?!

Now White forces mate, but Black was already out of playable options.

15 ♗xf7+! ♔xf7 16 ♘g5+ ♔e8 17 ♕e6+ 1-0

The Tel-Aviv Olympiad is won by the USSR, who score 36½/52 in the A-final, ahead of Yugoslavia (32) and West Germany (30½, beating the USSR 3-1 in their match). Wolfgang Uhlmann makes the best score on top board, helping East Germany achieve first place in the B-final, while Portisch's 12/16 is impressive. 50 teams compete.

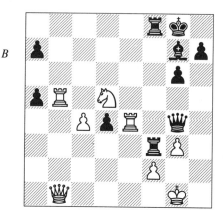

I. Aloni – M. Botvinnik
Tel-Aviv Olympiad 1964

29...♖xg3+! 30 fxg3 ♕xg3+ 31 ♔h1 d3!

The key idea – this pawn will also participate in the attack.

32 ♘e7+ ♔h8 33 ♕e1 ♕h3+ 34 ♔g1 d2! 35 ♘xg6+ hxg6 36 ♕h4+ ♔g8! 0-1

37 ♕xh3 (37 ♖b1 ♕b3 wins) 37...d1♕+ 38 ♔h2 ♖f2+ 39 ♔g3 ♕g1+ 40 ♔h4 ♗f6+ mates.

Viktor Korchnoi wins the 32nd USSR Championship (1964/5) with 15/19, ahead of Bronstein (13), Tal (12½) and Stein (12).

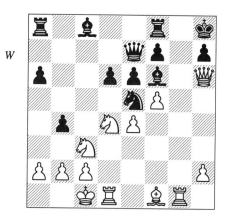

R. Kholmov – D. Bronstein
USSR Ch, Kiev 1964/5

White clearly needs to do something dramatic before Black consolidates.

18 ♘c6!!

The idea is to divert the black knight from e5, and then to free the e4-square for the other white knight by playing e5.

18...♘xc6 19 e5! ♗g5+?!

Black had to try 19...♗xe5 20 f6! ♗xf6 21 ♗d3 ♗g5+ 22 ♖xg5 f5 23 ♖dg1! ♖a7 24 ♘e2!, but here too White's attack is very strong.

20 ♖xg5 f6 21 exd6! ♕f7 22 ♖g3! bxc3 23 ♗c4!

Threatening 24 fxe6 ♗xe6 25 ♗xe6.

23...cxb2+ 24 ♔b1 ♘d8

24...♖e8 loses to 25 d7 ♗xd7 26 ♖xd7 ♖e7 27 fxe6 ♖b8 28 ♖c7, while after 24...♖d8 25 fxe6 ♕f8 26 e7 ♘xe7 27 dxe7 ♖xd1+ 28 ♔xb2 ♖b8+ 29 ♔c3, mate is forced.

25 ♖dg1?!

25 d7 is a more efficient route to victory.

25...♖a7 26 d7!

This move interferes with several black pieces at once, forcing one concession or another.

26...♖xd7 27 fxe6 ♘xe6 28 ♗xe6 ♖d1+ 29 ♖xd1 ♗xe6 30 ♔xb2 ♖b8+ 31 ♔a1 ♗xa2 32 ♖gd3 ♕e7 33 ♔xa2 ♕e6+ 34 ♖b3 1-0

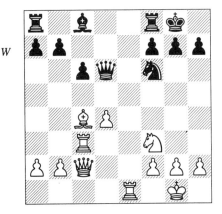

D. Marović – T. Tsagan
Student Olympiad, Krakow 1964

This is a known theoretical position. White now goes for a sharp attack.

16 ♘g5 ♗g4

The idea is to parry the threats by ...♗h5-g6.

17 ♖g3 ♗h5 18 ♖h3 ♗g6?

Allowing a combination worked out in 1938 by Kopaev and Chistiakov. 18...♕b4 is correct, and equal, as had been shown by Moiseev in 1949.

19 ♕xg6! hxg6 20 ♗xf7+! ♖xf7 21 ♖h8+! ♔xh8 22 ♘xf7+ ♔h7 23 ♘xd6 ♖d8 24 ♖e6 ♘d5 25 ♘f7 ♖f8 26 ♘g5+ ♔h6 27 ♘f3 ♖f4 28 h4

Marović smoothly exploited his extra pawn, winning 23 moves later.

Chess News in Brief

Boris Spassky wins the Belgrade tournament with 13/17, ahead of Korchnoi and Ivkov (11½).

Spassky wins the Moscow zonal; Stein and Bronstein also qualify. The result is very tight, with just two points separating the seven players in this double-round event.

Tal wins the Reykjavik tournament with 12½/13, ahead of Gligorić (11½), Olafsson and Johannessen (both 9).

Keres and Petrosian win the Buenos Aires tournament with 12½/17, ahead of R.Byrne (11½).

Fischer makes an extensive tour of the USA and Canada, playing a total of at least 1,882 games in more than 36 separate simultaneous displays. However, he plays in no major tournaments this year, even refusing to play at the Olympiad.

World News in Brief

Nikita Khrushchev is removed from power in the USSR, amid unease in the Communist Party about Khrushchev's impulsive decisions and failed schemes. The new leader is Leonid Brezhnev.

US Navy ships come under attack from North Vietnam, prompting a hardening of the American position.

China tests its first atomic bomb.

300 people die in rioting at a football match between Peru and Argentina.

Martin Luther King receives the Nobel Peace Prize for his work promoting civil rights in the USA.

A hurricane kills thousands in Ceylon and India.

1965

Spassky dominates the Candidates matches

Spassky convincingly wins the Candidates cycle, which has now taken the form of a series of matches, on a knock-out basis, between eight Candidates. The new formula is partly a response to Fischer's complaints, but the American chose not to compete in this cycle. Spassky beats Keres 6-4 in the quarter-final, Geller 5½-2½ in the semis, while Tal succumbs 7-4 in the final. This is the decisive game from Tal's 5½-4½ semi-final victory over Larsen:

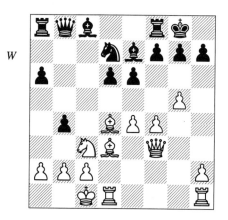

M. Tal – B. Larsen
Candidates match (game 10), Bled 1965

16 ♘d5!? exd5 17 exd5

White's threats include 18 ♕e4 and 18 ♗xh7+ ♔xh7 19 ♕h5+ ♔g8 20 ♗xg7! ♔xg7 21 ♕h6+ ♔g8 22 g6.

17...f5?!

17...g6! casts doubt over White's sacrifice. The key line is 18 ♖de1 ♗d8 19 ♕h3 ♘e5! 20 ♕h6 ♗b6!, when there is no clear path even to equality for White.

18 ♖de1 ♖f7

18...♗d8 19 ♕h5 ♘c5 20 ♗xg7! ♘xd3+ 21 ♔b1! ♕b7 22 ♗xf8 ♘xe1 23 ♖xe1 ♕f7 24 ♕xf7+ ♔xf7 25 ♗xd6 gives White three pawns for a piece, but the ending is somewhat unclear.

19 h4 ♗b7!

19...♘f8 loses to 20 h5 ♕c7 21 g6 ♖f6 22 h6!.

20 ♗xf5!? ♖xf5 21 ♖xe7 ♘e5

21...♖f7 lets White in: 22 ♖xf7 ♔xf7 23 g6+ hxg6 24 h5.

22 ♕e4 ♕f8 23 fxe5 ♖f4 24 ♕e3 ♖f3?

Black's last chance to put up resistance was 24...♗xd5 25 exd6 ♖xd4 26 ♕xd4 ♗xh1 27 b3 ♗f3 (27...♖e8? 28 ♕xg7+!!) 28 ♕c4+ ♔h8 29 ♖f7 ♕xd6 30 ♖xf3.

25 ♕e2 ♕xe7 26 ♕xf3 dxe5 27 ♖e1 ♖d8 28 ♖xe5 ♕d6 29 ♕f4! ♖f8 30 ♕e4 b3 31 axb3 ♖f1+ 32 ♔d2 ♕b4+ 33 c3 ♕d6 34 ♗c5!? ♕xc5 35 ♖e8+ ♖f8 36 ♕e6+ ♔h8 37 ♕f7 1-0

Leonid Stein wins the 33rd USSR Championship with 14/19, ahead of Polugaevsky (13½) and Taimanov (13).

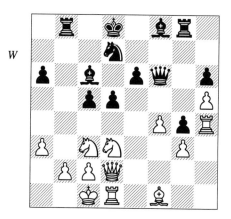

V. Korchnoi – P. Keres
USSR Ch, Tallinn 1965

Black has been fighting back after a difficult opening, and has some counterattacking chances.

22 ♘f2 c4 23 ♘xg4 ♕e7 24 ♖e1?

24 ♕e3 is a better defence, since if Black tries the same sacrifice, i.e. 24...♖xb2 25 ♔xb2 ♕xa3+ 26 ♔b1 ♗g7, then after 27 ♘e5 Black has problems bringing his rook into the attack.

24...♖xb2!! 25 ♔xb2 ♕xa3+ 26 ♔b1 ♗g7 27 ♘e5?!

27 ♖e3 d4 gives Black excellent winning chances.

27...♔c7! 28 ♘b5+

A necessary emergency measure in view of the threatened 28...♖b8+.

28...axb5

Now 29...♖a8 is the threat.

29 c3 ♗xe5! 30 fxe5 ♖xg3

The rook enters the attack from another angle.

31 ♖h3 ♖g5 32 ♖he3 ♘c5 33 ♖f3 ♗e8 34 ♕a2 ♕xa2+ 35 ♔xa2 ♖xh5 36 ♔a3 ♘e4 37 ♖f8 ♗d7 38 ♔b4 ♖xe5 39 ♖a1 ♖f5 40 ♖h8 ♖f2 0-1

Korchnoi wins the Erevan tournament with 9½/13, ahead of Petrosian and Stein (both 8½).

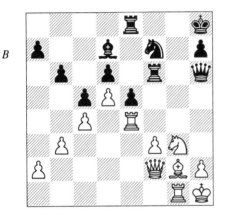

M. Filip – T. Petrosian
Erevan 1965

33...♘g5 34 ♖e3 ♕xh2+!! 35 ♔xh2 ♖h6+ 36 ♗h3

After 36 ♘h5 ♖xh5+ 37 ♔g3 ♖g8! Black forces mate.

36...♘xh3 37 ♘f5?!

37 ♔g2 ♘xf2 38 ♔xf2 is hopeless for White, but would enable him to resist for longer.

37...♖xf5 38 ♕f1 ♘f4+ 39 ♔g3 ♖g8+ 40 ♔f2 ♘h3+ 0-1

Chess News in Brief

Smyslov wins the Capablanca memorial tournament in Havana with 15½/21, ahead of Ivkov, Geller and Fischer (all 15). Fischer plays from New York by telephone-teletype, having been refused permission by the US State Department to travel to Cuba. This event marks Fischer's return to competitive chess after a period of semi-retirement. He later wins the US Championship, despite losing to Reshevsky and R.Byrne.

Ivkov and Uhlmann win the Zagreb tournament with 13½/19, ahead of Petrosian (12½).

Keres and Hort win the Marianske Lazne tournament.

The final of the European Team Championship takes place in Hamburg. The USSR wins, with 66/100, ahead of Yugoslavia and Hungary (both 57). Yugoslavia is second on tie-break.

Nona Gaprindashvili remains Women's World Champion by defeating her challenger, Alla Kushnir, 8½-4½.

Vladimir Zagorovsky wins the 4th Correspondence World Championship (1962-5).

Henrique Mecking (born 1952) is Brazilian Champion.

Nigel Short [World Championship Challenger in 1993] is born.

World News in Brief

The USA goes on the offensive in Vietnam, following attacks on its bases. Operation Rolling Thunder begins; it is a massive bombing campaign against military targets in North Vietnam.

Rhodesia makes a unilateral declaration of independence from Britain, after negotiations break down following Britain's insistence that an independent Rhodesia must have black majority rule.

Pakistan and India clash over Kashmir.

Mariner 4 transmits the first detailed pictures of the planet Mars.

Alexei Leonov becomes the first man to 'walk' in space, as he goes outside his *Voskhod 2* spacecraft.

Gemini 6 and *Gemini 7* make a rendezvous in orbit. The main purpose of NASA's Gemini programme is to develop the techniques that will be needed if there is to be a successful journey to the moon.

In the USA, civil rights leader Malcolm X is assassinated.

Race riots in the Los Angeles ghetto cause massive damage and about 30 deaths.

Evidence is found to support the view that the Vikings reached America well before Columbus's journey.

1966

Petrosian shows his class by retaining his title

Petrosian remains World Champion by defeating Spassky 12½-11½. This result does a great deal for Petrosian's credibility as World Champion, following a number of lacklustre tournament results during his first three years as Champion.

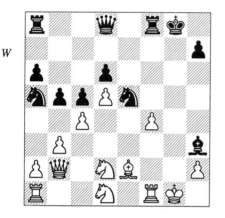

W

T. Petrosian – B. Spassky
World Ch match (game 10), Moscow 1966

21 ♘e3! ♗xf1

Spassky could hardly have taken much pleasure in winning the exchange. 21...♖xf4 22 ♖xf4 ♕g5+ 23 ♖g4! ♘xg4 24 ♘xg4 ♗xg4 25 ♗xg4 ♕xg4+ 26 ♔h1 leads to an unpleasant position for Black, but maybe there are drawing chances.

22 ♖xf1 ♘g6

22...♘d7 23 ♗g4 ♘f6 24 ♗e6+ gives White excellent play.

23 ♗g4!

Not 23 ♘g4 h5!.

23...♘xf4?

This allows a second exchange sacrifice, which is clearly favourable for White. However, even the superior 23...h6 24 ♘f5 is very uncomfortable for Black.

24 ♖xf4! ♖xf4 25 ♗e6+ ♔f7

25...♔f8 loses to 26 ♕h8+ ♔e7 27 ♕xh7+.

26 ♘e4 ♕h4 27 ♘xd6 ♕g5+

27...♕e1+ 28 ♔g2 ♕xe3 29 ♗xf7+ costs Black his queen.

28 ♔h1 ♖a7

Or 28...♕xe3 29 ♗xf7+ ♔f8 30 ♕h8+ ♔e7 31 ♘f5+, etc.

29 ♗xf7+ ♖xf7 30 ♕h8+!! 1-0

The black king is lured into a devastating knight fork.

Spassky wins the Second Piatigorsky Cup in Santa Monica, a strong ten-player double-round event, with 11½/18, ahead of Fischer (11) and Larsen (10). Petrosian is joint sixth with 9 points.

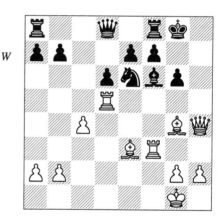

W

B. Larsen – T. Petrosian
Piatigorsky Cup, Santa Monica 1966

White has sacrificed a pawn to gain attacking chances. With his last move, 23...♗e5-f6?, Petrosian hoped to gain time by attacking the white queen in order to shore up his defences, but there is an unpleasant surprise in store for him.

24 ♕h6 ♗g7 25 ♕xg6!!

Not only strong, but also necessary. After 25 ♕h4? f5 Black beats off the attack.

25...♘f4

25...♘c7 is mated by 26 ♕xg7+! ♔xg7 27 ♖g5+ ♔h6 28 ♖h3#, while 25...fxg6 26 ♗xe6+ ♖f7 (or 26...♔h7 27 ♖h3+ ♗h6 28 ♗xh6) 27 ♗xf7+ ♔f8 28 ♗xg6+ ♗f6 29 ♖h5 gives White a winning attack.

26 ♖xf4 fxg6 27 ♗e6+ ♖f7

27...♔h7 28 ♖h4+ ♗h6 29 ♗xh6 leaves Black defenceless.

28 ♖xf7 ♔h8

28...♗e5 is met most elegantly by 29 ♖d4!.

29 ♖g5! b5 30 ♖g3 1-0

Leonid Stein wins the 34th USSR Championship (1966/7) with 13/20, ahead of Geller (12½), Gipslis, Korchnoi and Taimanov (all 12).

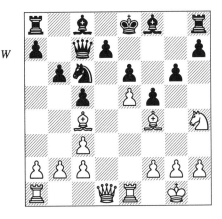

B. Gurgenidze – A. Lein
USSR Ch, Tbilisi 1966/7

Black's development is very backward, and disaster now strikes on an apparently well-defended square.

11 ♘xf5!! ♘a5

11...exf5 12 ♕d6! ♕d8 (12...♕xd6 13 exd6+ ♗e7 14 ♗d5) 13 ♕d5, intending e6, wins for White. 11...gxf5 12 ♕h5+ ♔d8 13 ♖ad1, followed by ♗xe6, leaves Black defenceless.

12 ♗d5!?

12 ♘d6+ ♗xd6 13 exd6 is also crushing.

12...♗b7

12...exd5 loses to 13 ♘d6+ ♔d8 14 ♗g5+ ♗e7 15 ♕g4.

13 ♘d6+ ♗xd6 14 exd6 ♕c8 15 ♗h6! ♖g8 16 ♕f3 ♗xd5 17 ♕xd5 ♘c6 18 ♖ad1 ♘d8 19 ♕g5 ♘c6 20 ♕f6 g5 21 ♖e5 1-0

Chess News in Brief

Petrosian comfortably wins a small tournament in Moscow two months before the Spassky match.

The Havana Olympiad is won by the USSR, who score 39½/52 in the A-final, ahead of the USA (34½), Hungary and Yugoslavia (both 33½). The American team arrived in Cuba having travelled via Mexico. The best score on top board is made by Petrosian (11½/13), just ahead, in percentage terms, of Fischer (15/17, including 14 wins), while Uhlmann's 13/18 is also notable. The best score of the Olympiad (not counting Ciric, who scores 100%, but only over 8 games) is made by Tal, playing on board 3: 12/13. The critical USSR-USA match is the subject of controversy, as the Soviets refuse to grant Fischer a two-hour delay to avoid playing on his Sabbath. The American team forfeits the match without play, but it is rescheduled to another day, and a 2½-1½ victory for the USSR recorded. 52 teams compete, thanks in part to the organizers paying the teams air travel expenses.

The Women's Olympiad, at Oberhausen, is won by the USSR, ahead of Romania.

Alexander Khalifman [1999 FIDE World Champion] is born.

Lembit Oll [Estonian grandmaster] is born.

World News in Brief

The 'Cultural Revolution' in China sees those considered to be resistant to Mao's revolutionary ideas systematically purged in a new wave of revolution.

An American H-bomb goes missing in the Atlantic Ocean. It is recovered two months later.

Opposition in the USA to the Vietnam War grows.

An unmanned American spacecraft, *Surveyor 1*, successfully lands on the moon and sends back data implying that the moon's surface is suitable for a manned spacecraft to land. The first pictures of the Earth from moon orbit are transmitted.

In Switzerland, the Sandoz corporation suspends distribution of the hallucinogenic drug LSD (lysergic acid diethylamide).

A rubella vaccine is developed.

Major oilfields are discovered in the North Sea.

At Aberfan in Wales, a coal tip slides into a primary school, killing 116 children and 28 adults.

1967

Fischer quits the Interzonal while leading

Larsen wins the Sousse Interzonal, but the sensation of the event is the withdrawal of Fischer while comfortably leading the event. The organizers had scheduled the games around Fischer and Reshevsky's religious holidays, not realizing that they observed different holidays. Impromptu rescheduling leaves Fischer playing four games on consecutive days. In protest, Fischer twice departs from the tournament, and twice returns, before finally leaving for good. At that point he is leading the tournament with 8½/10, and is clearly in great form. His results are erased from the tournament.

Larsen scores 15½/21, ahead of Geller, Gligorić, Korchnoi (all 14) and Portisch (13½). A three-way play-off for the final qualifying spot is a dead heat, so Reshevsky qualifies due to his better tie-break.

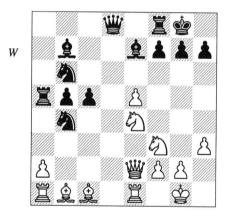

W

R. Fischer – L. Stein
Interzonal tournament, Sousse 1967

Stein has just played the inaccurate move 21...♘d7-b6?. Fischer now plays forcefully to exploit the exposed black kingside.

22 ♘fg5! ♗xe4

22...h6 loses to 23 ♘h7!, e.g. 23...♖e8 24 ♘hf6+ ♗xf6 25 ♘xf6+.

23 ♕xe4 g6 24 ♕h4 h5 25 ♕g3

Threatening 26 ♘e6 or 26 ♘xf7 ♖xf7 27 ♕xg6+ ♖g7 28 ♕e6+ ♔h8 29 ♕h6+ ♔g8 30 ♗f5.

25...♘c4 26 ♘f3?

26 ♘e6?! ♗h4 27 ♘xd8 ♗xg3 28 ♘b7 ♖a7 now gives White nothing.

26 e6 f5 27 ♘f3 ♔g7 (27...♕e8 avoids the transposition, but is unlikely to save Black) 28 ♕f4 ♖h8 transposes to the game, while avoiding the 28...♗f6 defence.

26 ♘xf7!? was not mentioned by Fischer, but might even be a clear win: 26...♖xf7 27 ♗xg6 (27 ♕xg6+ ♖g7 28 ♕e6+ ♔h8 29 ♕h6+ ♔g8 30 ♗f5 ♖a6 defends) 27...♖h7 (27...♖g7 28 ♗h6 ♕f8 29 a4) 28 ♕f3 ♖g7 29 ♕xh5.

26...♔g7 27 ♕f4 ♖h8 28 e6 f5?

28...♗f6 is better; then Fischer gives 29 exf7 ♗xa1 30 f8♕+ ♕xf8 31 ♕c7+ ♔g8 32 ♗xg6 ♘d5 33 ♕b7 ♘f6 34 ♗f4 ♖h7 35 ♗xh7+ ♘xh7 36 ♕d5+ ♕f7 37 ♕xf7+ ♔xf7 38 ♖xa1 as White's best, with a favourable ending.

29 ♗xf5 ♕f8

29...gxf5 30 ♕g3+ ♔h7 31 ♘g5+ ♗xg5 32 ♗xg5 ♕b8 (32...♕d3? loses to 33 ♕c7+ ♔g6 34 ♕f7+ ♔xg5 35 ♕g7+; 32...♕e8 33 ♖ad1 ♖a7 34 ♖d8 also wins) 33 ♕h4 ♕e8 34 ♖ad1 ♖a7 35 ♖d8 ♕g6 36 e7, followed by ♖e6, wins.

30 ♗e4?

30 ♘h4! should win, e.g. 30...♗xh4 31 ♕xh4 ♕xf5? 32 ♕e7+ ♔g8 33 ♕d8+ ♔g7 34 ♕c7+ ♔g8 35 e7.

30...♕xf4 31 ♗xf4 ♖e8?

31...♖xa2 32 ♖xa2 ♘xa2 gives Black better drawing chances.

32 ♖ad1 ♖a6 33 ♖d7 ♖xe6 34 ♘g5 ♖f6 35 ♗f3

White now wins efficiently, though 35 a3!? is also interesting.

35...♖xf4 36 ♘e6+ ♔f6 37 ♘xf4 ♘e5 38 ♖b7 ♗d6 39 ♔f1 ♘c2 40 ♖e4 ♘d4 41 ♖b6 ♖d8 42 ♘d5+ ♔f5 43 ♘e3+ ♔e6 44 ♗e2 ♔d7 45 ♗xb5+ ♘xb5 46 ♖xb5 ♔c6 47 a4 ♗c7 48 ♔e2 g5 49 g3 ♖a8 50 ♖b2 ♖f8 51 f4 gxf4 52 gxf4 ♘f7 53 ♖e6+ ♘d6 54 f5 ♖a8 55 ♖d2 ♖xa4 56 f6 1-0

Stein wins the very strong Alekhine Memorial tournament in Moscow with 11/17, ahead of

Smyslov, Gipslis, Bobotsov, Tal (all 10), Bronstein, Portisch, Spassky (all 9½), Geller, Najdorf, Keres and Petrosian (all 8½).

W. Uhlmann – B. Spassky
Alekhine memorial, Moscow 1967

Spassky shows how resilient his position is in the face of an all-out attack.

14...g6 15 g5 hxg5 16 h5?! ♔g7!

Improving on published theory of the day, which thought White's attack to be winning.

17 hxg6?

Uhlmann presses ahead, rather than trying to minimize the damage by 17 ♗b5.

17...fxg6 18 ♗b5 g4! 19 ♕d2?!

White's attack proves inadequate, but there was no good option. 19 ♖dg1 ♗g5+ 20 ♘xg5 ♕xg5+ 21 ♔b1 ♘xd4 and 19 ♗xc6 ♗xc6 20 ♖dg1 ♗d7 are both very good for Black.

19...gxf3 20 ♕h6+ ♔f7 21 ♕h7+ ♗g7 22 ♖h3 ♖h8! 0-1

After 23 ♖xf3+ ♕f6 24 ♖xf6+ ♔xf6 25 ♘xd5+ ♔f7 the white queen is trapped.

Chess News in Brief

Korchnoi wins the Leningrad tournament with 13/16, ahead of Kholmov (12).

Spassky wins the Beverwijk tournament with 11/15, ahead of Lutikov (10½), Cirić (9) and Larsen (8½).

Larsen wins the Capablanca memorial tournament in Havana with 15/19, ahead of Taimanov (13½) and Smyslov (13).

Fischer wins the Monte Carlo tournament with 7/9, ahead of Smyslov (6½).

Korchnoi wins the Budva tournament with 8/11, ahead of Tal and Gligorić (6½).

Darga and Larsen win the Winnipeg tournament with 6/9, ahead of Keres and Spassky (both 5½).

Polugaevsky and Tal share the 35th USSR Championship. For the first time it is played by the Swiss System (an experiment that isn't to be repeated until 1991): 130 players and 13 rounds. The two winners score 10 points, ahead of Vasiukov, Taimanov and Platonov (all 9½).

Robert Hübner (born 1948) jointly wins the West German Championship.

World News in Brief

Three NASA astronauts, Grissom, White and Chaffee, die as fire sweeps through their *Apollo 1* spacecraft during a rehearsal on the ground. The tragedy causes a major rethink of safety procedures, but the Apollo programme is to continue.

Tragedy also hits the Soviet space programme, as Vladimir Komarov dies as his craft crashes following re-entry.

Race riots ravage several US cities.

The Six Day War sees Israel capturing territory from its Arab enemies, reuniting Jerusalem and seizing Egyptian land up to the Suez Canal. The UN blames the conflict upon a build-up of forces by Egypt.

Civil war breaks out in Nigeria, as the Ibo people declare Biafra independent.

President de Gaulle of France causes international controversy, first by saying he will block British membership of the Common Market, and later by supporting "a free Quebec".

Oil from a massive tanker, the *Torrey Canyon*, causes enormous environmental damage after the ship runs aground off Land's End, England.

'Flower power' sweeps America, with San Francisco its focal point.

A prototype of Concorde, the Anglo-French supersonic passenger aeroplane, is unveiled.

In South Africa, the first human heart transplant is performed by a team led by Dr Christiaan Barnard, but the patient dies from complications 18 days later.

1968

Spassky is to challenge again • Dismay at another Fischer withdrawal

Fischer wins the Vinkovci tournament with 11/13, ahead of Matulović and Hort (9).

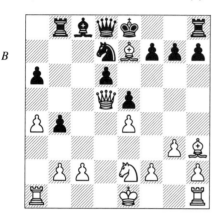

M. Matulović – R. Fischer
Vinkovci 1968

White is aiming to tie Black down to the defence of the d6-pawn.

13...♔xe7!

A surprising but very logical reply. The king is safe enough on e7, where it lends support to the d-pawn. Meanwhile the black queen can easily become active, and Black is able to exploit the loose white bishop on h3 – White must deal with the threat of 14...♘f6 or 14...♘b6. After 13...♕xe7 there would be no such threat.

14 ♕d2 ♘f6 15 ♗g2

A further time-losing retreat, but an exchange on c8 would help Black complete his mobilization.

15...♗b7 16 ♕d3 ♕b6 17 0-0 a5

White comes under fire on the f1-a6 diagonal.

18 ♖fd1 ♗a6 19 ♕d2 ♖hc8

Activating Black's remaining piece and threatening 20...♖c4.

20 h3! h5!

20...♖c4?! is met by 21 g4, when 21...♘xe4?! 22 ♗xe4 ♖xe4 23 ♘g3 obliges Black to give up an exchange by 23...♖f4 24 ♘f5+ (White could also try 24 ♘h5) 24...♖xf5.

21 b3

Stopping ...♖c4 at the cost of a new weakness at c3.

21...♗xe2! 22 ♕xe2 ♖c3

Attacking the g3-pawn.

23 ♖d3 ♖bc8 24 ♖xc3 ♖xc3 25 ♔h2 ♕c5 26 ♖a2 g6

White now has no constructive moves, so Fischer methodically improves his position.

27 ♗f1 ♕d4 28 f3?

This loses immediately, but after 28 ♗g2 h4, the black knight will break into some prime squares on the kingside.

28...♖e3 29 ♕g2 ♕d1 30 ♗c4 ♕xf3

30...♕b1 31 ♕f2 is less clear.

31 ♕xf3 ♖xf3 32 ♔g2 ♖e3 33 ♗d3 ♘xe4 34 ♗xe4 ♖xe4 35 ♔f2 d5 36 ♖a1 d4 37 ♖d1 ♖e3 38 h4 ♖c3 39 ♖d2 ♔e6 40 ♔g2 f5 0-1

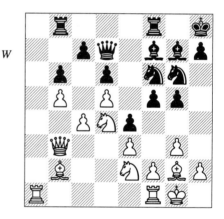

V. Smyslov – V. Liberzon
USSR Team Ch, Riga 1968

22 f4! exf3 23 ♖xf3 ♘e7 24 ♘c6 ♖be8 25 ♘ed4 ♘fxd5

Rather than allow White to turn the screws, Black initiates complications.

26 cxd5 ♗xd5 27 ♘xf5!!

This magnificent queen sacrifice gives White a powerful initiative.

27...♖xf5

27...♗xb3 28 ♗xg7+ ♔g8 29 ♘cxe7+ ♖xe7 30 ♗xf8 ♔xf8 31 ♖a8+ ♔f7 32 ♘d4+ and 33 ♘xb3 is good for White, while after 27...♘xf5 28 ♕xd5 ♗xb2 29 ♖af1, Black's position collapses.

28 ♗xg7+ ♔g8 29 ♖xf5! ♗xb3 30 ♖xg5

The main threat is 31 ♘xe7+.

30...♘g6

30...♕e6 31 ♘xe7+ ♖xe7 32 ♖a8+ ♖e8 33 ♗d4+ ♔f8 34 ♖a7 keeps the pressure on. 30...h6 31 ♗xh6+ ♔h7 32 ♘xe7 ♖xe7 33 ♗f8 ♖xe3 34 ♖g7+ ♕xg7 35 ♗xg7 ♔xg7 is an ending where White can play for a win.

31 ♗h6 ♕e6

31...♔h8 32 ♘d4 ♗c4 33 ♗c6 ♕h3 34 ♘f5 ♗e6 35 ♗g2 ♕xf5 36 ♖xf5 ♗xf5 37 ♖a7 and White should win the ending.

32 h4 ♕xe3+ 33 ♔h2 ♕c3 34 ♖f1 ♗c4 35 ♖f2 ♕e1 36 ♖gf5 ♗xb5 37 ♗d2 ♕b1 38 ♗d5+ ♔h8 39 ♗c3+ ♘e5 40 ♘xe5 dxe5 41 ♖xe5 1-0

Chess News in Brief

Spassky wins the Candidates cycle to become Petrosian's challenger for a second time. Spassky's victories, over Geller (quarter-final), Larsen (semi-final) and Korchnoi (final) are all convincing. Tal's progress is halted by Korchnoi, traditionally a difficult opponent for him, in a close semi-final.

Larsen wins the Monte Carlo tournament with 9½/13, ahead of Botvinnik (9), Hort and Smyslov (both 8½).

Uhlmann and Bronstein win the Lasker memorial tournament, played in East Berlin.

Korchnoi wins the Wijk aan Zee tournament with 12/15, three points ahead of Portisch, Hort and Tal (all 9).

Keres wins the Bamberg tournament with 12/15, ahead of Petrosian and Schmid (both 10).

The Lugano Olympiad begins with controversy, as Fischer refuses to play, complaining about the poor playing conditions, and in particular the lighting. The USSR is dominant, scoring 39½/52 in the A-final (having scored 27/28 in their preliminary group). Yugoslavia is second, with 31 points, ahead of Bulgaria (30) and the USA (29½, with Fischer's departure undoubtedly costing them medals). Petrosian makes the best score on top board (10½/12

with, as usual, no losses), while Penrose's 12½/15 (playing in the B-final) is impressive, as is Mecking's 11½/17 (also B-final). The best score of the Olympiad is Smyslov's 11/12 as second reserve. 53 teams compete.

Polugaevsky wins the 36th USSR Championship (1968/9), after a play-off against A.Zaitsev. They both score 12½/19, ahead of Lutikov (11½). Tal only manages 10½ points; illness and hospitalization have again been disrupting his chess.

Walter Browne (born 1949) is Australian Champion.

Hans Berliner wins the 5th Correspondence World Championship (1965-8).

Boris Gelfand [Belarussian grandmaster] is born.

Ilia Smirin [Belarussian grandmaster] is born.

World News in Brief

Following the Czechoslovakian government's introduction of new liberal policies, Soviet tanks roll into Prague to restore a hard-line regime. Czechs are horrified by the action of their 'ally', and many of them, though hopelessly outgunned, fight back against the tanks.

North Vietnamese and Viet Cong forces start a massive attack, the Tet offensive, throughout South Vietnam. Towards the end of the year, there are attempts to negotiate peace, with the US calling off the bombing of North Vietnam. Violent clashes break out in the USA between anti-war protestors and the National Guard.

Martin Luther King is assassinated in Memphis, and so becomes a martyr for the civil rights movement.

Senator Robert Kennedy, brother of the slain President John F. Kennedy, is assassinated in Los Angeles.

Immigration becomes a major issue in British politics, with Enoch Powell warning of 'rivers of blood'.

France is crippled by strikes and protests by students in Paris.

Apollo 8 is the first manned spacecraft to orbit the moon. The astronauts celebrate Christmas while orbiting about 70 miles (113 km) above the moon. It is a bright point at the end of a troubled year.

1969

Spassky is World Champion • Karpov – a new Soviet star

Petrosian loses the World Championship to Spassky, who scores a 12½-10½ victory. Spassky shows more ambition and tactical ingenuity in an otherwise fairly evenly balanced match.

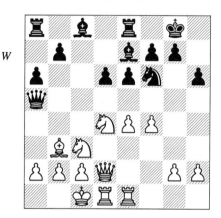

B. Spassky – T. Petrosian
World Ch match (game 19), Moscow 1969

14 ♔b1 ♗f8

The more natural 14...♗d7 is hit by 15 e5 dxe5 16 fxe5 ♘h7 17 ♘f5! ♗c6 18 ♘xe7+ ♖xe7 19 ♘d5 – here we see a point of White's 14th move.

15 g4!

This energetic pawn sacrifice makes good use of White's development advantage.

15...♘xg4

Otherwise White has simply gained time for his attack.

16 ♕g2 ♘f6

16...e5 17 ♘f5 forces Black to take on f5 with his bishop, aggravating his defensive problems.

17 ♖g1 ♗d7

17...♕c5 is met by 18 ♘f3! intending e5.

18 f5! ♔h8?

18...exf5 19 ♕g6 ♔h8 20 ♗xf7 is somewhat better for White. Note that 20...fxe4? loses to 21 ♖df1.

19 ♖df1

The immediate threat is fxe6 followed by ♖xf6.

19...♕d8?!

After 19...e5, 20 ♘de2 (but not the generally recommended 20 ♘e6? fxe6 21 fxe6, which loses to 21...♖xe6) favours White. White has a strong attack following 19...♕e5!? 20 ♘f3 ♕f4 (20...♕c5 is met by 21 h4 with ideas of ♘g5; 20...♕a5 21 fxe6 ♗xe6 22 ♗xe6 fxe6 23 e5 dxe5 24 ♘h4 is winning for White) 21 ♕h3 ♕e3 22 ♖g3 followed by ♘g5.

20 fxe6 fxe6

After 20...♗xe6 21 ♘xe6 fxe6 22 ♘e2 Black has no answer to White's ideas of ♘f4.

21 e5! dxe5 22 ♘e4 ♘h5

22...♘xe4 23 ♖xf8+ mates, while 22...exd4 loses to 23 ♘xf6.

23 ♕g6! exd4

23...♘f4 24 ♖xf4! exf4 25 ♘f3 ♕b6 26 ♖g5! ♕d8 (26...♗c6 27 ♘f6 forces mate) 27 ♘e5 and White wins.

24 ♘g5 1-0

24...hxg5 25 ♕xh5+ ♔g8 26 ♕f7+ and 27 ♖f3 is terminal.

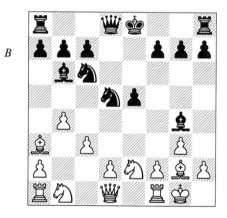

B. Jacobsen – L. Ljubojević
European Junior Ch, Groningen 1969/70

White has been asking for trouble with his eccentric development, but it is still surprising how viciously Ljubojević rips his position apart.

9...♘f4!? 10 gxf4 ♕d3 11 ♖e1

After 11 ♕a4 ♗xe2 12 ♗xc6+ ♔d8 (not 12...bxc6? 13 ♕xc6+ ♔d8 14 ♕xa8+ ♔d7 15

♕g2 defending) 13 ♗g2 exf4 Black has a very strong attack: 14 ♖e1 f3 15 ♗h3 ♕d6 16 d4 c6 17 b5 ♕h6 or 14 ♖c1 ♕g6 15 ♔h1 ♕g4.

11...0-0-0 12 b5

12 ♘c1? ♕g6 13 f5 ♕xf5 14 ♖e2 ♖d6 gives Black a winning attack, e.g. 15 b5 ♖g6 16 bxc6 ♗f3.

12...♘a5 13 ♗b4

White could try 13 ♘c1 ♕g6 14 f5 ♕xf5 15 ♖e2 ♕xf2+ (15...♖he8 is an aggressive alternative) 16 ♖xf2 ♗xd1, with an unclear ending.

13...♘c4 14 a4

Now 14 ♘c1? loses to 14...♕g6 15 f5 ♗xf2+! 16 ♔xf2 ♕b6+ 17 ♗c5 ♖xd2+!.

14...exf4 15 a5?!

15 ♘xf4 ♕f5 16 ♗f3?! (16 ♕c1 ♕xf4 17 d4 is safer) 16...h5 17 ♖e4 ♘e5 18 ♖xe5 ♕xe5 (18...♕xf4? 19 ♖e4) 19 ♘g2 ♕f5 20 ♘h4 ♕f4 (20...♕g5 21 ♘g2) 21 a5 ♗xf2+ 22 ♔xf2 ♖d3 gives Black a strong attack.

15...♗xf2+! 16 ♔xf2 ♘e3!

Now Black is clearly winning.

17 ♘a3

Or: 17 ♕c1 ♘xg2 18 ♔xg2 ♕f3+ 19 ♔g1 ♗h3 20 ♘xf4 ♕xf4 21 d4 ♕g4+ 22 ♔f2 ♕g2+ 23 ♔e3 ♖he8+; 17 ♘xf4 ♘xd1+ 18 ♖xd1 ♕f5 19 ♔g3 g5.

17...♘xd1+ 18 ♖axd1 f3 19 ♘c1 ♕f5 20 ♗h1 ♕f4 0-1

Chess News in Brief

A new Soviet star emerges: Anatoly Karpov wins the World Junior Championship in Stockholm with 10/11, three points clear of the field.

In a return to his best form, Petrosian wins the 37th USSR Championship after a play-off against Polugaevsky (played in early 1970). They both score 14/22, ahead of Geller, Smyslov and Taimanov (all 13½). Tal, about to have an operation to remove a kidney, only manages 10½ points. This is also a zonal event; Taimanov reaches the interzonal by winning a scrappy but exciting game against Lutikov in the last round.

Larsen wins the Palma de Mallorca tournament with 12/17, ahead of Petrosian (11½), Korchnoi, Hort (both 10½) and Spassky (10).

Geller and Botvinnik win the Wijk aan Zee tournament with 10½/15, ahead of Portisch and Keres (both 10).

Ulf Andersson (born 1951) wins the Swedish Championship for the first time.

The Women's Olympiad, played in Lublin, is won by the USSR with 26/28, ahead of Hungary (20½). It is the first time the USSR has dominated this event.

At the Büsum tournament, the veteran Fritz Sämisch loses all 15 of his games on time.

Viswanathan (Vishy) Anand [Indian grandmaster; Challenger in 1995] is born.

Vasily Ivanchuk [Ukrainian grandmaster] is born.

Jeroen Piket [Dutch grandmaster] is born.

World News in Brief

The *Apollo 11* mission is successful, and Neil Armstrong and Edwin (Buzz) Aldrin become the first men on the moon. The events are watched by about 600 million people around the world.

President Nixon plans a gradual disengagement from the Vietnam War, but massive anti-war protests continue. News emerges that a US platoon slaughtered nearly 600 residents in the Vietnamese village of My Lai.

Violence breaks out in Northern Ireland.

Yasser Arafat unites the Palestinian guerrilla groups into the Palestine Liberation Organization (PLO).

In France, De Gaulle's reforms are rejected in a referendum.

Troops from El Salvador invade Honduras following a dispute whose origin was a football match.

Colonel Gaddafi seizes power in Libya.

The Nigerian government refuses to let the Red Cross into Biafra, where there is mass-starvation.

British troops put down a rebellion on the Caribbean island Anguilla.

The Anglo-French supersonic airliner Concorde makes a successful maiden flight.

In Britain, scientists successfully fertilize a human egg in a test-tube.

1970

Fischer is back on track • USSR narrowly beats the Rest of the World

The USSR vs Rest of World match (ten boards, four rounds) results in a narrow 20½-19½ victory for the USSR. Larsen insists on playing top board above Fischer, and, despite one shockingly quick loss to Spassky, acquits himself well, scoring 2½/4. Fischer, on second board, trounces Petrosian 3-1. On boards 3 and 4, Portisch and Hort score 2½-1½ against Korchnoi and Polugaevsky respectively. However, the USSR's strength in depth swings the tie in their favour.

Fischer wins the Buenos Aires tournament with 15/17, well ahead of Tukmakov (11½) and Panno (11).

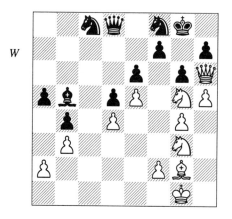

R. Fischer – O. Panno
Buenos Aires 1970

28 ♗e4!

Black could not tolerate the g3-knight coming to e4 and f6, so the bishop is safe on e4.

28...♕e7

After 28...dxe4 29 ♘3xe4 ♕e7 30 ♘f6+ ♔h8 31 ♘gxh7 White will force mate. 28...♗e8 29 hxg6 hxg6 30 ♘h5 gxh5 31 ♗h7+ ♘xh7 32 ♘xh7 f6 33 ♘xf6+ ♔f7 34 ♘xh5! is also hopeless for Black. However, letting the bishop live is no solution either.

29 ♘xh7 ♘xh7 30 hxg6 fxg6 31 ♗xg6 ♘g5

Or 31...♘f8 32 ♘h5 ♘xg6 33 ♘f6+ ♔f7 34 ♕h7+ ♔f8 35 ♕g8#.

32 ♘h5 ♘f3+ 33 ♔g2 ♘h4+ 34 ♔g3 ♘xg6 35 ♘f6+ ♔f7 36 ♕h7+ 1-0

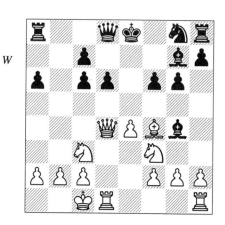

A. Ozsvath – J. Smejkal
Budapest 1970

Black has just played 10...♗c8-g4?, allowing a standard trick that is very surprising if you have never seen it before.

11 e5!! ♗xf3

11...fxe5 12 ♗xe5! gives White a large advantage, while 11...dxe5 12 ♕c4 ♗d7 13 ♖xd7 ♕xd7 14 ♖d1 ♕c8 15 ♕xc6+ is a winning attack.

12 exd6!

White's passed pawn will prove more valuable than a rook.

12...♗xd1 13 ♖e1+ ♔f8 14 ♕c5 ♕d7 15 dxc7+ ♘e7 16 ♖xe7! ♕xe7 17 ♗d6 ♔f7 18 ♗xe7 ♗g4 19 ♘e4

White has recouped the sacrificed material, while retaining his c7-pawn.

19...♖ae8 20 c8♕

This leads to a position where White's queen and knight will be deadly.

20...♗xc8 21 ♘d6+ ♔xe7 22 ♘xc8++ ♔d7 23 ♘b6+ ♔c7 24 ♘d5+ ♔d7 25 ♘b4 ♗h6+ 26 ♔d1 ♖e6 27 ♕a7+ ♔d6 28 ♕b6 ♖c8 29 ♘xa6 ♖e5 30 ♘b4 ♗f8 31 ♕a6 ♖c7 32 ♘d3 ♖e8

White has the position well under control, and now advances his pawns.

33 b4 ♔d7 34 a4 ♗d6 35 b5 ♖b8 36 b6
♖cc8 37 ♕a7+ ♔e6 38 b7 ♖d8 39 a5 c5 40 a6
c4 41 ♕b6 cxd3 42 a7 1-0

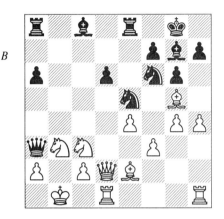

B. Bengtsson – C. Wahlblom
Swedish student Ch, Uppsala 1970

Black now plays an impressive combination.
20...♘exg4! 21 ♕xd6?
21 fxg4?? ♘xe4 is instantly terminal. 21 ♕c1
is necessary, but Black can be happy that he has
made very considerable positional gains.
21...♘xe4!! 22 ♕xa3?
22 fxe4 ♕xd6 23 ♖xd6 ♗xc3 gives Black all
the chances due to his better structure.
22...♘xc3+ 23 ♔c1 ♘xe2+ 24 ♔b1
24 ♔d2 ♗c3+ 25 ♔d3 ♗d7 is a massacre.
24...♘f2 25 ♖d8
25 ♗d2 ♗f5, threatening ...♖ec8, wins for
Black.
**25...♖xd8 26 ♗xd8 ♘xh1 27 ♕e7 ♘c3+ 28
♔c1 ♘xa2+ 29 ♔b1 ♘c3+ 30 ♔c1 h5 31
♕e8+ ♔h7 32 ♕xf7 ♗e6 33 ♕xe6 ♖xd8 34
♘d2 ♘g3 0-1**

Chess News in Brief
Fischer wins the Palma de Mallorca Interzonal by the large margin of 3½ points. He
scores 18½/23, ahead of Larsen, Geller, Hübner (all 15), Taimanov and Uhlmann (both 14).

Larsen wins the Lugano tournament with
9½/14, ahead of Olafsson (8½).

Fischer wins the Rovinj/Zagreb tournament
with 13/17, ahead of Hort, Smyslov, Gligorić,
Korchnoi (all 11) and Petrosian (10½).

Spassky wins a four-player tournament at
Leiden, ahead of Donner, Botvinnik and Larsen.

The Siegen Olympiad ends in a narrow victory for the USSR; in the A-final they score
27½/44, ahead of Hungary (26½), Yugoslavia
(26) and the USA (24½). Spassky makes the
best score on top board, just ahead of Fischer,
whom he defeated in their individual game.
England suffers the embarrassment of playing
in the C-final, having finished below Mongolia
in the preliminaries. 60 teams compete.

The final of the European Team Championship is played at Kapfenberg, with eight teams
competing. The USSR wins, with 52½/70, ahead
of Hungary (41) and East Germany (39½).

Korchnoi wins the 38th USSR Championship with 16/21, ahead of Tukmakov (14½) and
Stein (14). Karpov makes a solid debut at this
level, scoring 12 points.

Botvinnik retires from competitive chess to
concentrate on his work with chess-playing
computers.

Max Euwe becomes FIDE President.

FIDE adopts the Elo rating system, and the
first rating list is published.

Cosmonauts on *Soyuz 9* play a game of chess
against their ground crew.

World News in Brief
The *Apollo 13* mission almost ends in disaster as the craft is damaged by an explosion on
the way to the moon. Only extreme ingenuity,
both of the ground crew and of the astronauts,
enables the stricken craft to return safely to
Earth.

US planes bomb the Ho Chi Minh trail in
Laos, and US troops attack Communist military bases in Cambodia.

The IRA explodes bombs in Belfast and snip-
ers engage the British army in gun battles.

The Portuguese dictator Salazar dies.

Israeli troops raid Lebanon.

The Canadian government stands firm against
Quebec separatists, who are resorting to violence and kidnapping.

Biafra, lacking international support and
facing mass-starvation, surrenders to Nigeria.

A typhoon and tidal wave kill 150,000 in
East Pakistan.

1971

Fischer ruthless: 6-0 twice!

Fischer dominates the Candidates cycle. He scores unbelievable 6-0 (six wins, no draws, no losses) victories over first Taimanov and then Larsen. Petrosian (who edged out Korchnoi 5½-4½ in the semi-final, and whose quarter-final opponent, Hübner, resigned the match after seven games in protest at the playing conditions) initially holds Fischer at bay in the Candidates final, but four consecutive wins give Fischer victory in the match by the score 6½-2½. Thus Fischer qualifies to play Spassky for the World Championship.

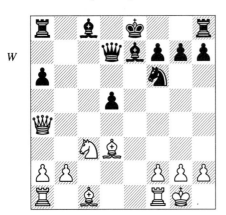

R. Fischer – T. Petrosian
Candidates match (7), Buenos Aires 1971

13 ♖e1!

Fischer is not interested in winning an exchange by 13 ♗b5?! axb5 14 ♕xa8 0-0, as this allows Black a good deal of counterplay.

13...♕xa4 14 ♘xa4

White aims to prove that the black a- and d-pawns are both serious weaknesses.

14...♗e6 15 ♗e3 0-0

15...♘d7 16 f4! g6 17 ♗d4 0-0 18 ♖ac1 is most unpleasant for Black.

16 ♗c5!

The dark-squared bishop is the most likely black piece to become active.

16...♖fe8 17 ♗xe7 ♖xe7 18 b4!

Both fixing Black's pawn on a6, and securing the c5-outpost.

18...♔f8 19 ♘c5 ♗c8 20 f3! ♖ea7?

Black's best chance of survival is 20...♖xe1+ 21 ♖xe1 ♘e8 22 ♔f2 ♘c7 23 ♔e3 ♔e7 24 ♔d4+ ♔d6.

21 ♖e5! ♗d7 22 ♘xd7+!!

Black's 'bad' bishop was holding Black's position together. Now his game disintegrates.

22...♖xd7 23 ♖c1 ♖d6 24 ♖c7 ♘d7 25 ♖e2 g6

After 25...♖e8 26 ♖xe8+ ♔xe8 27 ♖a7 ♘b8 28 a4 Black is tied up.

26 ♔f2 h5 27 f4 h4 28 ♔f3! f5 29 ♔e3 d4+ 30 ♔d2 ♘b6

Or 30...a5 31 bxa5 ♖xa5 32 ♖c8+ ♔g7 33 ♗c4 ♔f6 34 ♖ce8 ♘c5 35 ♖f8+ ♔g7 36 ♖f7+ ♔h6 37 ♖ee7 ♘e4+ 38 ♔d1 ♘f6 39 ♖f8 g5 40 ♖e5.

31 ♖ee7 ♘d5 32 ♖f7+ ♔e8 33 ♖b7 ♘xf4 34 ♗c4 1-0

Karpov and Stein share first place at the Alekhine Memorial tournament in Moscow with 11/17, ahead of Smyslov (10½), Tukmakov, Petrosian (both 10), Tal and Spassky (9½). One of Karpov's wins is especially beautiful:

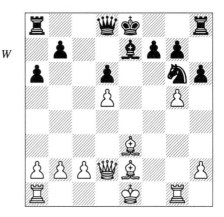

A. Karpov – V. Hort
Alekhine memorial, Moscow 1971

Black has just played 17...h6!?, attempting to remove the cramping g5-pawn.

18 gxh6 ♗h4+ 19 ♔d1

The white king turns out to be relatively safe here, whereas Black cannot castle safely.

19...gxh6 20 ♗xh6 ♗f6 21 c3 ♗e5 22 ♖g4!

The rook seems to be hanging in mid-air, yet it proves very well placed on the fourth rank.

22...♕f6 23 h4!

White consolidates his extra pawn, and now threatens 24 h5.

23...♕f5 24 ♖b4

Having secured White's kingside, the rook now probes the black queenside.

24...♗f6 25 h5 ♘e7

25...♘e5?? loses to 26 ♖f4.

26 ♖f4 ♕e5 27 ♖f3 ♘xd5 28 ♖d3

Again, the white rook finds an ideal regrouping.

28...♖xh6 29 ♖xd5 ♕e4 30 ♖d3!

Threatening the black rook and queen.

30...♕h1+ 31 ♔c2 ♕xa1 32 ♖xh6 ♗e5 33 ♕g5 1-0

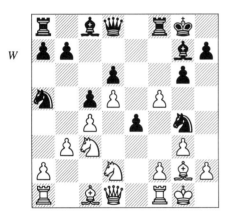

E. Geller – D. Velimirović
Havana 1971

Black has just played 12...e4?, a typical and ambitious King's Indian move.

13 f6!

This is the move that White 'wants' to play, from a positional viewpoint.

13...♘xf6 14 ♘dxe4

Geller's idea turns out to be a rook sacrifice. Instead, 14 ♗b2 e3 15 fxe3 ♘g4 gives Black good play, though 14 ♖b1 is reasonable.

14...♘xe4 15 ♘xe4 ♗xa1 16 ♗g5 ♗f6 17 ♘xf6+ ♖xf6 18 ♕a1 ♔f7 19 ♖e1 ♖b8 20 ♖e3!

20 ♖e8 ♔xe8 21 ♗xf6 ♕d7 22 ♗g5 ♕f5 gives White nothing better than a draw by 23 ♕h8+ ♕f8 24 ♕xh7 ♕f7 25 ♕h8+, etc.

20...b6

20...♗f5 21 h3 h6 (21...h5 22 g4 hxg4 23 hxg4 ♗xg4 24 ♗h3!) 22 ♗xh6 ♕h8 23 ♗g5 and g4 follows. 20...h6 is met by 21 ♗xh6 ♕h8 22 ♗g5 ♗f5 23 ♖f3 intending g4.

21 ♖f3 ♗f5 22 g4 ♕h8 23 ♗xf6 ♕xf6 24 ♕xf6+ ♔xf6 25 gxf5 gxf5 26 ♖e3

White has a winning advantage in this ending, due to the far superior placing of his pieces.

26...♘b7 27 ♖e6+ ♔f7 28 ♗f3 ♖g8+ 29 ♔f1 ♔f8 30 ♗h5 ♖g5 31 ♖e8+ ♔g7 32 ♖e7+ ♔h6 33 ♖xb7 ♖xh5 34 ♖xa7 ♖xh2 35 ♖d7 ♔g5 36 ♖xd6 ♔f4 37 ♔e2 b5 38 cxb5 ♔e5 39 ♖d7 ♖h4 40 a3 ♖h3 41 f3 ♔d4 42 b6 ♖h2+ 43 ♔e1 ♖h1+ 44 ♔f2 ♖h2+ 45 ♔e1 ♖h1+ 46 ♔f2 ♖h2+ 47 ♔g3 ♖b2 48 b7 ♖xb3 49 a4 c4 50 a5 c3 51 a6 1-0

Chess News in Brief

Korchnoi wins the Wijk aan Zee tournament with 10/15, ahead of Gligorić, Petrosian, Ivkov and Olafsson (all 9½).

Keres and Tal win the Tallinn tournament with 11½/15, ahead of Bronstein (11).

Korchnoi and Karpov share first place at the Hastings tournament (1971/2) with 11/15, ahead of Mecking and R.Byrne (9½).

Vladimir Savon is the surprising winner of the 39th USSR Championship, with 15/21, ahead of Smyslov, Tal (both 13½) and Karpov (13).

Horst Rittner wins the 6th Correspondence World Championship (1968-71).

Michael Adams [British grandmaster] is born.

World News in Brief

East Pakistan gains independence from Pakistan, with military support from India. The new nation is called Bangladesh.

Idi Amin seizes power in Uganda in a bloody coup.

China joins the United Nations.

Women are given the vote in Switzerland.

Apollo 15 astronauts use a moon rover to travel more extensively on the moon.

In Egypt, the Aswan High Dam is opened.

1972

Fischer is World Champion • Chess is headline news around the world

Fischer beats Spassky in one of the greatest sporting events of the century to become World Champion. There are grave doubts before the match whether Fischer will turn up, as there have been disagreements over the venue and financial conditions. When he finally arrives in Reykjavik, following persuasion by Henry Kissinger, and an addition to the prize-fund by Jim Slater, there are continuing disputes about various matters. Fischer loses the first game after a misguided attempt to liven up a drawish position. He then defaults the second game. Spassky refuses to follow an order to return home, and claim the match by default. Fischer's entourage manage to stop him leaving Iceland, and he returns to the chessboard – and dominates the rest of the match, scoring 7 wins, 1 loss and 11 draws, for an overall score of 12½-8½. There are plenty of further squabbles, which keep journalists happy, but do not seriously threaten the match.

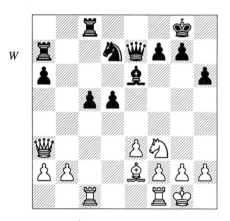

R. Fischer – B. Spassky
World Ch match (game 6), Reykjavik 1972

18 ♘d4! ♕f8

Now White brings about a favourable change in the structure. 18...♘f6 19 ♘b3 c4 20 ♕xe7 ♖xe7 21 ♘d4 a5! offers some counterplay.

19 ♘xe6! fxe6 20 e4!!

Now Black has no good way to resolve the central pawn structure.

20...d4

Now White can make progress without difficulty, but other lines are hardly more appealing: 20...♘f6 21 e5! ♘d7 22 f4, 20...dxe4 21 ♖c4 ♘f6 22 ♖fc1 or 20...c4 21 ♕h3! ♕f7 22 ♗h5! ♕e7 23 ♗g4! ♖e8 24 ♖fe1!.

21 f4 ♕e7 22 e5! ♖b8

Or 22...♘b6 23 ♕b3 ♘d5 24 f5! ♖b7 25 ♕a3! ♖cb8 26 f6 gxf6 27 exf6 ♘xf6 28 ♕g3+ ♔h8 29 ♕e5 ♖f8 30 ♖xc5 ♖xb2 31 ♖c6.

23 ♗c4 ♔h8

No better is 23...♘b6 24 ♕xc5 ♘xc4 25 ♕xc4 ♖xb2 26 ♕xd4.

24 ♕h3! ♘f8 25 b3 a5 26 f5 exf5 27 ♖xf5 ♘h7 28 ♖cf1! ♕d8 29 ♕g3 ♖e7 30 h4! ♖bb7 31 e6! ♖bc7 32 ♕e5! ♕e8

Black is mated after 32...♘f6? 33 ♖xf6 gxf6 34 ♖xf6.

33 a4 ♕d8 34 ♖1f2 ♕e8 35 ♖2f3 ♕d8 36 ♗d3 ♕e8 37 ♕e4 ♘f6

Or 37...♖xe6 38 ♖f8+ ♘xf8 39 ♖xf8+ ♕xf8 40 ♕h7#.

38 ♖xf6! gxf6 39 ♖xf6 ♔g8 40 ♗c4!? ♔h8 41 ♕f4 1-0

Mate follows shortly.

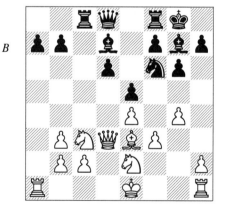

J. Bednarski – A. Adorjan
Varna 1972

We now see a display of extreme dynamism from a young Hungarian talent.

14...d5! 15 ♗g5

15 exd5 e4! 16 fxe4 (16 ♘xe4?! ♘xe4 17 ♕xe4 f5 18 ♕d3 fxg4 gives Black a great deal of activity) 16...♘xg4 17 ♗d4 ♗xd4 18 ♘xd4 f5 is a murky position, but in practice Black's chances must be preferred. 15 ♘xd5 ♘xd5 16 exd5 e4! 17 ♕xe4 f5 is likewise very good for Black.

15...d4 16 ♘d5

16 ♗xf6 ♗xf6 17 ♘d5 ♗h4+ 18 ♘g3 f5 is no safer for White.

16...♘xd5!!

This fantastic queen sacrifice is based on the poor position of the white king, and the white queen's inability to find an effective square.

17 ♗xd8 ♘b4 18 ♕d2 ♘xc2+ 19 ♔f2 ♘xa1 20 ♗e7?

20 ♖xa1 ♖fxd8 21 ♖xa7 ♗c6 (21...♗b5 22 ♖xb7 ♗xe2 23 ♔xe2 d3+ 24 ♔d1 is not at all clear) 22 g5 d3! 23 ♘c3 ♗f8 24 ♖a5 ♗b4 25 ♖xe5 ♖a8, intending ...♖a2, wins for Black.

20...♘xb3 21 ♕b4

21 ♕d1 ♖fe8 22 ♕xb3 ♖xe7 23 ♕xb7 ♗f8 is hopeless for White.

21...♗e6! 22 ♗xf8 ♗xf8

Black only has two bishops for the queen, but, together with his passed d-pawn, they overwhelm the uncoordinated white forces.

23 ♕xb7

23 ♕e1 ♖c2 24 ♔g3 ♗c4 also sees Black walking into White's position.

23...♖c2 24 ♔e1 ♗c4 25 ♘g3 d3 26 ♘f1 ♖e2+ 27 ♔d1 ♖xb2 0-1

28 ♔e1 ♖e2+ 29 ♔d1 ♘a5 is devastating.

Chess News in Brief

The Fischer-Spassky match makes headlines around the world, and features regularly on television news bulletins. Chess achieves a new status in the West, as it is suddenly seen as an exciting activity from which it is possible to make a living. Sales of chess sets and books increase dramatically. Fischer promises to be an active champion, but little does anyone realize that he is not to play again for twenty years.

The Skopje Olympiad finishes in victory for the USSR team, who score 42/60 in the A-final, ahead of Hungary (40½), Yugoslavia (38) and Czechoslovakia (35½). Hübner makes the best score on top board, just ahead of Hort. Karpov scores 13/15 as second reserve. Journalists report that a Mrs Grumer plays for the Virgin Islands team – while seven months pregnant! 62 teams compete. For the first time, the Women's Olympiad is played alongside (this practice has continued ever since); also for the first time, there are sufficient entries to necessitate preliminary groups. The USSR wins the A-final with 11½/14, ahead of Romania and Hungary (both 8).

Tal, in a period of excellent health and form, wins the 40th USSR Championship. He scores 15/21, ahead of Tukmakov (13).

Alexei Shirov [Latvian grandmaster] is born.

Loek van Wely [Dutch grandmaster] is born.

World News in Brief

The last US ground forces withdraw from Vietnam.

Following increasing sectarian violence in Northern Ireland, Britain imposes direct rule on the province, suspending the Protestant-dominated provincial government. Catholics applaud the move.

Britain, Ireland, Denmark and Norway join the European Common Market.

Richard Nixon wins a second term as President of the USA by a landslide, but a week later seven men, including former White House aides, are indicted for conspiracy to break into the Democratic Party's headquarters in Washington's Watergate complex.

The Olympic Games in Munich are marred by a massacre of Israeli athletes. Black September guerrillas shoot two Israelis and take nine hostage. In a failed rescue attempt, all nine are killed, together with four guerrillas and a German police officer.

Survivors of an aeroplane crash in the Andes admit to cannibalism during a 69-day ordeal.

An earthquake strikes Nicaragua, killing 100,000.

Apollo 16 astronauts John Young and Charles Duke spend 71 hours on the moon.

Pioneer 10 is launched. Its destination is the planet Jupiter.

1973

Karpov and Mecking become Candidates

For the first time, there are two interzonal tournaments, with three players qualifying from each. This is both to reduce the length of the tournaments, and to provide more places for qualifiers from zonal tournaments. The Leningrad Interzonal is won jointly by Korchnoi and Karpov with 13½/17, presaging their future rivalry, ahead of R.Byrne (12½). The Petropolis Interzonal is won by the new star Mecking with 12/17, ahead of Geller, Polugaevsky and Portisch (all 11½). Geller comes last in a three-way play-off, and so fails to qualify.

There follow three interesting games from various events.

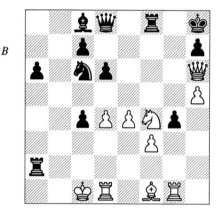

V. Bagirov – E. Gufeld
USSR Ch semi-final, Kirovabad 1973

This chaotic position has arisen from a Sämisch King's Indian. Everything now depends on the speed of both sides' respective attacks.

21...℟xf4! 22 ♕xf4 c3!

This pawn helps Black to generate mating ideas.

23 ♗c4

Black mates after 23 ♕f7 ♘b4 24 ♗d3 ℟a1+ 25 ♗b1 ♗e6! 26 ♕xe6 ♕g5+.

23...℟a3!!

This move is based on extremely fine calculation. 23...℟a4 24 ♗b3 ♘xd4 25 ℟xd4 ℟xd4 26 fxg4 allows White counterplay.

24 fxg4

24 ♔b1 ♗e6!, threatening 25...♕b8+, is a win for Black.

24...♘b4 25 ♔b1! ♗e6!!

25...c2+? 26 ♔b2 cxd1♕ 27 ℟xd1 allows White's own threats to come to the fore.

26 ♗xe6 ♘d3!

Not 26...♘d5? 27 exd5 ♕b8+ 28 ♔c2 ♕b2+ 29 ♔d3 c2+ 30 ♔e4, when Black will be mated.

27 ♕f7 ♕b8+ 28 ♗b3

Or 28 ♔c2 ♘b4+ 29 ♔b1 ℟a1+ 30 ♔xa1 ♘c2+ 31 ♔a2 ♕b2#.

28...℟xb3+ 29 ♔c2

It is Black to play and mate in eight moves!

29...♘b4+!! 30 ♔xb3

Or 30 ♔c1 ℟b1+! 31 ♔xb1 ♘d5+ 32 ♔c2 ♕b2+, etc.

30...♘d5+! 31 ♔c2 ♕b2+ 32 ♔d3 ♕b5+ 0-1

The finish is 33 ♔c2 ♕e2+ 34 ♔b3 ♕b2+ 35 ♔c4 ♕b5#.

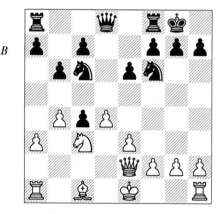

B. Rõtov – J. Timman
Tallinn 1973

12...b5! 13 ♘xb5 ♕d5 14 ♘xc7 ♕xg2 15 ♕f1?

Overlooking Black's follow-up. 15 ℟f1 ℟ac8 16 ♘b5 is essential; White can then hope to stay in the fight, as the following lines demonstrate: 16...℟fd8 17 f3 ♕xe2+ 18 ♔xe2; 16...e5 17 ♗b2 exd4 18 ♗xd4 ♘g4 (18...a6 19 ♗xf6; 18...♘xd4 19 ♘xd4) 19 f3 ♕xe2+ 20 ♔xe2.

15...♕f3! 16 ♘xa8 ♘xd4! 17 exd4

17 ♖a2 loses to 17...♘b3, while after 17 ♗b2 c3 18 ♗xc3 ♘c2+ 19 ♔d2 ♘xa1 20 ♗xa1 ♘e4+ Black's attack is quickly decisive.

17...♕c3+ 18 ♔e2 ♕xa1 19 ♕g2

19 ♘c7 ♕xd4 20 ♗e3 ♕d3+ 21 ♔e1 ♕b1+ 22 ♔e2 ♕c2+ 23 ♔f3 ♕e4+ 24 ♔e2 c3 will give Black a material advantage.

19...♕a2+ 20 ♔e1 ♕b1! 21 ♔d2 ♘e4+ 22 ♔e3 ♕d3+ 23 ♔f4 g5+ 24 ♔e5 ♖d8 0-1

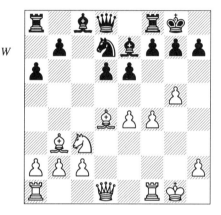

W

L. Yurtaev – E. Kengis
Junior event, Vilnius 1973

White now launches a crude but strong attack.

14 ♕h5 e5

14...♘c5 loses to 15 ♖f3 ♘xb3 16 ♖h3. There is no time for the standard defensive idea 14...♖e8 15 ♖f3 g6? because of 16 ♕xh7+! ♔xh7 17 ♖h3+ ♔g8 18 ♖h8#.

15 fxe5 g6 16 ♖xf7!!

A devastating queen sacrifice.

16...gxh5 17 ♖xe7+ ♔h8 18 exd6+ ♘f6

Yurtaev now complicates matters somewhat with a series of puzzling decisions, though he does not jeopardize the win.

19 ♖d1?! ♗g4 20 gxf6?! h6 21 ♖d3 ♕xd6 22 ♘d5 b5 23 ♔h1 a5 24 ♗e5 ♕c5 25 ♘f4 ♖g8 26 f7+ ♖g7 27 f8♕+ 1-0

Chess News in Brief

The final of the European Team Championship is held at Bath. The USSR wins, scoring 40½/56, ahead of Yugoslavia (34) and Hungary (33).

Szabo and Geller win the double-round Hilversum tournament with 9½/14, ahead of Ljubojević (8½).

Tal wins the Sochi tournament with 11/15, a point ahead of Spassky.

Karpov wins the Madrid tournament with 11/15, ahead of Tukmakov (10½) and Furman (10).

Tal wins the Wijk aan Zee tournament with 10½/15, ahead of Balashov (10).

Hecht, Andersson and Spassky share first place at the Dortmund tournament.

Spassky wins the 41st USSR Championship in the midst of a crackdown by the authorities. The top GMs have to play in the Championship, and are being made to work harder – draws before move 30 are not allowed. The result is slightly embarrassing for the authorities, if they were trying to show that Spassky's loss to Fischer was due to some weakness on Spassky's part. Spassky scores 11½/17, ahead of a group of five players on 10½ (Karpov, Korchnoi, Kuzmin, Petrosian and Polugaevsky).

Leonid Stein dies suddenly.

Joel Lautier [French grandmaster] is born.

World News in Brief

Several White House aides resign over the Watergate scandal. Vice President Agnew resigns after admitting to tax evasion.

Israeli jets shoot down a Libyan airliner.

Egypt and Syria launch an attack on Israel during Yom Kuppur, a Jewish religious holiday.

The Arab oil embargo, a retaliatory measure against the USA's support for Israel, causes widespread economic disruption. The price of oil soars, and in the USA, there are plans for fuel rationing. Together with industrial action in the mines, power stations and railways, the embargo prompts the British government to put the country on a three-day week. The silver lining for Britain is that the crisis increases the value of North Sea oil.

General Pinochet seizes power in Chile following a violent coup.

The army seizes power in Greece.

It is discovered that Saturn's rings are made of numerous fragments, ranging in size from large chunks down to dust grains.

1974

Karpov is Fischer's challenger

Karpov convincingly wins the Candidates cycle. His progress is smooth, and he seems to develop his skills and widen his repertoire with each match. He beats Polugaevsky 5½-2½ in the quarter-final, and then Spassky 7-4 in the semi-final – no less convincing than Fischer's win against the same player. The Candidates final is a long drawn-out war of attrition against Korchnoi. Karpov wins 12½-11½, including 19 draws.

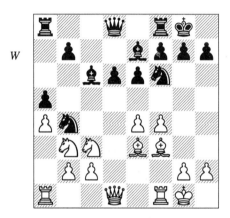

A. Karpov – B. Spassky
Candidates match (game 9), Leningrad 1974

13 ♘d4

Black will now need to guard the f5-square if he wishes to play ...e5.

13...g6 14 ♖f2 e5 15 ♘xc6 bxc6 16 fxe5 dxe5 17 ♕f1!

Karpov perceives that c4 is a key square for the queen.

17...♕c8 18 h3 ♘d7

18...♕e6 fails to keep White out of c4, since there follows 19 ♖c1 ♖fd8 20 ♗e2.

19 ♗g4 h5?! 20 ♗xd7 ♕xd7 21 ♕c4 ♗h4 22 ♖d2 ♕e7 23 ♖f1! ♖fd8 24 ♘b1!

White intends to find a more appropriate role for this knight. If Black exchanges on d2, the knight is immediately on a good circuit, and this fact gives White time to arrange his rooks most effectively.

24...♕b7 25 ♔h2! ♔g7 26 c3 ♘a6 27 ♖e2!

Karpov preserves his rook, as the plan now is to batter Black down the f-file.

27...♖f8 28 ♘d2 ♗d8 29 ♘f3 f6

Black has fortified the f-file at the cost of further weaknesses and loss of mobility, so White returns to the d-file.

30 ♖d2 ♗e7 31 ♕e6 ♖ad8 32 ♖xd8 ♗xd8

32...♖xd8 loses to 33 ♘xe5 ♕c7 34 ♕f7+ ♔h8 35 ♕xe7!.

33 ♖d1 ♘b8 34 ♗c5 ♖h8 35 ♖xd8! 1-0

A win by Portisch from his 6-7 quarter-final loss against Petrosian:

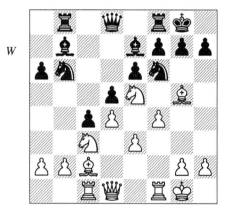

L. Portisch – T. Petrosian
Candidates match (game 10), Palma 1974

Petrosian's famous sense of danger has let him down here, and White has a very strong attack.

15 f5! ♘bd7 16 ♗f4 ♖c8

16...♘xe5 17 dxe5 ♘e8 18 f6 rips open the black kingside.

17 ♕f3

White's threats include both 18 fxe6 and 18 ♕h3.

17...exf5 18 ♗xf5 ♘xe5 19 dxe5 ♘e4 20 ♘xe4! dxe4 21 ♕h3 g6 22 ♖cd1 ♕b6 23 ♖d7 ♖ce8 24 e6!

White's threat of 25 exf7+ forces Black to respond.

24...gxf5

24...♗c6 loses to 25 ♗c7 followed by 26 exf7+ and 27 ♗e6.

25 ♖xe7 ♖xe7 26 ♕g3+ ♔h8 27 ♗h6 fxe6

27...♖g8 28 ♕e5+ f6 29 ♕xf6+ ♖eg7 30 ♖d1 is a win for White.

28 ♗xf8 ♖d7

After 28...♖f7 29 ♗d6 the bishop reaches e5.

29 ♗h6

Missing a clear win by 29 ♕e5+ ♔g8 30 ♗h6.

29...♕a5?

29...♕c5 is best met by 30 ♗g5 ♕f8 31 ♗f4!.

30 ♕b8+ ♕d8 31 ♕e5+ ♔g8 32 ♕xe6+ ♖f7 33 ♖xf5 1-0

An impressive attacking game from the final:

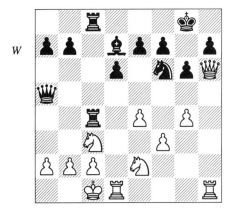

A. Karpov – V. Korchnoi
Candidates match (game 2), Moscow 1974

19 ♖d3!

Karpov introduces a novelty. The basic idea is to support the c3-knight before pressing ahead with play against the black king.

19...♖4c5?

It is little wonder that Korchnoi fails to find a good answer at the board, as there may not actually be one. 19...♗e6 20 g5 ♘h5 21 ♘g3 ♕e5! 22 ♘xh5 gxh5 23 ♖xh5! is good for White.

20 g5!

The move Black has just tried to prevent! The idea is to disrupt Black's coordination.

20...♖xg5 21 ♖d5! ♖xd5 22 ♘xd5

Now Black cannot keep a knight on f6.

22...♖e8 23 ♘ef4 ♗c6 24 e5! ♗xd5 25 exf6 exf6 26 ♕xh7+ ♔f8 27 ♕h8+ 1-0

Chess News in Brief

Evgeny Vasiukov wins the Manila tournament with 10½/14, ahead of Petrosian (9½) and Larsen (9).

The Nice Olympiad is won by the USSR, who score 46/60 in the A-final, ahead of Yugoslavia (37½), the USA and Bulgaria (both 36½). Karpov's 12/14 is the best score on top board; Torre's 14/19 is also notable. Three other Soviet players make the best score on their board, while Korchnoi's score is only bettered by Farooqi of Pakistan (16½/21), who plays in the D-final.

Tal and Beliavsky share the 42nd USSR Championship. They score 9½/15, ahead of Vaganian and Polugaevsky (both 9).

Walter Browne wins the United States Championship for the first of six times.

Tony Miles wins the World Junior Championship.

Gata Kamsky [Russian/Tartar, later American, grandmaster] is born.

Matthew Sadler [British grandmaster] is born.

World News in Brief

Turkish forces invade Cyprus, and divide the island in two. Greece is indignant that no assistance is forthcoming from its NATO allies.

President Nixon, convicted by grand jury and faced with impeachment, resigns from office.

Haile Selassie, ruler of Ethiopia for 58 years, is deposed in a bloodless coup.

Escalating violence in Northern Ireland brings the death toll since the troubles started in 1969 to over 1,000. The IRA takes its bombing campaign to the British mainland, notably killing 17 in two Birmingham pubs.

In Portugal, a military junta seizes power, and promises democratic reforms and elections, ending 40 years of dictatorial rule.

The British government is brought to its knees by the miner's strike, and calls a general election. By the end of the year inflation is at 20%.

Scientists Michael McElroy and Steven Wofsy claim that Freon gas, which is used as a propellant in aerosol spray cans, is damaging the atmosphere's ozone layer, which protects the Earth against harmful ultraviolet radiation.

1975

Karpov becomes World Champion by default to the dismay of Fischer's fans

Petrosian wins the 43rd USSR Championship with 10/15, ahead of a group of players with 9½ points (Vaganian, Gulko, Romanishin and Tal).

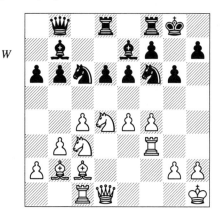

O. Romanishin – T. Petrosian
USSR Ch, Erevan 1975

16 ♘d5!? exd5 17 exd5!

For many years, Romanishin's combination was considered to be devalued because he 'missed' 17 ♘f5 '!! winning'. However, then 17...dxe4 18 ♘xe7+ (18 ♖g3 ♕c7 19 ♕h5 ♗c8 parries the threats) 18...♘xe7 19 ♕d4 d5! 20 ♕xf6 d4 is very unclear.

17...♘xd4 18 ♕xd4

White has just a pawn for his piece, but Black is bottled up and must address the threat of ♖e3.

18...♖de8 19 f5! ♗d8 20 ♕h4 ♖e5!

20...♘xd5? is mated by 21 ♕xh7+, while 20...♘h5? allows 21 ♕xh5.

21 ♕h6 ♕c7?

21...♘g4! is the correct defence, when White may have nothing better than 22 ♕f4 ♘f6 23 ♕h6, repeating.

22 ♖g3

Now White's attack is unstoppable.

22...♗c8

After 22...♘e8 23 ♖f1 ♕e7 24 ♖h3 ♘f6 25 ♗xe5 dxe5 26 fxg6 fxg6 27 ♗xg6 ♕g7 28 ♗xh7+ ♘xh7 29 ♕xg7+ ♔xg7 30 ♖xh7+ ♔xh7 31 ♖xf8 White wins a black bishop.

23 ♗xe5 dxe5 24 fxg6 fxg6 25 ♗xg6! ♘g4 26 ♗h5 ♖f6 27 ♕d2 ♖f4 28 d6 ♕g7 29 d7 ♗b7?

29...♕xd7 30 ♕xd7 ♗xd7 31 ♗xg4 ♖xg4 32 ♖d1 will give White a winning rook ending.

30 ♕xf4! 1-0

In view of 30...exf4 31 ♖xg4 ♗g5 32 ♖d1.

Ljubomir Ljubojević wins the Las Palmas tournament with 11/14, ahead of Mecking, Andersson and Tal (all 10).

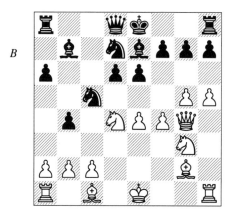

L. Ljubojević – M. Tal
Las Palmas 1975

Tal is under attack from a highly aggressive player.

14...h6!? 15 g6 0-0!

Intending 16...f5.

16 gxf7+ ♖xf7 17 ♗e3

17 ♘xe6? ♘xe6 18 ♕xe6 ♗h4 is good for Black.

17...♕c7 18 0-0!

The king is safer on the kingside, protected by a mass of pieces, than on the queenside.

18...♗f6

18...♘f6? 19 ♕g6 ♘cd7? loses to 20 ♘xe6 ♕c4 21 ♘f5 ♕xe6 22 ♘xh6+ ♔f8 23 f5.

19 ♘xe6 ♘xe6 20 ♕xe6 ♗xb2 21 ♖ad1 ♘f6 22 ♕xd6 ♘g4! 23 ♗b6 ♕xc2 24 ♕e6 ♘f6 25 ♘f5?!

25 ♕b3 ♕xb3 (25...♖c8?? loses to 26 ♖d8+) 26 axb3 gives White a pleasant ending.

25...♖e8 26 ♖d8 ♖xd8 27 ♗xd8 ♗xe4! 28 ♗xe4 ♘xe4

28...♕xe4? allows 29 ♕xf7+ ♔xf7 30 ♘d6+.

29 ♗b6

Not 29 ♕e8+? ♖f8 30 ♘e7+ ♔h7 31 ♕xf8?? ♗d4+ and Black forces mate.

29...♕d3

Now the game will end in perpetual check.

30 ♖e1 ♘d6 31 ♘xd6 ♕g3+ 32 ♔h1 ♕f3+ 33 ♔g1 ½-½

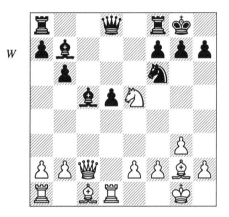

W

A. Karpov – B. Spassky
USSR Spartakiad, Riga 1975

Spassky has just taken on an isolated queen's pawn, but Karpov is ideally positioned to handle this structure.

14 ♘d3 ♗d6

Karpov considered 14...♖c8 15 ♘xc5 ♖xc5 a better defensive try.

15 ♗f4 ♖e8 16 e3 ♘e4 17 ♗xd6 ♕xd6 18 ♘f4 ♖ac8 19 ♕a4 ♕e7 20 ♕xa7!

Karpov has calculated that he can cope with Black's threats against f2.

20...♘xf2

20...d4 21 exd4! ♘xf2 fails to 22 ♖e1.

21 ♘xd5 ♗xd5 22 ♕xe7 ♘xd1

22...♖xe7 23 ♖xd5 ♘g4 24 ♗h3 ♘xe3 25 ♗xc8 ♘xd5 26 ♖d1 gives White a good ending.

23 ♖c1! ♖b8 24 ♕b4 ♗xg2 25 ♔xg2 ♘e3+ 26 ♔g1 ♖e6 27 ♕f4 ♖d8 28 ♕d4! ♖de8 29 ♕d7 ♘g4 30 ♖c8 ♘f6

Black isn't helped by 30...♖e1+ 31 ♔g2 ♖e2+ 32 ♔h3 ♘f2+ 33 ♔h4 ♖e4+ 34 g4 ♖xg4+ 35 ♕xg4, again exploiting the back rank.

31 ♖xe8+ ♖xe8 32 ♕b7 ♖e6 33 ♕b8+ ♘e8 34 a4 g6 35 b4 ♔g7 36 ♕b7 h5 37 h3 ♔f6 38 ♔g2 ♖d6 39 a5 bxa5 40 bxa5

Black's only hope is to give up his knight for the a-pawn and try to set up a blockade.

40...♖e6 41 a6 ♘c7 42 a7 ♖e7 43 ♕c6+ ♔e5 44 ♔f3 1-0

Chess News in Brief

Karpov is awarded the World Championship after Fischer and FIDE fail to agree terms.

Portisch wins the Wijk aan Zee tournament with 10½/15, ahead of Hort (10).

Karpov wins his first tournament as World Champion, in Milan.

Geller wins the Teesside tournament – the strongest in England for many years.

Ljubojević wins the Manila tournament.

Murray Chandler (born 1960) wins the New Zealand Championship (1975/6).

Paul Keres dies.

Fritz Sämisch dies.

Vladimir Kramnik [Russian GM] is born.

Veselin Topalov [Bulgarian GM] is born.

World News in Brief

Civil war between Moslems and Christians causes massive damage in Beirut.

The Vietnam War ends, as South Vietnam surrenders. Communist forces gain control of Cambodia, ending a five-year civil war.

Angola is granted independence by Portugal, but within the next two weeks about 40,000 people have been killed in fighting.

General Franco dies, and King Juan Carlos II becomes the new leader of Spain. He acknowledges the need for reforms.

In Britain, Margaret Thatcher becomes leader of the Conservative Party.

In a referendum, the British electorate decides to remain in the Common Market.

American *Apollo* astronauts and Soviet *Soyuz* cosmonauts dock their crafts in space in an unprecedented international mission. To avoid misunderstandings, the Americans speak Russian and the Soviets speak English.

1976

Karpov proves he is a worthy Champion by dominating tournament chess • Korchnoi defects

Karpov wins the Skopje tournament with a score of 12½/15, ahead of Uhlmann (11) and Timman (10½).

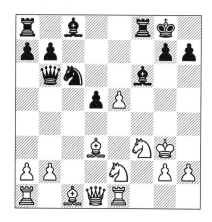

S. Reshevsky – R. Vaganian
Skopje 1976

16...♗h4+!! 17 ♔xh4 ♖xf3!

Now that the king has been dragged up the board, Black eliminates its best defender.

18 ♖f1

18 gxf3 is met by 18...♕f2+ 19 ♔g5·h6+ 20 ♔g6 ♘e7+ 21 ♔h5 ♕xh2#.

18...♕b4+ 19 ♗f4

19 ♘f4 ♕e7+ 20 ♔h5 ♕xe5+ 21 ♔h4 ♕f6+ 22 ♔h5 ♕h6# is another way to be mated.

19...♕e7+ 20 ♗g5

Or 20 ♔h5 ♕e6 21 gxf3 ♕h3+ 22 ♔g5 ♕h6#.

20...♕e6!

White must now return the piece to avoid mate.

21 ♗f5 ♖xf5 22 ♘f4

22 ♖xf5 ♕xf5 23 ♕xd5+ ♗e6 24 ♕f3 ♕xe5 25 ♗f4 g5+! 26 ♗xg5 ♕xh2+.

22...♕xe5 23 ♕g4 ♖f7 24 ♕h5 ♘e7 25 g4 ♘g6+ 26 ♔g3 ♗d7 27 ♖ae1 ♕d6 28 ♗h6 ♖af8 0-1

An excellent finish by Julian Hodgson (born 1963):

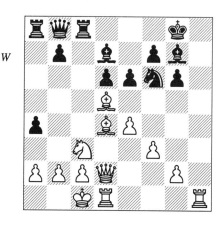

W

J. Hodgson – D. Paunović
London-Belgrade telex match, 1976

17 ♕g5! e5

17...exd5 18 ♕xf6! forces mate.

18 ♖h8+!! ♔xh8

After 18...♗xh8 White forces mate by 19 ♕xg6+ ♗g7 20 ♕xf7+ ♔h8 21 ♖h1+ ♘h7 22 ♖xh7+ ♔xh7 23 ♕h5+ ♗h6+ 24 ♗e3.

19 ♗xf7 ♖g8 20 ♖h1+ 1-0

An impressive game from one Garry Kasparov (born 1963):

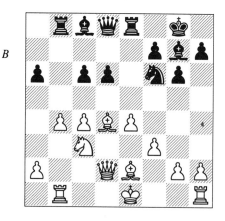

B

S. Lputian – G. Kasparov
Caucasus Youth Games, Tbilisi 1976

15...c5!

Kasparov has spotted the possible vulnerability of the white rooks on b1 and h1.

16 bxc5

16 ♗xf6 ♗xf6 17 ♘d5 is safer.

16...♘xe4!! 17 fxe4

Not 17 ♘xe4? ♖xb1+.

17...♕h4+ 18 g3?!

18 ♔f1 ♖xb1+ 19 ♘xb1 ♕xe4 20 ♗xg7 ♕xb1+ 21 ♕d1 ♕f5+ 22 ♗f3 ♔xg7 23 cxd6 gives White better drawing chances.

18...♖xb1+ 19 ♔f2 ♖b2!!

Now White is forced into a rotten ending.

20 gxh4 ♖xd2 21 ♗xg7 ♔xg7 22 ♔e3 ♖c2 23 ♔d3 ♖xc3+!

23...♖b2 24 cxd6 ♗b7 25 ♗f3 f5 is messier.

24 ♔xc3 dxc5 25 ♗d3 ♗b7 26 ♖e1 ♖e5! 27 a4 f5 28 ♖b1 ♗xe4 29 ♖b6 f4! 30 ♖xa6 f3 31 ♗f1 ♗f5! 32 ♖a7+ ♔h6 33 ♔d2 f2 34 ♗e2 ♗g4! 35 ♗d3 ♖e1 36 ♖f7 ♗f5! 37 a5 ♗xd3! 38 ♖xf2 ♖f1! 0-1

Chess News in Brief

Karpov is an active champion; he enhances his credibility as Champion with a series of impressive tournament results.

Korchnoi and Miles win the IBM tournament in Amsterdam with 9½/15, ahead of Sax (9). After the tournament, Korchnoi asks the Dutch authorities for asylum. He is subsequently regarded as a non-person by the Soviet authorities, who boycott tournaments where he plays. His wife and son remain in the Soviet Union.

Ljubojević and Olafsson win the Wijk aan Zee tournament with 7½/11, ahead of Kurajica and Tal (both 6½).

Karpov wins a four-man tournament in Amsterdam, but is second behind Eugenio Torre in a similar event in Manila.

The Haifa Olympiad is blighted by a Soviet boycott. The USA takes first place with 37/52, ahead of the Netherlands (36½), England (35½) and Argentina (33). Jan Timman makes the best score on top board. Only 48 teams compete. Israel wins the Women's Olympiad.

There are again two interzonals, each with three qualifying places for the Candidates matches. The Manila Interzonal is won by Mecking, with Polugaevsky and Hort joint second. The Biel Interzonal is won by Larsen ahead of Petrosian, Portisch and Tal. Tal loses out in a three-way play-off and fails to qualify for the Candidates matches.

Karpov wins the 44th USSR Championship with 12/17, ahead of Balashov (11), Petrosian and Polugaevsky (10½).

Tony Miles becomes Britain's first over-the-board grandmaster.

Yakov Estrin wins the 7th Correspondence World Championship (1972-6).

Peter Svidler [Russian grandmaster] is born.

Judit Polgar [Hungarian, who is to become the strongest woman player, and the youngest grandmaster, in history] is born.

Vadim Zviagintsev [Russian grandmaster] is born.

Chess computers, capable of giving social players a reasonable game, become commercially available.

World News in Brief

In Guatemala, an earthquake kills 22,000 and leaves a million homeless.

Israeli commandos make a daring raid at Entebbe Airport in Uganda, to rescue 105 hostages held by pro-Palestinian hijackers.

Mao Zedong dies. Subsequently, his widow and three other prominent officials, the 'Gang of Four', are officially denounced as "like dog dung".

Unrest sweeps the black townships in South Africa, culminating in rioting in Soweto. The police brutally restore order.

Rhodesia moves towards majority rule.

Britain and Iceland make an agreement to end the third Cod War. Icelandic ships had been cutting British trawlers' lines inside Iceland's 200-mile exclusion zone.

The British government applies for a $3.9 billion loan from the International Monetary Fund. It is a humiliating moment for the country.

The USA celebrates its bicentenary.

In China, a massive earthquake devastates Tangshan.

A boycott by African nations mars the Montreal Olympics.

Viking 1 lands on Mars, and sends back pictures from the surface.

1977

Korchnoi wins through a tempestuous Candidates cycle

Spassky and Korchnoi contest a politically charged Candidates final. Korchnoi dominates the first part of the match, but then loses four in a row after Spassky adopts the policy of only coming to the board to make his moves, and analysing from his box on the demonstration board. This is argued to be against the rules, and an enormous row develops. Korchnoi wins in the end by 10½-7½ (with just 7 draws). Korchnoi's previous matches had seen him narrowly win a grudge match against Petrosian (both men had hated each other for years) 6½-5½, and overwhelm Polugaevsky 8½-4½. Spassky scored a fortunate victory over Hort in the quarter-final, and then beat Portisch 8½-6½ in the semi-final.

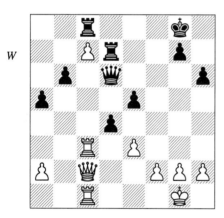

V. Korchnoi – B. Spassky
Candidates match (game 7), Belgrade 1977

Korchnoi brilliantly proves that his passed pawn is the stronger.

26 ♖c6 ♕d5 27 ♕b1 d3 28 ♕xb6 d2 29 ♖d1 ♕xa2

Many grandmaster commentators considered Black to be winning at this point.

30 h3!!

With perfect timing, Korchnoi secures his back-rank. 30 ♕b7 ♕a4! 31 ♕xc8+ ♔h7 32 ♕h8+ (32 h3 ♕xc6 gives White no advantage) 32...♔xh8 33 c8♕+ ♔h7 34 ♖c2 loses to the unexpected 34...♕a1!.

30...♕a4 31 ♖xd2! ♖xd2 32 ♕b7 ♖dd8

Not 32...♖xc7? 33 ♖xc7, when g7 collapses, as 33...♕a1+ 34 ♔h2 e4 35 ♕c8+ ♔h7 36 ♕f5+ forces mate.

33 cxd8♕+ ♖xd8 34 ♖c7 ♕a1+ 35 ♔h2 e4

Black's a-pawn is not far enough advanced to cause White any real problems.

36 ♕xe4 ♕f6 37 f4 ♕f8 38 ♖a7 ♕c5 39 ♕b7 ♕c3 40 ♔e7 ♖f8 41 e4 ♕d4 42 f5 h5

42...a4 43 ♖d7 ♕f6 (else 44 e5) 44 ♕xf6 and 45 ♖a7 wins the a-pawn.

43 ♖xa5 ♕d2 44 ♕e5 ♕g5 45 ♖a6 ♖f7 46 ♖g6 ♕d8 47 f6 h4 48 fxg7 1-0

Karpov dominates the Las Palmas tournament, scoring 13½/15, ahead of Larsen (11) and Timman (10).

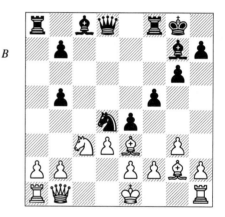

S. Tatai – A. Karpov
Las Palmas 1977

18...b4 19 ♘d1 ♖e8 20 dxe4 fxe4 21 ♗xd4

21 ♗xe4? loses to 21...♖xe4 22 ♕xe4 ♗f5.

21...♕xd4 22 a3

22 0-0 ♕d2 23 ♗xe4 ♗h3 24 ♗g2 ♗xg2 25 ♔xg2 ♖xe2 puts White under great pressure.

22...♗g4

Discouraging White from castling, and also threatening 23...♗f3.

23 ♕c2 ♕d3!

A powerful temporary queen sacrifice.

24 exd3

This leads to disaster, but there was no real solution to White's problems. 24 ♘e3 ♕xc2 25 ♘xc2 ♗xb2, 24 ♖c1 bxa3 and 24 ♕d2 ♕xd2+ 25 ♔xd2 ♖ac8! all favour Black.

24...exd3+ 25 ♔d2 ♖e2+ 26 ♔xd3 ♖d8+ 27 ♔c4

27 ♗d5+ ♖xd5+ 28 ♔c4 ♖xc2+ 29 ♔xd5 ♗f3+ forces mate.

27...♖xc2+ 28 ♔xb4 ♖cd2 29 f3 ♗f8+ 30 ♔a5 ♗d7! 0-1

The white king will be mated.

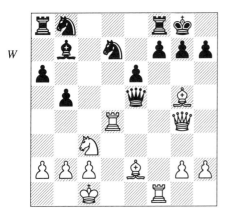

H. Westerinen – G. Sigurjonsson
New York 1977

White has given up a pawn for a strong attack.
16 ♖d3 f5 17 ♕h4 b4

Or: 17...h6 18 ♗xh6 gxh6 19 ♖g3+! ♔h7 20 ♕e7+ ♔h8 21 ♖g6 ♕e3+ 22 ♔b1 ♖g8 23 ♗h5! and Black suffers a catastrophe; 17...♘f6 loses material to 18 ♗f4 ♕c5 19 ♗d6; 17...♘c5 18 ♖h3 h6 19 ♗xh6 is a win for White.

18 ♕xb4 ♗xg2 19 ♖g1 ♗e4

19...♕xh2 20 ♕d4 leaves Black with no answer to the threats against g2 and g7.

20 ♘xe4 fxe4 21 ♖dg3

Black now conceives a desperate but ingenious plan of counterattack.

21...♘c6 22 ♕b7!

Westerinen decides he can fall into the 'trap'.

22...♖ab8 23 ♕xd7 ♕xb2+ 24 ♔d1 ♘d4

24...♘b4 is dealt with by 25 ♗f6! ♕b1+ 26 ♔d2 e3+ 27 ♔xe3 ♘d5+ 28 ♔d3!? ♘f4+ 29 ♔d2, winning. After 24...♖fd8 25 ♗xd8 ♖xd8 26 ♖xg7+ ♕xg7 27 ♖xg7+ White wins a rook.

25 ♕xg7+!! ♔xg7 26 ♗d8+!

Only this square will do. 26 ♗e7+ ♔f7 and 26 ♗h4+ ♔h6 both let the king escape.

26...♔h8 27 ♖g8+! ♖xg8 28 ♗f6+ ♖g7 29 ♗xg7+ ♔g8 30 ♗xd4+ ♔f7 31 ♖f1+ ♔e7 32 ♗xb2 1-0

Chess News in Brief

Karpov dominates the Bad Lauterberg tournament, scoring 12/15; Timman's second place, two points adrift, is also an excellent performance.

Larsen wins the Geneva tournament with 8½/13, ahead of Andersson (8).

Larsen wins the Ljubljana/Portorož tournament with 9½/13, edging out Hort and Savon (both 9).

Romanishin and Tal win a strong tournament in Leningrad, scoring 11½/17; Karpov's equal fourth place is his first (relative) failure as World Champion.

Karpov wins the Tilburg tournament with 8/11, ahead of Miles (7).

The final of the European Team Championship is played in Moscow. The USSR wins, with 41½/56, ahead of Hungary (31) and Yugoslavia (30).

Dorfman and Gulko win the 45th USSR Championship, scoring 9½/15, ahead of Petrosian and Polugaevsky (both 9).

Jon Arnason (born 1960) is Icelandic Champion and World Under-16 Champion.

World News in Brief

Thousands of refugees flee from Vietnam crowded aboard ships of various sizes. Many of these 'boat people' are stranded in the South China Sea, refused permission to land in Hong Kong.

Egypt and Israel move towards peace.

A military coup brings General Zia to power in Pakistan.

Two jumbo jets collide on the ground at Tenerife airport. 574 people die.

The American Space Shuttle makes its first test flights, piggybacking on a Boeing 747, in order to test the vehicle's ability to glide down to Earth.

The Trans-Alaskan pipeline begins operation.

1978

Karpov remains Champion after a thrilling match • Hungary wins the Olympiad

Karpov wins a tense World Championship match against Korchnoi by 6 wins to 5 with 21 draws. Korchnoi, whose wife and son are still in the USSR, is convinced that the KGB is making every effort to ensure he loses. There are many disputes during the match; the most famous is the claim that Karpov being brought a yoghurt could be an instruction to offer a draw, etc. The issue that most seriously riles Korchnoi, though, is the presence of the parapsychologist, Dr Zoukhar, who stares at him continually during the games.

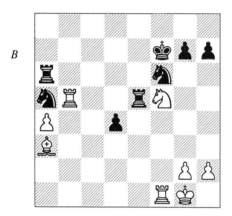

B

V. Korchnoi – A. Karpov

World Ch match (game 17), Baguio City 1978

Korchnoi has been going slightly astray after achieving a large advantage from the opening.

27...♘c4!

Karpov seeks maximum activity so as to give Korchnoi some awkward decisions in his time-trouble. Korchnoi had spent 11 minutes at the start of the game persuading the organizers to move Dr Zoukhar back from his fifth-row seat.

28 ♖b7+!

The only way to play for a win. Not 28 ♘d6+? ♖xd6 29 ♖xe5 ♘xa3.

28...♔e6 29 ♘xd4+

29 ♗f8 d3 30 ♘xg7+ ♔d5 31 ♖b5+ ♔e4 32 ♖e1+ wins material, but Black's powerful d-pawn provides compensation.

29...♔d5! 30 ♘f3

30 ♘c2 ♖xa4 31 ♗f8 is better.

30...♘xa3 31 ♘xe5 ♔xe5 32 ♖e7+ ♔d4

At this point, Karpov realized that he had some mating ideas, but was only hoping that they would save the game for him.

33 ♖xg7?!

33 ♖d1+ ♔c3 34 ♖c7+ ♔b3 35 ♖xg7 enables White to play for a win.

33...♘c4! 34 ♖f4+?! ♘e4!

A surprise. Karpov surrenders his last pawn in search of activity.

35 ♖d7+

35 ♖xh7 ♘d2 and then ...♔e3 gains time on the rook.

35...♔e3 36 ♖f3+ ♔e2 37 ♖xh7

White seems safe, now that he has eliminated Black's last pawn.

37...♘cd2 38 ♖a3?! ♖c6! 39 ♖a1??

This obvious response is an outright blunder. He had to move the g-pawn.

39...♘f3+! 0-1

It is mate: 40 ♔h1 ♘f2# or 40 gxf3 ♖g6+ 41 ♔h1 ♘f2#. An absolute tragedy for Korchnoi.

Karpov and Spassky win the Bugojno tournament with 10/15, ahead of Timman (9).

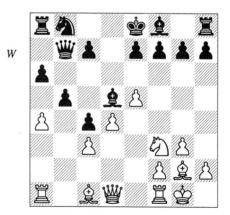

W

Y. Balashov – A. Miles

Bugojno 1978

White must find a way to make use of Black's lack of development.

12 e6! ♗xe6

12...fxe6 13 ♘h4 g6 (13...♗xg2 14 ♘xg2 is good for White) 14 ♖e1 threatens ♖xe6.

13 ♘g5

13 ♘e5 ♗d5 14 ♗xd5 ♕xd5 15 axb5 was later shown to be more accurate.

13...♗d5 14 ♗xd5 ♕xd5 15 axb5 axb5?

15...h6 and 15...e6 both give Black better prospects of survival.

16 ♖xa8 ♕xa8 17 ♕g4! ♘c6

There is nothing better: 17...e6? 18 ♘xe6 fxe6 19 ♕xe6+ ♗e7 20 ♗g5 ♘c6 21 ♖e1 is a massacre; after 17...♕b7 18 ♕f5 f6 19 ♘e6 Black will not be able to develop; 17...♘d7 18 ♘xf7! is just miserable for Black.

18 ♕f3!

18 ♕f5 ♘d8 enables Black to hold on.

18...f6 19 ♘e6 ♕b7 20 ♕d5! g5

20...♘a5 21 ♕d8+ ♔f7 22 ♕d7! wins.

21 ♗f4!! ♗h6

21...gxf4 22 ♕h5+ ♔d7 23 ♘c5+ wins the black queen.

22 ♖e1! ♕b6 23 ♘xc7+ ♔f8 24 ♖e6! gxf4 25 ♖xc6 ♕b8 26 ♘e6+ ♔e8 27 ♖c7 ♔f7 28 ♘xf4+ ♔f8 29 ♕c5 1-0

Chess News in Brief

The young Kasparov achieves remarkable successes, qualifying for the USSR Championship, in which he makes a level score.

Portisch wins the Wijk aan Zee tournament, just ahead of world no. 2 Korchnoi. This tournament is one of many during this period boycotted by the Soviets due to Korchnoi's participation. Tournament organizers have a clear choice: invite Korchnoi, or invite Soviets.

Gulko and Timman win the Nikšić tournament with 8/11, ahead of Vaganian (6½).

Timman wins the IBM tournament in Amsterdam with 9½/13, ahead of Ribli (8½).

Portisch wins the Tilburg tournament with 7/11, ahead of Timman (6½).

Maya Chiburdanidze becomes the Women's World Champion at the age of 17.

The Buenos Aires Olympiad, a 14-round Swiss system event, is won by Hungary with 37/56, ahead of the USSR (36) and the USA

(35). The Soviets are without Karpov, resting after his exertions in Baguio, but it is nevertheless a remarkable achievement for the Hungarians. Korchnoi, thirsting for battle, makes the best score on top board, with 9/11, though his opposition is not so strong, since he is playing for the Swiss team. Portisch's 10/14 is a major factor in Hungary's victory, while Tarjan's 9½/11 for the USA is the best score of the Olympiad. A team from China, which has not hitherto taken part in international chess, finishes in 20th place. 65 teams compete. The Women's Olympiad is won by the USSR, ahead of Hungary.

Tal and Tseshkovsky share the 46th USSR Championship, scoring 11/17, ahead of Polugaevsky (10).

Paul Motwani (born 1962) wins the Scottish Championship for the first time.

Carlos Torre dies.

Tal Shaked [American grandmaster] is born.

FIDE introduces the FIDE Master title.

Fridrik Olafsson is elected FIDE President.

World News in Brief

Soviet-backed army officers seize power in Afghanistan.

Prime Minister Begin of Israel and President Sadat of Egypt reach agreement on a peace process at Camp David with the assistance of President Carter. Begin and Sadat are later awarded the Nobel Peace Prize.

Martial law is imposed in Iran following demonstrations against the Shah.

Sandinista rebels fight for control of Nicaragua.

Aldo Moro, the former prime minister of Italy, is kidnapped and murdered by Red Brigade terrorists.

More than 900 followers of Rev Jim Jones die in a mass suicide in Guyana.

In London, a Bulgarian defector, Georgy Markov, is killed by a pellet containing ricin, which is injected into him from a modified umbrella.

Karol Wojtyla from Poland becomes the first non-Italian pope for more than 400 years.

The first test-tube baby, Louise Brown, is born in England. Subsequently, the technique becomes standard.

1979

Garry Kasparov achieves sensational results • Tal has a great year

There are two interzonals, with three qualifying from each. At the Riga Interzonal, Tal is in top form, and scores a fantastic 14/17. Polugaevsky is second, while Adorjan also qualifies on tie-break after a play-off match against his compatriot Ribli is drawn. At the Rio de Janeiro Interzonal, Portisch, Petrosian and Hübner share first place and so qualify.

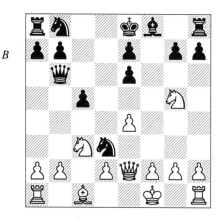

L. Polugaevsky – M. Tal
Interzonal tournament, Riga 1979

It seems implausible that Black can really cause White problems, as his d3-knight looks insufficiently supported. However, all it takes for Tal to work his magic are a few inaccuracies from White.

10...c4! 11 b3 h6 12 ᘒf3?!

12 ᘒa4 ♕d4 13 ♗b2! is best, because after 13...ᘒxb2 14 ᘒf3 Black must relinquish the b2-knight.

12...ᘒc6 13 bxc4 0-0-0 14 g3?

14 ᘒe1 looks like White's best chance.

14...g5 15 ♔g2 ♕c5! 16 ♖b1 ♗g7 17 ᘒb5 ♕xc4 18 ♕e3 ♖hf8 19 ♖f1

19 ᘒxa7+ loses to 19...ᘒxa7 20 ♕xa7 ♕xe4.

19...g4! 20 ᘒh4 ᘒxf2! 21 ᘒg6

21 ♖xf2 ♖xf2+ 22 ♔xf2 ♖f8+ is also winning for Black.

21...♖d3! 22 ᘒa3 ♕a4 23 ♕e1 ♖df3 24 ᘒxf8 ᘒd3 25 ♕d1

25 ♕e2 ᘒd4 26 ♕d1 ♕xd1 27 ♖xd1 ♖f2+ 28 ♔h1 ᘒf3 and mate next move.

25...♕xe4 26 ♖xf3 gxf3+ 27 ♔f1 ♕f5 28 ♔g1 ♗d4+ 0-1

Tal and Karpov share first place at the elite ten-player double-round Montreal tournament.

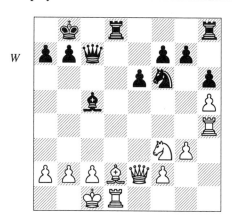

M. Tal – R. Hübner
Montreal 1979

Tal now plays an unusual combination.

20 ♗f4 ♗d6 21 ♖xd6! ♖xd6 22 ᘒe5!

Tal was very pleased with this idea – a sacrifice to set up a pin on a diagonal, followed by a move that temporarily interferes with the pin. One tempo is not enough to evacuate three pieces from the h2-b8 diagonal, and White threatens 23 ᘒxf7 and 23 ᘒc4.

22...♔a8

22...ᘒd5 23 ᘒxf7 ᘒxf4 24 ♖xf4 exploits a fork to win material, while 22...♖hd8 23 ᘒc4 ᘒe8 24 ♖g4 decisively probes Black's kingside.

23 ᘒc4! ᘒe8

With the knight on c4, 23...e5? fails to 24 ♗xe5 ♖e6 25 ♗xc7! ♖xe2 26 ᘒb6+ axb6 27 ♖a4#.

24 ♖g4! ♕e7

24...♖g8 25 ᘒxd6 ᘒxd6 26 ♕d3 ♖d8 27 ♖xg7 is also hopeless for Black.

25 ᘒxd6 ᘒxd6 26 ♖xg7 ᘒf5 27 ♖g4 ♖d8 28 ♗e5 f6 29 ♗c3

White has consolidated his extra pawn.

29...e5 30 b3 a6 31 ♔b2 ♕e6 32 ♕c4 ♕e8 33 ♖g6 ♖c8 34 ♕a4! ♕d8 35 ♕e4! ♘d6 36 ♕d3 ♕c7!? 37 ♗b4

Not 37 ♖xf6?, when 37...e4! draws, thanks to ideas of ...♘b5.

37...♘b5

37...e4 38 ♕xd6 (not 38 ♗xd6?? losing after 38...exd3 39 ♗xc7 d2) 38...♕xc2+ 39 ♔a3 ♕c1+ 40 ♔a4 is a win for White.

38 ♖xf6 a5

38...♘d4 loses to 39 ♖xa6+! bxa6 40 ♕xa6+ ♔b8 41 ♗d6.

39 ♗d6 ♘xd6 40 ♖xd6 e4 41 ♕d2 1-0

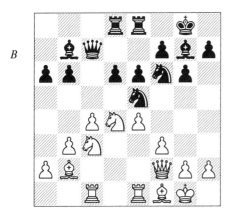

R. Byrne – U. Andersson
IBM tournament, Amsterdam 1979

Andersson now uses thematic Hedgehog pawn-breaks to generate an instant attack from a seemingly cramped position.

17...d5! 18 exd5

18 cxd5 is also met by 18...♘fg4!, e.g. 19 ♕g3 ♘d3! 20 ♕xc7 ♗xd4+ 21 ♔h1 ♘df2+ 22 ♔g1 ♘h3++ 23 ♔h1 ♘gf2#.

18...♘fg4! 19 ♕g3 ♘xf3+!! 20 gxf3

20 ♘xf3 ♕c5+ 21 ♔h1 ♘f2+ 22 ♔g1 ♘e4+ costs White his queen.

20...♗xd4+ 21 ♔h1 ♕xg3 22 hxg3 ♘e3

Black's spectacular combination has shattered White's position.

23 ♗d3 exd5 24 cxd5 ♘xd5 25 ♖xe8+ ♖xe8 26 ♗e4 ♗xc3 27 ♗xc3 ♘xc3 28 ♗xb7 ♘xa2 29 ♖c6 a5 30 ♖xb6 ♖b8

This pin makes Black's task straightforward.

31 ♔g2 ♔f8 32 ♖b5 ♘b4 33 ♔f2 ♔e7 34 ♔e3 ♔d6 35 ♔d4 ♘c7 36 ♖xb4 axb4 37 ♗d5 ♔d6 38 ♗xf7 ♖f8 39 ♗d5 ♖f5 40 ♗e4 ♖g5 41 g4 h5 0-1

Chess News in Brief

Kasparov dominates a top-class GM tournament at Banja Luka.

Karpov wins the Tilburg tournament.

Geller wins the 47th USSR Championship with 11½/17, ahead of Yusupov (10½), Balashov and Kasparov (both 10). Tal's poor result, equal 14th, comes at the end of an otherwise superb year for him.

Nigel Short (aged 14) is equal first in the British Championship, but loses on tie-break.

Niaz Murshed becomes Champion of Bangladesh at the age of 12.

Cecil Purdy dies.

Peter Leko [Hungarian player who breaks Judit Polgar's record to become the youngest grandmaster in history] is born.

World News in Brief

A bloody revolution brings Ayatollah Khomeini to power in Iran. The new regime is ruthless in executing hundreds of those who worked for the Shah's government. Iranian militants take a strong anti-US stance, and, late in the year, seize the American embassy in Tehran, taking 90 hostages.

Pol Pot is forced from power in Cambodia. It becomes clear that his Khmer Rouge regime committed genocide against his own people, with millions of Cambodians murdered since he came to power in 1975.

Idi Amin is forced to flee from Uganda.

Carter and Brezhnev sign the SALT-2 (Strategic Arms Limitation Treaty) agreement.

Margaret Thatcher becomes Britain's first woman prime minister, on a radical platform of reductions in income tax and curbing the power of the trades unions.

The Sandinistas are victorious in Nicaragua, but the conflict has left the country in ruins.

At the end of year, Soviet troops invade Afghanistan in support of the new president.

The worst nuclear accident in US history occurs at Three Mile Island.

1980

A mixed year for Karpov • England emerges as a chess power

The final of the European Team Championship is played at Skara, Sweden. The USSR wins, with 36½/56, ahead of Hungary (29) and England (28½). The USSR's victory is mainly due to good performances on the lower boards, in particular Kasparov's 5½/6 as second reserve. Karpov, Tal and Polugaevsky fail to win any games. England's third place is a milestone achievement for a nation that is emerging as a major chess power. Miles's victory over Karpov (answering Karpov's 1 e4 with the bizarre 1...a6) and Nunn's victory over Polugaevsky help England achieve a 4-4 draw in their match with the USSR.

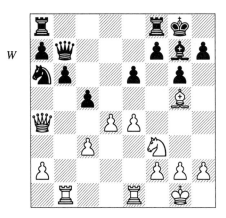

W

G. Kasparov – J. Přibyl
European Team Ch, Skara 1980

16 d5!

16 ♖ed1 f5! breaks up White's centre.

16...♗xc3 17 ♖ed1 exd5 18 exd5

Black's pieces, in particular his knight, are poorly placed to blockade White's d-pawn.

18...♗g7

18...♘c7 19 ♗e7 ♖fe8 20 ♕d7 keeps Black bottled up.

19 d6 f6 20 d7!!

It is worth a piece to split Black's position in two, and bring the pawn closer to promotion.

20...fxg5

20...♘b4 21 ♕b3+ ♔h8 22 ♘e5! fxe5 23 d8♕ ♖axd8 24 ♖xd8 ♖xd8 25 ♗xd8 is good

for White, while after 20...♖ad8 21 ♕c4+ ♔h8 22 ♘e5! fxe5 23 ♗xd8 ♖xd8 24 ♕e6! ♘c7 (or 24...♕b8 25 ♖b3 c4? 26 ♖h3 with a winning kingside attack) 25 ♕e7 ♕b8 (25...♕a8 26 ♖b3) 26 ♖b3 e4 27 ♖d6 Black cannot hope to defend.

21 ♕c4+ ♔h8 22 ♘xg5 ♗f6

22...♗d4? loses to 23 ♖xd4.

23 ♘e6 ♘c7

23...♘b4 24 ♖d6 (24 ♕f4?! ♕b8) 24...♗e7 25 ♕c3+ ♗f6 (25...♖f6 26 ♖bd1 ♘c6 27 ♖xc6 ♕xc6 28 d8♕+ ♖xd8 29 ♖xd8+ ♗xd8 30 ♘xd8 and Black loses his rook – an unusual tactic!) 26 ♕xf6+! ♖xf6 27 d8♕+ ♖f8 28 ♕h4 gives White a winning attack.

24 ♘xf8 ♖xf8 25 ♖d6 ♗e7

25...♗d8 26 h4 ♕a6 27 ♕c3+ ♔g8 28 ♕c2 keeps Black tied up.

26 d8♕!

Most unexpected, but highly effective.

26...♗xd8

26...♖xd8 27 ♖xd8+ ♗xd8 28 ♖d1 wins.

27 ♕c3+ ♔g8 28 ♖d7 ♗f6 29 ♕c4+ ♔h8 30 ♕f4 ♕a6?

After 30...♗g7 31 ♕xc7, 31...♕xc7 32 ♖xc7 ♗d4 33 ♖f1 is a hopeless ending for Black; 31...♕e4 32 ♖f1 ♗d4 33 ♖f7 is hardly better.

31 ♕h6 1-0

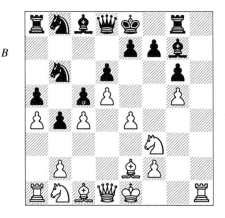

B

V. Kovačević – Y. Seirawan
Wijk aan Zee 1980

White has gone to considerable lengths to open the h-file. While this has disrupted any ideas Black may have had of castling kingside, the plan's overall merits are less clear.

14...♔d7!

This marvellous and surprising move is based on the simple logic that the king will be completely safe on the queenside, and that Black will now be in a strong position to fight for control of the h-file. Development of the queenside minor pieces will follow when the best squares for these pieces become apparent.

15 ♘bd2 ♖h8 16 ♖g1 ♔c7 17 ♖b1 ♖h3 18 b3 ♕h8

The queen exerts powerful influence in two directions. White is already in deep trouble.

19 ♘f1 ♘8d7 20 ♗f4 ♘e5 21 ♘xe5 ♗xe5 22 ♗xe5 ♕xe5 23 f3 ♗d7 24 ♕c2 ♕d4 25 ♖g2 ♖h1 26 ♖f2 ♕h8 27 f4 ♕h4 28 ♖d1 f6 29 gxf6 exf6 30 e5

Desperation; otherwise White will have e-file pressure and a passed black g-pawn to deal with.

30...fxe5 31 fxe5 ♖f8 32 exd6+

One line that illustrates White's problems is 32 ♗d3 ♖e8 33 e6 ♗xe6 34 dxe6 ♖xe6+ 35 ♗e2 ♖xf1+ 36 ♔xf1 ♕h1#.

32...♔b7 33 ♗d3 ♖e8+ 0-1

Chess News in Brief

Miles shares first place with Andersson and Korchnoi at the London tournament – the strongest in Britain for many years. The young Nigel Short suffers badly, achieving just four draws from the 13 games.

Karpov wins the Bugojno, Amsterdam and Tilburg tournaments.

Kasparov wins the Baku tournament.

Larsen wins the Buenos Aires tournament; Karpov's joint fourth place, two points off the lead, is by his standards a failure.

At the Malta Olympiad, the USSR and Hungary both finish on 39/56, ahead of Yugoslavia (35) and the USA (34). The USSR finishes first on tie-break. Karpov scores 9/12 on top board, against Portisch's total of 9½/13. Kasparov scores 9½/12 as second reserve. 82 teams compete. The Women's Olympiad is won by the USSR, a point ahead of Hungary. A team from China, competing for the first time, finishes an impressive 6th.

Beliavsky and Psakhis share the 48th USSR Championship (1980/1), scoring 10½/17.

Johann Hjartarson (born 1963) is Icelandic Champion.

Kasparov is World Junior Champion.

Jørn Sloth wins the 8th Correspondence World Championship (1975-80).

Alberic O'Kelly de Galway dies.

World News in Brief

There is international fury at the Soviet intervention in Afghanistan. The Islamic Conference calls for their withdrawal, while the USA provides covert support for the Mujahedeen, who are fighting a guerrilla war against the Soviet invaders. The USA leads a boycott of the Moscow Olympics.

The newly-founded free trade union, Solidarity, under the leadership of Lech Walesa, wins concessions from the Polish government.

An American attempt to rescue the hostages from its embassy in Iran ends in dismal failure. The crisis continues, blighting Jimmy Carter's final year as US president.

A siege at the Iranian embassy in London is brought to an end as the SAS (Special Air Service), an elite branch of the British army, storms the building.

War breaks out between Iran and Iraq. It is a bitter, savage conflict.

Rhodesia is formally granted independence with majority rule, and takes the name Zimbabwe.

Mount St Helens, in Washington State, erupts with tremendous force. The blast is equivalent to 17,000 Hiroshima bombs, and makes a cloud in the atmosphere that travels all the way around the globe. The pyroclastic explosion literally blows the top off the mountain, which is now 375 metres (1,235 feet) lower.

Unemployment in Britain reaches two million.

Earthquakes kill about 3,500 people in Algeria.

Smallpox is eradicated worldwide.

Voyager 1 sends back pictures from Saturn and its moons.

1981

Karpov comfortably defends his title • Great results for Timman

The very strong Moscow tournament is won by Karpov with 9/13. Polugaevsky, Smyslov and Kasparov are 1½ points behind in second place. For Kasparov this is a successful, if quiet, debut in 'super-GM' events.

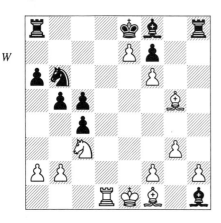

W

L. Polugaevsky – E. Torre
Moscow 1981

17 h4!!

White's idea becomes clear with the next move.

17...♗h6 18 f4!!

If Black exchanges on g5, then the string of white pawns (g3-h4-g5-f6-e7) will brick in the h8-rook, so compensating White for the fact that he is a rook down!

18...b4 19 ♖d6! ♖b8!

Or 19...bxc3 20 ♖xb6 cxb2 21 ♗xc4!?.

20 ♘d1 ♗xg5 21 fxg5 ♘d5!

Black's best chance, as White must play accurately to win the ending.

22 ♗xc4 ♘xe7 23 fxe7 ♔xe7 24 ♖f6!

24 ♖xa6 ♖he8! is less clear.

24...♖hf8 25 ♘e3 ♗e4 26 ♖xa6 ♖bd8 27 ♖f6 ♖d6 28 ♖f4 ♖d4 29 h5 ♗d3! 30 ♘d5+! ♔d6 31 ♖xd4 cxd4 32 ♗b3?!

32 ♗xd3! ♔xd5 33 h6! is a clear win.

32...♗c2! 33 ♗xc2 ♔xd5 34 ♗b3+? ♔e5 35 g4 ♔f4?

Black could secure a draw by 35...d3!.

36 g6! ♔e3

Or 36...♔g5 37 ♗xf7 ♔h6 38 g5+, and White wins.

37 g7 ♖c8 38 ♔f1 d3 39 ♔g2 ♔f4 40 h6 1-0

Beliavsky wins the Tilburg tournament. Kasparov only manages a level score (5½/11), which he regards as a terrible failure.

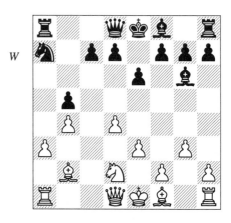

W

G. Kasparov – U. Andersson
Tilburg 1981

Black intends to play ...d5, whereupon his position would be quite attractive. However, Kasparov is not going to give him time.

13 h4!

White wants to provoke a weakening of Black's kingside before sacrificing his d-pawn.

13...h6 14 d5! exd5 15 ♗g2 c6 16 0-0

White's pawn sacrifice has liberated his pieces, and stymied his opponent's.

16...f6

How else is Black to develop?

17 ♖e1! ♗e7 18 ♕g4 ♔f7 19 h5 ♗h7 20 e4 dxe4 21 ♗xe4 ♗xe4 22 ♘xe4 ♘c8

22...d5 is more resilient.

23 ♖ad1 ♖a7 24 ♘xf6! gxf6

24...♗xf6 loses to 25 ♕g6+ ♔f8 26 ♗xf6 gxf6 27 ♖e6.

25 ♕g6+ ♔f8 26 ♗c1! d5 27 ♖d4! ♘d6 28 ♖g4 ♘f7 29 ♗xh6+! ♔e8

29...♘xh6 30 ♕g7+ ♔e8 31 ♕xh8+ ♔d7 32 ♕xh6 is also an easy win.

30 &g7 1-0

White's h-pawn will run through to queen.

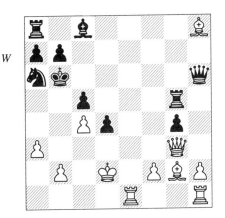

I. Kopylov – S. Koroliov
Correspondence 1981-3

White's king moves are a remarkable feature of this game.

26 &d1! Wxh8

Otherwise the white bishop would escape.

27 Wd6+ &a5 28 &d2!

Threatening 29 b4+ &a4 30 &c6+.

28...&f5!

After 28...d3 29 b4+ &a4 30 &c6+ bxc6 31 Wxc6+ &b3 32 Rb1+ White also forces mate.

29 &xb7!

29 b4+ &a4 30 &c6+ bxc6 31 Wxc6+ &b3 32 Rb1+ &a2! 33 Wa4 Wh3! saves the black king.

29...Rg6 30 b4+ &a4 31 &c6+ &b3 32 Wg3+ &b2 33 Rb1+! &xb1 34 Rxb1+ &xb1 35 Wb3+ &a1 36 &c1!

36 &c2 d3+, and 37...Wb2, rescues Black.

1-0

36...Wh6+ 37 &c2 d3+ 38 Wxd3 Wg7 39 Wd1+ &a2 40 Wb1+ &xa3 41 Wb3#.

Chess News in Brief

Karpov wins a one-sided World Championship match against Korchnoi by 6 wins to 2, with 10 draws.

Karpov and Christiansen share first place at the Linares tournament – for the former it is a return to form; for the latter a sensational achievement.

Korchnoi devastates the opposition in a reasonably strong tournament at Bad Kissingen, scoring 9/10.

Timman wins the Amsterdam tournament, half a point ahead of Karpov and Portisch.

Timman dominates the Las Palmas tournament, scoring 8½/10; this time the field contains Larsen and Korchnoi.

Andersson wins a four-man tournament in Johannesburg – a controversial event in view of South Africa's policy of apartheid.

Kasparov and Psakhis share the 49th USSR Championship, scoring 12½/17.

Max Euwe dies.

Alexander Kotov dies.

World News in Brief

President Reagan is shot and seriously wounded, but makes a full recovery.

Pope John Paul II survives an attempted assassination by an escaped murderer.

Iran releases the American hostages.

Martial law is declared in Poland as the government crushes several strikes.

There is rioting in a number of British cities, as unemployment soars.

There are protests in Western Europe against the deployment of American nuclear missiles.

Israeli planes destroy Iraq's nuclear reactor.

The space shuttle *Columbia* makes a successful orbital flight.

IBM launches its PC (Personal Computer). Although it is no real advance on similar machines from other manufacturers, the fact that it is from the company that is dominant in the computer industry leads to standardization of specifications, and other manufacturers develop 'IBM compatible' computers. The machine uses the MS-DOS operating system and various computer languages developed by a relatively small corporation called Microsoft.

AIDS (Acquired Immune Deficiency Syndrome) is identified. The disease destroys the body's immune system, and so leads to the patient succumbing to common infections. There is no known cure, nor is it known what causes the disease.

A solar-powered aircraft crosses the English Channel.

1982

Kasparov gathers momentum, but political storms are brewing

Kasparov achieves a brilliant result, winning the Bugojno tournament with 9½/13, 1½ points clear of a world-class field.

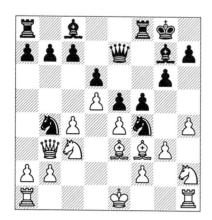

L. Kavalek – G. Kasparov
Bugojno 1982

Kavalek has just played 14 ♕d1-b3, an error since the black knights are able to maintain their advanced positions for just long enough.

14...♘fd3+ 15 ♔e2 f4 16 ♗d2 fxg3?!

16...♘xf2! 17 ♔xf2 ♘d3+ 18 ♔g2 (or 18 ♔e2 ♘c5) 18...fxg3 19 ♔xg3 ♖f4! gives Black a massive attack.

17 fxg3 ♖xf3! 18 ♘xf3 ♗g4 19 ♖af1 ♖f8 20 ♘d1?

20 ♗e3! was analysed by Kasparov as leading to a draw by perpetual check:

a) 20...♕f7? 21 ♗d2! (Kasparov cited 21 a3, but then 21...♘c1+!! 22 ♗xc1 ♗xf3+ 23 ♔e1 ♘d3+ 24 ♔d2 ♘c5 gives Black a winning attack) 21...♗xf3 22 a3 is good for White.

b) 20...♗h6! 21 ♗xh6 ♖xf3 22 ♖xf3 ♗xf3+ 23 ♔xf3 ♕f6+ 24 ♔g2 ♕f2+ 25 ♔h3 ♕f3 26 ♖h2 g5! 27 ♗xg5 ♕f1+ 28 ♔g4 h5+! 29 ♔xh5 ♕f3+ 30 ♔h6 ♕f8+ 31 ♔h5 ♕f3+, etc.

20...♕f7! 21 ♗e3 ♗xf3+ 22 ♔d2 ♕d7 23 ♖hg1

23 a3 ♗xh1 24 ♖xh1 a5 25 axb4 ♘xb4 is winning for Black.

23...♕h3 24 a3 ♗xe4! 25 ♖xf8+ ♗xf8 26 axb4 ♕h2+ 27 ♔c3 ♘c1! 0-1

The Lucerne Olympiad is won by the USSR with 42½/56, ahead of Czechoslovakia (36) and the USA (35½). The USSR's renewed dominance is due to strong performances by Karpov (6½/8) and Kasparov (8½/11) on the top two boards, while on the lower boards, Tal and Yusupov both score at least 80%. 92 teams compete. The Women's Olympiad is won by the USSR, ahead of Romania.

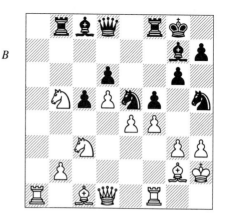

V. Korchnoi – G. Kasparov
Lucerne Olympiad 1982

This very sharp position has arisen from a then topical line of the Modern Benoni.

19...fxe4!

If Black retreats, his position will rapidly collapse, so Kasparov relies on tactics.

20 ♗xe4

20 fxe5 ♗xe5, 20 ♘a7 ♘f3+ 21 ♗xf3 exf3 and 20 ♘xd6 ♕xd6 21 ♘xe4 ♕b6 22 fxe5 ♖xf1 23 ♕xf1 ♗xe5 are all rather unclear.

20...♗d7 21 ♕e2

21 ♘xd6?! ♖b6 22 fxe5 ♗xe5 23 ♘e2 (23 ♘c4 ♗xg3+ 24 ♔h1 ♖bf6 25 ♖xf6 ♕xf6 favours Black) 23...♖xd6 is dangerous for White.

21...♕b6 22 ♘a3 ♖be8

It is logical for Black to put pressure on the e-file, where the white queen resides.

23 ♗d2?

23 ♕g2 is the move Kasparov feared at the board; some years later he concluded that the

best reply is 23...♛b4 24 ♘c2 ♛b8 25 ♘e3 ♘f7 26 ♘c4 ♝xc3 27 bxc3 ♘f6 28 ♝f3 ♝f5 29 ♘e3 ♝d3 30 ♖d1 c4. The crude 23 g4 looks like it should allow Black good play by 23...♘xg4+ 24 hxg4 ♛d8 (as given by Kasparov), but after the simple 25 gxh5 ♛h4+ 26 ♚g1 ♝d4+ 27 ♝e3 ♛g3+ 28 ♚h1, it is hard to see a satisfactory continuation for Black.

23...♛xb2! 24 fxe5?

24 ♖fb1?? loses to 24...♘f3+!, which Korchnoi presumably missed when deciding upon 23 ♝d2. 24 ♘c2 ♛b8 25 fxe5 is a better idea though.

24...♝xe5 25 ♘c4 ♘xg3! 26 ♖xf8+ ♖xf8 27 ♛e1 ♘xe4+ 28 ♚g2 ♛c2

28...♖f2+! wins directly: 29 ♚h1 ♖h2+ 30 ♚g1 ♘xd2 or 29 ♛xf2 ♝xh3+ 30 ♚f3 ♝g4+ 31 ♚g2 ♛xa1.

29 ♘xe5 ♖f2+?

29...♝xh3+ 30 ♚xh3 ♘xd2 is a clear win for Black.

30 ♛xf2 ♘xf2

30...♝xh3+!? 31 ♚g1 ♘xf2 32 ♖a2 ♛b3 33 ♖a8+ ♚g7 34 ♖a7+ ♚f6 (otherwise it's a draw) 35 ♘f3 g5! (the only move) 36 ♚xf2 ♛c2 is distinctly double-edged, but Black's g-pawn may prove useful.

31 ♖a2 ♛f5

31...♝xh3+!? 32 ♚g1 transposes to the previous note.

32 ♘xd7 ♘d3

White has regained material, and it is now a question of whose attack is the stronger.

33 ♝h6?

33 ♖a8+ ♚g7 34 ♖a7 ♛f2+ 35 ♚h1 ♛xd2 36 ♘e5+ gives White perpetual check, e.g. 36...♚f8 37 ♖a8+ ♚e7 38 ♖a7+ ♚d8 39 ♖a8+ and Black must go back, since 39...♚c7?? loses to 40 ♘b5+.

33...♛xd7 34 ♖a8+ ♚f7 35 ♖h8?!

35 ♘e4 is best met by 35...♛e7, when White has no adequate continuation.

35...♚f6 36 ♚f3?

Panic in time-trouble.

36...♛xh3+ 0-1

Chess News in Brief

This year there are three interzonals, with two qualifying places from each. The Las Palmas Interzonal is won by Ribli; Smyslov also qualifies. At the Toluca Interzonal, Portisch and Torre share first place and qualify – an especially impressive result for Torre. The Moscow Interzonal is comfortably won by Kasparov, ahead of Beliavsky.

Balashov and Nunn share first place at the Wijk aan Zee tournament.

Timman wins the Mar del Plata tournament; Karpov is two points behind in third place.

Andersson and Karpov share first place at the London tournament; Seirawan beats Karpov and is just half a point behind.

Karpov wins the Tilburg tournament.

There are increased political tensions in the USSR chess establishment, as it seems that Kasparov's progress is being blocked. Krogius's comment to Kasparov is notable: "We have one World Champion and we don't need any other."

Lembit Oll (born 1966) is Estonian Champion.

Simen Agdestein (born 1967) is Norwegian Champion.

Florencio Campomanes is elected FIDE President.

World News in Brief

Argentina invades the Falkland Islands (a crown colony of the UK), a group of small islands in the South Atlantic with a population of about 2,000. Britain sends a large task force and recaptures the territory by force. The final death toll for the conflict is 255 Britons and 712 Argentines. The leader of the ruling Argentine military *junta*, General Leopoldo Galtieri, resigns.

The Polish government outlaws Solidarity. The trade union continues its activities in secret, partly thanks to covert assistance from the USA.

In Beirut, Christian militiamen murder hundreds of Palestinians in the Sabra and Shatila refugee camps.

Iran recaptures territory in the war against Iraq.

Israel drives the PLO out of Beirut.

Doctors in Salt Lake City install an artificial heart in a patient, but he dies a few weeks later.

1983

Candidates cycle in crisis • Kasparov faces a stern challenge from Korchnoi

Spassky wins the Linares tournament on 6½/10, ahead of Karpov and Andersson (both 6).

A. Karpov – G. Sax
Linares 1983

Black now attempts to liberate his pieces with a little piece of tactics.

14...♘xe4 15 ♘xe4 d5 16 ♕b3!

Karpov plays for the attack.

16...dxe4 17 ♗c4 ♖f8

After 17...0-0, 18 g5 makes good use of White's earlier pawn advances.

18 ♖d5!!

Devastating. Black's king will be too exposed on the light squares if he takes the rook.

18...♗xd5

18...♕c7 19 ♗b5 keeps some advantage.

19 ♗xd5 ♖d8

19...♕b4 20 ♗xb7 ♕xb3 21 axb3 ♖b8 22 ♗c6+ ♔d8 23 ♗xa7 leads to a terrible ending.

20 ♗c4! ♗b4 21 c3 b5 22 ♗e2 ♗d6 23 ♕d5! ♔e7?

Now White wins by a prolonged attack. 23...♕c7 24 ♗xb5+ ♔e7 25 ♕xe4 gives White good play, while 23...♕xc3+ 24 ♔b1 only opens lines for White.

24 ♗c5! ♗xc5

24...f6? loses to 25 ♗c4!.

25 ♕xe5+ ♔d7 26 ♕xc5 ♕c7 27 ♕f5+ ♔e7 28 ♕xe4+ ♔d7 29 ♕f5+ ♔e7 30 ♖e1 ♖d6 31

♗c4+ ♔d8 32 ♗xb5 a6 33 ♗a4! g6 34 ♕f3 ♔c8 35 ♖e7! ♖d1+

Or 35...♕xe7 36 ♕a8+ ♔c7 37 ♕a7+ ♔d8 38 ♕b8#.

36 ♔xd1 ♕xe7 37 ♕a8+ ♔c7 38 ♕a7+ ♔d6 39 ♕b6+ 1-0

39...♔e5 40 ♕d4+ ♔e6 41 ♗b3#.

After the quarter-finals (in which Kasparov convincingly defeats Beliavsky 6-3), politics disrupt the Candidates cycle. The USSR Chess Federation rejects FIDE's proposed venues for the semi-finals, and defaults on behalf of Kasparov and Smyslov! While attempts are being made to rectify the situation, Kasparov annihilates the opposition at the Nikšić tournament, scoring 11/14, two points ahead of Larsen, for whom this result is a welcome return to form.

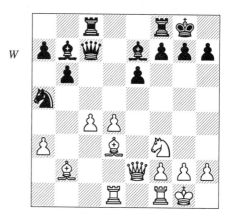

G. Kasparov – L. Portisch
Nikšić 1983

Kasparov now smashes lines open so as to activate his bishops against the poorly defended black kingside.

17 d5! exd5

After 17...♘xc4 18 ♕e4 g6 19 ♗xc4 ♕xc4 20 ♕e5 f6 21 ♕xe6+ ♖f7 22 ♖c1 ♕a6 23 ♘d4 White has strong threats.

18 cxd5 ♗xd5 19 ♗xh7+ ♔xh7 20 ♖xd5 ♔g8

20...♕c2 21 ♖d2 ♕c5 22 ♘e5 leaves Black defenceless.

21 ♗xg7!!

This is the best way to make progress. White demolishes more of the black king's pawn-cover.

21...♔xg7 22 ♘e5 ♖fd8

Other moves are no better. For example: 22...♖h8 23 ♕g4+ ♔f8 24 ♕f5 f6 25 ♖e1 ♘c6 26 ♘d7+ ♔f7 27 ♖xe7+! or 22...♖cd8 23 ♕g4+ ♔h7 24 ♘d7 f5 25 ♘xf8+ ♖xf8 26 ♖xf5 ♖xf5 27 ♕xf5+ ♔g7 28 ♖e1.

23 ♕g4+ ♔f8 24 ♕f5 f6

24...♗d6 loses to 25 ♕f6!.

25 ♘d7+

25 ♘g6+ is met by 25...♔f7!, when White has made no progress.

25...♖xd7 26 ♖xd7 ♕c5 27 ♕h7 ♖c7! 28 ♕h8+!

28 ♖d3? falls into a trap: 28...♕xf2+!!, when 29 ♔xf2 ♗c5+ 30 ♔g3 ♖xh7 31 ♖xf6+ is about equal.

28...♔f7 29 ♖d3 ♘c4 30 ♖fd1! ♘e5?!

30...♗d6 is better, though after 31 ♖h3! Black is very unlikely to survive.

31 ♕h7+ ♔e6

31...♔f8 32 ♖d8+ mates, as does 31...♔e8 32 ♕g8+ ♗f8 33 ♕e6+ ♗e7 34 ♖d8#.

32 ♕g8+ ♔f5 33 g4+ ♔f4

White also wins after 33...♘xg4 34 ♖f3+ ♔e5 35 ♕xg4, and mate in two more moves.

34 ♖d4+ ♔f3 35 ♕b3+ 1-0

35...♕c3 36 ♕d5+ ♔e2 37 ♕e4+ ♕e3 38 ♕xe3#.

Chess News in Brief

Eventually, both Candidates semi-finals are played in London. Kasparov wins a tough match against Korchnoi after losing the first game. The veteran Smyslov surprisingly beats Ribli.

Karpov wins the Tilburg tournament.

The Wijk aan Zee tournament is won by Andersson with 9/13, ahead of Ribli (8½), Browne and Hort (both 8).

The final of the European Team Championship is played at Plovdiv. The USSR wins, ahead of Yugoslavia and Hungary.

Karpov wins the 50th USSR Championship with 9½/15, ahead of Tukmakov (9). Kasparov does not play, as his match against Beliavsky has only just finished.

Curt Hansen (born 1964) wins the Danish Championship for the first time.

Tõnu Õim wins the 9th Correspondence World Championship (1977-83).

Etienne Bacrot [French grandmaster; briefly the youngest player ever to hold the title] is born.

Ruslan Ponomariov [Ukrainian grandmaster, who beats Bacrot's record] is born.

World News in Brief

President Reagan proposes the Strategic Defence Initiative (SDI), which becomes known as 'Star Wars', after the popular film. The idea is that orbiting satellites would use lasers, particle beams and missiles to intercept and destroy incoming missiles. Although the stated purpose is defensive, it is viewed by Soviet leaders as a major threat to world peace, as it would disturb the situation of 'mutual assured destruction' that has maintained an uneasy peace during the Cold War.

In Beirut, a bomb at the US embassy kills 40 people. Later in the year, 216 US marines, in Beirut as part of an international peace-keeping force, are killed as a suicide bomber drives a truck filled with explosives into the marine headquarters. A similar attack claims the lives of 58 French peacekeepers.

The USA backs the Contra rebels, who are fighting against the Marxist Sandinista government in Nicaragua.

Soviet fighter planes shoot down a Korean passenger plane that had gone off course, and strayed into Soviet air space. 269 people are killed.

Violence breaks out between Sinhalese and Tamils in Sri Lanka.

Mount Etna erupts; explosives are used to divert the lava flow away from two towns.

There is severe famine in Ethiopia.

In the USA, Martin Luther King's birthday is made a national holiday.

Microsoft introduces its 'mouse' pointing device, the word-processing program Word and announces the graphical interface Windows.

Sally Ride becomes the first US woman in space, aboard the space shuttle *Challenger*.

1984

Kasparov fights desperately for survival in a marathon match

Kasparov scores an impressive 8½-4½ victory over Smyslov in the Candidates final, and so becomes Karpov's challenger.

Karpov dominates the early stages of the World Championship match, scoring four wins in the first nine games, but Kasparov digs in, and Karpov is unable to score the sixth victory necessary to win the match. Kasparov scores his first win in game 32. By the end of 1984, the score is Karpov 5 wins, Kasparov 1 win, with 30 draws, and so the match drags on into the next year. The organizers had not anticipated such a lengthy match, and there are various postponements of games due to prior bookings of the hall, and, just before Christmas, for the lying-in-state of Marshal Ustinov.

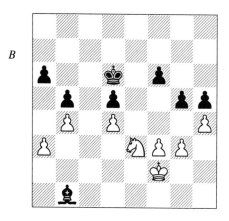

B

A. Karpov – G. Kasparov
World Ch match (game 9), Moscow 1984/5

After an arduous defence, Kasparov is close to achieving a hard-earned draw. However, his next move is careless.

46...gxh4?

Both 46...♗g6 and 46...♚e6 47 g4 hxg4 48 hxg5 fxg5 49 ♘xg4 ♗a2 are more reliable.

47 ♘g2!!

Rather than routinely recapturing, Karpov is willing to give up a pawn to open a route for his king. With hindsight, this move is extremely logical, but was very difficult to see in advance.

47...hxg3+

After 47...h3 48 ♘f4 the black pawns fall.

48 ♚xg3 ♚e6 49 ♘f4+ ♚f5 50 ♘xh5

With material level and his pieces penetrating, White is firmly in control and will make further progress without undue difficulty.

50...♚e6 51 ♘f4+ ♚d6 52 ♚g4 ♗c2 53 ♚h5 ♗d1 54 ♚g6 ♚e7 55 ♘xd5+ ♚e6 56 ♘c7+ ♚d7 57 ♘xa6 ♗xf3 58 ♚xf6 ♚d6 59 ♚f5 ♚d5 60 ♚f4 ♗h1 61 ♚e3 ♚c4 62 ♘c5 ♗c6 63 ♘d3 ♗g2 64 ♘e5+ ♚c3 65 ♘g6 ♚c4 66 ♘e7 ♗b7 67 ♘f5 ♗g2

After 67...♚c3 68 ♚f4 ♚b3 69 ♘e7 ♚xa3 70 d5 White keeps enough of his pawns to win.

68 ♘d6+ ♚b3 69 ♘xb5 ♚a4 70 ♘d6 1-0

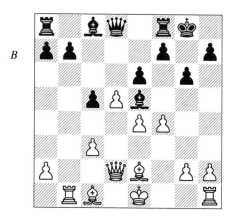

B

V. McCambridge – J. Hjartarson
Grindavik 1984

This position, highly topical in 1984, comes from a main line of the Exchange Grünfeld.

13...♗h8

The problem with the natural 13...♗g7 is shown by 14 c4 ♖e8 15 e5 f6 16 d6 fxe5 17 ♗b2 exf4 18 ♗xg7 ♚xg7 19 0-0 ♖f8 20 ♖xf4 ♖xf4 21 ♕xf4 ♕f6 22 ♕e4 ♖b8 23 ♖f1 ♕d4+ 24 ♕xd4+ cxd4 25 ♖b1 ♗d7 26 ♗f3 b6 27 c5 ♖c8 28 c6 ♗xc6 29 ♖c1 ♗d7 30 ♖xc8 ♗xc8 31 ♗c6 ♚f6 32 d7 ♗xd7 33 ♗xd7 e5 34 ♚f2 e4 35 ♗c6 ♚e5 36 h4! (a prepared novelty at move 36!) with a technically winning ending for White, Novikov-Tukmakov, USSR Ch, Lvov

1984. With the bishop on h8, the various tactical devices along White's 7th rank throughout the sequence do not work.

14 c4 ♖e8 15 e5 f6 16 f5!!

White finds a way to take advantage of the position of the bishop on h8.

16...gxf5

16...fxe5 17 fxg6! hxg6 18 0-0 exd5 19 ♕h6! gives White a winning attack, while 16...exd5 17 fxg6 hxg6 18 cxd5 ♖xe5 19 0-0 is also very good for White.

17 ♖b3 ♖e7

17...fxe5 18 0-0! exd5 (18...f4 19 d6) 19 cxd5 f4 20 d6 ♖b8 21 d7 ♗xd7 22 ♖d3 ♖e7 23 ♖d6 gives White a strong bind.

18 d6! ♖g7 19 exf6 ♕xf6 20 ♗b2 e5

Now for a marvellous sacrifice.

21 ♗xe5!! ♕xe5 22 ♖e3 ♕e6

After 22...♕a1+ 23 ♔f2 ♕xh1 24 ♖e8+ ♔f7 25 ♗h5+ ♖g6 26 ♖e7+! ♔g8 27 ♖e8+ ♔g7 28 ♗xg6 ♕a1 29 ♗h5 ♕d4+ 30 ♕xd4+ cxd4 31 ♗f3! White's d-pawn is too strong.

23 ♖xe6 ♗xe6 24 ♕e3 ♖e8 25 ♕xc5

White went on to win 23 moves later.

Chess News in Brief

Karpov wins the London tournament. Murray Chandler is joint second – an excellent result. The tournament brings to an end the Soviet boycott of events featuring Viktor Korchnoi.

Timman wins the Bugojno tournament.

Miles wins the Tilburg tournament.

The Thessaloniki Olympiad ends in a narrow victory for the USSR, who are without Karpov and Kasparov, though superb performances by Beliavsky and Vaganian compensate. The USSR scores 41/56, ahead of England (37) and the USA (35). England's silver medals are a sensation for a country that until 1976 had no grandmasters. England's hero is John Nunn, whose 10/11 on board 2 is the best individual result of the Olympiad. On a rest day, Nunn also wins the problem-solving competition. Roman Dzindzichashvili's 8/11 on top board is a major factor in the USA's result. The USSR wins the Women's Olympiad, ahead of Bulgaria.

In a repeat of the 1970 match, the USSR beats the Rest of the World 21-19. Beliavsky's 3½-½ score is decisive.

Andrei Sokolov (born in 1963 at the Vorkuta mining/penal settlement in the extreme north of Russia) wins the 51st USSR Championship – a startling result, albeit in a relatively weak event. He scores 12½/17, ahead of Lerner (11½) and Eingorn (10½).

Short wins the British Championship for the first time.

Vytas Palciauskas wins the 10th Correspondence World Championship (1978-84).

Tigran Petrosian dies.

World News in Brief

In Britain, a bitter industrial dispute begins, as the National Union of Mineworkers (NUM), the union that was instrumental in bringing down the Conservative government a decade earlier, takes national strike action against planned pit closures. It becomes clear that there is going to be no negotiated settlement, and Margaret Thatcher's government is digging in for a prolonged confrontation.

An IRA bomb explodes at the hotel in Brighton where leading members of the British government are staying during the Conservative party conference. Three people are killed and several injured, but Margaret Thatcher is unharmed.

In China, reforms introduce a degree of capitalism into the economy. The Chinese government agrees that Hong Kong can retain its capitalist system after it is ceded back to China by Britain in 1997.

Shots are fired from inside the Libyan embassy in London, at protesters on the street outside. Several are wounded, and a British policewoman, Yvonne Fletcher, is killed. It is to be 15 years before Libya apologizes for the attack.

Neutral ships in the Persian Gulf come under attack as a result of the ongoing Iran-Iraq war.

In the Philippines, there are mass demonstrations against President Marcos.

Over 2,000 people die after toxic gas leaks from an insecticide plant at Bhopal, India.

The Los Angeles Olympics are boycotted by the USSR and other communist countries.

The HIV virus, which is thought to cause AIDS, is identified.

Genetic fingerprinting is pioneered.

1985

Outrage as match is cancelled • Kasparov is the new Champion

After a further sequence of ten draws followed by two wins for Kasparov, the World Championship match is abandoned in unclear and controversial circumstances, at the instigation of FIDE President Campomanes. It is claimed that the players are exhausted, but both declare themselves willing to continue the match. There is to be a new match later in 1985, limited to 24 games and with the score starting at 0-0. Both players have grounds for complaint: Karpov because his 5-3 lead has been wiped out; and Kasparov because he was finally scenting victory. FIDE's handling of the match damages its credibility as organizer of the World Championship, and starts a bitter feud between Kasparov and Campomanes.

Kasparov emerges as convincing 13-11 winner in the second match (5 wins, 3 losses). Karpov has a right to a return match in 1986.

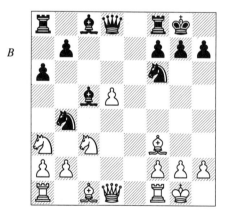

B

A. Karpov – G. Kasparov
World Ch match (game 16), Moscow 1985

Kasparov's dubious gambit idea has not been punished, and he now obtains good play by preparing to sink his knight into d3.

13...♗f5! 14 ♗g5 ♖e8! 15 ♕d2

15 ♘c4!? ♗d3 16 a3 ♗xc4 17 axb4 ♗xb4 18 ♖e1 ♖xe1+ 19 ♕xe1 leads to an unclear position. However, Karpov sees no need to return the material.

15...b5! 16 ♖ad1 ♘d3! 17 ♘ab1?!

Now White has problems getting any play at all. However, 17 d6 ♕xd6! 18 ♗xa8 ♖xa8 gives Black good compensation.

17...h6! 18 ♗h4 b4! 19 ♘a4?!

White should try 19 ♘e2 g5 20 ♗xg5 ♘xf2 21 ♖xf2 ♗xf2+ 22 ♔xf2 hxg5 23 ♕xg5+ ♗g6 24 ♘d2.

19...♗d6

Astonishingly, Kasparov had reached this position in his pre-game preparation.

20 ♗g3

20 ♕c2? ♖c8 21 ♕b3 ♘f4 22 ♖c1 ♖xc1 23 ♖xc1 g5! 24 ♗g3 g4 takes advantage of White's weak back rank.

20...♖c8! 21 b3 g5!!

This rules out White's intended ♘b2.

22 ♗xd6

22 h4 ♘e4! 23 ♗xe4 ♗xe4 is good for Black.

22...♕xd6 23 g3

23 ♗e2 ♘f4 24 ♗c4 ♘g4! 25 g3 ♖xc4! 26 bxc4 ♖e2 is a win for Black.

23...♘d7!! 24 ♗g2

24 ♘b2 is met by 24...♕f6!! 25 ♘c4 (25 ♘xd3 ♗xd3 26 ♕xd3 ♘e5! traps the queen mid-board) 25...♘7e5 26 ♗e2 ♗h3 27 ♘xe5 ♘xe5 28 f4 ♕b6+ 29 ♖f2 ♘g4 30 ♗xg4 ♗xg4 31 ♖e1 ♖xe1+ 32 ♕xe1 gxf4 33 gxf4 ♗f3!? 34 d6 ♗a8, and the white king is suffering.

24...♕f6!

White is completely tied up.

25 a3 a5 26 axb4 axb4 27 ♕a2 ♗g6! 28 d6 g4! 29 ♕d2 ♔g7 30 f3

Now White succumbs to a burst of tactics.

30...♕xd6 31 fxg4 ♕d4+ 32 ♔h1 ♘f6! 33 ♖f4 ♘e4! 34 ♕xd3 ♘f2+ 35 ♖xf2 ♗xd3 36 ♖fd2 ♕e3! 37 ♖xd3 ♖c1! 38 ♘b2 ♕f2! 39 ♘d2 ♖xd1+ 40 ♘xd1 ♖e1+ 0-1

There are three interzonals, with four from each going forward to a Candidates tournament. In the Tunis Interzonal, Yusupov wins ahead of Beliavsky; Portisch and Chernin also qualify. Vaganian wins the Biel Interzonal ahead of Seirawan and A.Sokolov. Nigel Short picks up the fourth qualifying place following a play-off. The Taxco Interzonal is won by Timman, with Nogueiras, Tal and Spraggett qualifying.

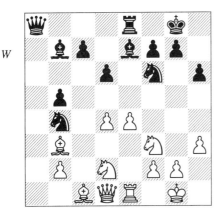

N. de Firmian – P. Nikolić
Interzonal tournament, Tunis 1985

In this unbalanced, tense Lopez position, de Firmian initiates forcing play.

16 e5 dxe5 17 dxe5 ②fd5 18 ②e4 c5 19 e6!
fxe6

19...f5 20 ②g3 gives White a powerful attack.

20 ②e5 ②c6

White smashes through after 20...c4 21 ♕h5 ♖f8 22 ♗xh6.

21 ♗xd5 exd5

21...②xe5? loses to 22 ♗xe6+.

22 ♕xd5+ ♔h7 23 ♕d3 ♔g8 24 ♕d5+ ♔h7
25 ♕d3 ♔g8 26 ②d7 ②b4?

26...♔h8 is more resilient.

27 ②ef6+!! ♔f7

27...♗xf6 loses to 28 ②xf6+ ♔f7 29 ♕d7+.

28 ②e5+ ♔e6 29 ②eg4+ ♔f7 30 ②e5+ ♔e6
31 ②eg4+ ♔f7 32 ②xh6+! gxh6 33 ♕h7+
♔xf6 34 ♕xh6+ ♔f7 35 ♕h7+ ♔f6 36 ♗g5+!
♔xg5 37 ♕g7+ 1-0

Chess News in Brief

For the first time since 1962, a Candidates tournament is played, in Montpellier. There are four qualifying places available for a mini-cycle of matches, the winner of which is to face the loser of the 1986 world championship match in a 'Candidates Super-final'. These places are taken by Yusupov, Vaganian and A.Sokolov,

who share first place, and Timman, on tie-break, after a play-off against Tal is drawn.

Timman wins the Wijk aan Zee tournament, ahead of Nunn and Beliavsky.

Karpov wins the Amsterdam tournament, ahead of Timman.

Miles, Hübner and Korchnoi share first place at the Tilburg tournament; controversy rages over the fact that Tony Miles, due to back problems, plays many of his games lying down.

The first World Team Championship is played in Lucerne. The idea is to have ten teams of six players: the Champions of Asia, Europe, the Americas, and Africa, together with the host nation and five qualifiers from the previous Olympiad. The USSR wins with 37½/54, ahead of Hungary (34½), England (30½), France and Romania (both 28½).

Mikhail Gurevich is declared winner of the 52nd USSR Championship after a play-off with Gavrikov and Chernin is drawn, apparently due to his better tie-break in the original event, although the rules made no such provision.

World News in Brief

Mikhail Gorbachev becomes the leader of the USSR. He is a new brand of Soviet leader, who wishes to make reforms in his country and favours a more open form of government. There is optimism in the West that relations with the USSR are set to improve dramatically.

Britain and Ireland reach an agreement whereby the Irish Republic has a consultative role in the government of Northern Ireland. Unionist politicians are outraged.

In Britain, the miners call off their strike.

Thousands are killed in Bangladesh as a cyclone and tidal wave hit the coast.

A volcanic eruption in Colombia kills about 20,000 people.

A powerful earthquake in Mexico causes devastation and thousands of deaths.

Palestinian terrorists kill El Al passengers at Rome and Vienna airports.

Many pop music stars respond to Bob Geldof's call to help raise money for famine-stricken Ethiopia, culminating in the Live Aid concerts, held in London and Philadelphia, which raise millions of dollars.

1986

Kasparov defends his title • Startling successes by Andrei Sokolov

Kasparov defends the World Championship in a return match against Karpov. The final score is 12½-11½ in Kasparov's favour, but there is a dramatic episode when Karpov draws level with three consecutive wins in games 17 to 19. Kasparov immediately accuses one of his team, Evgeny Vladimirov, of treachery, and dismisses him. However, he provides no evidence to back up his allegation.

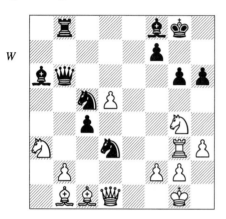

G. Kasparov – A. Karpov
World Ch match (game 16), Leningrad 1986

A very sharp position has arisen. Black is dominating the queenside, but it is not clear how potent White's kingside play is.

28 ♗xh6 ♕xb2 29 ♕f3! ♘d7?!

Karpov plays for a win, and as a result gets into trouble. 29...♕xa3 30 ♘f6+ ♔h8 31 ♕h5 ♖xb1+ 32 ♗c1+ ♔g7 33 ♘e8+ ♔g8 would be one way to settle for a draw.

30 ♗xf8 ♔xf8 31 ♔h2!

This move will undoubtedly be necessary, so it is most flexible to play it first.

31...♖b3!

31...♕xa3? 32 ♘h6, 31...♔g7? 32 ♘xc4! and 31...♕c1? 32 ♗xd3 cxd3 33 ♘f6! all favour White.

32 ♗xd3! cxd3?!

Karpov chases the mirage of victory. He could guide the game towards a draw by 32...♖xd3 33 ♕f4 ♕xa3 34 ♘h6 ♕e7 35 ♖xg6 ♕e5.

33 ♕f4 ♕xa3?

Now White's attack becomes devastating. The critical line runs 33...d2! 34 ♘h6 ♘f6 35 ♖xb3 ♕xb3 36 ♕xf6 ♕xd5 37 ♕h8+ ♔e7 38 ♘g8+ ♔d6 39 ♘f6 ♕e5+ 40 g3 ♕e2 41 ♕d8+ ♔e6 42 ♕b6+ ♔e7 43 ♘d5+ ♔f8 44 ♘b1 d1♕ 45 ♘bc3, when Black may survive the ending.

34 ♘h6 ♕e7 35 ♖xg6 ♕e5

35...♔e8 loses to 36 d6.

36 ♖g8+ ♔e7 37 d6+!

The move Karpov had missed. Now Black loses a lot of material.

37...♔e6 38 ♖e8+ ♔d5 39 ♖xe5+ ♘xe5 40 d7 ♖b8 41 ♘xf7 1-0

Glenn Flear, brought in as a last-minute reserve, is the surprise winner of the London GLC tournament (the last such event, due to changes in local government in London).

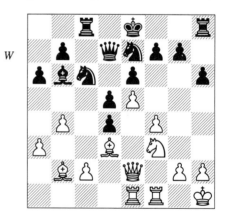

M. Chandler – R. Vaganian
London 1986

17 g4! g6 18 ♘h4 h5?! 19 f5! hxg4 20 fxg6

20 fxe6 ♕xe6! 21 ♖f6 ♖xh4 gives Black enough for his queen.

20...♖xh4 21 gxf7+ ♔f8 22 ♗c1!

Threatening 23 ♗g5 and 23 ♕f2.

22...♘f5 23 ♗xf5 d3!?

23...exf5 24 e6 wins for White: 24...♕e7 25 ♖xf5 or 24...♕d6 25 ♗f4 ♕e7 26 ♕d2.

24 ♗xd3 g3 25 ♕g2!!

This queen sacrifice is an effective way to eliminate the black rook, and so break through to the enemy king.

25...♖xh2+ 26 ♕xh2 gxh2 27 ♗h6+ ♔e7 28 ♗g5+ ♔f8 29 ♗h6+ ♔e7 30 ♗g6!

Threatening 31 f8♕+ ♖xf8 32 ♗g5+ ♖f6 33 exf6+.

30...♗c7

30...♖f8 allows 31 ♗g5#; 30...♘xe5 is the only way to defeat the threat, but White will have too great a material advantage.

31 ♗g5+ ♔f8 32 ♗h6+ ♔e7 33 f8♕+ ♖xf8 34 ♗xf8+?!

Good enough, but 34 ♗g5+ ♖f6 35 exf6+ ♔d6 36 f7 is more devastating.

34...♔d8 35 ♖f7 ♕e8 36 ♗g7 ♘xe5 37 ♗f6+ 1-0

Chess News in Brief

A.Sokolov beats Yusupov 7½-6½ in the Candidates final, thanks to three consecutive victories against the run of the play, after being two games adrift. Sokolov will play Karpov in the Super-final for the right to challenge Kasparov.

Karpov wins the double-round Bugojno tournament with 8½/14.

Kasparov wins the double-round Brussels tournament with 7½/10, ahead of Korchnoi (5½).

Beliavsky wins the double-round Interpolis tournament at Tilburg with 8½/14, ahead of Ljubojević and Karpov.

Short achieves an impressive victory at the Wijk aan Zee tournament.

The superbly well organized Dubai Olympiad is won by the USSR with 40/56, just ahead of England (39½) and the USA (38½). England's tremendous performance (Short's 10/13 and Chandler's 9/11 being valuable) pushes a full-strength USSR team all the way to the finish. Going into the last round, the USSR has a half-point lead, and after England completes a 4-0 victory over Brazil, the USSR needs to do likewise against Poland – and succeeds. Yusupov's 10/12 is especially noteworthy, as he has Black in many of his games, after A.Sokolov refuses to play with Black following a shattering loss to Nunn. 108 teams compete. The USSR wins the Women's Olympiad ahead of Hungary.

Tseshkovsky wins the 53rd USSR Championship with 11/17, ahead of a group of six players with 10 points.

World News in Brief

In the world's worst nuclear accident, a fire in the reactor core at the Chernobyl power plant in Ukraine leads to the release of a large amount of radiation. Contamination in the surrounding area, including Kiev, is serious; thousands are expected to die of cancer over the forthcoming years. Nuclear fallout is spread over a very large area; rain falling as far away as the British Isles has a significantly increased level of radiation.

The American space shuttle *Challenger* explodes a little over a minute after blast-off from Cape Canaveral, killing all seven crew members. This tragedy is a major setback to the space programme, and shatters any ideas that space travel can become routine in the foreseeable future.

President Marcos flees from the Philippines after being forced to accept the results of a general election that he lost. The new leader is Corazon (Cory) Aquino, widow of the former opposition leader Benigno Aquino who was gunned down on his return to the Philippines in 1983.

There is political scandal in the USA, as it becomes known that arms had been sold to Iran in return for hostages (contrary to stated policies), and some of the proceeds had been diverted to help the Contra rebels in Nicaragua (in violation of a congressional ban).

The USA bombs Libya in retaliation for terrorist attacks on its forces in Germany.

Dictator Jean-Claude 'Baby Doc' Duvalier flees from Haiti.

A summit in Reykjavik between Reagan and Gorbachev, aimed at arms reduction, ends in failure. News reports on the summit mention the Fischer-Spassky match in 1972 as the last event of global importance in Reykjavik.

The Soviet space station *Mir* begins operation.

Halley's Comet is again visible from Earth, though it is less bright than it had been during its previous appearance, in 1910.

1987

Kasparov survives a scare in Seville

There are three interzonals, each with three qualifying places. At the Subotica Interzonal, Short, Sax and Speelman share first place – a triumph for British chess. The Szirak Interzonal ends in victory for Salov and Hjartarson, with Portisch taking the final qualifying place after a play-off match against Nunn. Korchnoi, playing with great energy, wins the Zagreb Interzonal, ahead of Ehlvest and Seirawan.

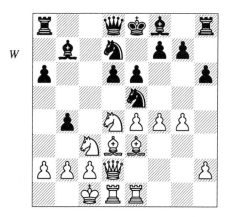

J. Nunn – M. Marin
Interzonal tournament, Szirak 1987

Black has just erred with 13...b4?, forcing White to make a strong sacrifice.
14 ♘d5! ♘xd3+
14...exd5 15 fxe5 is good for White, while 14...♘xg4 15 ♕xb4 ♖b8 16 ♕a4 is difficult for Black, since taking on d5 remains risky, and it is hard for him to develop if he leaves the knight there.
15 ♕xd3 exd5
15...♘c5 16 ♕c4 is good for White.
16 exd5 ♗e7?
16...♘c5 makes a fight of it.
17 ♘c6! ♗xc6 18 dxc6 ♘f6?
Now White wins by force. 18...♘f8?! 19 f5! is also winning for White, e.g. 19...♖b8 20 ♗f4 or 19...♘h7 20 ♗b6! ♕xb6 21 ♖xe7+ ♔f8 22 ♕d5, while 18...0-0 (best) 19 cxd7 ♕xd7 20 ♗d4 is obviously good for White.
19 ♗b6!

Diverting the queen from protecting e7 just happens to work here because White has the follow-up of advancing his g-pawn.
19...♕xb6
19...♕b8 loses to 20 ♕d4!, intending c7.
20 ♖xe7+ ♔f8 21 ♕xd6 ♔g8 22 g5
White's immediate target, if Black rescues his knight, is the f7-pawn.
22...hxg5 23 fxg5 ♖c8
23...♘f2 is met by 24 c7! ♖xh2 25 ♕d8+ ♔h7 26 ♕d3+ ♔g8 27 gxf6. After 23...♘g4 24 g6!, Black's king position is ripped open.
24 c7!
White's other major idea is revealed: the powerful passed c-pawn is hard to stop.
24...♕xd6 25 ♖xd6 ♘g4
25...♔f8 is neatly answered by 26 ♖e3!, e.g. 26...♔g8 27 ♖d8+ ♔h7 28 ♖h3+.
26 ♖d8+ ♔h7 27 ♖ed7! 1-0

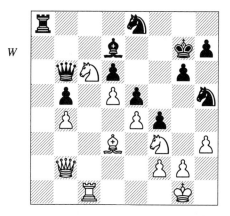

M. Tal – J. Hjartarson
Reykjavik 1987

Tal now crowns a powerful attacking performance with a wonderful and surprising sacrifice.
36 ♖c5!!
Exploiting the vulnerability of Black's king on the long diagonal to step up the pressure on the b5-pawn.
36...♕a6

36...dxc5 37 ♘fxe5 ♘hf6 38 ♘xd7 ♕a6 39 ♘xc5 and 36...♗xc6 37 ♖xc6 ♕b7 38 ♘g5 are hopeless for Black.

37 ♖xb5 ♘c7

37...♗xc6 38 dxc6 ♘c7 loses to 39 ♖a5!.

38 ♖b8! ♕xd3 39 ♘cxe5!

Finally, a sacrifice on the long diagonal wins.

39...♕d1+

The only chance, as 39...dxe5 40 ♕xe5+ is winning for White.

40 ♔h2 ♖a1 41 ♘g4+! ♔f7 42 ♘h6+ ♔e7 43 ♘g8+ 1-0

In view of 43...♔f7 44 ♘g5#.

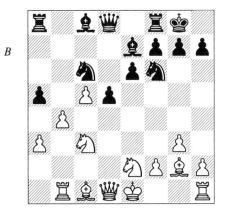

V. Salov – M. Gurevich
Leningrad 1987

13...♖b8! 14 ♗f4?!

14 ♕a4 and 14 ♘d4 are better.

14...axb4!

It is more important to shatter White's pawn majority than to cling on to an exchange.

15 ♗xb8 bxc3 16 ♕a4?

16 ♗d6 ♗xd6 17 cxd6 ♕a5 18 0-0 ♕xa3 19 ♕c2 gives White good chances of survival.

16...♘xb8 17 ♖xb8

Black now manages to play a series of active moves with gain of tempo.

17...♘d7 18 ♖a8 ♘xc5 19 ♕b5 ♕d6!

Threatening 20...♗a6.

20 ♗f3 ♗a6 21 ♖xf8+ ♗xf8 22 ♕a5 ♘d3+ 23 ♔f1 ♘e5 24 ♕xc3

Otherwise Black's c- and d-pawns are too strong.

24...d4 25 ♕b3 ♗c4 0-1

Chess News in Brief

Karpov beats A.Sokolov 7½-3½ in the Candidates Super-final. Kasparov remains World Champion by drawing 12-12 against Karpov at Seville. The finish is exciting, with Kasparov winning the 24th game to level the match.

Karpov and Timman win the double-round Amsterdam tournament with 4/6.

Kasparov and Ljubojević win the Brussels (S.W.I.F.T.) tournament with 8½/11.

Timman wins the Tilburg tournament.

Ljubojević wins the Belgrade tournament.

Short and Korchnoi win the Wijk aan Zee tournament.

Beliavsky wins the 54th USSR Championship after a play-off against Salov.

Viswanathan (Vishy) Anand wins the World Junior Championship.

Yakov Estrin dies.

World News in Brief

President Reagan is criticized by the Iran-Contra report, but it does not claim that the president was directly responsible. The strong performance at the hearings by Colonel Oliver North is a factor in the American public's relatively calm reaction to the scandal.

Gorbachev and Reagan sign an arms reduction treaty.

The New York stock exchange suffers its biggest single-day fall since 1929, but this time it does not lead to a global depression.

A car ferry heading for Dover, the *Herald of Free Enterprise*, capsizes shortly after setting off from Zeebrugge. 193 people perish in the tragedy, which is caused by the ship setting off with its bow doors open.

31 people die in a fire at King's Cross underground station in London.

A 19-year-old West German novice pilot, Matthias Rust, flies a small plane into the USSR from Helsinki and lands near the Kremlin, in Red Square. The pilot is sentenced to four years' imprisonment, and the Soviet defence minister is dismissed.

Los Angeles is hit by a major earthquake, but damage is relatively minor, since buildings designed to be earthquake-proof behave as intended.

1988

The GMA makes chess more democratic and organizes the World Cup

The Thessaloniki Olympiad is convincingly won by the USSR with 40½/56, ahead of England and the Netherlands (both 34½ – England win the silver medals on tie-break), the USA and Hungary (both 34). Kasparov's 8½/10 and Karpov's 8/10, on boards 1 and 2 respectively, are both dominating performances. 107 teams compete. The Women's Olympiad is won by Hungary, half a point ahead of the USSR. The Hungarian team includes the three Polgar sisters – Judit scores 12½/13 on second board. The top-scorer for the USSR is Elena Akhmylovskaya (8½/9), who makes the headlines by eloping with the USA team captain, John Donaldson.

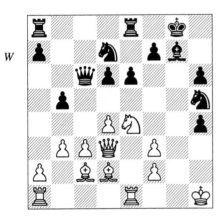

W

C. Høi – B. Gulko
Thessaloniki Olympiad 1988

White has been attacking vigorously after a modest opening, and now embarks upon a surprising sacrificial sequence.

24 ♖g1 ♔f8

After 24...f5 25 ♗xh6 fxe4 26 ♕e3 ♖e7 27 ♗xe4 d5 28 ♕g5 ♘df6 29 ♗g6 ♗xh6 30 ♕xh6 ♘g7 31 ♕xh4 White has a strong attack.

25 ♖xg7!! ♔xg7

25...♘xg7 26 ♗xh6 f5 27 ♗xg7+ ♔xg7 28 ♖g1+ gives White more than enough attack for the exchange.

26 ♗xh6+! ♔xh6 27 ♖g1 f5

27...♘f4 28 ♘g5! f5 29 ♕e3 wins for White.

28 ♕e3+ f4 29 ♘xd6! ♕xd6

29...♘g3+ also loses after 30 ♖xg3 ♕xd6 (30...fxe3 31 ♘f7+ ♔h5 32 ♖g5#) 31 ♖g6+ ♔h7 (31...♔h5 32 ♕c1 and the queen comes round via g1 to give mate) 32 ♕d3 ♘e5 33 ♖h6++ ♔xh6 34 ♕h7+ ♔g5 35 ♕g7+ ♔h5 36 dxe5.

30 ♕d3 ♘f8

This allows a beautiful mate, but 30...♘g3+ 31 ♖xg3 ♘f8 32 ♖g6+ ♔h5 33 ♖f6 is hopeless.

31 ♕h7+! 1-0

Owing to 31...♘xh7 32 ♖g6#.

The World Cup cycle begins. It is organized by the Grandmasters Association (GMA), an association of top grandmasters who are working together to further the interests of players. There are to be six tournaments during 1988-9; each player can play in four, with the best three results counting. The first tournament, at Brussels, is won by Karpov with 11/16, ahead of Salov (10). The second tournament, at Belfort, sees both 'Ks' in action, with Kasparov scoring 11½/15 ahead of Karpov's 10½. Next, at Reykjavik, Kasparov wins with 11/17, ahead of Beliavsky (10½).

A series of GMA Opens also begins, the purpose of which is to enable players to qualify for the second World Cup.

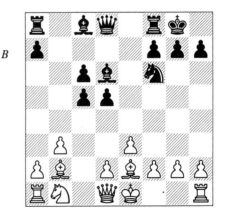

B

M. Taimanov – G. Kaidanov
GMA Open, Belgrade 1988

White has just unwisely declined a speculative pawn sacrifice by 10 ♗b5-e2?!. White's attempt to play cautiously permits Black time to organize his attack.

10...♖e8 11 0-0 ♖b8 12 d3 ♖b4!

A daring scheme. The rook is heading for h4, and White could only stop it by advancing his d-pawn, which would waste a tempo, block off his bishop, and hand Black the e4-square.

13 ♘d2?!

Nevertheless, 13 d4 is the lesser evil.

13...♖h4! 14 g3? ♘g4! 15 ♗xg4

15 ♘f3 ♖h3 16 ♖e1 ♘xh2 17 ♘xh2 ♖xh2 18 ♔xh2 ♕h4+ 19 ♔g1 ♗xg3 20 fxg3 ♕xg3+ 21 ♔h1 ♖e6 gives Black a winning attack. 15 gxh4 loses to 15...♕xh4 16 ♘f3 ♕h3 17 ♔h1 ♘xh2.

15...♗xg4 16 f3

After 16 ♕e1 ♖h6 17 f3 ♗h3 18 ♖f2 f5 Black redirects his attention to the e-file, and the sickly e3-pawn.

16...♖xh2!! 17 fxg4 ♖xe3! 18 ♗f6!?

White desperately tries to keep the black queen out, but it turns out the rooks can do enough damage on their own.

18...♖h3! 19 ♖f3

19 ♗xd8 loses to 19...♖exg3+ 20 ♔f2 ♖h2+ 21 ♔e1 ♖e3+.

19...♖xg3+ 20 ♔h1 gxf6 21 ♖xg3 ♗xg3 22 ♘f3 ♕d7 0-1

Chess News in Brief

Fourteen players contest seven preliminary matches in Saint John, Canada; the winners (Spraggett, Hjartarson, Portisch, Timman, Yusupov, Short and Speelman) are joined by Karpov to make up the normal complement of 8 players for the Candidates quarter-finals.

Kasparov wins the quadruple-round Amsterdam tournament with 9/12, ahead of Karpov (6½).

Karpov wins the Tilburg tournament; Short is second.

Timman wins the Linares tournament with 8½/11, ahead of Beliavsky (7).

Karpov wins the Wijk aan Zee tournament with 9/13, ahead of Andersson (8½).

Short wins the Hastings tournament (1988/9) ahead of Korchnoi.

Kasparov and Karpov share the 55th USSR Championship. There is supposed to be a play-off, but neither player finds the proposed terms to be acceptable. It is a very strong event; the winners score 11½/17, ahead of Yusupov, Salov (both 10), Eingorn and Ivanchuk (both 9½).

Fritz Baumbach wins the 11th Correspondence World Championship (1983-8).

World News in Brief

The Soviets pull out of Afghanistan, following successes by the Mujahedeen rebels. The turning point in the war came when the rebels obtained American *Stinger* anti-aircraft missiles.

The Iran-Iraq War ends, as Iran accepts the UN's cease-fire proposals. A few weeks earlier, Iraq admitted to using chemical weapons.

32 months after the *Challenger* disaster, space shuttle flights resume.

A new, highly addictive form of the drug cocaine, known as crack, sweeps across the USA. This adds to the already serious drug problem and strengthens the political resolve to cut off the supply at source.

There is conflict between Armenia and Azerbaijan over the disputed region of Nagorno-Karabakh.

Yasser Arafat announces that the PLO renounces violence.

A Libyan bomb explodes on board a Pan Am jumbo jet, wreckage from which showers down onto the town of Lockerbie in southern Scotland. In total, 270 people are killed, including 11 on the ground. An eye-witness describes the scene as "raining liquid fire".

An Iranian airliner is shot down in the Persian Gulf by a US warship.

In the North Sea, there is an explosion on the *Piper Alpha* oil rig. 167 die.

57 die in a train crash at the Gare de Lyon, Paris.

Chile votes to remove General Pinochet from power. While his rule has brought prosperity, there have also been human rights violations.

A massive earthquake causes devastation in Armenia. 25,000 are killed and about half a million are made homeless.

1989

Kasparov wins the World Cup

The World Cup develops into a race between Kasparov and Karpov. Kasparov and Ljubojević are joint first at Barcelona with 11/16, after Kasparov wins in the last round to preserve his eight-year record (after Tilburg 1981) of coming first or joint first in every tournament he has played. Timman wins the Rotterdam tournament with 10½/15, ahead of Karpov (9½, including three losses). Kasparov and Karpov win the final tournament at Skellefteå, with 9½/15. Kasparov is overall winner of the World Cup, just ahead of Karpov. Salov is third, Ehlvest fourth, Ljubojević fifth and Nunn sixth.

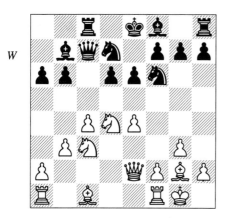

G. Kasparov – V. Salov
World Cup, Barcelona 1989

The fact that the opening has been a 'quiet' English may have lulled Salov into thinking a delay in development would go unpunished.

12 ♘d5! ♕b8

12...exd5 13 exd5+ ♔d8 14 ♗b2 gives White excellent play for the piece.

13 ♖d1 g6

After 13...exd5 14 exd5+ ♔d8 15 ♘c6+ ♗xc6 16 dxc6 ♘c5 17 b4 White keeps a powerful initiative. 13...e5 14 ♘xf6+ ♘xf6 15 ♘f5 g6 16 ♗g5 ♘d7 17 ♘h6 is good for White.

14 ♗g5 ♗g7

14...exd5 15 exd5+ ♗e7 16 ♘c6 ♗xc6 17 dxc6 ♘e5 18 f4 turns out well for White.

15 ♗xf6! ♘xf6

15...♗xf6 16 ♘xf6+ ♘xf6 17 e5 gives Black no good reply.

16 ♘xb6 ♖d8?!

16...♖c7 is more resilient.

17 e5! ♗xg2

17...dxe5 18 ♘c6 ♗xc6 19 ♗xc6+ ♔e7 20 c5 is no more palatable for Black.

18 exf6 ♗xf6 19 ♘xe6! fxe6

19...♗xa1 loses to 20 ♘xd8+ ♔xd8 21 c5.

20 ♕xe6+ ♗e7 21 c5! ♗b7

21...♗c6 is met by 22 ♖ac1.

22 ♖e1 ♕c7 23 c6! ♗xc6 24 ♖ac1 ♖d7 25 ♘xd7 ♕xd7 26 ♕c4! ♗b7 27 ♕c7 ♖f8 28 ♕b8+ ♔f7 29 ♖c7! 1-0

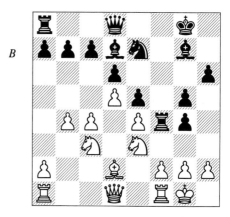

L. Portisch – J. Nunn
World Cup, Skellefteå 1989

16...♘g6

16...♕f8?! led to a draw in the earlier game Kasparov-Nunn from the same tournament.

17 ♖c1 ♘h4 18 ♔h1?!

18 f3 gxf3 19 g3 ♕f6 (or 19...g4) 20 ♖f2 ♖f8 was given by Nunn as totally unclear.

18...♕e8 19 f3 gxf3 20 g3 ♕h5! 21 gxh4?!

21 gxf4? is bad due to 21...exf4!, but 21 ♖f2 ♖af8 is unclear.

21...♖xh4

White's extra piece is now little consolation for Black's devastating attack.

22 ♖f2 g4 23 ♘f1 ♖h3 24 ♔g1 ♕g6

The threat is 25...g3.

25 ♘g3 ♖f8 26 ♘f5

Now White's game collapses very quickly, but there was no answer to ...h5-h4.

26...♖xf5! 27 exf5 ♗xf5 28 ♘e2 fxe2 29 ♕xe2 ♗d3 30 ♕d1 g3 31 hxg3 ♗e4 0-1

Chess News in Brief

Karpov qualifies for the Candidates final, edging out Yusupov 4½-3½ in the semi-final, after being in trouble in some games. Timman defeats Speelman in the other semi-final, a scrappy affair, by the same score.

Ivanchuk wins the Linares tournament with 7½/10, ahead of Karpov (7).

Kasparov dominates the double-round Tilburg tournament, scoring 12/14, ahead of Korchnoi (8½).

Kasparov wins at Belgrade with 9½/11, ahead of Timman and Ehlvest (both 6½).

Ehlvest wins the Reggio Emilia tournament (1989/90) with 7½/10, ahead of Ivanchuk (6½).

Gelfand wins the GMA Open at Palma de Mallorca.

The European Team Championship is played at Haifa. The qualifying rounds have now been dispensed with, and it is a nine-round Swiss system event open to national teams of six players. The USSR, without Kasparov and Karpov, wins with 36/54, ahead of Yugoslavia (33) and West Germany (31½). England performs badly, due in part to internal disagreements in what hitherto has been a very cohesive, and successful, team.

The World Team Championship, again held in Lucerne but now with teams of four players, is won by the USSR with 27½/36, ahead of Yugoslavia (22½) and England (21½). Ivanchuk's 6½/7 is the best score of the event.

Vaganian wins the 56th USSR Championship with 9/15, ahead of four players on 8½ (Beliavsky, Gelfand, Dolmatov and Eingorn).

Michael Adams (aged 17) wins the British Championship.

Zsofia Polgar scores 8½/9 in the Rome Open, to record one of the best tournament rating performances ever.

Kasparov thrashes the super-computer Deep Thought 2-0 in New York.

World News in Brief

Chinese forces brutally put down a pro-democracy movement, killing or injuring thousands of those who had gathered in Tiananmen Square, Beijing.

In the wake of Gorbachev's measured democratic reforms in the Soviet Union, communist governments across Eastern Europe collapse. Mostly, the transitions are peaceful, as governments feel obliged to hold, or at least move towards, free elections. First, Solidarity wins an election in Poland by a huge majority. Then Hungary opens its borders with Austria. Next, in East Germany the hard-line regime of Erich Honecker is replaced by a more moderate government, which opens the country's borders and renders the Berlin Wall a relic of the Cold War; the people start to dismantle it, with lumps of 'The Wall' becoming popular souvenirs for tourists. Public demonstrations oblige the Czechoslovakian government to resign. However, in Romania, Nicolae Ceausescu has no intention of stepping down, probably fearing a backlash against his cruel and repressive years in power. A week before Christmas there are bloody clashes between demonstrators and tanks, with Ceausescu's troops murdering unarmed civilians. On Christmas Day, Ceausescu and his wife are summarily executed; the gruesome scene is filmed, and broadcast around the world.

Presidents Bush and Gorbachev announce an official end to the Cold War.

The USA sends 24,000 troops to Panama in order to oust General Noriega and restore democracy.

A massive earthquake hits the San Francisco Bay area. About 270 are killed, and the cost of the damage runs into billions of dollars.

The *Exxon Valdez* runs aground in Alaska, spilling more than a million barrels of crude oil, causing an environmental disaster.

Voyager 2 transmits pictures of Neptune and its moons.

Scientists at CERN, the European Particle Physics Laboratory, start to develop the World Wide Web. It is a means of instantaneously exchanging electronic information, including both text and graphics, via the Internet.

1990

Kasparov prevails in exciting World Championship match

Karpov defeats Timman in the Candidates final 6½-2½ to become Kasparov's challenger yet again. The fifth Karpov-Kasparov World Championship match is close, but Kasparov ends up the 12½-11½ winner. The match features some excellent fighting chess.

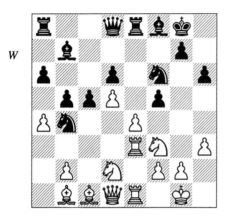

G. Kasparov – A. Karpov
World Ch match (game 20), Lyons 1990

In a very sharp line of the Ruy Lopez, Kasparov now tries a new move.

19 ♘h2!? ♚h8

19...♕d7 was later played by Karpov, with more success.

20 b3!

On b2, the bishop will be a fine attacking piece.

20...bxa4 21 bxa4 c4 22 ♗b2 fxe4 23 ♘xe4 ♘fxd5

Black has destroyed White's pawn-centre, but the exposure of his king is too great a cost.

24 ♖g3

24 ♕h5 c3 is less clear.

24...♖e6 25 ♘g4 ♕e8?!

Karpov plays ambitiously, but he is heading for annihilation. 25...♘d3 is better.

26 ♘xh6! c3

26...♖xh6 27 ♘xd6! wins for White: 27...♕h5 (27...♕xe1+ 28 ♕xe1 ♖xd6 29 ♕e4) 28 ♖g5! ♕xd1 29 ♘f7+ ♚g8 30 ♘xh6+ ♚h8 31 ♖xd1 c3 32 ♘f7+ ♚g8 33 ♗g6 with mating ideas.

27 ♘f5! cxb2 28 ♕g4! ♗c8

28...g6 loses to 29 ♚h2!, e.g. 29...♕d7 30 ♘h4.

29 ♕h4+ ♖h6 30 ♘xh6 gxh6 31 ♚h2

Preparing ♘f6.

31...♕e5 32 ♘g5! ♕f6 33 ♖e8 ♗f5 34 ♕xh6+

This wins, but 34 ♘f7+! is a forced mate.

34...♕xh6 35 ♘f7+ ♚h7 36 ♗xf5+ ♕g6 37 ♗xg6+ ♚g7 38 ♖xa8 ♗e7 39 ♖b8 a5 40 ♗e4+ ♚xf7 41 ♗xd5+ 1-0

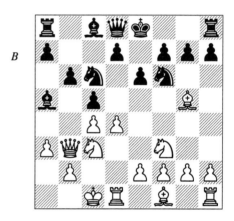

Y. Seirawan – J. Timman
Match (game 5), Hilversum 1990

White has just bravely castled queenside, in order to quicken his play in the centre.

8...♗xc3 9 d5! exd5?

9...♗e5 offers better chances of equality.

10 cxd5 ♗e5 11 dxc6 ♕e7 12 cxd7+ ♗xd7 13 e3

Black now has severe problems due to his inability to develop quickly enough.

13...♖d8

13...0-0? loses a piece after 14 ♘xe5 ♕xe5 15 ♗xf6. 13...h6 loses to 14 ♖xd7! ♚xd7 15 ♘xe5+ ♕xe5 16 ♕xf7+.

14 ♖xd7! ♖xd7

14...♚xd7 loses to 15 ♗b5+.

15 ♗b5 ♗d6 16 ♖d1 0-0 17 ♗xd7 ♕xd7 18 ♗f4 c4 19 ♕c2! ♘e8 20 ♘g5!

By creating threats of ♕xh7# and ♘e4, White overloads Black's defences.

20...f5 21 ♕xc4+ ♔h8 22 ♗xd6 ♘xd6 23 ♕d5 ♖d8 24 ♘e6 ♕c8+ 25 ♔b1 ♖d7 26 ♕xd6! 1-0

After 26...♖xd6 27 ♖xd6 White regains his queen with an extra piece.

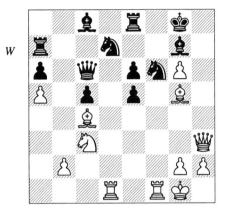

A. Shirov – A. Hauchard
Paris 1990

23 ♘d5! exd5 24 ♖xd5! ♔f8 25 ♕h7 ♖e6 26 ♗h6 ♔e8 27 ♕xg7 ♘xd5 28 ♕h8+ ♔e7 29 g7 ♖xh6 30 ♖f7+! ♔xf7 31 g8♕+ ♔e7 32 ♕d8+ 1-0

Chess News in Brief

The Manila Interzonal is a 64-player 13-round Swiss. Gelfand and Ivanchuk are joint first with 9/13. Anand and Short both score 8½, after recovering from poor starts.

Kamsky and Ivanchuk win the double-round Tilburg tournament with 8½/14.

Kasparov wins the Linares tournament with 8/11, ahead of Gelfand (7½).

Seirawan wins the Haninge tournament with 8½/11, ahead of Ehlvest and Karpov (both 7½).

The final of the GMA Opens, bringing together the qualifiers from each, is played in Moscow. Speelman, M.Gurevich, Khalifman, Azmaiparashvili and Bareev are joint winners.

The Novi Sad Olympiad is won by the USSR with 39/56, ahead of the USA and England (both 35½; the USA win the silver medals on tie-break) and Czechoslovakia (34½). Ivanchuk scores 7/10 on top board, while Chandler makes 9/11 as first reserve. 107 teams compete. The Women's Olympiad is won by Hungary on tie-break from the USSR. China picks up the bronze medals. Arakhamia scores 12/12 as reserve.

The Reykjavik Summit features four teams of ten. The USSR wins, with 31½/60, ahead of England (31), the USA (30) and a combined Nordic team (27½). The event features England's only match victory over the USSR: 6-4.

Beliavsky wins the 57th USSR Championship on tie-break from Yudasin, Bareev and Vyzhmanavin.

FIDE bans smoking at all its events.

World News in Brief

Germany is reunited. In effect, it is a take-over of East Germany by West Germany.

There are riots in Britain, as large numbers of people protest against the community charge (known as the 'poll tax'), which is widely seen as unfair, since ability to pay is only partly taken into account. Later in the year, Margaret Thatcher resigns as Prime Minister, amid disagreements with her colleagues on European policy and the poll tax.

In the USSR, Boris Yeltsin is elected president of the Russian republic; it is clear that he is favoured by the people, rather than the increasingly unpopular Gorbachev.

In Britain, customs officers seize sections of large-calibre piping that, it is claimed, is to be used for an Iraqi 'supergun'.

Lithuania declares its independence from the USSR, which imposes an economic blockade.

Iraq invades Kuwait. President Bush receives UN support for military action to drive Iraqi forces out of Kuwait, and an international force is assembled.

In Poland, Lech Walesa is elected president.

In South Africa, the ANC leader, Nelson Mandela, is freed after 27 years in prison.

An earthquake devastates northern Iran.

English and French excavations for the Channel Tunnel meet up under the sea.

The Hubble Space Telescope is put into orbit, but there is a fault with the main mirror, reducing its effectiveness.

1991

Anand enters the world elite • The World Cup collapses

Ivanchuk, Anand, Timman, Gelfand, Short, Korchnoi and Yusupov qualify for the Candidates quarter-finals. The quarter-final match Karpov-Anand is noteworthy, as Anand comes very close to winning. The 'crown princes' Ivanchuk and Gelfand are both eliminated at this stage.

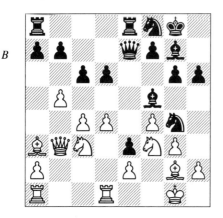

V. Ivanchuk – A. Yusupov
Candidates match (game 9), Brussels 1991

Yusupov has handled the opening aggressively, and now goes for broke on the kingside.

17...g5! 18 bxc6 bxc6 19 ♘e5?!

White should exchange pawns on g5 before playing this.

19...gxf4 20 ♘xc6 ♕g5 21 ♗xd6 ♘g6

Not 21...♘xh2? 22 ♗xf4! ♕h5 23 ♘d5.

22 ♘d5 ♕h5!?

The alternatives are easier to meet:

a) 22...fxg3? 23 ♗xg3 h5 24 h4! is good for White (based on the tactic 24...♘xh4?? 25 ♗f4 ♕g6 26 ♘ce7+).

b) 22...♘xh2 23 ♗xf4! leaves Black fighting for a draw: 23...♕h5 24 ♕b7 ♘g4 25 ♘ce7+ ♘xe7 26 ♘xe7+ ♖xe7 27 ♕xe7 ♗f6 28 ♕b7 ♖e8.

23 h4 ♘xh4?

Objectively, this is a mistake, but it does lead to a fantastic finish. 23...fxg3 24 ♗xg3 ♘xh4 25 ♘f4 ♕g5 26 ♘h3 ♕f6! is promising for Black.

24 gxh4 ♕xh4 25 ♘de7+?

The wrong knight! 25 ♘ce7+! ♔h8 26 ♘xf5 ♕h2+ 27 ♔f1 ♗e5!? 28 dxe5! is winning for White: 28...♖g8 29 ♘dxe3! fxe3 (29...♘xe3+ 30 ♘xe3 fxe3 31 ♕b7) 30 e6!; or 28...f3 29 exf3 e2+ 30 ♔xe2 ♕xg2+ 31 ♔d3.

25...♔h8 26 ♘xf5 ♕h2+ 27 ♔f1 ♖e6! 28 ♕b7?

28 ♘ce7 is a better try, but Black wins by the spectacular 28...♖g8!!: 29 ♘xg8 ♖g6 30 ♕xe3 ♘xe3+ 31 ♘xe3 ♖xd6 32 ♘g4 ♕g3 33 ♘8xh6 ♗xh6 34 ♘e5 f3 35 exf3 ♗e3 36 ♘g4 ♗xd4; 29 ♕d3 ♗f8 30 ♘xg8 ♖g6 31 ♘xe3 ♘xe3+ 32 ♔e1 ♗xd6 33 c5 f3! 34 ♗xf3 ♘c4! or 29 ♕b2!? ♗e5!! 30 ♗xe5+ ♘xe5 31 ♘xg8 ♖g6 32 ♕b7 f3, forcing mate.

28...♖g6!! 29 ♕xa8+ ♔h7

Threatening 30...♕h1+!! 31 ♗xh1 ♘h2+ 32 ♔e1 ♖g1#.

30 ♕g8+! ♔xg8 31 ♘ce7+ ♔h7 32 ♘xg6 fxg6 33 ♘xg7 ♘f2!!

Now the threat is 34...♘h3.

34 ♗xf4 ♕xf4 35 ♘e6 ♕h2 36 ♖db1 ♘h3 37 ♖b7+ ♔g8 38 ♖b8+ ♕xb8 39 ♗xh3 ♕g3 0-1

Kasparov wins the double-round Tilburg tournament with 10/14.

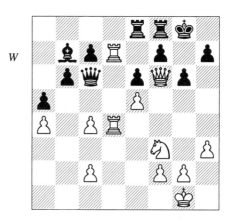

N. Short – J. Timman
Tilburg 1991

Black is paralysed, but it is not obvious how White is to make further progress; after all, his pieces all appear to be optimally placed.

30 h4!

Threatening h5, but this seems easy enough for Black to meet.

30...h5 31 ♔h2!!

Astonishingly, the king is heading for h6!

31...♖c8

Timman perhaps fails to perceive White's evil intentions. Otherwise he might have played 31...♗c8, when White has to find some accurate moves to win, starting with 32 g4!:

a) 32...♗xd7 33 gxh5 ♔h7 34 ♘g5+ ♔h6 35 ♘xf7+! ♖xf7 36 ♕xg6#.

b) 32...hxg4 33 ♘g5! g3+ (33...♗xd7 34 h5 g3+ 35 fxg3 ♕xa4 36 h6 ♕xc2+ 37 ♖d2!) 34 ♔xg3 ♗xd7 35 ♔h2!! ♕xa4 36 h5 gxh5 37 ♖h4 followed by ♖xh5 and ♖h8#.

32 ♔g3! ♖ce8 33 ♔f4 ♗c8 34 ♔g5 1-0

White's next move will be 35 ♔h6, unless Black plays 34...♔h7, when 35 ♕xg6+ ♔h8 36 ♕h6+ ♔g8 37 ♔f6 is one way to win.

Chess News in Brief

Ivanchuk wins the Linares tournament with 9½/13, ahead of Kasparov (9).

Salov and Short win the Amsterdam tournament with 6/9, ahead of Karpov and Kasparov (both 5½); these four players are all undefeated.

Ivanchuk and Karpov win at Reykjavik with 10½/15. It is the first tournament in the second World Cup, but it turns out to be the only such event, as the series is abandoned after Kasparov (and then Karpov) demand appearance fees, contrary to the principles of the World Cup, which Kasparov had been instrumental in setting up in the first place. It is a sad end to what had been one of the most exciting developments in the chess world for many years, and leads to a decline in the role of the GMA.

Karpov wins the double-round Reggio Emilia tournament (at the start of 1991) with 7½/12.

Gelfand wins the Belgrade tournament with 7½/11, ahead of Kamsky and Nunn (both 7).

Shirov wins the double-round Biel tournament with 9½/14, ahead of Bareev (8½).

Nunn wins the Wijk aan Zee tournament with 8½/13.

Christiansen wins the Munich tournament with 9½/13.

Anand wins the Reggio Emilia tournament (1991/2) with 6/9, ahead of Gelfand and Kasparov (both 5½).

The 58th and last USSR Championship is the second to be played using the Swiss System. Minasian surprisingly wins, on tie-break from Magerramov. 64 players compete; they include rising stars such as Kramnik and Shirov.

Gata Kamsky wins the USA Championship.

Judit Polgar wins the Hungarian Championship, and so breaks Fischer's record to become the youngest grandmaster in history.

Xie Jun beats Maya Chiburdanidze 8½-6½ to become Women's World Champion.

Grigory Sanakoev wins the 12th Correspondence World Championship (1984-91).

World News in Brief

The Gulf War sees the US-led forces wage a surgical campaign with hi-tech weapons. Precision bombing is followed by a brief ground offensive, which pushes Iraq out of Kuwait. There are just over 200 Allied casualties, compared to about 150,000 Iraqi dead. Before retreating, the Iraqis set on fire hundreds of oil wells, causing enormous environmental damage. After the war, Iraqi leader Saddam Hussein turns his forces against the Kurds, in the north of Iraq, forcing them to flee.

The Warsaw Pact is dissolved.

Estonia and Latvia declare their independence from the USSR.

A attempted coup against Mikhail Gorbachev fails, after Boris Yeltsin rallies the public against the conspirators. However, Gorbachev's standing is fatally weakened, and the Soviet Union is formally wound up in late December by agreement between the leaders of 11 Soviet republics. Yeltsin is the leader of Russia.

Slovenia and Croatia both declare independence from Yugoslavia. The Belgrade government opposes the break-up of the country, and takes military action, leading to civil war.

In South Africa, all remaining Apartheid laws are abolished.

A cyclone causes devastation and claims about 120,000 lives in Bangladesh.

1992

Fischer is back • Short beats Karpov

Anand wins a match against the other leading member of the young generation of super-GMs, Ivanchuk, by the score of 5-3.

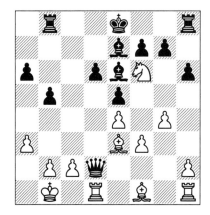

V. Ivanchuk – V. Anand
Match (game 1), Linares 1992

17...gxf6!!

A surprising recapture, but Anand has seen a way to gain the initiative on the kingside.

18 Rxd2 h5! 19 Rg1

After 19 Be2 hxg4 20 fxg4 Rh3, the black rook becomes very active.

19...hxg4 20 fxg4 Bc4!!

Denying White time to consolidate with h3 and Rg3.

21 b3

21 Bxc4 bxc4 22 Rg3 is met by 22...c3.

21...Bxf1 22 Rxf1 Rh3

Black's plan is to play ...d5 and to end up with two connected passed pawns, while White will be left with split pawns on c2 and h2.

23 Re2?!

23 Bg1 Kd7 24 Rd3 Rh4! favours Black.

23...Kd7 24 g5 Ke6 25 gxf6 Bxf6 26 Bd2 Be7! 27 Re1 f6 28 Bg3 d5 29 exd5+ Kxd5 30 Rf5! Kc6 31 Ref2?

31 Rf3! Rh7 32 Rc3+ Kb7 gives Black a harder technical task.

31...Rh6 32 Kb2 Kd7 33 Re2 Bd6 34 Rf3 Rc8! 35 Be1 Ke6 36 Rd3 Rh7 37 Rg3 Bc5 38 Ka2 Rd7 39 Rc3 Rcc7 40 h4 Rd1 41 Bf2 Bd6

42 Rg3 e4! 43 Rxe4+ Be5 44 Rxe5+ fxe5 45 Kb2 Rd2 0-1

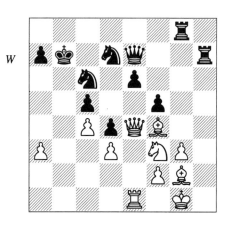

D. Norwood – S. Marsh
Walsall 1992

28 Qxc6+!! Kxc6 29 Nxd4++ Kb6 30 Rb1+ Ka6 31 Bb7+ Ka5 32 Bd2+ Ka4 33 Bc6+ Kxa3 34 Bc1+ Ka2 35 Rb2+ Ka1 36 Nc2#
(1-0)

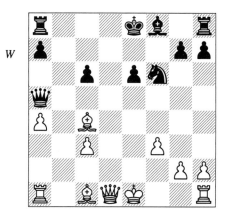

P. van der Sterren – M. Petursson
San Bernardino 1992

14 Qe2!! Qxc3+ 15 Kf1 Qxa1

Otherwise White has a powerful attack without any sacrifice.

16 ♕xe6+ ♔d8

16...♗e7 17 ♕xc6+ ♔f8 18 ♕xa8+ ♘e8 19 ♔e2 ♕xa4 leaves White much better.

17 ♔e2! ♕xa4

Or 17...♕c3 18 ♖d1+ ♔c7 19 ♗f4+! ♔b6 20 ♖b1+! ♔c5 21 ♖b5+! cxb5 22 ♕f5+, etc.

18 ♖d1+ ♕xd1+

Now the white queen will be dominant. 18...♔c7 loses to 19 ♕f7+ ♔b6 20 ♗e3+.

19 ♔xd1 ♗c5 20 ♕f7! ♖e8 21 ♕xg7 ♘d7 22 ♗f7 ♖f8 23 ♗e6 ♘f6 24 ♕b7 ♖e8 25 ♕xa8+ ♔c7 26 ♗f4+ 1-0

Chess News in Brief

In the Candidates semi-finals, Short excels himself to beat Karpov.

Fischer emerges after 20 years to play a match with Spassky. He wins by 10 wins to 5 (with 15 draws), but does not play subsequently. The match makes headlines, not least due to Fischer's defiance of the US State Department's instructions that he should not play in war-torn Yugoslavia, which is subject to UN sanctions. The quality of the play is uneven, but Fischer produces a few games that are reminiscent of his earlier glories.

Anand and Gelfand win the Moscow tournament with 4½/7.

Kasparov (despite losing two games) and Ivanchuk win the Dortmund tournament.

Kasparov wins the Linares tournament with 10/13, ahead of Timman and Ivanchuk (both 8).

M.Gurevich wins the Munich tournament with 7/11.

Anand and Short win the double-round Amsterdam tournament with 3½/6.

Adams wins the Tilburg knockout tournament.

Karpov wins the double-round Biel tournament with 10½/14. Shirov is next to last, with 5½ points – a set-back for a player who has jumped to third place in the world rankings.

The Manila Olympiad is won by Russia with 39/56, ahead of Uzbekistan (35), Armenia (34½) and the USA (34). Kasparov scores 8½/10 on top board, but the sensation of the Olympiad is new star Vladimir Kramnik's 8½/9 as first reserve. The break-up of the Soviet Union has brought many strong chess nations into the battle for medals, though Uzbekistan's second place is a great surprise, given that their team contains no world-class players. 102 teams compete. The Women's Olympiad is won by Georgia (no surprise, as most of the USSR's top women players come from this republic) ahead of Ukraine (led by Galliamova, a Russian/Tartar, who is now married to Ivanchuk) and China (with Xie Jun on top board). The Hungarian team does not include any Polgars.

The European Team Championship is played at Debrecen, with teams of four. Russia wins with 25/36, ahead of Ukraine (22½) and England (21½). Kasparov and Kramnik are again high-scorers. The women's event is won by Ukraine, ahead of Georgia.

The first Melody Amber tournament is contested, at Roquebrune (Monaco). These yearly events bring together some of the world's top players to contest rapidplay and, in later years, blindfold rapidplay games.

Mikhail Tal dies.

Samuel Reshevsky dies.

World News in Brief

Bosnia votes for independence from Yugoslavia. Bosnian Serbs, opposed to independence, resort to violence, and begin the process of 'ethnic cleansing', i.e. forcibly removing Croats and Moslems from areas they wish to make Serbian. The world is shocked by reports of mass-murders by Serbs.

The Maastricht agreement brings Europe a step closer to unity, but in many countries the politicians will have a hard time convincing the public that it is the right course.

There are severe riots, leaving 58 dead and causing enormous damage, in Los Angeles after four white policemen are acquitted of a savage beating of a black man, Rodney King, despite the event being captured on videotape.

US troops are deployed in Somalia to enable food and medicine to be brought in to relieve the severe famine.

In Afghanistan, rebels occupy the capital, Kabul.

The British economy is in crisis, following the pound's exit from the Exchange Rate Mechanism (ERM) sending its value into free-fall.

1993

Kasparov and Short split from FIDE

Kasparov convincingly wins the very strong Linares tournament with 10/13.

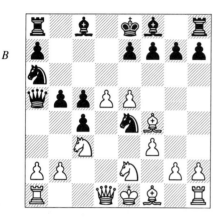

B

B. Gelfand – V. Anand
Linares 1993

It looks as if Black's activity will be short-lived, but Anand finds a superb way to keep the initiative.

9...♘b4!

Improving over an earlier game where Anand had suffered after 9...♘xc3?! 10 ♙xc3 ♗f5 11 g4 ♗g6 12 a4.

10 fxe4 ♘d3+ 11 ♔d2 g6!!

Black does not grab material by 11...♘f2?! 12 ♕e1 ♘xh1, as then White's active minor pieces and powerful central control would prevail. Instead, Anand's idea is to activate all his pieces and target the white king. The knight on d3 plays a central role, paralysing White's position. The immediate intention is ...♗g7 and ...♘xe5.

12 b3?

Gelfand, impressed by Anand's idea, plays a somewhat defeatist move. There are many alternatives, but it is hard for White to change the nature of the position. Black is for preference after 12 d6!? exd6 13 a4 b4! 14 ♘d5 ♗g7 or 12 ♔e3 ♗g7 13 ♘g3 (intending ♗xd3) 13...♘xf4 14 ♔xf4 ♗xe5+ 15 ♔e3 (15 ♔xe5? g5! forces mate) 15...♗d4+.

12...♗g7 13 bxc4 ♘xf4 14 ♘xf4?

Now Black takes full control, though 14 cxb5 ♗xe5 15 ♕b3 ♘xe2 16 ♗xe2 0-0 is quite unpleasant for White.

14...♗xe5 15 ♘fe2 b4 16 ♕a4+ ♕xa4 17 ♘xa4 ♗xa1 18 ♘xc5 0-0! 19 ♘d3 a5

It would be easy for White's central pawns to become menacing, but Anand plays very precisely to keep them under control.

20 g3 ♗g7 21 ♗g2 ♗a6! 22 c5 ♖ac8 23 c6 ♖fd8 24 ♖c1 ♗h6+ 25 ♘ef4 ♗xd3 26 ♔xd3 e5 27 ♔c4 exf4 28 ♖e1 fxg3 29 e5 ♗f4 30 hxg3 ♗xg3 31 ♖e3 ♗f4! 32 ♖e4 ♗h2 33 ♗h3 ♖c7 34 ♖e2 ♗g3 35 ♖e3 ♗f4 36 ♖e4 g5 37 ♔c5 ♖e7 38 ♔d4 f6! 39 d6 ♗xe5+ 40 ♖xe5 ♖xd6+ 0-1

The World Team Championship, played at Lucerne, ends in victory for the USA, who score 22½/36, ahead of Ukraine (21) and Russia (20½, losing two matches – to Armenia and Iceland).

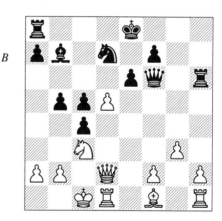

B

G. Kamsky – A. Shirov
World Team Ch, Lucerne 1993

This position comes from the insanely sharp Botvinnik System of the Semi-Slav.

16...♔f8!

This move had been suggested by Yusupov as an improvement over an earlier game, in which he had played White against Shirov. The move may not solve Black's theoretical difficulties, but it opens up some very interesting possibilities. The idea is that if White's knight goes to e4, then it will not be threatening to move to d6 with check. As a result, Black can now answer 17 ♗g2 or 17 dxe6 with 17...♘e5, and 17 ♘e4 with 17...♕g6.

17 f4

A rather crude way to prevent ...♘e5.

17...♘b6! 18 ♗g2 exd5 19 ♕f2 ♖c8!

Shirov calmly gathers his pieces for a massive queenside attack.

20 ♘xb5?!

This brings matters to a head, but 20 g4 ♖g6 21 h3 b4 22 ♘xd5 ♗xd5 23 ♗xd5 c3 is also grim for White.

20...♘a4! 21 ♕c2 ♕a6! 22 ♘a3 c3!!

This sensational move allows White some apparent activity, but once it is quelled, Black's attack will be unstoppable.

23 ♗xd5

23 bxc3 ♕a5! 24 ♘b1 ♖b8, intending ...♗a8 and ...♖hb6, offers White no hope.

23...♘xb2 24 ♕f5

24 ♗xb7? ♕xa3! 25 ♗xc8 ♘d3++ mates.

24...♖f6!?

24...♗xd5 25 ♖xd5 ♖b8 also wins.

25 ♕h7 ♕xa3! 26 ♕h8+ ♔e7 27 ♖he1+ ♔d7!

White has all manner of discovered and double checks, but nothing that rescues his king.

28 ♕h3+ ♔d6! 29 ♗xb7+ ♘xd1+ 30 ♔xd1 ♕xa2 31 ♕g2 ♕b1+ 0-1

Chess News in Brief

Short emerges as World Championship Challenger by beating Timman 7½-5½ in the Candidates final. Kasparov and Short break away from FIDE, starting a period of chaos in international chess. Kasparov wins comfortably 12½-7½ against Short, in a match held in London under the auspices of a controversial new organization, the Professional Chess Association (PCA).

FIDE strips Kasparov of his title and, in rather petty fashion, removes Kasparov and Short from the FIDE rating list. FIDE holds a rival world championship match between Karpov and Timman (who had both been defeated by Short), which is won 12½-8½ by Karpov.

FIDE's Biel Interzonal is won by Boris Gelfand with 9/13, ahead of a group of eight players on 8½. Anand gets the tenth qualifying place on tie-break.

The PCA qualifier (the equivalent of FIDE's interzonal) at Groningen is won by Adams and Anand. The other qualifiers for the PCA Candidates matches are Kamsky, Kramnik, Tiviakov, Gulko and Romanishin.

Karpov wins the Dortmund tournament with 5½/7, ahead of Kramnik and Lutz (both 4).

Shirov wins the Munich tournament with 8/11, ahead of Gelfand (7½).

Beliavsky wins the Belgrade tournament with 7½/9, ahead of Kramnik (6).

Morović wins the Las Palmas tournament with 6/9, ahead of Anand and Khalifman (both 5½).

Karpov wins the Tilburg knockout tournament, beating Ivanchuk in the final.

World News in Brief

A violent rebellion by hard-liners against Boris Yeltsin is defeated as the army backs the President.

Czechoslovakia splits into two new nations: the Czech Republic and Slovakia. The transition is wholly peaceful, and is the result of a democratic vote.

White rule ends in South Africa, as the parliament votes itself out of existence. President de Klerk and Nelson Mandela are awarded the Nobel Peace Prize for their roles in guiding South Africa through a very difficult period.

A peace agreement between Israel and the PLO is reached.

There is civil war in the former Soviet republic of Georgia.

A huge bomb damages the 110-storey World Trade Centre in New York. Damage is extensive, but the building survives.

115 die as blizzards sweep the eastern USA.

The Mississippi bursts its banks, causing severe flooding.

NASA loses contact with its *Mars Observer* craft.

The crew of the space shuttle *Endeavor* successfully repair the Hubble Space Telescope in orbit.

1994

The PCA organizes a series of high-profile events •
Karpov dominant at Linares

Karpov achieves a remarkable victory in the Linares tournament. He scores 11/13, ahead of Kasparov and Shirov (8½). Kasparov's stated view prior to the event was that the winner of Linares could be regarded as the World Champion of tournament chess.

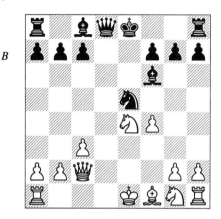

B

V. Topalov – E. Bareev
Linares 1994

White has just played the unwise move 10 f2-f4?!, which leaves his position very exposed.

10...♘g6 11 g3 0-0 12 ♗d3

The more natural 12 ♗g2 has the drawback that 12...♖e8 13 ♘e2 ♗f5 pins the knight against the queen.

12...♕d5!

Stopping White castling queenside.

13 a3?

Preparing 0-0-0 in any case, but Topalov should have been thinking more about his immediate survival. 13 ♘e2 ♗e7 14 a3 is probably best, when White is hanging on.

13...♘xf4!

Now there is no way out; Black has a winning attack.

14 ♘xf6+

Accepting the piece is no better. 14 gxf4 ♗h4+ gives Black a large advantage after 15 ♔d2 ♖d8, 15 ♔e2 ♗g4+ 16 ♘f3 f5 or 15 ♔f1 f5.

14...gxf6 15 ♗xh7+ ♔g7 16 ♕e4

Desperately trying to stop Black bringing a rook to e8. However, the queen is White's only good defensive piece, so Black can play the move White has just 'prevented' in order to denude the white king.

16...♖e8!

16...♘d3+ is less clear.

17 ♕xe8 ♗f5!! 18 ♕xa8

Now Black forces mates in nine moves, but 18 ♕a4 ♘d3+ 19 ♔f1 ♔xh7 is no good for White either.

18...♕e4+ 19 ♔f2

19 ♔d2 ♕g2+! 20 ♔e3 ♘d5+ 21 ♔d4 ♕d2+ mates.

19...♕g2+ 20 ♔e3 ♘d5+ 21 ♔d4 ♕d2+ 22 ♔c5 ♕e3+ 23 ♔c4 ♘b6+ 0-1

It is mate in three more moves.

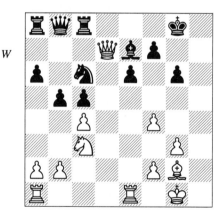

W

A. Karpov – V. Topalov
Linares 1994

Karpov now crowns some powerful positional play with a devastating sacrificial sequence.

20 ♖xe6!! ♖a7!

20...fxe6 21 ♗xc6 ♖a7 22 ♕xe6+ (this is the reason White needed to sacrifice on e6 before taking on c6) 22...♔g7 23 ♗e4 ♗f6 24 ♕g4 is terrible for Black.

21 ♖xg6+! fxg6

Now Black has to take the rook. 21...♔h7 loses to 22 ♕h3+! ♔xg6 23 ♗e4+.

22 ♕e6+ ♔g7 23 ♗xc6 ♖d8 24 cxb5 ♗f6

Now White has too many pawns for the exchange, but 24...axb5 loses to 25 ♘xb5.

25 ♘e4 ♗d4 26 bxa6 ♕b6 27 ♖d1 ♕xa6 28 ♖xd4! ♖xd4 29 ♕f6+ ♔g8 30 ♕xg6+ ♔f8 31 ♕e8+ ♔g7 32 ♕e5+ ♔g8 33 ♘f6+ ♔f7 34 ♗e8+ ♔f8 35 ♕xc5+ ♔d6 36 ♕xa7 ♕xf6

36...♖d1+ 37 ♔g2 ♖g1+!? should be met not by 38 ♔xg1? ♕d1+ 39 ♔g2 ♕h1+!, but by 38 ♔h3 ♖h1+ 39 ♔g4, winning.

37 ♗h5 ♖d2 38 b3 ♖b2 39 ♔g2 1-0

Chess News in Brief

A major sponsorship deal with Intel enables the PCA to hold a series of Grand Prix events (quickplay knockout tournaments with large prizes). Anand wins the Moscow Grand Prix. Kramnik beats Kasparov in the final to win the New York event. At London, the Pentium Genius (Richard Lang's *Chess Genius* program running on Intel's new Pentium chip) beats Kasparov, but is then convincingly subdued by Anand, who goes on to lose to Ivanchuk in the final. Kasparov finally manages to win a Grand Prix event, in Paris.

In the PCA World Championship cycle, Anand and Kamsky score clear victories over Adams and Short respectively, thus reaching the final of the PCA cycle.

The qualifiers for FIDE's quarter-finals are Timman, Salov, Gelfand, Anand, Kamsky and Kramnik. Kamsky then scores a surprising victory over Anand (6-4 after two tie-break games), after Anand seemed to have the match wrapped up. Kramnik is eliminated by Gelfand.

Notable tournaments: Kasparov and Ivanchuk win the double-round Novgorod tournament with 7/10, ahead of Kramnik (5). Kasparov wins the double-round Amsterdam tournament with 4/6. Kamsky wins the Las Palmas tournament with 6½/9, ahead of Karpov (6). Kasparov wins the Horgen tournament with 8½/11. Piket wins the Dortmund tournament with 6½/9, ahead of Adams (5½). Ivanchuk wins the Munich tournament with 7½/11. Gelfand wins the Dos Hermanas tournament with 6½/9, ahead

of Karpov (6). J.Polgar wins the Madrid tournament with 7/9. Salov wins the Tilburg knockout event.

Alexander Morozevich wins the last Lloyds Bank Masters in London with a phenomenal 9½/10 score.

The Olympiad, originally planned for Thessaloniki, is hurriedly rearranged in Moscow, where security, amongst other things, is poor. Russia wins with 37½/56, ahead of Bosnia & Herzegovina (35), Russia II and England (both 34½). 124 teams compete. The Women's Olympiad is won by Georgia, ahead of Hungary. The FIDE Congress is held under an oppressive atmosphere, and is anything but democratic.

Peter Svidler (born 1976) wins the Russian Championship.

Salov wins the double-round Buenos Aires tournament with 9/14. The rules for this tournament are that every game must start with an Open Sicilian.

Vladimir Zagorovsky dies.

World News in Brief

NATO planes bomb Serbian targets in Bosnia, after Bosnian Serb aircraft defy a UN no-fly zone. It is the first military action taken by NATO in its 45-year history. Late in the year, a cease-fire is agreed in Bosnia.

Russian forces, equipped with tanks, but mainly composed of conscripts, move into the breakaway province of Chechnia, but meet fierce resistance from experienced Chechen guerrillas.

The first free elections in South Africa bring the ANC to power.

The IRA declares a complete cease-fire, though British politicians are concerned that the declaration does not refer to a permanent cessation.

Civil war in Rwanda escalates, leaving more than 100,000 dead.

Los Angeles is seriously damaged by an earthquake. 34 people die, and tens of thousands are made homeless.

The car ferry *Estonia* sinks in the Baltic Sea. 912 die.

The Channel Tunnel, linking Britain and France, opens.

1995

Kasparov retains the PCA title • FIDE's Karpov-Kamsky match is postponed

Anand scores a convincing 6½-4½ victory over Kamsky to qualify for the PCA World Championship match. After a good start for Anand (5-4 up after nine games), Kasparov scores three wins in the next four games, effectively sealing his victory. The final score is 10½-7½.

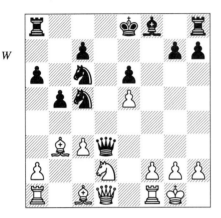

G. Kasparov – V. Anand
PCA World Ch match (10), New York 1995

This position had been seen in an earlier game of the match, and indeed had cropped up in the 1978 world championship match.

14 ♗c2! ♕xc3 15 ♘b3!!

Kasparov unleashes his prepared idea, which is a massively complicated rook sacrifice.

15...♘xb3

15...♖d8 16 ♗d2 ♖xd2 might be a better try for Black.

16 ♗xb3 ♘d4

16...♕xa1 17 ♕h5+! g6 18 ♕f3 ♘d8 19 ♕f6 ♖g8 20 ♗xe6! is good for White.

17 ♕g4 ♕xa1 18 ♗xe6 ♖d8?

The critical line is 18...♕c3! 19 ♗d7+ ♔f7 20 ♗e3 ♗c5 21 e6+ ♔g8 22 e7 g6 23 ♕e4! ♘e2+ 24 ♔h1 ♔g7!.

19 ♗h6! ♕c3

19...♕xf1+ 20 ♔xf1 gxh6? 21 ♕h5+ mates.

20 ♗xg7 ♕d3 21 ♗xh8 ♕g6

Anand returns the material, when White's task becomes a technical one. 21...♘e2+ 22

♔h1 ♘g3+ 23 hxg3 ♕xf1+ 24 ♔h2 leaves Black defenceless.

22 ♗f6 ♗e7 23 ♗xe7 ♕xg4 24 ♗xg4 ♔xe7 25 ♖c1!

Very accurate. Black will not be able to advance his pawns at all quickly.

25...c6 26 f4 a5 27 ♔f2 a4 28 ♔e3 b4 29 ♗d1 a3 30 g4 ♖d5 31 ♖c4 c5

31...♘e6 32 ♗b3 ♘c5 is met by 33 ♗c2.

32 ♔e4 ♖d8 33 ♖xc5 ♘e6 34 ♖d5 ♖c8 35 f5 ♖c4+ 36 ♔e3 ♘c5 37 g5 ♖c1 38 ♖d6 1-0

Kasparov wins the Tal memorial tournament in Riga with 7½/10, ahead of Anand (7).

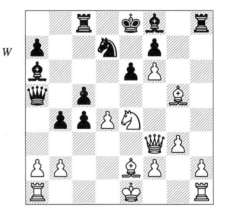

V. Kramnik – J. Ehlvest
Tal memorial, Riga 1995

16 d5!? exd5 17 ♕f5!? dxe4?!

17...♗b7 is a tougher defence.

18 0-0-0 ♖c7

18...♕c7 is best met by 19 ♕xe4+ ♕e5 20 ♕xe5+ ♘xe5 21 ♖he1 ♖d8 22 h4, when White will regain the piece with advantage.

19 ♗g4! ♗b5

After 19...♕xa2 20 ♖xd7 ♕a1+ 21 ♔d2 ♕xb2+ 22 ♔e3 ♕c3+ 23 ♔f4 White wins.

20 ♕xe4+ ♔d8 21 ♗xd7 ♗xd7

21...♖xd7 loses to 22 ♗f4 ♕a6 23 ♕a8+ ♕c8 24 ♕xa7 ♖xd1+ 25 ♖xd1+ ♗d7 26 ♕b6+ ♔e8 27 ♗c7!.

22 ♖he1 ♗h6 23 ♕a8+ ♖c8 24 ♖xd7+!
♔xd7 25 ♕d5+ 1-0

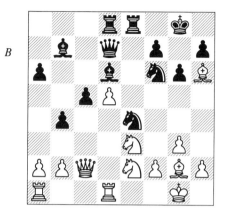

R. Cifuentes – V. Zviagintsev
Open tournament, Wijk aan Zee 1995

24...♘xf2! 25 ♔xf2 ♖xe3! 26 ♗xe3

26 ♔xe3 ♘g4+ 27 ♔d2 ♘xh6 is very good for Black, as the white king remains a target.

26...♘g4+ 27 ♔f3 ♘xh2+ 28 ♔f2 ♘g4+ 29 ♔f3 ♕e6! 30 ♗f4

30 ♗c1 c4! threatens both 31...♗c5 and 31...♗xd5 32 ♖xd5 ♕xd5+, with a mating attack.

30...♖e8 31 ♕c4

Now Black forces mate with a spectacular queen sacrifice.

31...♕e3+! 32 ♗xe3 ♖xe3+ 33 ♔xg4 ♗c8+ 34 ♔g5 h6+! 35 ♔xh6 ♖e5 0-1

36...♗f8# or 36...♖h5# follows.

Chess News in Brief

In the FIDE semi-finals, Kamsky beats Salov 5½-1½, and Karpov achieves a 6-3 victory over Gelfand. Under new FIDE rules, the defending champion enters the competition a stage earlier than previously was the case. The final, lacking a suitable venue or sponsorship, is postponed to 1996.

Lautier wins the double-round Amsterdam tournament with 4/6, ahead of Kasparov (3½).

Kamsky, Karpov and Adams win the Dos Hermanas tournament with 5½/9.

Kramnik wins the Dortmund tournament with 7/9, ahead of Karpov (6½).

Kasparov wins the Novgorod tournament with 6½/9.

Kramnik and Ivanchuk win the Horgen tournament with 7/10. Kasparov only manages fifth place, with 5 points. Anand does not play, having declined his invitation after publicity material described him as the defeated challenger, before his match with Kasparov was over.

Ivanchuk wins the Linares tournament with 10/13, ahead of Karpov (9).

Gelfand and Kramnik win the Belgrade tournament with 8/11.

Korchnoi wins the Madrid tournament with 6½/9, ahead of Salov (6).

Korchnoi wins the San Francisco tournament with 8/11, ahead of Nunn and Gulko (both 7½).

Ivanchuk wins the Moscow Grand Prix event. Kasparov wins at New York, and Adams at London. Kasparov is the winner of the concluding event of the series, in Paris.

Kasparov gains revenge over the Pentium Genius, winning a two-game rapidplay match in Cologne. A later match against Fritz is rendered farcical when the referee, Stewart Reuben, rules that an operator's error in entering a move must stand.

Mikhail Umansky wins the 13th Correspondence World Championship (1989-95).

Mikhail Botvinnik dies.

Lev Polugaevsky dies.

World News in Brief

The Dayton Accord brings an imperfect peace to Bosnia. The country is to be divided into two self-governing regions, one for Croats and Moslems, the other for Serbs, by a zigzag line that separates the country along racial lines.

A bomb, planted by a far-right extremist, devastates the federal building in Oklahoma City, killing 167.

Hutu refugees are massacred in Rwanda.

Israel gives Palestinians on the West Bank a degree of autonomy.

An earthquake, measured at 6.9 on the Richter Scale, kills about 5,400 people in Kobe (Japan) after many 'earthquake-proof' buildings collapse.

The US space shuttle *Discovery* docks with the Russian space station *Mir*.

1996

Kasparov beats Deep Blue, after losing the first game •
Topalov has a great year

Kasparov wins a match against IBM's Deep Blue, after losing the first game. The match score is 4-2 in Kasparov's favour; by the end of the match he has started to outclass the machine. The match receives an enormous amount of media attention around the world.

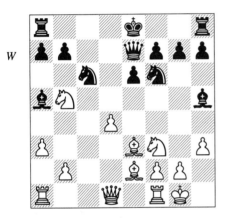

Deep Blue – G. Kasparov
Match (game 1), Philadelphia 1996

Kasparov has just played 13...♕d6-e7?!, an inaccuracy the machine punishes with a series of powerful moves to seize the initiative.

14 ♘e5! ♗xe2 15 ♕xe2 0-0 16 ♖ac1 ♖ac8 17 ♗g5

The pin on the h4-d8 diagonal is extremely awkward.

17...♗b6

Black could try instead 17...♖fd8 18 ♗xf6 gxf6 19 ♘c4 a6 20 ♘xa5 ♘xa5.

18 ♗xf6! gxf6

18...♕xf6? loses an exchange to 19 ♘d7.

19 ♘c4! ♖fd8

The d-pawn is defended by tactical means: 19...♘xd4? 20 ♘xd4 ♗xd4 21 ♕g4+.

20 ♘xb6! axb6 21 ♖fd1 f5 22 ♕e3! ♕f6 23 d5!

This is the type of move an experienced human grandmaster might play to smash apart Black's pawn-structure – a decision based on experience and intuition. Poor Deep Blue had only its phenomenal calculating power to guide it towards the move.

23...♖xd5 24 ♖xd5 exd5 25 b3!

Deep Blue secures its pawns, and prepares to feast on Black's weaklings.

25...♔h8?

Kasparov goes for a desperate counter-attack that might have frightened a human opponent. Objectively 25...♘e7 26 ♖xc8+ ♘xc8 27 ♕e8+ ♔g7 28 ♕xc8 ♕a1+ 29 ♔h2 ♕e5+ 30 g3 ♕e2 is better, when White must try to win a queen ending.

26 ♕xb6 ♖g8 27 ♕c5 d4 28 ♘d6 f4 29 ♘xb7

Deep Blue has calculated that Black's threats come to nothing.

29...♘e5 30 ♕d5 f3 31 g3 ♘d3

31...♕f4 32 ♖c8! ♕g5 33 ♖c5! ends Black's attack.

32 ♖c7 ♖e8 33 ♘d6 ♖e1+ 34 ♔h2 ♘xf2 35 ♘xf7+ ♔g7 36 ♘g5+ ♔h6 37 ♖xh7+ 1-0

In view of 37...♔g6 38 ♕g8+ ♔f5 39 ♘xf3.

Ivanchuk wins the Wijk aan Zee tournament with 9/13, ahead of Anand (8) and Topalov (7½).

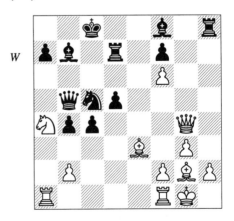

V. Ivanchuk – A. Shirov
Wijk aan Zee 1996

21 ♕g7!?

A stunning piece of over-the-board inspiration by Ivanchuk.

21...♗xg7 22 fxg7 ♖g8 23 ♘xc5

White has just two pieces for the queen, but various threats on the queenside, while the g7-pawn is a nuisance too.

23...d4?!

Now Black gets into trouble. The critical line is 23...♖xg7!? 24 ♗d4! f5 25 ♘xd7 ♖xd7 26 ♖xa7, resulting in a messy position.

24 ♗xb7+ ♖xb7 25 ♘xb7! ♕b6!

After 25...♔xb7 26 ♗xd4 White's rooks penetrate decisively.

26 ♗xd4!! ♕xd4 27 ♖fd1! ♕xb2

27...♕xg7 28 ♖xa7 (threatening 29 ♘d6+) 28...♔b8 29 ♖da1 ♖e8 (29...♕d4 30 ♘a5!!) 30 ♘d6 ♖e1+ 31 ♖xe1 ♔xa7 32 ♘xc4 is a winning ending for White.

28 ♘d6+ ♔b8 29 ♖db1 ♕xg7

Black has no adequate continuation. For example, 29...♕e5 30 ♖xb4+ gives Black problems; one line is 30...♔c7 31 ♖b7+ ♔xd6 32 ♖a6+ ♔c5 33 ♖a5+.

30 ♖xb4+ ♔c7 31 ♖a6! ♖b8 32 ♖xa7+! ♔xd6 33 ♖xb8 ♕g4 34 ♖d8+ ♔c6 35 ♖a1 1-0

Chess News in Brief

Karpov defends the FIDE World Championship against Kamsky, winning by 10½-7½. The match is played in Elista, following protests about FIDE's intended venue, Baghdad.

Kasparov wins the double-round six-player Las Palmas tournament, one of the strongest of all time (average rating 2757), with 6½/10, ahead of Anand (5½), Kramnik, Topalov (both 5), Ivanchuk and Karpov (both 4).

Other major tournaments: Kramnik and Topalov win the Dos Hermanas tournament with 6/9, ahead of Anand and Kasparov. Topalov wins the double-round Novgorod tournament with 6/10. Gelfand, Topalov and Karpov win the Vienna tournament with 5½/9. Topalov and Kasparov win the Amsterdam tournament with 6½/9. Kramnik and Anand win the Dortmund tournament with 7/9. Adams wins the Chess in the Schools tournament in New York.

The Erevan Olympiad is won by Russia with 38½/56, ahead of Ukraine (35), the USA and England (both 34). Notable performances are Kasparov's 7/9, Ivanchuk's 8½/11 (both on top board), Svidler's 8½/11 on board 4, and Sadler's 10½/13 as first reserve for England. 114 teams compete. Georgia wins the Women's Olympiad, ahead of China and Russia.

Zsuzsa Polgar becomes Women's World Champion by beating Xie Jun 8½-4½, but the contest is marred by match organizer Luis Rentero sending the players a letter they find insulting.

French prodigy Etienne Bacrot (born 1983) wins a match against Smyslov by a 5-1 score.

Grand Prix events are held in Moscow (won by Kramnik) and Geneva (won by Anand).

World News in Brief

The IRA ends its cease-fire, exploding a massive bomb in London's Canary Wharf.

In Israel, there is renewed violence on the West Bank.

In Operation Desert Strike, US Cruise missiles are fired on southern Iraq.

The US State Department finds no evidence for Gulf War syndrome. It had been claimed that the treatment given to soldiers to protect them against possible Iraqi chemical and biological weapons has seriously damaged their health. In Britain, the Ministry of Defence admits that troops were exposed to dangerous chemicals.

A TWA airliner explodes off Long Island, New York. 228 die.

A gunman kills 16 primary school children and a teacher in Dunblane, Scotland. Subsequently, Britain outlaws all but the smallest handguns.

In Port Arthur (Australia), a gunman kills 35 tourists.

A European Space Agency Ariane-5 rocket veers off course shortly after blast-off, and has to be destroyed. It is carrying four spacecraft, and is not insured.

There are fears that bovine spongiform encephalopathy (BSE, the so-called 'mad cow disease') is linked to a human brain disease, Creutzfeldt-Jakob Disease (CJD).

There is a major fire in the Channel Tunnel.

The ferry *MV Bukova* capsizes in Lake Victoria, Tanzania. About 1,000 drown.

1997

Kasparov loses a bizarre rematch against Deep Blue

Kasparov loses his return match against the super-computer Deep(er) Blue in ludicrous fashion. In game 6, he falls into an opening trap of which he has been well aware for years. Chess-players are just bemused, but outside the chess world it is viewed as a highly significant event. The final score is 3½-2½. Afterwards, Deep Blue is 'retired' from competitive chess.

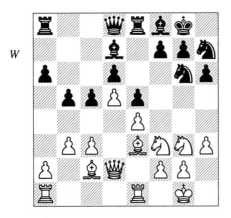

W

Deep Blue – G. Kasparov
Match (game 2), New York 1997

Kasparov has played a passive opening, doubtless expecting the computer to be unable to find coherent plans in such a blocked position. However, there are ways for White to make nuggets of progress that come within its calculation range.

19 a4 ♘h4 20 ♘xh4 ♕xh4 21 ♕e2! ♕d8 22 b4 ♕c7 23 ♖ec1

With ideas of playing c4.

23...c4 24 ♖a3 ♖ec8 25 ♖ca1 ♕d8 26 f4!

Making gains on the kingside.

26...♘f6 27 fxe5 dxe5 28 ♕f1

Possibly intending to triple on the a-file.

28...♘e8

With ideas of ...♘d6 and ...bxa4 or ...a5, and also granting the queen access to h4. Deep Blue now changes plan to meet this.

29 ♕f2 ♘d6 30 ♗b6 ♕e8 31 ♖3a2! ♗e7

31...bxa4 32 ♗xa4 ♘b5 is smoothly met by 33 ♕e3.

32 ♗c5 ♗f8 33 ♘f5 ♗xf5 34 exf5 f6 35 ♗xd6 ♗xd6 36 axb5 axb5 37 ♗e4!

Rather than going for material gains by ♕b6, the computer first blocks out any possible counterplay by ...e4. Quite how the computer made this decision is unclear – maybe the programmers had made it doubly wary of Kasparovian pawn sacrifices. In any case, as a result of these moves Kasparov became convinced that something improper was going on.

37...♖xa2 38 ♕xa2 ♕d7 39 ♕a7 ♖c7 40 ♕b6 ♖b7 41 ♖a8+ ♔f7 42 ♕a6 ♕c7 43 ♕c6 ♕b6+ 44 ♔f1?

44 ♔h1 ♖b8 45 ♖a6 wins comfortably for White.

44...♖b8 45 ♖a6?

45 ♕xb6 is still good for White.

1-0??

In fact, Black can draw: 45...♕e3! 46 ♕xd6 ♖e8! 47 h4 (47 ♗f3 ♕c1+ 48 ♔f2 ♕d2+ is perpetual) 47...♕xe4 48 ♖a7+ ♔g8 49 ♕d7 ♕d3+ 50 ♔g1 ♕e3+ 51 ♔h2 ♕f4+ 52 ♔h3 ♖e7! 53 ♖a8+ ♔h7 54 ♕c8 ♖e8! 55 ♕xe8 ♕xf5+ and Black gives perpetual check.

Anand wins the double-round Biel tournament with 7/10.

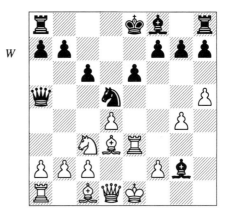

W

V. Anand – J. Lautier
Biel 1997

15 f3! ♗b4

After 15...♘xe3 16 ♗xe3 ♕b6 17 ♔f2 ♗h3 18 ♖b1 White's bishops work well.

16 ♔f2! ♗xc3 17 bxc3 ♕xc3 18 ♖b1 ♕xd4

18...♗xf3 19 ♕xf3 ♕xd4 20 ♖xb7 0-0 21 ♕e4 gives White an extra piece.

19 ♖xb7 ♖d8

19...0-0? fails to 20 ♗xh7+, while 19...♗h3 20 ♖xf7! c5 21 ♖f5! and 19...♘f4 20 ♔g3 ♕d6 21 ♗a3! are very good for White.

20 h6!

Black survives after 20 ♗g6 ♕xd1 21 ♖xe6+ ♔f8, so Anand seeks an improved version.

20...gxh6?

20...g6? 21 ♗xg6! ♕xd1 22 ♖xe6+ ♔f8 23 ♖xf7+ ♔g8 24 ♖g7+ forces mate. Black's best is 20...♘xe3 21 ♗xe3 ♕e5 22 hxg7 ♖g8, although 23 ♕c1! strongly favours White.

21 ♗g6!! ♘e7

The key line is 21...♕xd1 22 ♖xe6+ ♔f8 23 ♗xh6+ ♔g8 24 ♗xf7#.

22 ♕xd4 ♖xd4 23 ♖d3! ♖d8 24 ♖xd8+ ♔xd8 25 ♗d3! 1-0

Chess News in Brief

FIDE brings in a new knockout format for its Championship. Anand wins the knockout stage at Groningen at the end of the year, and then has two days before he starts play against Karpov immediately after New Year in Lausanne. FIDE has made no travel arrangements for him or his seconds.

Kasparov wins the double-round Novgorod tournament with 6½/10.

Anand and Kramnik win the Dos Hermanas tournament with 6/9.

Kasparov wins the Linares tournament with 8½/11, ahead of Kramnik (7½).

Kramnik wins the Dortmund tournament with 6½/9, ahead of Anand (5½).

Anand and Ivanchuk win the Belgrade tournament with 6/9.

Svidler, Kasparov and Kramnik win the Tilburg tournament with 8/11.

Salov wins the Wijk aan Zee tournament with 8½/13.

Topalov and Shirov win the Madrid tournament with 6½/9.

The European Team Championship, played at Pula, is won by England, on tie-break from Russia. Both teams score 22½/36, ahead of Armenia (22). England's star performer is Sadler (7/9). Georgia wins the women's event, ahead of Romania and England.

The World Team Championship, played in Lucerne, is won by Russia with 23½/36, ahead of the USA (23), Armenia (21) and England (20½). Instead of an African team, this time there is a Georgian women's team.

Miguel Najdorf dies.

Erich Eliskases dies.

World News in Brief

A state of emergency is declared in Albania, after the country's pyramid savings schemes collapse.

Britain hands Hong Kong over to China.

The IRA reinstates its cease-fire.

Russia and Chechnia sign a peace treaty.

A NATO-Russian cooperation charter is signed.

Diana, Princess of Wales, dies in a car crash in Paris. There is a great outpouring of grief, both in Britain and around the world.

The Russian space station *Mir* collides with a supply craft, causing major damage, but the crew survive.

The Hale-Bopp comet is seen brightly from Earth. The ancient Egyptians had recorded the comet's previous appearance, about 4,000 years earlier. 39 people in the Heaven's Gate cult commit mass-suicide, believing they will be taken up by a UFO that is hiding behind the comet.

58 tourists are killed in a massacre at Luxor in Egypt.

Scientists in Edinburgh succeed in cloning a sheep. The lamb, named Dolly, is an exact genetic copy of her mother. In principle, the same procedure could be used to clone humans.

The *Pathfinder* probe lands on Mars, and releases a six-wheeled robot, *Sojourner*.

The Petronas Tower in Kuala Lumpur, Malaysia, becomes the world's highest building. It is 452 metres (1,480 feet) high.

ThrustSSC sets a new land speed record of 763 miles per hour (1,229 km/h), in the process breaking the sound barrier.

The world's oldest person, Jeanne Caldwell, dies, aged 122.

1998

Anand dominates tournament chess •
World Championship Cancelled?

Gelfand wins the Polanica Zdroj tournament with 6½/9, ahead of Shirov (5½). Karpov is joint seventh, with 4 points.

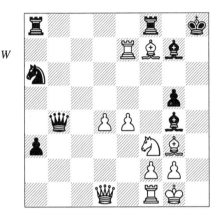

B. Gelfand – A. Shirov
Polanica Zdroj 1998

23 ♖d7!! ♗xd7

Else 24 ♗d6, but now White can bring his queen and knight into the attack.

24 ♘xg5 ♕b6 25 ♗e6!

Stopping the black queen defending the kingside by moving to h6.

25...♕xe6

The only move, as 25...♗e8 26 ♕g4 is hopeless for Black.

26 ♘xe6 ♗xe6

If White can safely remove the black a-pawn, and keep the black king exposed, his swarm of passed pawns should carry the day.

27 ♗e5 ♖f7

27...♗xe5 28 ♕h5+ ♔g8 29 ♕xe5 ♗c4 30 ♕g5+ ♔f7 31 ♖b1 wins for White.

28 ♕h5+ ♔g8 29 ♕g6 ♗d7 30 ♗xg7 ♖xg7 31 ♕d6 ♔h7

31...♘c7 32 ♕xc7 ♗h3 33 ♕c6 ♖a5 34 ♖c1 ♖xg2+ 35 ♔h1 a2 36 ♕e8+ ♔h7 37 ♕e7+ ♔h6 38 ♖c6+ ♖g6 39 ♕f8+ picks up the a5-rook.

32 ♕xa3 ♘c7 33 ♕e3 ♘e6 34 d5 ♘g5 35 f4 ♘h3+ 36 ♔h1 ♖a2 37 f5! ♘g5 38 f6 ♖g6 39 f7
1-0

Anand wins the elite double-round Linares tournament (average rating 2752) with 7½/12, ahead of Shirov (7), Kasparov and Kramnik (6½). Kasparov manages only one win in the event, though it is against Anand.

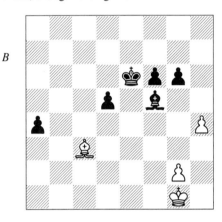

V. Topalov – A. Shirov
Linares 1998

The opposite-coloured bishops make it hard for Black to exploit his material advantage.

47...♗h3!!

Black needs to advance his a- and d-pawns as quickly as possible, with the support of his king. Moving the bishop with gain of tempo is therefore logical, but it needs a creative leap to see that this might be done by putting the bishop *en prise*! Black's a-, d- and f-pawns, if well enough supported by the king, will overpower the white bishop. Neither 47...a3 48 ♔f2 a2 49 ♔e3 nor 47...♗e4 48 ♔f2 ♔f5 49 g3 is a clear win for Black.

48 gxh3

After 48 ♔f2 ♔f5 49 ♔f3 (no better is 49 g3 ♔e4) 49...♗xg2+ 50 ♔xg2 ♔e4 Black penetrates, overloading the white bishop.

48...♔f5 49 ♔f2 ♔e4! 50 ♗xf6

After 50 ♔e2 a3 51 ♔d2 d4 52 ♗a1 f5 White cannot stop all three passed pawns.

50...d4 51 ♗e7 ♔d3! 52 ♗c5 ♔c4! 53 ♗e7 ♔b3 0-1

Chess News in Brief

Karpov wins the FIDE Championship match against Anand, but there is wide-spread criticism of the fact that Anand had to play against a rested and prepared Karpov so soon after a gruelling knockout event. Subsequently, Anand has a great year, winning a series of top-level events, whereas Karpov plays few major events, with no notable successes.

Kasparov's efforts to arrange a new World Championship defence, under the auspices of the WCC (World Chess Council; later wittily dubbed 'World Championship Cancelled') hit major problems. Anand refuses to play in the proposed match with Kramnik (with the winner to challenge Kasparov), so Shirov is chosen to replace him. When Shirov unexpectedly beats Kramnik 5½-3½, the main weakness of the system becomes apparent. As there was no real qualifying cycle, winning this match isn't enough to make Shirov an obviously legitimate challenger, and there are problems finding sponsorship, especially as an arrangement apparently made by Luis Rentero falls through. Shirov comes off very badly: he received no money for the Kramnik match; his 'prize' was the right to challenge Kasparov, and that evaporates, leaving him with nothing. Kasparov then invites World no. 2 Anand to challenge him directly. The rating list has become, it seems, the most credible and democratic way of selecting a challenger.

Notable tournaments: Kramnik, Adams and Svidler win the Dortmund tournament with 6/9. Anand wins the Tilburg tournament with 7½/11, ahead of Leko (7). Anand and Kramnik win the Wijk aan Zee tournament with 8½/13. Karpov can only manage a 50% score. Anand wins the Madrid tournament with 6½/9. Morozevich wins the Pamplona tournament (1998/9) with 8/9. This is one of a number of outstanding results that catapult him high in the world rankings.

The Elista Olympiad is won by Russia with 35½, ahead of the USA (34½), Ukraine and Israel (both 32½). The Russian team consists predominantly of young players; Morozevich is their top scorer, with 8/10 on board 4. 110 teams compete. The Women's Olympiad is won by China, ahead of Russia and Georgia.

Kasparov and Topalov draw an 'Advanced Chess' match 3-3. In these rapidplay games, the players are allowed to use a computer, both as a database, and for analytical assistance.

Efim Geller dies.

Laszlo Szabo dies.

World News in Brief

Following Iraq's refusal to allow UN arms inspections, there is an Anglo-American bombing campaign against suspected weapons factories and stockpiles in Iraq.

Trouble is brewing in Kosovo, a province in the south of Serbia where the majority of the people are ethnic Albanians. There are reports of massacres by Serbs.

The Good Friday agreement sets a timetable for permanent peace in Northern Ireland. The deal is backed by politicians and gains strong support from the public in referenda in both Eire and Ulster. John Hume and David Trimble, the leaders of the main Catholic and Protestant parties respectively, receive the Nobel Peace Prize.

India and Pakistan both conduct nuclear tests.

Bomb attacks on US embassies in Nairobi and Dar-es-Salaam leave 240 dead.

There is political scandal in the USA as President Clinton first denies, and then admits to an 'inappropriate relationship' with Monica Lewinsky, a White House intern. The affair is related to accusations of perjury and obstruction of justice. The House of Representatives votes to institute impeachment proceedings against the president. Two articles of impeachment are passed.

The Japanese government announces a massive aid package to rejuvenate the country's ailing economy.

Microsoft becomes the largest company in the USA.

Benoit Lecomte becomes the first person to swim the Atlantic.

An appalling train crash at Eschede (Germany) kills 96. A faulty wheel is the primary cause.

Hurricane Mitch devastates Central America.

Water is discovered on the moon.

1999

Kasparov reconfirms his dominance • Three World Championships now in disarray

Kasparov wins at Wijk aan Zee with 10/13, ahead of Anand (9½) and Kramnik (8). He then wins the very strong (average rating 2735) double-round Linares tournament with 10½/14, ahead of Kramnik and Anand (both 8). These emphatic victories reconfirm that Kasparov's period of dominance in world chess has by no means finished.

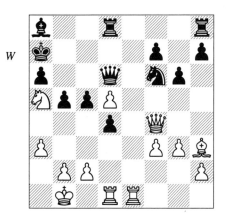

G. Kasparov – V. Topalov
Wijk aan Zee 1999

24 Rxd4! cxd4?

Topalov plays the ambitious move. 24...♔b6! 25 ♘b3 ♗xd5 26 ♕xd6+ Rxd6 is level.

25 Re7+ ♔b6

25...♔b8 loses to 26 ♕xd4 ♘d7 27 Rxd7.

26 ♕xd4+ ♔xa5

26...♔c5 27 ♕xf6+ ♕d6 28 ♗e6!! wins; the point is 28...♔xa5 29 b4+ ♔a4 30 ♕c3 ♗xd5 31 ♔b2! intending ♕b3+, mating.

27 b4+ ♔a4 28 ♕c3

More accurate is 28 Ra7! ♗b7 (or 28...♘xd5 29 Rxa6+! ♕xa6 30 ♕b2) 29 Rxb7 ♕xd5 30 Rb6! a5 31 Ra6 Ra8 32 ♕e3 Rxa6 33 ♔b2 and Black suffers ruinous losses.

28...♕xd5 29 Ra7 ♗b7 30 Rxb7! ♕c4

30...Rhe8 31 Rb6 Ra8 32 ♗f1!, preventing ...♕c4, is winning for White. The key threat is Rd6, and 32...Re1+ 33 ♕xe1 ♘d7 34 Rb7! wins; for example, 34...♕xb7 35 ♕d1 ♔xa3 36

c3. Instead, 30...♘e4 31 fxe4 ♕c4 32 Ra7! Rd1+ 33 ♔b2 ♕xc3+ 34 ♔xc3 Rd6 35 e5 Rb6 36 ♔b2 Re8 37 ♗g2 Rd8 38 ♗b7 Rd7 39 ♗c6! Rd8 (39...Rxa7 40 ♗d5 and 41 ♗b3#) 40 ♗d7, with c4 to follow, is also a win for White.

31 ♕xf6 ♔xa3

Or 31...Rd1+ 32 ♔b2 Ra8 33 ♕b6 ♕d4+ 34 ♕xd4 Rxd4 35 Rxf7 winning more prosaically.

32 ♕xa6+ ♔xb4 33 c3+! ♔xc3 34 ♕a1+ ♔d2 35 ♕b2+ ♔d1 36 ♗f1! Rd2

36...♕xf1 is mated by 37 ♕c2+ ♔e1 38 Re7+. The text-move apparently throws a spanner in the works, but Kasparov has the perfect answer ready.

37 Rd7! Rxd7 38 ♗xc4 bxc4 39 ♕xh8 Rd3 40 ♕a8 c3 41 ♕a4+ ♔e1 42 f4 f5 43 ♔c1 Rd2 44 ♕a7 1-0

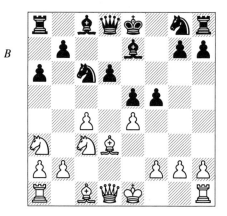

J. Nunn – I. Nataf
French League 1999

9...f4!? 10 g3 ♘f6!? 11 gxf4 exf4 12 ♗xf4 0-0 13 ♗g3 ♘g4

Black's compensation for the pawn looks highly nebulous, but his play against the weakness of f2 is very real.

14 ♗e2?

14 0-0 is necessary, but Black will definitely have compensation due to the exposed position of the white king.

14...♘xf2!!

14...♘ge5 is met by 15 ♕d5+ and 16 0-0-0.

15 ♕d5+

Striving to control g5. 15 ♗xf2 ♖xf2 16 ♔xf2 ♗h4+ 17 ♔g2 ♕g5+ 18 ♗g4 ♘e5 will amount to a very good exchange sacrifice by Black.

15...♔h8 16 ♗xf2?

After the superior 16 ♖f1 ♘g4 White is fighting for a draw.

16...♘b4!

This drives the white queen from d5, but seems to misplace the knight. However, it turns out later to be in just the right place!

17 ♕h5

17 ♕d4 ♖xf2! 18 ♔xf2 ♗h4+ 19 ♔f3 ♗h3! gives Black a winning attack.

17...♖xf2! 18 ♔xf2 ♗h4+ 19 ♔g2

19 ♔e3 g6 20 ♕f3 ♕g5+ 21 ♕f4 ♕c5+ 22 ♔d2 ♗g5 wins the white queen.

19...g6

Now White's queen must cede control of g5.

20 ♕f3 ♕g5+ 21 ♔f1 ♗h3+! 22 ♕xh3 ♖f8+ 23 ♗f3 ♕e3 24 ♕xh4 ♘d3!!

This forces mate in 7 more moves, but it is highly surprising that neither of the immediate captures on f3 is the correct move. The threat is 25...♖xf3+ 26 ♔g2 ♘f4+ 27 ♕xf4 ♕f2#.

25 ♘d5 ♕xf3+

25...♖xf3+! 26 ♔g2 ♕e2+ 27 ♔g1 g5 mates.

26 ♔g1 ♘f2 27 ♔f1 ♕xh1+ 28 ♔e2 ♕xa1

0-1

Chess News in Brief

The FIDE Championship in Las Vegas is won by Alexander Khalifman. For various reasons, many of the world's leading players are absent (e.g. Kasparov, Anand, Morozevich and Karpov, who is threatening legal action against FIDE), while the top players who are present fall by the wayside in the knockout process.

The 'Ultimate Championship' Kasparov-Anand is postponed, after sponsorship collapses. It is rescheduled to early 2000.

The FIDE Women's World Championship is in chaos. Zsuzsa Polgar is stripped of her title, and then Xie Jun plays Alisa Galliamova (who had already defaulted in the Candidates final) for the World Championship. Xie Jun wins.

In a career-best result, Michael Adams wins the Dos Hermanas tournament with 6/9, ahead of Kramnik (5½). Anand is in joint last place, with 3½ points.

Kasparov wins the Sarajevo tournament with 7/9, ahead of Bareev and Shirov (both 6).

Anand routs Karpov 5-1 in an 'Advanced Chess' match. However, it is clear that Karpov has no useful experience with databases, and he is unable to make any real use of the computerized analytical assistance.

Chess publishers Batsford fold.

Kasparov plays against the World on the Internet.

Tõnu Õim wins the 14th Correspondence World Championship (1994-9).

Lembit Oll dies.

World News in Brief

There is war between NATO and Yugoslavia (which now comprises just Serbia and Montenegro) over Kosovo. Serbian forces are eventually forced out of Kosovo, but there is a massive humanitarian crisis, as Serbian forces had driven most of Kosovo's Albanians from their homes, killing thousands. Damage throughout Serbia is also extreme.

The European single currency (the Euro) comes into effect from the start of the year. 11 EU countries are involved, but Britain, having opted out, retains the pound.

There is trouble in East Timor, as Indonesian militias terrorize the public, who have voted for independence.

The Senate acquits President Clinton on both charges (perjury and obstruction of justice).

There is a series of terrorist explosions in Moscow.

A large earthquake causes widespread devastation in north-west Turkey, possibly killing as many as 40,000 people.

The world's human population reaches six billion.

In a major and costly embarrassment for NASA scientists, a sophisticated unmanned probe to the planet Mars is lost after instructions are sent to it using Imperial, rather than Metric, measurements.

Conclusion

The 20th Century has seen a remarkable, and ever-quickening growth in the popularity of chess. The game itself has never looked healthier. Electronic tools to help with preparation and analysis have sharpened the play of top grandmasters. Elaborate opening preparation, far from making chess sterile, has given scope for great creativity. Chess, once considered a game of 'rules' and principles, which might occasionally be broken, has been transformed into a struggle where concrete considerations are paramount.

Chess lends itself very naturally to electronic media, so it is no surprise that it has flourished during the computer boom. Home computers and the Internet have provided the means for enthusiasts to play chess where they want, when they want.

So, will chess simply keep on growing and developing in the new millennium? We may like to think so, but it is by no means certain.

Firstly, there is the issue of computer domination. During the early part of the 21st Century, computers will become so good at chess that no human will stand a chance against them. It is impossible to predict how people will react to that. Even if chess-players are unperturbed, it could downgrade the public's perception of chess as a worthwhile activity.

Secondly, the chess community needs to promote itself more effectively. In particular, chess needs to have a universally recognized and credible world championship, as it did for much of the 20th Century. As the new century dawns, the world championship is in crisis; if it falls into decay, chess will have lost its most powerful publicity vehicle.

As we have seen throughout this book, the fortunes of chess are closely intertwined with political support. Whatever one thought of the USSR, it was a superpower that supported chess, and this fact pushed chess higher up the agenda in the USA. Currently there is no major nation providing significant state support for chess.

However, predicting the future is virtually impossible, and technology can quickly develop in directions that had not previously even been contemplated. Maybe the Internet, or some highly evolved version of it, will occupy a dominant place in a future global society, in which case chess may well be set to thrive.

Index of Games

Numbers refer to years. When the second player's name appears in **bold**, that player has White.

ADORJAN, A. – **Bednarski, J.** 1972

ALATORTSEV, V. – Boleslavsky, I. 1950; **Tolush, A.** 1947

ALEKHINE, A. – Alexander, C. 1936; **Bogoljubow, E.** 1922; Bogoljubow, E. 1934; Böök, E. 1938; **Capablanca, J.** 1913, 1927; **de Rozynski** 1913; Euwe, M. 1937; **Grigoriev, N.** 1915; Junge, K. 1942 (2); Koltanowski, G. 1932; Maroczy, G. 1931; Nimzowitsch, A. 1931; Réti, R. 1922; **Réti, R.** 1925; **Rubinstein, A.** 1926; Steiner, H. 1929; Sterk, K. 1921; Sultan Khan 1932; Yates, F. 1923

ALEXANDER, C. – **Alekhine, A.** 1936

ALONI, I. – Botvinnik, M. 1964

ANAND, V. – **Gelfand, B.** 1993; **Ivanchuk, V.** 1992; **Kasparov, G.** 1995; Lautier, J. 1997

ANDERSSON, U. – **Byrne, R.** 1979; **Kasparov, G.** 1981

ARONIN, L. – Estrin, Y. 1957

AVERBAKH, Y. – Kotov, A. 1953

BAGIROV, V. – Gufeld, E. 1973

BALASHOV, Y. – Miles, A. 1978

BARANOV, K. – Rokhlin, Y. 1935

BARCZA, G. – Keres, P. 1957

BAREEV, E. – **Topalov, V.** 1994

BEDNARSKI, J. – Adorjan, A. 1972

BEHTING, C. – **Nimzowitsch, A.** 1919

BEILIN, M. – Lipnitsky, I. 1950

BELOV, L. – Nezhmetdinov, R. 1961

BELSITZMAN – Rubinstein, A. 1917

BENGTSSON, B. – Wahlblom, C. 1970

BENKO, P. – **Fischer, R.** 1963

BERNSTEIN, O. – **Capablanca, J.** 1911; Najdorf, M. 1954

BOBRISCHEV-PUSHKIN, A. – Timofeev, N. 1908

BOGOLJUBOW, E. – Alekhine, A. 1922; **Alekhine, A.** 1934; Capablanca, J. 1928; Monticelli, M. 1930; Rellstab, L. 1940; **Réti, R.** 1924; **Rotlewi, G.** 1910

BOLESLAVSKY, I. – **Alatortsev, V.** 1950; Lilienthal, A. 1941; **Vinogradov** 1943

BONDAREVSKY, I. – Lisitsyn, G. 1940; **Panov, V.** 1937

BÖÖK, E. – **Alekhine, A.** 1938

BOTVINNIK, M. – **Aloni, I.** 1964; Bronstein, D. 1951; Capablanca, J. 1938; Gligorić, S. 1956; **Keres, P.** 1941, 1955; Keres, P. 1948, 1952; Konstantinopolsky, A. 1943; **Najdorf, M.** 1946; **Rabinovich, I.** 1927; **Rauzer, V.** 1933; Smyslov, V. 1944; Smyslov, V. 1954

BRONSTEIN, D. – **Botvinnik, M.** 1951; **Kholmov, R.** 1964; **Spassky, B.** 1960

BURN, A. – **Marshall, F.** 1907

BYRNE, D. – Fischer, R. 1956

BYRNE, R. – Andersson, U. 1979; Fischer, R. 1963

CAPABLANCA, J. – Alekhine, A. 1913, 1927; Bernstein, O. 1911; **Bogoljubow, E.** 1928; **Botvinnik, M.** 1938; **Corzo, J.** 1901, 1913; Corzo, J. 1901; **Keres, P.** 1938; Lasker, Em. 1921; Lilienthal, A. 1936; **Marshall, F.** 1931; Marshall, F. 1909; **Nimzowitsch, A.** 1914; **Rubinstein, A.** 1928; Spielmann, R. 1911; Steiner, H. 1933; **Tartakower, S.** 1924

CARDOSO, R. – **Rossetto, H.** 1958

CHAJES, O. – **Janowski, D.** 1916

CHANDLER, M. – Vaganian, R. 1986

CHIGORIN, M. – **Maroczy, G.** 1903; **Marshall, F.** 1905; **Mieses, J.** 1906; Mortimer, J. 1900; **Rubinstein, A.** 1906; Rubinstein, A. 1903

CIFUENTES, R. – Zviagintsev, V. 1995

COLLE, E. – Grünfeld, E. 1926; O'Hanlon, J. 1930

CORZO, J. – **Capablanca, J.** 1901; Capablanca, J. 1901, 1913

DE FIRMIAN, N. – Nikolić, P. 1985

DE ROZYNSKI – Alekhine, A. 1913

DEEP BLUE – Kasparov, G. 1996, 1997

DENKER, A. – Smyslov, V. 1946

DULANTO, A. – **Yanofsky, D.** 1939

EHLVEST, J. – **Kramnik, V.** 1995

ELJASCHOFF, M. – **Spielmann, R.** 1903

ENGELS, L. – **Grohmann, G.** 1934

ESTRIN, Y. – **Aronin, L.** 1957

EUWE, M. – **Alekhine, A.** 1937; Keres, P. 1939; Lasker, Em. 1934; Najdorf, M. 1953;

Tartakower, S. 1948; **Vidmar, M.** 1929
FILIP, M. – Petrosian, T. 1965
FINE, R. – Steiner, H. 1945
FISCHER, R. – Benko, P. 1963; **Byrne, D.** 1956; **Byrne, R.** 1963; **Matulović, M.** 1968; Panno, O. 1970; Petrosian, T. 1971; Spassky, B. 1972; Stein, L. 1967
FLAMBERG, A. – **Réti, R.** 1912
FLOHR, S. – **Horowitz, I.** 1945; Kashdan, I. 1933; **Keres, P.** 1937
FUDERER, A. – Gligorić, S. 1949
FÜSTER, G. – **Steiner, L.** 1948
GELFAND, B. – Anand, V. 1993; Shirov, A. 1998
GELLER, E. – **Keres, P.** 1952; **Korchnoi, V.** 1954; Korchnoi, V. 1960; **Kotov, A.** 1949; Velimirović, D. 1971
GEREBEN, E. – Troianescu, O. 1951
GIBAUD, A. – **Lazard, F.** 1909
GLIGORIĆ, S. – **Botvinnik, M.** 1956; **Fuderer, A.** 1949
GRIGORIEV, N. – Alekhine, A. 1915
GROHMANN, G. – Engels, L. 1934
GRÜNFELD, E. – **Colle, E.** 1926
GUFELD, E. – **Bagirov, V.** 1973; Kavalek, L. 1962
GULKO, B. – **Høi, C.** 1988
GUREVICH, M. – **Salov, V.** 1987
GURGENIDZE, B. – Lein, A. 1966
HALPRIN, A. – Pillsbury, H. 1900
HAUCHARD, A. – **Shirov, A.** 1990
HECHT, H.-J. – **Tal, M.** 1962
HENNIG – **Taube, A.** 1933
HJARTARSON, J. – **McCambridge, V.** 1984; **Tal, M.** 1987
HODGSON, J. – Paunović, D. 1976
HØI, C. – Gulko, B. 1988
HOROWITZ, I. – Flohr, S. 1945
HORT, V. – **Karpov, A.** 1971; Keres, P. 1961
HROMADKA, K. – **Rubinstein, A.** 1923
HÜBNER, R. – **Tal, M.** 1979
IDIGORAS, G. – Panno, O. 1955
IVANCHUK, V. – Anand, V. 1992; Shirov, A. 1996; Yusupov, A. 1991
JACOBSEN, B. – Ljubojević, L. 1969
JANOWSKI, D. – Chajes, O. 1916; **Pillsbury, H.** 1902; Salwe, G. 1906; Sämisch, F. 1925; Schlechter, C. 1902; Tarrasch, S. 1905
JOHNER, P. – Nimzowitsch, A. 1926
JUNGE, K. – **Alekhine, A.** 1942 (2)
KAIDANOV, G. – **Taimanov, M.** 1988
KAMSKY, G. – Shirov, A. 1993

KARPOV, A. – Hort, V. 1971; **Kasparov, G.** 1986, 1990; Kasparov, G. 1984, 1985; Korchnoi, V. 1974; **Korchnoi, V.** 1978; Sax, G. 1983; Spassky, B. 1974, 1975; **Tatai, S.** 1977; Topalov, V. 1994
KASHDAN, I. – **Flohr, S.** 1933
KASPAROV, G. – Anand, V. 1995; Andersson, U. 1981; *Deep Blue* 1996, 1997; **Karpov, A.** 1984, 1985; Karpov, A. 1986, 1990; **Kavalek, L.** 1982; **Korchnoi, V.** 1982; **Lputian, S.** 1976; Portisch, L. 1983; Přibyl, J. 1980; Salov, V. 1989; Topalov, V. 1999
KAVALEK, L. – **Gufeld, E.** 1962; Kasparov, G. 1982
KENGIS, E. – **Yurtaev, L.** 1973
KERES, P. – **Barcza, G.** 1957; **Botvinnik, M.** 1948, 1952; Botvinnik, M. 1941, 1955; Capablanca, J. 1938; **Euwe, M.** 1939; Flohr, S. 1937; Geller, E. 1952; **Hort, V.** 1961; **Kholmov, R.** 1959; **Korchnoi, V.** 1965; Levenfish, G. 1947; Petrovs, V. 1940; Richter, K. 1942; **Ståhlberg, G.** 1936; Tolush, A. 1957; Winter, W. 1935
KHOLMOV, R. – Bronstein, D. 1964; Keres, P. 1959; **Uhlmann, W.** 1960
KLAVESTAD, G. – **Rojahn, E.** 1944
KOFMAN, R. – Kogan, E. 1944
KOGAN, E. – **Kofman, R.** 1944
KOLTANOWSKI, G. – **Alekhine, A.** 1932
KONSTANTINOPOLSKY, A. – **Botvinnik, M.** 1943
KOPYLOV, I. – Koroliov, S. 1981
KORCHNOI, V. – Geller, E. 1954; **Geller, E.** 1960; **Karpov, A.** 1974; Karpov, A. 1978; Kasparov, G. 1982; Keres, P. 1965; Spassky, B. 1977
KOROLIOV, S. – **Kopylov, I.** 1981
KOTOV, A. – **Averbakh, Y.** 1953; Geller, E. 1949; **Tolush, A.** 1945; Yudovich, M. 1939
KOVAČEVIĆ, V. – Seirawan, Y. 1980
KRAMER, E. – **Nićifor, A.** 1921
KRAMNIK, V. – Ehlvest, J. 1995
L'HERMET, R. – **Spielmann, R.** 1927
LARSEN, B. – Petrosian, T. 1966; **Tal, M.** 1965
LASKER, EM. – **Capablanca, J.** 1921; **Euwe, M.** 1934; **Marshall, F.** 1907; Napier, W. 1904; **Pillsbury, H.** 1904; Pirc, V. 1935; **Rubinstein, A.** 1909; **Schlechter, C.** 1904; **Tarrasch, S.** 1908; **Torre, C.** 1925
LAUTIER, J. – **Anand, V.** 1997
LAZARD, F. – Gibaud, A. 1909

LEIN, A. - **Gurgenidze, B.** 1966
LEVENFISH, G. - **Keres, P.** 1947; **Verlinsky, B.** 1924
LEVITSKY, S. - Marshall, F. 1912
LIBERZON, V. - **Smyslov, V.** 1968
LILIENTHAL, A. - **Boleslavsky, I.** 1941; **Capablanca, J.** 1936; Najdorf, M. 1948, 1950; Romih, M. 1930
LIPNITSKY, I. - **Beilin, M.** 1950
LISITSYN, G. - **Bondarevsky, I.** 1940
LJUBOJEVIĆ, L. - **Jacobsen, B.** 1969; Tal, M. 1975
LPUTIAN, S. - Kasparov, G. 1976
MARCO, G. - Mieses, J. 1901
MARIN, M. - **Nunn, J.** 1987
MAROCZY, G. - **Alekhine, A.** 1931; Chigorin, M. 1903; **Rubinstein, A.** 1920; Tarrasch, S. 1905; Tartakower, S. 1922
MAROVIĆ, D. - Tsagan, T. 1964
MARSH, S. - **Norwood, D.** 1992
MARSHALL, F. - Burn, A. 1907; **Capablanca, J.** 1909; Capablanca, J. 1931; Chigorin, M. 1905; Lasker, Em. 1907; **Levitsky, S.** 1912; **Nimzowitsch, A.** 1928; **Rubinstein, A.** 1908
MATTISON, H. - Rubinstein, A. 1929
MATULOVIĆ, M. - Fischer, R. 1968
MCCAMBRIDGE, V. - Hjartarson, J. 1984
MIESES, J. - Chigorin, M. 1906; **Marco, G.** 1901; Møller, J. 1906; **Reggio, A.** 1903; **Spielmann, R.** 1910
MILES, A. - **Balashov, Y.** 1978
MOISEEV, O. - Simagin, V. 1951
MØLLER, J. - **Mieses, J.** 1906
MONTICELLI, M. - **Bogoljubow, E.** 1930
MORTIMER, J. - **Chigorin, M.** 1900
NAJDORF, M. - **Bernstein, O.** 1954; Botvinnik, M. 1946; **Euwe, M.** 1953; **Lilienthal, A.** 1948, 1950
NAPIER, W. - **Lasker, Em.** 1904; **von Bardeleben, C.** 1902
NATAF, I. - **Nunn, J.** 1999
NEZHMETDINOV, R. - **Belov, L.** 1961; **Polugaevsky, L.** 1958; Suetin, A. 1947; Tal, M. 1961
NIĆIFOR, A. - Kramer, E. 1921
NIKOLIĆ, P. - **de Firmian, N.** 1985
NIMZOWITSCH, A. - **Alekhine, A.** 1931; Behting, C. 1919; Capablanca, J. 1914; **Johner, P.** 1926; Marshall, F. 1928; **Sämisch, F.** 1923; Tarrasch, S. 1914
NORWOOD, D. - Marsh, S. 1992

NOWARRA, H. - **Schmidt, P.** 1941
NUNN, J. - Marin, M. 1987; Nataf, I. 1999; **Portisch, L.** 1989
O'HANLON, J. - **Colle, E.** 1930
O'KELLY DE GALWAY, A. - **Rossolimo, N.** 1949
OZSVATH, A. - Smejkal, J. 1970
PADEVSKY, N. - **Tal, M.** 1963
PANNO, O. - **Fischer, R.** 1970; **Idigoras, G.** 1955
PANOV, V. - Bondarevsky, I. 1937; **Ravinsky, G.** 1943
PAUNOVIĆ, D. - **Hodgson, J.** 1976
PETROSIAN, T. - **Filip, M.** 1965; **Fischer, R.** 1971; **Larsen, B.** 1966; **Portisch, L.** 1974; **Romanishin, O.** 1975; **Spassky, B.** 1969; Spassky, B. 1966; **Szabo, L.** 1952
PETROVS, V. - **Keres, P.** 1940
PETURSSON, M. - **Van der Sterren, P.** 1992
PILLSBURY, H. - **Halprin, A.** 1900; Janowski, D. 1902; Lasker, Em. 1904
PILNIK, H. - **Spassky, B.** 1955
PIRC, V. - **Lasker, Em.** 1935
POLUGAEVSKY, L. - Nezhmetdinov, R. 1958; **Spassky, B.** 1958; Tal, M. 1979; Torre, E. 1981
PORTISCH, L. - **Kasparov, G.** 1983; Nunn, J. 1989; Petrosian, T. 1974; **Stein, L.** 1962
PŘIBYL, J. - **Kasparov, G.** 1980
RABINOVICH, I. - Botvinnik, M. 1927
RAGOZIN, V. - Solin, I. 1946
RAUZER, V. - Botvinnik, M. 1933
RAVINSKY, G. - Panov, V. 1943
REGGIO, A. - Mieses, J. 1903
RELLSTAB, L. - **Bogoljubow, E.** 1940
RESHEVSKY, S. - Vaganian, R. 1976
RÉTI, R. - **Alekhine, A.** 1922; Alekhine, A. 1925; Bogoljubow, E. 1924; Flamberg, A. 1912; Tartakower, S. 1910
RICHTER, K. - **Keres, P.** 1942
RIUMIN, N. - **Slonim, S.** 1931
ROJAHN, E. - Klavestad, G. 1944
ROKHLIN, Y. - **Baranov, K.** 1935
ROMANISHIN, O. - Petrosian, T. 1975
ROMIH, M. - **Lilienthal, A.** 1930
ROSSETTO, H. - Cardoso, R. 1958
ROSSOLIMO, N. - O'Kelly de Galway, A. 1949
ROTLEWI, G. - Bogoljubow, E. 1910; Rubinstein, A. 1907
RÕTOV, B. - Timman, J. 1973
RUBINSTEIN, A. - Alekhine, A. 1926; **Belsitzman** 1917; Capablanca, J. 1928; **Chigorin, M.**

1903; Chigorin, M. 1906; Hromadka, K. 1923; Lasker, Em. 1909; Maroczy, G. 1920; Marshall, F. 1908; **Mattison, H.** 1929; **Rotlewi, G.** 1907; Spielmann, R. 1912; Vidmar, M. 1918

SALOV, V. – Gurevich, M. 1987; **Kasparov, G.** 1989

SALWE, G. – **Janowski, D.** 1906

SÄMISCH, F. – **Janowski, D.** 1925; Nimzowitsch, A. 1923

SAX, G. – **Karpov, A.** 1983

SCHLECHTER, C. – **Janowski, D.** 1902; Lasker, Em. 1904

SCHMID, L. – Udovčić, M. 1953

SCHMIDT, P. – Nowarra, H. 1941

SEIRAWAN, Y. – **Kovačević, V.** 1980; Timman, J. 1990

SHIROV, A. – **Gelfand, B.** 1998; Hauchard, A. 1990; **Ivanchuk, V.** 1996; **Kamsky, G.** 1993; **Topalov, V.** 1998

SHORT, N. – Timman, J. 1991

SIGURJONSSON, G. – **Westerinen, H.** 1977

SIMAGIN, V. – **Moiseev, O.** 1951; **Tal, M.** 1956

SLONIM, S. – Riumin, N. 1931

SMEJKAL, J. – **Ozsvath, A.** 1970

SMYSLOV, V. – Botvinnik, M. 1944; **Botvinnik, M.** 1954; **Denker, A.** 1946; Liberzon, V. 1968; **Tal, M.** 1959

SOLIN, I. – **Ragozin, V.** 1946

SPASSKY, B. – Bronstein, D. 1960; **Fischer, R.** 1972; **Karpov, A.** 1974, 1975; **Korchnoi, V.** 1977; **Petrosian, T.** 1966; Petrosian, T. 1969; Pilnik, H. 1955; Polugaevsky, L. 1958; **Uhlmann, W.** 1967

SPIELMANN, R. – **Capablanca, J.** 1911; Eljaschoff, M. 1903; L'Hermet, R. 1927; Mieses, J. 1910; **Rubinstein, A.** 1912; **Stoltz, G.** 1932

STÅHLBERG, G. – Keres, P. 1936

STEIN, L. – **Fischer, R.** 1967; Portisch, L. 1962

STEINER, H. – **Alekhine, A.** 1929; **Capablanca, J.** 1933; **Fine, R.** 1945

STEINER, L. – Füster, G. 1948

STERK, K. – **Alekhine, A.** 1921

STOLTZ, G. – Spielmann, R. 1932

SUETIN, A. – **Nezhmetdinov, R.** 1947

SULTAN KHAN – **Alekhine, A.** 1932

SZABO, L. – Petrosian, T. 1952

TAIMANOV, M. – Kaidanov, G. 1988

TAL, M. – Hecht, H.-J. 1962; Hjartarson, J. 1987; Hübner, R. 1979; Larsen, B. 1965; **Ljubojević, L.** 1975; **Nezhmetdinov, R.** 1961; Padevsky, N. 1963; **Polugaevsky, L.** 1979; Simagin, V. 1956; Smyslov, V. 1959; Tringov, G. 1964

TARRASCH, S. – **Janowski, D.** 1905; Lasker, Em. 1908; **Maroczy, G.** 1905; **Nimzowitsch, A.** 1914

TARTAKOWER, S. – Capablanca, J. 1924; Euwe, M. 1948; **Maroczy, G.** 1922; **Réti, R.** 1910

TATAI, S. – Karpov, A. 1977

TAUBE, A. – Hennig 1933

TIMMAN, J. – **Rõtov, B.** 1973; **Seirawan, Y.** 1990; **Short, N.** 1991

TIMOFEEV, N. – **Bobrischev-Pushkin, A.** 1908

TOLUSH, A. – Alatortsev, V. 1947; **Keres, P.** 1957; Kotov, A. 1945

TOPALOV, V. – Bareev, E. 1994; **Karpov, A.** 1994; **Kasparov, G.** 1999; Shirov, A. 1998

TORRE, C. – Lasker, Em. 1925

TORRE, E. – **Polugaevsky, L.** 1981

TRINGOV, G. – **Tal, M.** 1964

TROIANESCU, O. – **Gereben, E.** 1951

TSAGAN, T. – **Marović, D.** 1964

UDOVČIĆ, M. – **Schmid, L.** 1953

UHLMANN, W. – Kholmov, R. 1960; Spassky, B. 1967

VAGANIAN, R. – **Chandler, M.** 1986; **Reshevsky, S.** 1976

VAN DER STERREN, P. – Petursson, M. 1992

VELIMIROVIĆ, D. – **Geller, E.** 1971

VERLINSKY, B. – Levenfish, G. 1924

VIDMAR, M. – Euwe, M. 1929; **Rubinstein, A.** 1918

VINOGRADOV – Boleslavsky, I. 1943

VON BARDELEBEN, C. – Napier, W. 1902

WAHLBLOM, C. – **Bengtsson, B.** 1970

WESTERINEN, H. – Sigurjonsson, G. 1977

WINTER, W. – **Keres, P.** 1935

YANOFSKY, D. – Dulanto, A. 1939

YATES, F. – **Alekhine, A.** 1923

YUDOVICH, M. – **Kotov, A.** 1939

YURTAEV, L. – Kengis, E. 1973

YUSUPOV, A. – **Ivanchuk, V.** 1991

ZVIAGINTSEV, V. – **Cifuentes, R.** 1995